S0-BRE-081

WITHDRAWN

Gettell's

HISTORY OF POLITICAL THOUGHT

THE CENTURY
POLITICAL SCIENCE SERIES

Edited by FREDERIC A. OGG

———

Frederic A. Ogg and P. Orman Ray, *Introduction to American Government*, Tenth Edition, and *Essentials of American Government*, Seventh Edition.

Hillman M. Bishop and Samuel Hendel, *Basic Issues of American Democracy*, Second Edition.

Clyde F. Snider, *American State and Local Government*.

Arthur W. Bromage, *Introduction to Municipal Government and Administration*.

Joseph P. Chamberlain, *Legislative Processes: National and State*.

Howard R. Penniman, *Sait's American Parties and Elections*, Fifth Edition.

Andrew C. McLaughlin, *A Constitutional History of the United States*.

Percy Thomas Fenn, Jr., *The Development of the Constitution*.

John M. Mathews, *American Foreign Relations: Conduct and Policies*, Revised Edition.

Graham H. Stuart, *Latin America and the United States*, Fourth Edition.

Pitman B. Potter, *An Introduction to the Study of International Organization*, Fifth Edition.

Charles G. Fenwick, *International Law*, Third Edition.

Frank M. Russell, *Theories of International Relations*.

Edward M. Sait, *Political Institutions: A Preface*.

W. F. Willoughby, *The Government of Modern States*, Revised Edition.

Francis W. Coker, *Recent Political Thought*.

Lawrence C. Wanlass, *Gettell's History of Political Thought*, Second Edition.

Raymond G. Gettell, *History of American Political Thought*.

J. Mark Jacobson, *The Development of American Political Thought*.

Anna Haddow, *Political Science in American Colleges and Universities, 1636–1900*.

Everett S. Brown, *A Manual of Government Publications: United States and Foreign*.

Gettell's

History of
Political Thought

By LAWRENCE C. WANLASS

Mount Holyoke College

SECOND EDITION

New York

APPLETON-CENTURY-CROFTS, INC.

KLINCK MEMORIAL LIBRARY
Concordia Teachers College
River Forest. Illinois

COPYRIGHT, 1953, BY

APPLETON-CENTURY-CROFTS, INC.

*All rights reserved. This book, or parts
thereof, must not be reproduced in any
form without permission of the publishers.*

5103-1

Library of Congress Card Number: 54-5423

Copyright, 1924, by The Century Co.

PRINTED IN THE UNITED STATES OF AMERICA

43801

PREFACE

Because the earlier edition of this book, written by the late Professor Raymond Garfield Gettell, was so well received, no attempt has been made in this revision to alter its general character. Many of the chapters remain much as they were. Where changes do occur they will be found primarily in the chapters dealing with Greek political philosophy and in the concluding chapters on liberalism, fascism, and communism. To give emphasis to these latter subjects, I have reorganized the book into parts, eliminating in the process a number of chapters on nineteenth century thought which now seem expendable. New chapter-end bibliographies have also been provided which contain recent, more available material.

In carrying out these modifications I have incurred many obligations. I am under a debt to other scholars on whose works I have relied. Professor Charles McIlwain's *The Growth of Political Thought in the West* has influenced my thinking about Greek political philosophy. A. J. and R. W. Carlyle's *A History of Medieval Political Theory in the West* has been of great value in revising those sections dealing with medieval thought. Elie Halévy's *The Growth of Philosophic Radicalism* has conditioned my thinking about British Utilitarianism. And George H. Sabine's *A History of Political Theory* has afforded me numerous insights into the form as well as the general content of political philosophy. I am also indebted to friends and associates who have offered advice and encouragement during the preparation of the typescript. My thanks are due especially to Harold U. Faulkner of Smith College, Roger W. Holmes of Mount Holyoke College, and Dwight Waldo of the University of California. My greatest debt, however, is to my wife Anita, who devoted long hours to this, our joint undertaking. This revision would not have been possible without her unfailing coöperation and support.

L. C. W.

CONTENTS

PART III

MEDIEVAL POLITICAL THOUGHT

PART IV

THE BEGINNINGS OF MODERN
POLITICAL THOUGHT

PART V

MODERN LIBERAL THOUGHT

PART VI

THE GROWTH OF FASCISM

PART VII

THE LEGACY OF MARX

CONTENTS

PART I

Introductory

CHAPTER I ⟿

The Nature of Political Thought

Origin of Political Thought

All living creatures except man are largely at the mercy of their surroundings. They live under conditions which are not of their making and which are but little changed by their efforts. No conscious purpose nor definite idea of progress is possible among them. They live in a world of nature and are controlled by its conditions, being unable to conquer it or to change their own destiny by their own deliberate actions.

The relation of man to his environment is essentially different. Although in primitive times man, like the lower creatures, lived at the mercy of nature and developed in accordance with the law of natural evolution, and although man is still in many ways affected by conditions which he is powerless to change, a point was nevertheless reached in human development when man became conscious of his environment and set his reason to work to explain it and to plan modifications and improvements. Natural phenomena were investigated and understood, and conscious direction and purpose gradually replaced the purely physical relation between man and nature.

This was the case not only with the physical environment, composed of those geographic and climatic conditions and their resultant natural resources within which all life exists, but also with the social environment, composed of those ideas, associations, and institutions that make up the non-physical life of man. In the same way that man began to investigate nature, learn her laws, bring her powers under his control, and utilize her resources, so man began to question his intellectual beliefs and his social customs and institutions, to examine their nature, to question their authority, and finally to plan deliberate change and progress. All early social institutions, therefore, arose and for a long time developed unconsciously.

3

Only gradually did man realize their existence and the possibility of directing or improving them by his own purposeful efforts.

Of all social institutions the state has been the most universal and most powerful. Some form of organization and authority has been found wherever human life has existed, and a sanction of some kind has enforced some sort of rules. In the process of human development, it was, therefore, inevitable that man should investigate this institution, should attempt to discover its origin, should question or uphold its authority, and should dispute over the proper scope of its function. As the outcome of this process, political thought arose. Government and law, springing up naturally and growing at first without conscious direction, came later under the scrutiny of man's reason. Man became conscious of the state and made attempts, crude enough in the beginning, to explain the nature of political phenomena. Increasing powers of observation and of logical analysis built up a constantly widening sphere of political speculation, and the development of the state in its objective phase of organization and activity was, accordingly, accompanied by its subjective phase—the theory of the state —in the minds of men and in the records of tradition and literature.

Political Thought and Political Institutions

It is evident that a close relation will exist between the political thought of any given period and the actual political conditions then existing. Most political theories arose either to explain and justify the authority that men obeyed or to criticize it in the hope of accomplishing change. Sometimes, it is true, political philosophers speculated concerning the ideal state, or drew imaginative pictures of political conditions as, in their opinion, they should be. Even this type of political theory, however, will, if closely examined, prove to be based on the political ideals of its time, and will usually be aimed at certain specific evils to which the conditions then prevailing gave rise. Plato's *Republic* has little meaning unless viewed in the light of the conditions that existed during the decline of the Greek city-states. More's *Utopia* depends upon the background of social unrest during the change from agriculture to sheep raising in England. Bellamy's *Looking Backward* presupposes the modern city and modern problems of capital and labor.

Ordinarily, political theories are the direct result of objective political conditions. They reflect the thoughts and interpret the motives that underlie actual political development. At least they represent what men believe to be the nature and spirit of their institutions. They indicate the conditions and the intellectual point of view of their age. At the same time, political theories also influence political development. They are not only the outgrowth of actual conditions, but they, in turn, lead men to modify their political institutions. Sometimes theory has preceded, sometimes it has followed, the corresponding institution or activity. Political theories are thus both cause and effect. Changing conditions create new theories; these in turn influence actual political methods. Magna Carta and the Declaration of the Rights of Man were more than mere statements of principle. They were programs of action whose effects are felt to this day.

Political theory is connected not only with the political institutions of its time but also with other categories of thought. Just as an abstract political or economic man cannot be separated from man in all his interests, so political thought cannot be divorced from science, philosophy, ethics, religion, economic theory, and literature, or even from tradition, dogma, prejudice, and superstition. The nature of political thought depends largely upon the stage of intellectual development. At one period men's intellectual interests place emphasis on one phase; at another, upon a different phase. The primary influence of religious doctrines on the political thought of the Middle Ages, and the connection between economic doctrines and political theory at the present day are at once suggested. Accordingly, the historical survey of political thought must keep in mind not only the actual development of political institutions but also the parallel progress of human thought in other fields, in order that the political principles of any given time may be understood and appreciated.

There are, therefore, two phases in the evolution of the state. One is the objective, concrete development of states as manifested in their governments, their administration of law, and their international relations; the other is the subjective development of ideas concerning the state as an abstraction. In political theory as in actual political organization, a continuous growth may be traced. Political principles, like devices of government, are handed down from age to age, each state by its experience and in the light of its conditions modifying former concepts and devices, and these in turn influencing the states that follow.

It remains to add that political thought is essentially relative in its nature and lays no claim to absolute truth. In the past it grew out of actual conditions and existing modes of thought; at present it represents problems with which we must deal. Concerning these problems political thinking is never unanimous. After the lapse of a considerable period of time, when a proper historical perspective may be secured, past problems stand out clearly, and uncritical people often judge harshly the apparent blindness of earlier generations and the inadequacy or futility of their attempted solutions. So no doubt many of our problems will appear simple to future generations and our groping remedies will seem equally blundering. But when judged in the light of prevailing conditions and prevailing methods of thought, the difficulties involved are more apparent.

Intelligent men differ honestly in their opinions concerning the beneficial or injurious effects of certain phases of political life. Even when all agree concerning the nature of the problems, agreement is lacking concerning their causes or the proper methods of solution. Many such differences of opinion underlie political issues, create political parties and their contests, and form the motive forces of government. Many others are involved in the international policies of states and lead to dispute or to warfare in which both parties to the conflict are honestly convinced of the justice of their cause. There are times when the clash of political issues is mild, when men and states agree fairly well on fundamental questions, and when governmental and international relations run smoothly and effectively. At other times differences of opinion are sharp, parties assume hostile attitudes, revolution is in the air, and international relations are strained or openly hostile.

Although some of the fundamental principles of political theory have been stated and restated, hammered out and refined, and have gained in the process a quality of explanatory power that seems universal, no theory of the state can be considered as ultimate truth. It is a fundamental weakness of a certain type of reformer that he believes that his scheme of reorganization would be perfect and permanent. A century hence, under the changed conditions of that time, our present attitude toward political problems may seem as crude and absurd as many of the theories that arose in the past now seems to us. This does not, however, diminish the necessity that each age should build up for itself a philosophy of the state, based upon its development to the point then reached, upon the actual conditions then existing, and upon the ideals of the future then held.

Problems of Political Thought

If an analysis be made of the questions with which political thought has been concerned, it is found that emphasis was placed at various periods upon widely different types of problems. In the medieval period controversy centered in the contest for supremacy between spiritual and temporal authorities; in the seventeenth and eighteenth centuries the dominant interest was in the contest between monarchic and democratic theories of political organization; at present the extent of state activities has come into prominence and the connection between political and economic interests is especially close.

Political conditions have changed so greatly from age to age that the same problem has also had quite different meanings at different periods. Thus eighteenth century liberal thinkers favored individualism because they wished to limit the activities of governments controlled by irresponsible monarchs. To-day the same type of thinker is likely to hold a moderate socialistic point of view and to favor the extension of governmental regulation and control. When political power was transferred from king to people, much of the reason for fearing it disappeared; and government came to be looked upon as a servant whose actions promoted general welfare and should be extended, rather than as a tyrant whose power should be curbed.

Moreover, few thinkers have attempted to build up a consistent and comprehensive theory of the state. Men have usually been interested in some particular phase of political existence that seemed important to their time. It is therefore difficult to make a complete and logical outline of the problems that political theory has attempted to solve. Some of the most important, and some that have appeared most frequently, may however be pointed out.

Considerable attention has been given to the origin of the state. In the uncritical past, when historical knowledge was slight, numerous attempts were made to account for the beginnings of political institutions. Among the most widely held theories were the divine theory, which considered the state to be established by the authority of God; the force theory, which found the origin of the state in the compulsory subjection of the weak to the strong; and the social-contract theory, which viewed the state as the deliberate creation of individuals by means of voluntary agreement or consent. Only recently have the expansion of historical knowledge, the rise of a critical historical attitude, and the acceptance of the principles of evolution made possible a satisfactory theory of state origin. Even yet our knowledge of the early period of political life is incomplete, and many important points are in dispute. In general, however, the modern evolutionary theory views the state neither as divinely created nor as the deliberate work of man through either conquest or agreement. It sees the state coming into existence gradually as the natural result of the needs of men for order and protection.

Closely allied with the question of origin has been the question of obligation to state authority. With the exception of isolated anarchists, most writers have agreed that some form of governmental power is necessary. They have been unable to agree, however, on the nature of this authority. This has raised the question of legitimacy which is at the heart of all political thought. In its clearest terms the question was put by Rousseau when he asked, "Man is born free and everywhere he is in chains. . . . What can render it legitimate?" [1]

[1] Jean-Jacques Rousseau, *The Social Contract,* trans. by Henry J. Tozer (1924), p. 100.

To this query, various answers have been given. Some theorists have rested man's obligation to the state on divine ordination, Burke proclaiming that God, "Having disposed and marshalled us by a divine tactic, not according to our will, but to His ... had ... vitally subjected us to act the part which belongs to the place assigned us." [2] Some, including Aristotle, have considered the state to be the necessary result of the innate political character of men. The Utilitarians have justified it because of its obvious usefulness, holding that obedience to the state secures the greatest happiness of the greatest number. Others, such as Locke and Rousseau, have based its authority on the consent involved in the original compact by which the body politic was created. Theorists like Treitschke have rested its authority frankly on force, thus explaining and at the same time justifying its existence. To them might makes right. And still others have found in the state the crystallization of man's "real" will. Only through living within the state's compass and under its direction is the highest form of human development possible. From this point of view the state represents the more universal and permanent aspect of the individual's own will, so that in obeying the state he is obeying his own best self.

Since the Middle Ages, political theory has also been concerned with the idea of sovereignty. The earliest political philosophers wrote of the sovereignty of the law, but the rise of national monarchies caused the state to be personified in the ruler and its essential relationship to be conceived of as that between sovereign and subject. Attacks on royal power led to the theory of popular sovereignty, attributing ultimate political power to the entire body of citizens, and associating the concept of sovereignty with the state as a legal person rather than with the ruler as an individual. The vague and non-legal nature of popular sovereignty led, during the nineteenth century, to elaborate attempts to locate sovereignty in various organs of government, on the basis of the separation of powers established by a written constitution. Endless difficulties, especially in federally organized states, were encountered in this attempt. Besides, the concept of the absolute, supreme, and indivisible sovereignty of the state met difficulties, both in the existence of organizations within the state which seemed to have a juristic life and authority of their own, and in the relations among states, where the theory of the equality and independence of sovereign states conflicted with actual inequalities and with various degrees of dependence.

Similarly, the concept of law has undergone various transformations. Originating as custom, supported by immemorial tradition and the pre-

[2] Edmund Burke, *Reflections on the Revolution in France* (1790), *Works,* Vol. III, p. 361. Reference is to Little, Brown edition (1866).

vailing belief in divine sanction, law was later considered as existing in nature, to be discovered and applied by human reason. When national monarchies were established, the will of the sovereign became a source of law. Finally, modern democracies have attained to the idea that law, as the will of the state, should be formulated and administered by popular governmental organs, and should be modified as occasion demands new rules to meet new social needs.

The form of government and the location of authority within the state have been other sources of controversy in political theory. Whether political power should be centered in a single head, or limited to an aristocratic few, or widely distributed among the democratic masses has furnished much ground for discussion.

Also, wide differences of opinion have arisen over the proper scope of state activities. At one extreme is found an individualism that would limit the state to the narrowest exercise of authority and leave to its individual citizens the widest possible sphere of free action. At the other extreme is a paternalistic socialism that would extend state action to the widest limits and submerge the individual in the political mass. Between these extremes all shades of opinion may be found. Certain activities are recognized by all as essential to state existence, but over a wide range of optional functions a great controversy is being waged. In the United States this controversy has centered in the efforts of recent administrations to control our free-enterprise system without destroying it. This has brought the charge of socialism and the assertion that more controls will result in the destruction not only of free enterprise but of all freedoms.

Finally, a considerable section of political thought has been devoted to relations among states. At first states held the belief that they owed no obligations to any except peoples of their own race and religion. Strangers were enemies and had no rights, hence the existence of principles to regulate the relations among states was not admitted. Then, after the establishment of the Roman Empire, the ideal of world unity and of supreme authority vested in emperor or pope prevented for centuries the rise of a sound theory of international relations. However, commercial activities, diplomatic intercourse, and the waging of war gradually developed their own customs and principles. General doctrines were laid down concerning the independence and equality of states, the rights of neutrals, and the methods of carrying on hostilities by land and sea. Peace under generally accepted rules rather than unregulated war came to be considered the normal relation among states. The nature of treaties, of confederations, and of international law gave rise to much political speculation; and ideals of world empire or world federation and of universal peace attracted the best thinkers of all ages.

Conservative and Critical Political Thought

Since political thought usually aims either to support or to attack existing political institutions and methods, it may be classified broadly as
either conservative or critical. Theories of the conservative type arise
from the attempts of men to explain and justify the political system under
which they live and to maintain the *status quo*. Such theories are usually
created or supported by the class in power and by those who benefit
under the existing régime. They also represent the natural mental attitude of those who love law and order, and dislike confusion and change.
The best example of this type of theory is the doctrine of divine right,
by which the religious authority of the church was added to the political
authority of the state, a supernatural sanction was given to law, and the
position of the rulers made sacred and inviolable. This theory, which
made resistance to the powers that be a sin as well as a crime, was
mutually advantageous to the officials of the state and to the leaders of
the church, and appeared frequently in the history of political thought
as the support of autocratic authority and the opponent of reform.

Milder forms of conservative theory were represented in the laudation
of the British Constitution during the eighteenth century in the writings
of Montesquieu, Blackstone, and De Lolme, and in the general praise
accorded to the American Constitution by almost all American writers
during the nineteenth century. By establishing a widespread belief in
the perfection of existing institutions, they made change more difficult.
Similarly, political policies may be crystallized into dogmas or shib-
boleths and receive unthinking support because, by constant repetition,
they become imbedded in the national tradition. The Monroe Doctrine
is an example of a conservative theory created by this process.

Those who hold conservative theories view changing conditions with
emotions ranging from regret to alarm. When their theory no longer corresponds with actual conditions, they picture a golden age in the past,
believe that the world is going to ruin, and long to return to the good old
days. In this form conservative theories become reactionary and usually
disappear, though they often die hard in their last efforts to resist inevitable change.

Critical theories arise in opposition to the *status quo* and support efforts
to change existing political institutions and methods. Such theories range
from philosophical and imaginative utopias that have little apparent connection with actual life and no likelihood of practical application, to the
concrete ideals of reformers who are aiming to remedy certain evils or
to accomplish desired reconstruction. These latter vary from attempts to
change some single device of organization or to make minor readjust-

ments in governmental activities, to wide-sweeping schemes of political reorganization or the creation of new political systems. Some of their advocates are willing to work slowly and through legal channels; others believe in immediate and revolutionary methods. Liberal theories thus shade off into various degrees of radicalism.

It is obvious that critical theories could not arise and become widespread until men had reached a considerable degree of political intelligence and were permitted freedom of thought and of discussion. Such theories are usually held by those who are not in power, who are not prosperous and happy under the existing régime, and who hope to better their condition by change. Critical theory at its best is always constructive, since it includes not only a generalization of facts but also a valuation of tendencies. In destroying outworn and obsolete ideas, critical political thought implies an ideal of what ought to replace them. Such doctrines are dangerous to the powers that be, and during the greater part of human history have been forbidden and suppressed. Only occasionally, as in the Greek cities or in modern democracies, has it been possible to build up, without serious opposition, a critical political philosophy or to accomplish by legal methods the reform desired.

An important example of critical political thought was the doctrine of social contract and natural rights as set forth by Locke and Rousseau. This theory served as the basis for the English Revolution of the seventeenth century and the French and American Revolutions of the eighteenth century. It attacked the divine right of kings and justified revolution and popular sovereignty. Modern socialistic doctrines furnish other examples of critical theory.

It is interesting to observe that when a critical theory is generally accepted and becomes successful in practice, it tends to become a conservative theory, making certain concessions to practical necessity but endeavoring to maintain what it has accomplished and to prevent further change. Thus the doctrine of natural rights, with its emphasis on individualism and on the safeguarding of personal and property rights, was a critical theory in the eighteenth century, attacking the autocratic and paternalistic governments of that day. At present the theory is used as a conservative support for the vested interests in an effort to prevent the extension of state regulation and control that the socialists demand. This thesis is further substantiated by recent developments in Russia. Communist theory, having been adjusted to meet existing conditions by Lenin and Stalin, has now taken on a marked rigidity which will tend to maintain the prevailing order and to oppose further change.

Both conservative and critical theories have points of strength and weakness. Conservative theories, valuable in maintaining public peace and stability, frequently prevent or delay much-needed reform. Critical theories, necessary to prevent stagnation and to secure healthy political progress, frequently represent the panaceas of fanatics or lead to political chaos and anarchy. The proper compromise in political thought between undesirable extremes of conservatism and radicalism is difficult to maintain, and a swing too far in one direction is likely to be followed by a reaction toward the opposite extreme.

Sources of Our Knowledge of Political Thought

Knowledge concerning the political thought of the past must be drawn from many sources. The theory of the state at any given time was not a simple and unanimous set of principles. On some questions there was such a consensus of political opinion as to justify one in speaking definitely of the political theory of the time. On other questions opponents were sharply divided, with the issue clearly defined. On still other questions thought was fragmentary and indecisive, and showed all shades of opinion. In tracing the development of political thought, therefore, attention must be focused chiefly on the doctrines that were so generally held that they formed a part of the intellectual atmosphere of their times, and upon the conflicting points of view as they centered around the dominant issues of each period.

The main source of our knowledge of political theory is the writings of those political philosophers who attempted to put into systematic form the political thought of their times. This includes a long list of conspicuous men from Plato to the present. Some devoted their attention exclusively to political philosophy; others dealt with the state incidentally as a part of their larger interest in philosophy as a whole. The writings of these men not only crystallized the thought of those who preceded them and of their own day, but they also frequently marked out new lines of theory that secured general adherence later.

The chief objection to depending exclusively upon this source is that it gives a history of political literature rather than of political thought. Political philosophers are often too much removed from practical political life, or too close to their own institutions to get a proper perspective, or too much influenced by past doctrines or by personal bias and prejudice to give a true picture of the political thought of their day. In any attempt to view political thought in connection with the history, institutions, and general intellectual background of its time, this source must, therefore, be supplemented by others.

Much political theory is never put into definite statement. It is found tacitly underlying the form of actual organization and methods. It is taken for granted, or sometimes deliberately suppressed. A study of the history of political institutions and of the actions and policies of states is therefore essential, as they occasionally show more clearly than words the actual principles that dominated men's minds. Quite often in political doctrines, as in other phases of human endeavor, a wide discrepancy is found between the principles professed and those that are acted upon. The political theory of the Middle Ages would certainly give a most unsatisfactory idea of the actual nature of medieval political institutions; and many motives that are influential in practical politics today are seldom put into party platforms or into campaign orations.

A knowledge of the general intellectual background of each period is also essential to an understanding of political ideas. The thought of men in other fields affects their ideas concerning the state; hence the history of philosophy, of science, of religion, of ethics, and of economic theory contributes to the history of political thought.

A considerable amount of information concerning the theory of the state may be derived from the writings and speeches of men who occupy official positions in government, or who exercise leadership in public opinion. Such materials, though often colored for public consumption, nevertheless reveal, sometimes quite unintentionally, important political principles. They have both the merits and the defects that result from being in close contact with the realities of political life.

The official documents of states furnish a most valuable source of political thought. These include written constitutions, statutes and ordinances, court decisions, charters, departmental reports, treaties, diplomatic correspondence, state papers, and the like. Although these must be supplemented by observation of the actual practices of the states concerned, with which they do not always correspond, they are nevertheless an important guide to political theory.

In former times political thinking was limited to a comparatively small part of the population. The masses were ignorant and indifferent or suppressed. More recently, public opinion has come to play an important part in political thought and to exert a powerful influence in actual government. Accordingly, methods have been devised to influence it or to give it means of expression. Newspapers, magazines, pamphlets, posters, cartoons, and other forms of publicity have thus become important sources of political theory.

Finally, literature, in its narrower sense, often deals directly or indirectly with political life and problems. This is especially true of the essay, poetry, fiction, and the drama. Because they are less self-conscious and less partisan than the writings of political publicists, such sources may often give the truest picture of the political thought of a period.

Value of Political Thought

Political theory has been accused not only of being barren in practical results but even of being fertile with disaster to actual politics. Burke said that one sure symptom of an ill-conducted state was the tendency of the people to revert to theories. Leslie Stephen believed that political philosophy was generally the offspring of a recent, or the sign of an approaching, revolution. Professor Dunning observed that the crystallization of a political system into political philosophy usually sounded the knell of that system. It is true that theories that have outlived their usefulness have often stood in the way of progress, and that the fanatical ideas of ill-informed and unbalanced zealots have worked confusion. Against these criticisms may be set the fact that revolutions furthered by political principles have usually been of ultimate benefit to mankind, and that progress toward democracy, individual liberty, and international justice owes much to the doctrines of a long line of able thinkers.

It is sometimes urged that political philosophy, like all speculative thought, ignores reality, cannot be applied in practice, and utilizes legal fictions and absolute concepts which are untrue and dangerous. As with all social theory, the complexity of the problems with which it deals prevents exactness. Political theories express tendencies rather than absolute principles, and when applied in practice must take into consideration modifying circumstances. Likewise political concepts, such as the absolute sovereignty of the state or the equality of states, useful as working hypotheses, must not be pushed to extremes against obvious limitations in actual facts.

It is also said that political theory is incapable of giving definite answers to disputed questions, and that if one holds strong views concerning the rights of the individual or the best form of government, he cannot prove his position with any degree of finality. First principles in political theory, as in ethical theory, cannot be proved. They are the results of intellectual judgments or emotional intuitions. What the study of political theory can achieve is to bring men together in a common enterprise of reflection and discussion so that they can define their terms and understand one another's view point. If the result is mutual respect and toleration, the study of political principles is justified.

On the positive side, political theory may justly lay claim to certain values. It gives precision and definiteness to the meaning of political terms. This is a necessity for every science, but is especially valuable for political science, since its fundamental concepts, such as liberty, independence, democracy, nationality, and the like, are used freely by the average man as well as by the student of politics. Moreover, political thought examines the actual meanings behind these terms, and this is conducive to clarity and honesty of thought. It is a common device of demagogues to influence men's minds by the use of words that have acquired desirable or undesirable associations. Thus at present to call a thing "democratic" is to praise it, whereas to accuse a thing of being "radical" or "un-American" is, in the minds of most persons, to attach to it a certain stigma. Many a word which has now become commonplace was once the embodiment of a great political passion; others are still effective forces in shaping history.

Political theory is valuable also as an aid to the interpretation of history. It gives an insight into the intellectual atmosphere of the past, and explains the motives underlying important political movements. In order to understand the past, one must know not only what men did, but also what men believed and what they hoped for. In so far as the events of the past were shaped by human will, it is necessary to know the ideals which guided the will. Institutions are what they are in virtue of the ideas they embody. No one can understand the Middle Ages unless he is familiar with the controversy in political thought between the rival claims of emperor and pope. Nor can one appreciate the middle period of American history unless he understands the issue between the North and the South in terms of the political theory of sovereignty.

A knowledge of past political thought is also essential to an understanding of present-day politics and international relations. The problems of the present have grown up out of conditions in the past, and the political principles that are now being applied are the result of the evolution of past political thought. The theory of separation of powers has had a constant effect on actual government in the United States, and the principle of the balance of power remains fundamental in international politics.

Every state must have its political theory. Some general principles will guide the statesman and the citizen; every readjustment of governmental organization and every policy of governmental action will be based on some general scheme, more or less definite and systematic. The study of political thought, therefore, has practical value in that it aids the formation of habits of more thorough and candid examination of the meaning and tendency of our political undertakings. To a large extent, the future is in the present, as the present was once in the past, as a hope or ideal. Any successful attempt at constructive political progress must rest upon a sound and comprehensive political theory, applicable to present-day conditions and needs.

Finally, political thought represents a high type of intellectual achievement and, like other forms of philosophic thought, has an interest and a value entirely apart from any practical application of its principles. Intelligent men naturally wish to understand the authority under which they live, to analyze its organization and its activities, and to speculate concerning the best form of political existence. The fact that many of the greatest thinkers of all time—Plato, Aristotle, Aquinas, Locke, Rousseau, Kant, Mill, and others—were concerned with the political aspects of philosophy is an indication of its importance as a form of intellectual effort.

There have long been two conflicting theories concerning the nature of political evolution. According to the one theory, government is not a matter of human choice, but is an inevitable natural growth in which the deliberate purposes of man have little part. After making some effort to untangle the bewildering facts of social life, Burke said, "I doubt whether the history of mankind is yet complete enough, if it ever can be so, to furnish ground for a sure theory on the internal causes which necessarily affect the fortune of a state.... We are therefore obliged to deliver up that operation to mere chance, or more piously, perhaps more rationally, to the occasional interposition and irresistible hand of the Great Disposer." If this be true, the study of political theory, aside from its academic interest, is futile.

According to the other theory, government is merely a problem in human ingenuity, of determining what is best and adapting the means to the desired end. If this be true, no study can be more valuable than political theory. Each of these doctrines is untenable if pushed to its logical conclusion, yet in some compromise between them lies essential truth. "Long the victim of material forces, man has, by taking thought, made himself master of wind and wave and storm. May he not, by taking thought, lift himself above the social conflicts that destroy civilizations, and make himself master of his social destiny?" [3]

REFERENCES

BEARD, C. A., *The Economic Basis of Politics*, 3rd ed. (New York, Knopf, 1945), Chap. 1.

BURNS, C. D., *Political Ideals*, 4th ed. (London, Oxford Univ. Press, 1929), Chap. 1.

CASSIRER, Ernst, *The Myth of the State* (New Haven, Yale Univ. Press, 1946), Part I.

D'ENTRÈVES, A. P., *The Medieval Contribution to Political Thought* (Oxford, Oxford Univ. Press, 1939), Chap. 1.

ELLIOT, W. Y., and McDONALD, N. A., *Western Political Heritage* (New York, Prentice-Hall, 1949), Introduction.

FIGGIS, J. N., *Political Thought from Gerson to Grotius* (Cambridge, Cambridge Univ. Press, 1907), Lecture I.

[3] C. A. Beard, *The Economic Basis of Politics*, 3rd ed. (1945), p. 3.

GETTELL, R. G., "Nature and Scope of Present Political Theory," *Proceedings of the American Political Science Association*, Vol. 10 (1913).

HALLOWELL, J. H., *Main Currents in Modern Political Thought* (New York, Holt, 1950), Chap. 1.

LERNER, Max, *Ideas Are Weapons* (New York, Viking, 1939), Chap. 1.

McILWAIN, C. H., *The Growth of Political Thought in the West* (New York, Macmillan, 1932), pp. 1-3.

ORTON, W. A., *The Liberal Tradition* (New Haven, Yale Univ. Press, 1945), Chap. 1.

WILLOUGHBY, W. W., "The Value of Political Philosophy," *Political Science Quarterly*, Vol. 15 (March, 1900).

PART II

Ancient Political Thought

CHAPTER II ⬿

The Beginnings

Primitive Political Ideas

From the earliest times men have had ideas concerning the external control to which they submitted their lives and actions. While our knowledge of early thought is scant, yet certain principles that primitive men believed to underlie their political institutions may be discovered by reasoning back from later periods, by investigating the beliefs and customs of the earliest peoples of whom we have knowledge, and by observing the remnants of primitive peoples surviving today.

The most universal and striking feature of early political thought was the failure to differentiate religion, custom, and law. Divine prohibition or divine sanction accompanied almost every act, customary obligation regulated conduct, and the idea of change was abhorrent. The bond of unity within the group was essentially a religious one, and the ultimate authority behind every rule of action, whatever its origin, was the will of the gods.

Primitive law was purely negative in character. It consisted of a list of things that were forbidden or *taboo*. The origin of these prohibitions was ordinarily connected with the apprehension of danger. They resulted from the savage's ignorance of natural phenomena and his general belief in malevolent spirits. Magic and ceremonial rites played a large part in primitive thought, and the power of the sorcerer or "medicine man" was enormous.

In addition to the religious bond, and closely connected with it, was the tie of kinship. The earliest social units were "totem groups" distinguished by the sign of some natural object, which was often worshiped. Within these groups intermarriage was forbidden, descent was traced through the mother, and definite rules regulated marriage outside the group and determined the system of relationships.

21

The next stage of social development, brought about largely by the domestication of animals and the rise of pastoral life, was the patriarchal tribe, a stronger and more permanent form of organization with more definite political ideas. In this system the woman became a member of her husband's group, and descent was traced through the father, whose power became well-nigh despotic. Authority within the group was personal, all members being connected by real or fictitious ties of kinship. In the patriarchal system, slavery appeared, since with the increasing food supply cannibalism became unnecessary and captives were kept alive to work for their captors. Ancestor worship, arising from belief in the spirit world and from deference to parental authority, became the dominant religion and added its sanction to the power of the patriarch or chief and to the observance of law. The negative idea of taboo was replaced by the positive idea of custom. Law was not a thing to be made, but a thing to be discovered. The practices followed in life by the revered ancestors were declared by the chief or elders, and those who refused to observe the customs were outlawed and banished from the tribe. Injuries to other members of the group were settled by the blood-feud or by money payments.

Under both of these systems of kinship organization there was need for a stronger and wider authority than the family could give, for the purpose of maintaining internal peace and order through the settlement of private disputes, and the guarantee of safety against external danger through united action in war. These needs gave rise to the chieftain, sometimes the patriarchal head, more often a champion renowned for physical prowess, who exercised political authority within the tribe and whose right to rule received the sanction of his subjects as well as the support of religion. Beginning with a jurisdiction that included little except authority in time of war and limited right of judgment in time of peace, the political organization of the tribe gradually increased its executive and judicial functions; later it assumed legislative power; and finally it developed into the sovereign body of modern times. In this process the family, retaining its organization and a certain control over its members, was subordinated to the growing state. The most important steps in the increasing political power of the group took place when, with the growth of agriculture, the tribe became fixed upon a definite portion of the earth, with the result that its sovereignty became territorial rather than personal, and when it finally assumed the function through its rulers of creating new law.

Political units were formed in early times either by the disintegration of larger units or by consolidation resulting from force. Tribes divided when too large, or were conquered and their lands incorporated with those of the conqueror. Alliances were temporary and difficult to maintain, and permanent unions based upon consent were unknown. Voluntary coöperation among groups required a considerable degree of political advancement. The Oriental empires were formed by conquest, not by confederation. Even the Hebrews, in spite of the unifying influence of their common faith, and the Greeks, in spite of pride in their common Hellenic race and culture, were not able to form permanent unions.

Oriental Political Thought

The Oriental empires—Egypt, Babylonia, Assyria, and Persia—were prevented by the general conditions of their social environment from creating a systematic political philosophy. A simple and predominantly rural economic system, superstitious and inflexible religious dogmas, social classes crystallized into castes, and minute regulation of everyday life [1] gave a fixity and sanctity to established institutions which discouraged speculation concerning their origin, nature, or possible improvement. Oriental social life was undifferentiated. Family, church, state, and industrial organization were inextricably bound together. Consequently political thought was not separated from religion, ethics, philosophy, and economic doctrines. The dominant influence was religious in character, and the ideas that prevailed were created, preserved, and handed down by the priestly class.

Morality and law were not clearly distinguished; ideas were based on tradition and dogma rather than on reason; and political liberty sufficient to permit questioning was never allowed. A certain amount of individualism seems necessary to the development of political theory. Oriental thought was paternalistic. It exalted the institution, glorified political and religious despotism, and denied the personal worth of the individual. Discontent, which has played such a large part in modern progress, was of little influence. Happiness was generally arrived at by decreasing one's desires rather than by demanding increased satisfaction of growing needs. Passivity and fatalism, resulting in political stagnation, logically resulted. Static ideals dominated. The general aim was to maintain the social equilibrium; and modern ideals of progress and reform were unknown. The Oriental had no right to question, in thought or in word, the ethical basis upon which his political institutions were founded. His belief in the

---

[1] "The sacred laws of the Brahmanic civilization regulated everything from the cleaning of one's teeth to one's funeral oblations; and the Mosaic code, with its express directions concerning the sowing of vineyards, eating, and trimming hair and beard, show the same tendency." L. H. Haney, *History of Economic Thought*, 3rd ed. (1936), p. 51.

perfection of existing institutions, and the fixity of all customary political obligations, prevented any real inquiry into the nature and source of authority, any discussion of the best form of governmental organization and administration, or any conception of individual liberty.

Eastern peoples have generally held a less materialistic view of life, not striving so eagerly as the peoples of the West for industrial progress or personal prosperity. Moral and religious codes have played a more direct and practical part in shaping their ideas. The fulfillment of the law has always been an essential idea in Oriental thought, the law consisting of an elaborate code which included religious ceremonies and observances and moral precepts as well as rules of human conduct.

Fragmentary sentences and aphoristic sayings upon political matters may be found in the early writings of Brahmins, Buddhists, and Confucians. They were, however, confused with religious and ethical principles and were never worked out into any system of political philosophy. Some Oriental peoples engaged extensively in speculative thought, but their inquiries resulted mainly in the formulation of elaborate cosmologies or in schemes to justify the existing régime as being in accordance with the sanctions of a revealed religion or of the superior ancestral wisdom of the past. The Hindus and the Chinese alone seem to have reached doctrines of human equality and ideals of political democracy.

The general form of state that the Oriental world created was a theocratic, despotic monarchy, with conquest or religion the sanction for authority. Monarchs either were, as in Egypt, worshipped as being themselves gods, or, as in Assyria and Persia, were considered the agents of the gods. The monarchs were aided by an elaborate body of administrative officials and supported by a priestly class that controlled men's minds and sometimes, as in Egypt, exercised the real governing power in the state.

The unity of the Oriental state was based not upon race and language, as in the modern world, but upon the worship of common gods. These supported the authority of the rulers within the state and gave aid to their worshippers in wars of aggression and defense. The gods, except in the case of the Hebrews, were associated with particular places, and a people emigrating or transported to an alien land were obliged to abandon their gods and adopt the worship of the gods of their new home. Similarly, a conquered people, while continuing the worship of their own gods, were compelled to acknowledge the supremacy of the gods of their conquerors.

The Orient contributed to political thought the imperial idea. Its empires were, however, collections of loosely united states rather than well-integrated political units. Weaker states sometimes placed themselves under the protection of stronger states by formal alliance, bringing gifts as a token of their good will. More often, empires were built up by conquest, the defeated peoples acknowledging the suzerainty of the victorious monarch and paying him tribute and military aid. Subject nations that were not rebellious were allowed to retain their national identity and their peculiar customs and laws. If they tried unsuccessfully to revolt, heavier tribute might be required, or their autonomy might be destroyed by placing them under officials sent out from the central state, or in extreme cases deportation or wholesale slaughter might threaten their national existence.

These loose-jointed Oriental empires never developed a well-organized administrative system, such as was later built up by Rome. Where conquered peoples retained their own political institutions, national aspirations were encouraged and revolt occurred whenever opportunity offered. Even when imperial officials were sent out to rule the subject provinces, their obligation to the central authority was limited to the customary yearly tribute and aid in war. The temptation of the officials to make themselves independent rulers, with the support of the people they governed, was always present; and the most advanced system of centralized control consisted in the sending of royal emissaries to spy upon the officials and report concerning their loyalty. Distance and the absence of effective communication were serious obstacles to unity in the ancient world.

The Oriental peoples whose ancient writings contain the greatest amount of political thought and whose political principles exhibit the most advanced ideas were the Hindus, the Chinese, and the Hebrews. While none of these peoples distinguished political from ethical ideas, as has been done in the western world, their contribution demands further consideration.

Hindu Political Thought

India, with an area as extensive as Europe minus Russia, and with a large and diverse population, has had an active political history. The existence of autonomous oligarchic city states is recorded in the earliest Hindu tradition. As early as the fourth century B.C. a Hindu empire was established which included a more extensive territory than the present India. In the following centuries kingdoms and empires rose and fell, warfare among the various principalities was almost constant, and frequent attempts were made by ambitious rulers to unite India into a world empire. State systems were not long-lived, and dynastic revolutions were numerous. The political development of India resembled in many ways that of Europe, and was marked by a growing political consciousness and by the creation of a considerable amount of political philosophy.

In contrast to the other Oriental political systems, the Hindu states were not theocratic. Religion in India did not dominate politics. The state was independent of the church, and the priests did not interfere in administration. The dictates of religion were limited to principles of moral guidance for ruler and subject alike. Because of this condition, political speculation was permissible and was able to reach advanced conceptions. Political philosophy was recognized as a distinct field of knowledge, created an extensive literature,[2] and was considered by some of its founders the most important of sciences.

Hindu political thinkers viewed the original nature of man as essentially selfish and wicked. They agreed with the Church Fathers and with Hobbes, rather than with Locke and Rousseau, in considering the state of nature a condition of violence, injustice, and the rule of might. They had no rosy conceptions concerning a Golden Age or a Garden of Eden. In the absence of authority, they believed that "the stronger would devour the weak like fishes in water," and this figure of the struggle for existence, known as the "logic of the fish," frequently recurs in both political and popular literature.

To prevent this condition, authority and punishment were required. Law, supported by force, was necessary to prevent private violence, to safeguard property, and to secure justice. The state arose, therefore, because of needs growing out of the original nature of man, and its authority rested upon its ability to coerce and to impose penalties. The Hindu theory of sanction and punishment corresponds closely to the *majestas* of Bodin, the *summa potestas* of Grotius, and the modern concept of sovereignty.

According to Hindu political thought, authority was personified in the ruler of the state, but the ruler as a person was subject to restraint and liable to punishment as was every other individual.[3] Hence the dilemma of royal power in Hindu theory. The king was possessor of sovereignty. He presided over and regulated the state, bringing evil doers to justice and correcting abuses. On the other hand, the possession of this power was dangerous to the ruler. If he exercised it wisely, it was conducive to the greatest good of the people, but if he exercised it thoughtlessly or arbitrarily, he was himself liable to removal and punishment. Hindu thinkers usually advocated active resistance to arbitrary authority. They justified revolution and frequently put the theory into practice. One of

[2] See B. K. Sarkar, "Hindu Political Philosophy," *Political Science Quarterly*, Vol. 33 (December, 1918), pp. 488-491.

[3] *Ibid.*, pp. 497-499.

43801

their greatest political writers said "the unity of opinion possessed by the many is more powerful than the king. The rope that is made of many threads is strong enough to drag the lion."

In order to prevent unwise and hasty action, the ruler was expected to take advice from the best minds and to associate with himself a council of ministers. The Hindu theory thus upheld a limited rather than an absolute monarchy, and a system of checks and balances was favored. Many Hindu writers upheld democratic institutions, popular assemblies, communistic undertakings, and personal liberty. The ideal of human brotherhood and of personal equality was frequently expressed. Buddha, in the fifth century B.C., was a staunch supporter of democratic views, taught the people that their prosperity depended upon the maintenance of their popular local assemblies, and carried on an active propaganda against monarchy.

Although Hindu ethics assigned a low place to the military virtues and taught a pacifist fatalism, Hindu political thought was often decidedly militaristic and sometimes Machiavellian. It emphasized the values of preparedness, praised the military virtues, frankly based political authority upon force, and extolled the judicious use of guile and secret diplomacy. The military aspects of Hindu theory resembled the Lycurgan creed of Sparta, the Bushido of Japan, and the modern doctrines of Treitschke.

Chinese Political Thought

In many respects the political thought of the Chinese resembled that of the Hindus rather than that of the other Oriental peoples. China was isolated, fairly free from warfare, and never united under a monarch powerful enough to crush freedom of thought and local independence. The worship of Heaven, the supreme deity, was a state function, performed by the magistrates. Ancestor worship was the popular cult cared for by the head of the family. Filial piety was the root of all virtue. From it was derived the duty of obedience and reverence toward all authority. There was, therefore, no powerful national priesthood. Their place was taken by the learned class, who gave considerable attention to political principles, especially in their moral aspects. The golden age in Chinese thought appeared in the Chou dynasty, between the eleventh and third centuries B.C. Among the most important thinkers were Confucius, Mencius, Moh-Ti, Lao-Tze and numerous commentators on their ideas.

The Chinese philosophers taught the necessity of law in order to restrain the innate depravity of man. "Man who is by nature wicked needs teaching and discipline in order to be right.... The ancient rulers understood the native viciousness of man ... and therefore created morals and laws and institutions in order that human instincts and impulses might be disciplined and transformed." [4] Chinese theory also taught equality among men, democracy in government, and the right to revolt against arbitrary authority. In the writings of Confucius were found political ideas that were not only democratic but even radical and revolutionary. Local institutions were always vigorous in China and maintained the ideals of self-government.

The great religious teacher Moh Ti (c 500-420 B.C.) was the preacher of universal brotherhood. Mencius was the author of the dictum that "the most important element in a state is the people; next come the altars of the national gods; least in importance is the king," and that "by observing the nature of the people's aspirations we learn the will of Heaven." *Vox populi vox dei* was a truism to the Chinese. It was quite logical that the pre-revolutionary writers in France should view Chinese philosophy and institutions with great admiration. It was treated almost as a constitutional principle in China that, when the king misbehaved, it was the duty of the most virtuous and powerful of his princes to depose and succeed him; and ministers sometimes confined the sovereign temporarily "until he gave proof of reformation."

The aim of the state was conceived, as by the Greeks, to be virtue, not wealth or power; and a high ideal of character and benevolence was set for rulers. The qualities of the warrior held a low place in Chinese esteem and the principles of militarism were bitterly opposed.[5] In contrast to the general Chinese conception of the perfection of the past, and the emphasis which they placed upon conformity to ancient custom, the political philosophy of ancient China was often advanced and liberal.

Hebrew Political Thought

Like most Oriental peoples, the Jews held a theocratic conception of the state, believing that political authority was divine in origin and sanction; but they early reached the conception of a single deity, worshipped in common by all their tribes. Their god, Jehovah, was not associated with a particular place; on the contrary, he became the god of the Hebrew people, guiding and protecting them wherever they went, even during political captivity. Hence, although the Jews were not able to form a

[4] Hsun Tze (B.C. 305-235?) cited and translated by Shih Hu, *The Development of the Logical Method in Ancient China* (1922), p. 156. Mencius, however, taught that "The tendency of man's nature to good is like the tendency of water to flow downwards," and the dogma that "Man commences life with a virtuous nature" was generally accepted by Taoists and Confucians.

[5] The writings of Mencius were largely devoted to an attack on the evils of warfare.

sovereign state, they had a stronger feeling of national unity and of national destiny than other Oriental peoples.

They considered the state as divinely established, and all law as derived from the will of Jehovah. This law was absolute and permanent, binding upon rulers and subjects alike, and could not be made or changed by man. Nevertheless, the Hebrews added to the usual Oriental belief in theocratic authority the idea of popular consent. The people voluntarily and formally accepted the rule of Jehovah. They entered into a covenant of obedience in return for divine favor. When they disobeyed the law, they were guilty not only of disregarding the will of God but also of breaking their solemn agreement.

The Hebrews also believed that Jehovah might be consulted on important questions, and that He would give response through his chosen agents. Thus prophets and judges, whose words were believed to voice the will of God, appeared from time to time. These leaders did not gain their position by heredity, nor did they form a separate class. They arose to power through natural ability and force of character, and their duties were moral, not political. In spite of the theocratic basis of the Hebrew state, it was not governed by its priests, most of the kings and of the judges coming from outside that group. But the influence of the priest, though indirect, was powerful, even after the establishment of the monarchy. When the Hebrew tribes, forced into union and compelled to adopt a more centralized government because of common danger from the Philistines, appealed to God for a king, He granted the request, according to priestly interpretation, reluctantly. The first king, Saul, was chosen by God through Samuel as a priestly intermediary, and when Saul proved unfit it was Samuel as priest who deposed him and chose his successor.

The democratic element in Hebrew political thought was shown not only in the idea of a voluntary covenant with God but also in the influence of public opinion upon the kingship. The Hebrews did not hesitate to criticize their rulers. David was reproved by the prophet Nathan and Ahab by Elijah. The prophets openly voiced and stimulated popular discontent with royal misconduct and misrule. The people resented Solomon's imperial designs and strict government, with its taxes, military service, and forced labor; and after his death, the northern tribes refused to accept his son and chose another king. There was a distinct socialistic element in the teachings of the prophets. Theirs was the first passionate plea for the poor, the wretched, and the heavy-burdened, and the first definite statement of the brotherhood of man.

The people also played a considerable part in reducing the law to a definite code. The law at first was conceived to be the direct will of

Jehovah, manifested through his priests in deciding disputes brought before them. These decisions, or "torahs," naturally created precedents upon which general rules could be based. Secular courts were established later by Moses to try ordinary cases in which well-established rules could be applied, and new or difficult questions only were referred to the priests. However, the need for an authoritative code was increasingly felt, partly to secure uniformity in the decisions of the local judges, partly to restore principles which the people were in danger of disregarding. Accordingly, the Book of the Covenant,[6] consisting of a collection of decisions, was drawn up in the eighth century B.C. This put into definite form established rules and contained no new principles, but in the second half of the seventh century B.C. the Deuteronomic Code [7] was promulgated. This was a privately prepared code and included such early laws as its authors considered worth perpetuating. It aimed to recall the people to the customs of their fathers and to offset the degrading influence of Assyria. It contained such extensive changes from existing law that years of priestly exhortation were needed to prepare the way for its acceptance. It was adopted in a formal mass meeting, in which king and people solemnly agreed to "perform the words of this covenant that were written in this book." [8] In the fifth century B.C., the codification was practically completed by the adoption by the people in a great assembly of the Priestly Law, brought to Jerusalem from Babylon by Ezra the scribe.[9]

Later Hebrew thought was characterized by an intolerant, rigid ritualism and by a war ethics that deepened intertribal hatreds and intensified the barbarities of war. As modified later by Hellenism and by Christianity, many of its principles spread to Europe and have come down to the modern world.

Ancient Theory of International Relations

Certain principles of interstate relations may also be found in ancient literature or may be deduced from the external dealings of early peoples. Although the modern idea of international law among sovereign and independent states did not develop until the rise of national monarchies at the close of the Middle Ages, yet ancient peoples carried on foreign relations according to certain customs and rules, usually under religious sanction. The intergroup relations of antiquity were based in the main upon force. Ancient states were formed by constant conflict with neighboring

[6] Exodus 21-23.
[7] II Kings 23:1-3.
[8] Deut. 12-25.
[9] Ezra 7; Nehemiah 8-9.

states and with surrounding barbarians. Their idea of the normal condition of interstate relations would naturally differ from those of the modern world, which grew out of the Roman Empire with its *Pax Romana*. War was regarded as the natural condition of mankind; peace, as an exceptional condition secured by special agreement. Negotiation between states was Machiavellian in character and was employed as an aid to war or as a substitute for it; and the foreigner was regarded as an enemy, without legal rights or obligations. Certain ties were acknowledged among those of the same race and religion, but states as such possessed no rights and were under no legal obligations one to another. The Hebrews recognized mutual rights in their intertribal dealings, considered other peoples as natural enemies, and were especially bitter against the original occupiers of the Promised Land.[10]

War was waged ruthlessly. The persons and property of the conquered were at the mercy of the victors, and the religions of the period usually urged the extermination or enslavement of defeated peoples. The bodies of the slain were often mutilated, captives were subjected to horrible tortures, and the victors carved boasting records of their atrocities upon their monuments. Religion was conceived as an alliance of the gods and their worshipers against other peoples and their gods. "Let us go up against them, for our God is greater than their God," was a characteristic battle cry. Oriental states considered it one of their chief duties to extend the authority of their gods over as many peoples as possible, the method of its achievement being military force. Victory was ascribed to the gods, and the punishments inflicted upon the vanquished were declared to be commanded by divine authority.

However, the pressure of frequent life and death struggles among primitive peoples, together with the strong emphasis placed upon unity of kinship and religion, had a marked effect upon the inner spirit of the group. Loyalty to comrades, self-sacrifice, and devotion to the common cause were called into constant activity. Nearly all early peoples attained ideals of closer brotherhood and unity within national bounds than have obtained in western countries. Competition in primitive times was between groups, not between individuals. Within the group communistic ideas prevailed. An injury to any member was considered an injury to the group, and the group was held responsible for the activities of its members.

Friendly relations among primitive peoples were not entirely lacking. Mutual aid was exchanged, even among savages.[11] Early empires ex-

---

[10] Deut. 7:1-3; 20:10-17.

[11] See Margaret Mead, ed., *Coöperation and Competition Among Primitive Peoples* (1937).

changed letters,[12] presents, and embassies; and alliances, cemented by intermarriages, were sometimes concluded. Bribery was also used to corrupt the officials of neighboring states. Hospitality to visitors and messengers was extended under certain conditions and according to rigid rules and formalities.

In the second half of the eighth century B.C., the Assyrian Empire, absorbing the smaller states of western Asia, became a world power. Political unity then, as later under Rome, suggested the idea of world law and peace. The Hebrew prophets of that period, convinced of the supremacy of their God and their religion, conceived of a world-wide kingdom in which all nations should acknowledge the suzerainty of Jehovah. They put forth the ideal of universal peace and spoke of the time when "nation shall not lift up sword against nation, neither shall they learn war any more." [13] The ideal of arbitration was referred to by Herodotus, who relates that one of the Persian satraps compelled the cities of Ionia "to make agreements among themselves so that they might give satisfaction for wrongs and not plunder one another's land." [14] Early Hindu political philosophy, growing up under conditions of active intertribal life, worked out the concepts of external sovereignty, balance of power, and world organization, and urged humane methods of warfare.[15] The Chinese philosopher Mencius maintained that the same rules of morality apply in the relations of nations as in those of individuals, and taught that differences between nations should be settled by arbitration and by considerations of justice, not by force.

Commerce, in its origin, was scarcely distinguished from war or robbery. Piracy was regarded as an honorable undertaking. The hope of plunder was a guiding motive in foreign policy; and commercial peoples like the Carthaginians and the Phoenicians organized trade as a government enterprise, carried on systematic commercial exploitation of weaker peoples, and waged relentless war against all rivals in order to secure a monopoly of trade. Early commerce was largely trade of civilized with less civilized or barbarous peoples. The latter distrusted and feared the former, and warfare ending in annihilation, slavery, or colonial dependence was generally the fate of the less civilized combatant. Ancient peoples usually extolled agriculture and looked upon commerce with distrust, permitting foreign trade only under stringent restrictions.

[12] For an example of early diplomatic correspondence see the Tell el-Amarna letters. W. M. F. Petrie, *A History of Egypt*, 3rd ed. (1899), Vol. II, pp. 259-320. See also J. Baikie, *The Amarna Age* (1926), Chap. 10.

[13] Isaiah 2:4; and Micah 4:3.

[14] Herodotus, vi. 42.

[15] B. K. Sarkar, "Hindu Theory of International Relations," *American Political Science Review*, Vol. 13 (August, 1919), pp. 400-414.

Friendly commercial relations were, however, sometimes carried on, especially by the Egyptians, and commercial treaties were occasionally made and observed. Under Solomon, Jewish trading vessels engaged in commerce with distant ports; later kings of Israel secured the right to establish trading quarters in foreign cities, and granted similar privileges to alien merchants.

REFERENCES

Primitive Political Thought

BOWLE, John, *Western Political Thought* (New York, Oxford, 1948), Chap. 1.
BREASTED, J. H., *The Conquest of Civilization* (New York, Harper, 1926), Chap. 1.
FRAZER, J. G., *Aftermath* (New York, Macmillan, 1937).
MAINE, H. S., *Ancient Law* (London, J. Murray, 1907).
MEAD, Margaret, ed., *Coöperation and Competition among Primitive Peoples* (New York, McGraw, 1937).
WILLOUGHBY, W. W., *Political Theories of the Ancient World* (New York, Longmans, 1903), Chap. 1).

Oriental Political Thought

BAIKIE, J., *The Amarna Age* (New York, Macmillan, 1926).
BOWLE, John, *Western Political Thought*, Chap. 2.
BREASTED, J. H., *The Dawn of Conscience* (New York, Scribner, 1934).
———, *The Conquest of Civilization*, Part II.
DAVIES, W. W., *The Codes of Hammurabi and Moses* (New York, Methodist, 1905).
FRANKFORT, H., and others, *The Intellectual Adventure of Ancient Man* (Chicago, Univ. of Chicago Press, 1946).
HANEY, L. H., *History of Economic Thought,* 3rd ed. (New York, Macmillan, 1936), pp. 37-88.
HU, Shih, *The Development of the Logical Method in Ancient China* (Shanghai, Oriental, 1922).
MAXEY, Chester, *Political Philosophers,* rev. ed. (New York, Macmillan, 1948), Chap. 2.
PETRIE, W. M. F., *A History of Egypt,* 3rd ed. (London, Methuen, 1899), Vol. II.
SARKER, B. K., "Hindu Political Philosophy," *Political Science Quarterly,* Vol. 13 (December, 1918).
———, "Hindu Theory of International Relations," *American Political Science Review,* Vol. 13 (August, 1919).
———, *Political Institutions and Theories of the Hindus* (Leipzig, Markert and Petters, 1922).
THOMAS, E. D., *Chinese Political Thought* (New York, Prentice-Hall, 1927).
ZIMMER, Heinrich, *Philosophies of India* (New York, Pantheon, 1951).

CHAPTER III ~

The Greek City-State

Although the political ideas and institutions of the Orient are of interest, it is primarily to Greece that we must look for an understanding of the origins of western culture. In literature, in art, and in the sciences inquiries into our past begin with the great names of early Greek society. Sophocles and Euripides, Phidias and Polycletus, Euclid and Hippocrates, are only a few of those that might be mentioned. This is even more true in political philosophy. In spite of notable refinements made over the centuries, we must still return to the great age of Plato and Aristotle for answers to political questions which continue to plague mankind. Nowhere, for instance, have the questions of reason and authority, justice, and rule of law been subjected to closer scrutiny. This will be illustrated when we consider the dialogues of Plato and the *Politics* of Aristotle. But to place such a study in perspective, it will first be desirable to consider the institutional background provided by the unique πολις, or city-state.

Greek Political Institutions

The Hellenic world consisted of a group of cities, scattered among the valleys of Greece and on the neighboring coasts and islands. These cities had a tradition of common origin and possessed common social and religious institutions. Politically, however, they were independent, save for impermanent alliances and the efforts of certain cities to dominate their neighbors. Colonies were frequently sent out, but they soon severed political ties with the home land, becoming autonomous.

Kingship in the Homeric tradition appears very early in the political organization of these city-states. But by the seventh century B.C. oligarchies, composed of the heads of the leading clans or tribes, controlled most of the cities. These oligarchies, grown lazy and quarrelsome, were themselves replaced from 700 to 500 B.C. by "tyrants," who appeared first as champions of the people. Soon, however, it became evident that the corruption and arbitrary rule of the oligarchies had been mild in comparison with the capriciousness of these ambitious men. Uniting with the aristocracy the people successfully rebelled in city after city, driving the tyrants out. There then ensued a long period of democratic control punctuated by contests with the aristocracy. It was during this period that Greek political thought had its beginning.

Of the city-states, two stand out in importance—Sparta and Athens early asserting their leadership. It was to these cities that the Greeks turned when the Persian invasion compelled united action, and it was Sparta and Athens whose later rivalry ended in the Peloponnesian War.

The government of Sparta was based upon a rigid social system which divided the population into three classes. The most numerous were the Helots, or serfs, whose agricultural labor supported the population, but who had no share in civil or political rights. The Perioikoi, or middle class, engaged mainly in industry and commerce, possessed civil rights, but had no share in the political life of the state. The Spartans proper, descendants of the original Dorian conquerors, though few in numbers, had absolute control in public affairs. They owned the land, were forbidden to engage in trade, and devoted their energy mainly to military service until the maturity of physical life was passed, after which they assumed the duties of government. Their life was rigidly regulated and communistic. Children at the age of seven were placed in the hands of state officials for uniform training; the adult males ate at the public mess hall. Physical perfection and eugenics were emphasized, and all forms of luxury and inequality were prohibited. In every dispute the judgment of the magistrate was final, written laws being expressly forbidden. Intercourse with foreigners was narrowly limited.

The governmental system consisted of an assembly composed of the whole body of Spartans; a senate of twenty-eight members, elected for life; two kings, equal in authority; and an annually elected board of five ephors. The ephors, intended originally as a check upon the power of the kings and senate, gradually acquired political supremacy. As the number of landowners decreased, and many of the Spartans, unable to furnish their share for the public tables, were excluded from participation in government, real power fell into the hands of a narrow oligarchy.

With such conditions prevailing, it is not surprising that Sparta contributed little directly to Greek political thought. But indirectly its importance must not be underestimated. The philosophers of Athens were writing at a time when Athens was rapidly disintegrating. Lacking social stability and military success, they turned to Sparta, drawing heavily on Spartan institutions.

In many respects Athens and Sparta provided a striking contrast. During a major part of its history, Athens was intensely democratic in both organization and spirit. Moreover, Athens was maritime and commercial, not agricultural; it had no traditional social distinction between conqueror and conquered; it admitted a large alien population into social and economic privileges; and it did not exercise a vise-like control over the lives of its citizens.

Social classes in Athens included slaves, resident foreigners, and Athenian citizens. The slaves constituted a full third of Athens' inhabitants and were completely without rights. Much of the manual labor, of course, fell to their lot. But it would be a mistake to assume that all of it did, leaving the citizens as a leisure class. "It is quite false," as Sabine' points out, "to imagine that in a city like Athens the citizens were typically men whose hands were unsoiled by labor." [1]

Nonetheless, most of the mines and larger farms were worked by slaves, and they were employed by the city in carrying out the menial functions of the administration. The abuses which such a system entailed were not widely discussed. Slavery existed everywhere and was largely taken for granted.

The second class, the resident foreigners or metics, also constituted a sizeable segment of Athens' population. As some of them were transients, their numbers varied. But many families remained who had lived for generations in Athens without acquiring citizenship. Citizenship was granted through birth to Athenian citizens only,[2] so that aliens had little hope of assuming a share in the control of Athens. Otherwise, however, they were not discriminated against. They were possessed of full civil and social rights and were, as a group, rather prosperous.

All political power was vested in the last group, the citizens.[3] They in turn were divided into nobles and commons, the former representing the distinguished families in the city. Originally all political authority had belonged to the nobles, but in the seventh century B.C. a conflict between nobles and commons led to the reforms of Solon. These made wealth instead of birth the basis of political power, and opened to all citizens some share in public life. When the tyrants were expelled in 510 B.C., the legislation of Cleisthenes gave a further impulse toward democracy; and in the next century, under Pericles, Athenian democracy approached its final form.

To be a citizen in Athens was to hold an active membership in the

---

[1] G. H. Sabine, A History of Political Theory, rev. ed. (1950), p. 5.

[2] To this rule there were certain exceptions. For extraordinary service, citizenship could be conferred by decree of the people.

[3] Citizens here refers only to men. Women had no political rights.

business of governing. If a citizen did nothing else, he participated in the assembly, which was the supreme organ of government.[4] More than ten times each year [5] citizens over twenty met together to consider the state of public affairs. Decrees of this assembly were law and superseded action taken by the Council of Five Hundred or by the magistrates.

While the assembly was supreme, it seldom attempted to formulate or execute policy. This was left to other organs of government, held responsible by the assembly.

Chief among these was the Council of Five Hundred. This body was representative in character. Members were nominated by local districts called demes. From those nominated, five hundred were chosen by lot to serve for a year. The use of lots in this connection has always interested later democratic countries. Athenians considered their system to be more democratic than merely voting, because the use of lots gave every nominated citizen a chance to be elected. As the council was to represent the *people*, it was felt that elected officials should be representative of a cross-section of the population—not chosen because of special merits which distinguished them from others. The theory was that "each is ruled by all and in his turn each rules over all." [6] Powers of the council included those now associated with the executive branch of government. It sent and received ambassadors, it controlled the navy and lesser administrative bodies, and it formulated a legislative program to be presented to the assembly.

Associated with the council were boards of magistrates, composed of ten members who were chosen from each of the ten tribes into which Athens was divided. They, too, served short terms and were chosen by lot. Such administrative powers as they had were severely limited by the assembly, the council, and the courts. Their accounts were audited monthly by a committee of the council. Their tenure of office was subject to monthly review by the assembly. And an "information" might be brought against them at any time by private citizens,[7] leading in some cases to their dismissal.

More favorably situated was the Board of Generals. This group of ten military leaders held a special place in Athenian society. It answered to a considerable degree the need for security felt by the people. Its members were not chosen by lot, but were elected directly by the citizens. Moreover, members of this board could be reëlected indefinitely. Legally its

[4] Not all the citizens, of course, attended every meeting. Often only a few thousand were present. For important votes 6000 constituted a quorum. See G. Glotz, *The Greek City and Its Institutions* (1929), p. 153.

[5] *Ibid.*, p. 154.

[6] Ernest Barker, *The Political Thought of Plato and Aristotle* (1906), p. 447.

[7] *Ibid.*, p. 457.

powers were restricted to purely military matters, but in periods of crisis it assumed a place of first importance in the control of foreign policy as well.

Finally, there were the courts. These differed greatly from our system of courts, being completely democratic in organization and spirit. They were composed of "judgment-finders," who were selected from a jury panel of six thousand. Often as many as four or five hundred citizens served at once and on the same jury. The theory behind such large numbers was that the Courts *were* the people, acting in particular cases to register popular approval or disapproval. These juries had power to reach decisions in both civil and criminal cases and to impose penalties from which there was no appeal. They also had power to try laws. Laws held contrary to custom or to the Athenian constitution could be nullified by court action. This gave to the courts, as a similar power gives to the U.S. Supreme Court, a marked degree of legislative authority.

Sense of Community: Pericles

Other factors were equally important in shaping Greek political thought. Foremost among these were a sense of community and spirit of camaraderie which have few modern parallels.

The lives of Athenians were not as compartmentalized as ours often are. Distinctions between public and private interests melted away into a common concern for the community. They would not, moreover, have been able to understand the wide distrust of government which we have not yet completely lost. They sought happiness through government, not in spite of it. Added to this was a sense of neighborliness and friendship which is known by people intimately sharing the same problems under isolated and often adverse circumstances. Much of this has been lost in our impersonal world where many people scarcely know their nextdoor neighbors. But the life of the market-place,[8] the love of discussion, and the values people shared left no room for such an occurrence in Athens.

[8] Charles McIlwain is at his best when commenting on the life of the market-place. "The polis was in a sense his [the citizen's] home, for he never, at least in the later period of Greek development, allowed his household to draw him away from the every-day association with his fellow citizens. For him there was nothing quite comparable with the English love of home to keep him from the market-place where his real life was to be lived, and it was there that his days were actually passed. Women's sphere might be the home, and silence their chief virtue, but his place was in the assembly or the market-place. A woman, says Aristotle, who was only as modest as a good man would be considered a chatter-box, and one of the bad features of extreme democracy is that the wives of the poor cannot be kept from going out of doors." *The Growth of Political Thought in the West* (1932), p. 9. By permission of The Macmillan Company.

Of the common values, none was more important than religion. Gods were community gods, presiding over the city in a personal and compassionate way. Legends relate that they laughed and cried, loved and hated, and in other ways acted not very differently from ordinary people. More than this, Athenian religion was surprisingly undogmatic when compared with its Oriental counterpart. Little was actually required of its adherents, religion being a matter of individual conscience. The Greeks therefore had no priestly caste controlling thought or exercising authority. This left room for all to play a greater or lesser part as they desired, with the result that religion became more of a ceremonialized expression of unity and love of city than a more formal expression of fixed religious beliefs.

Other things were held in common as well. Greek architecture was always a matter of public concern, as were other forms of art. And many commercial enterprises were owned and operated by the city, such as the mines. But these facts only serve to illustrate the fundamental conclusion that Greek life was a life in common. "The vividness of the feeling of community, the approximation of neighborliness and citizenship, the living realization of a true *res publica* or common weal": these were the deepest roots from which Athens drew its life.[9]

Nowhere is this sense of community better expressed than in Pericles' Funeral Oration,[10] as related by Greece's greatest historian, Thucydides. The war with Sparta has just begun. The first of the dead have been returned home. And in commemoration of their service Pericles, the foremost Athenian, begins his public accounting of the greatness of Athens and the men who died for her.

Our constitution does not copy the laws of neighbouring states; we are rather a pattern to others than imitators ourselves. Its administration favours the many instead of the few; this is why it is called a democracy. If we look to the laws, they afford equal justice to all in their private differences; if to social standing, advancement in public life falls to reputation for capacity, class considerations not being allowed to interfere with merit; nor again does poverty bar the way, if a man is able to serve the state, he is not hindered by the obscurity of his condition. . . . If we turn to our military policy, there also we differ from our antagonists. . . . Our rivals from their very cradles by a painful discipline seek after manliness, at Athens we live exactly as we please, and yet are just as ready to encounter every legitimate danger. . . . Nor are these the only points in which our city is worthy of admiration. We cultivate refinement without extravagance and knowledge without effeminacy; wealth we employ more for use than for show, and place the real disgrace of poverty not in owning to the fact but in declining the struggle against it. Our public men have, besides politics, their private affairs to attend to, and our ordinary citizens, though occupied with the pursuits of industry, are still fair judges of public matters; for,

[9] *Ibid.*, p. 8.
[10] Thucydides, *History of the Peloponnesian War*, ii. 34-46.

unlike any other nation, regarding him who takes no part in these duties not as unambitious but as useless, we Athenians are able to judge at all events if we cannot originate, and instead of looking on discussion as a stumbling-block in the way of action, we think it an indispensable preliminary to any wise action at all. . . . In short, I say that as a city we are the school of Hellas.

In these memorable passages Pericles summed up all that was best in Athenian democracy. Much, of course, was left unsaid, as Plato in condemning democracy was later to point out.[11] But as the statement of an ideal and as evidence of pride in community, it leaves little to be desired.[12]

Nature of Greek Political Thought

Perhaps the chief characteristic of Greek thought was its concern for first principles or for the central rules controlling the universe. One early Greek philosopher, as evidence of this spirit, declared that he would rather discover one causal law than be king of Persia. The Greeks conceived the universe as the product of creative reason. Consequently, it only remained for them to search out the controlling principles if they were to understand it. In seeking these principles, the Greeks first turned to the external world. But by the fifth century B.C., man's intellectual curiosity had turned toward man himself. The Greeks were struck by differences between their culture and that of the barbarians, as they loved to call all non-Hellenic peoples. This led to speculation over the causes of this difference. Later, as Athens disintegrated before Sparta and then before the armies of Philip of Macedon, further impetus was given to this search for cause and effect relationships—this search after rules governing men's lives.

Added to this inquiring mind and faith in reason, was a strong conviction that few things were fatalistically determined and so out of men's control. Because of their religious background the Greeks feared little. Instead, they were impressed with man's ability to shape his own society in spite of those "unseen powers" which in other ages have ruled man's mind.

Freed by his society to think and to inquire, the Greek's intellectual frontiers were almost limitless. Catlin catalogues only a few of the more discussed subjects. Here is his list: "Democracy, the freedom of writing and thought, censorship, the relation of democracy and the expert, feminism, eugenics, abortion, the problem of leisure, whether the prolongation

---

[11] Against Pericles' ideal of "happy versatility," Plato set the ideal of each person playing the particular role assigned to him by reason.

[12] For additional comment on this subject see Sabine, *op. cit.*, pp. 11 ff.

of life by medicine cannot be carried to excess, nudism, psychoanalysis, revolution, the proletariat, the class war, what comes after popular dictatorship." [13] In the field of politics alone the subjects discussed were innumerable. But for the purposes of this discussion, attention can be confined to a few of the more important questions.

According to the ideas of the Greeks, men's lives should be lived in accordance with nature and with right reason. It was the duty of men to use the powers that nature had given them and to develop their potentialities. Since men were gifted with reason, they should not only live but live well. Their lives should correspond to the highest ideals that their reason could conceive. To accomplish this end, social and political life was essential. Man was, by nature, "a political animal." Only a god or a beast could do without society. Hence the state, being necessary for man's highest development, was as much a product of nature as man himself, and it needed no further justification. Man and the state were thus bound together in a living social whole; neither could have interests contrary to the other. The state was conceived to be a living personality, absorbing in its life all individual personalities; and political existence was considered to be the highest form of life. "While the Oriental, in his subjection to the law and to the state, viewed his subordination as an obedience rendered to an alien and external power, the Greek saw in it but the yielding to a higher self, a giving up of his will to a will in the formation of which he participated." [14]

The Greek conception of the state as an entity of which every individual was an integral part demanded active political participation by each citizen. This was possible in the small city-states of the Hellenic world. Hence, the Greek theory of the nature of the state led logically to democracy, since all men must exercise political authority in order to realize their best life; and to the city-state ideal, since under the conditions of transportation and communication in the ancient world, democracy could exist only in a state small in territory and population. Their ideal state was a small, compact community in which the citizens were personally known one to another and in which all could assemble in one place.

Furthermore, since only through the state could man achieve his highest ends, no logical limit could be set to the activities undertaken by the state. Whatever was for the best interests of man was a legitimate public function, and the state might find it desirable to regulate even the smallest details of life. The idea that the state existed to safeguard the rights of

[13] George Catlin, *The Story of The Political Philosophers* (1939), p. 28.
[14] W. W. Willoughby, *Political Theories of the Ancient World* (1903), p. 37.

its citizens, as worked out in the Roman theory of private law, or that the citizen had rights which the state was bound to respect, as developed in the eighteenth century theory of natural rights, was alien to Greek thought. Since the individual and the state were one, no distinction between public and private affairs could be made. The conception of public law, which defines the relation between state and individual, had no place in Greek political theory. Greek democracy contributed the idea of political rights, but not that of civil rights.

The Greek idea of law went through several stages. The writings of Homer and Hesiod portrayed a theocratic organization of the state, in which custom and tradition governed, law and religion were not distinguished, and the will of the gods, spoken through the king, was the source of authority. Commands were issued as distinct inspirations, unconnected by general principles. The customs of the ancestors were held in great reverence, though a crude idea of abstract justice and reason occasionally appeared.

When monarchy was replaced by aristocracy, the theocratic idea was weakened. The nobles could not claim the divine inspiration which the kings had asserted, and when they abused their custody of the unwritten customs, a demand for written rules arose. Hence appeared the codes. In Sparta, the fundamental laws of Lycurgus came into being. And in Athens, the criminal code of Draco was developed, later being supplemented by the civil and political code of Solon. Law was thus secularized, the theocratic idea was excluded, and the human element made more important.

However, the Greeks never attained to the idea of law as the deliberate creation of a legislative organ in the state. The enactment of a new law was made difficult even in the height of democracy at Athens. The later Greeks believed that law was to be found, in the form of a complete system, in reason itself. It grew out of the very nature of the state, spontaneously voicing its needs. The general principles of law were believed to be perfect and permanent, not subject to change at the will of the people.[15] Nature was the source of law, and human reason the means through which nature's wishes could be discovered. Accordingly, changes were needed only when the general nature of the political system was modified, and the duty of the state was ordinarily considered to be the application rather than the creation of the law. The highest function of the state, according to the Greek conception, was the judicial; it was the popularization of the law courts that marked the final step in Athenian democracy.

---

[15] This statement must be modified to the degree that Sophistic ideas gained acceptance. This problem will be more fully discussed later.

The Sophists

Traces of political thought appear in the earliest literature of the Greeks. Homer portrayed a patriarchal regime in which kings were descended from the gods, exercised despotic authority, and held the mass of the people in contempt. In Hesiod and in the fragmentary writings of the Seven Sages, the supports of monarchy were somewhat weakened. The duties as well as the rights of kings were emphasized, and the acts of rulers were judged by the same standards as those of other men. The growth of a more liberal theory of the state was both a cause and a result of the political movement from monarchy to aristocracy.

The fifth century B.C., beginning with the Persian and ending with the Peloponnesian War, gave the Hellenic world experience in every phase of politics. Close contact with Persian despotism and the bitter struggle between Spartan oligarchy and Athenian democracy stimulated political reflection. The religious faith of the Greek world was disappearing; democracy was quickening popular intelligence, but also bringing danger of deterioration in administration and lack of stability in public policy. Old restraints were disappearing, freedom of thought permitted the most revolutionary ideas,[16] and intellectual life was in general ferment. A contest for political power was also waged between the old landowning aristocracy and a new wealthy class engaged in commerce, influenced by foreign ideas, and disposed to innovation.

The way was thus opened for the employment of the arts of the demagogue, and for the rise of a group of teachers who gave lessons in politics, teaching men how to appeal effectively, through eloquence and the art of disputation, to the public mind. The Sophists,[17] representing in their point of view the disintegrating tendencies of the times, aimed to supply the instruction that would fit a young man for a successful career in the practical life of a citizen. They rejected the ideas of universal truth and of abstract principles of justice. They taught that "man is the measure of all things," each individual being qualified to judge, according to his own beliefs and desires, what was right. In denying fixed rules of conduct, they attacked the rationality of nature, which had been the basis of Greek philosophy and ethics. They pointed out that such rules or laws varied widely, differing from government to government. So far were they from agreeing, that some laws expressly forbade what others com-

---

[16] A good expression of this attitude is found in Greek drama, especially the comedies.

[17] The term *Sophist* was the name of the profession, not of a school of philosophic thought. The Sophists were characterized by a common method and point of view, rather than by common ideas. The most noted were Protagoras, Gorgias, and Prodicus.

manded. Laws were thus mere conventions, not unchangeable laws of nature.

The Sophists, in holding that men were by nature selfish and unequal in strength, based political authority upon might. Political rule resulted, either from an agreement among the strong to oppress the weak, or from a combination among the weak to defend themselves against the strong. This view is clearly expressed by Thrasymachus in the *Republic*. Thrasymachus, as the representative in the dialogue of the Sophists, is asked by Socrates to define justice. His reply is "that everywhere there is one principle of justice, which is the interest of the stronger." [18] The Sophists thus believed that might makes right. They also believed that men were naturally nonsocial, that the state rested upon an artificial and individualistic basis, and that political authority was essentially selfish in its aims. The Sophists were the first teachers of individualism, and originated the idea that the state rests upon a social compact. They also drew a distinction between morality and law, and showed that law, because of the nature of political authority, often forces men to act contrary to the dictates of reason.

To what degree these ideas were accepted, it is difficult to say. But probably the Sophists were more convincing than Plato and later critics would have us believe. On the basis of existing evidence, it appears that by the middle of the fifth century B.C. these ideas had made so much progress that they were receiving general assent. McIlwain points to several examples of this.[19] Athenian envoys in Thucydides are quoted as saying, "you and we should say what we really think, and aim only at what is possible for we both alike know that into the discussion of human affairs the question of justice only enters where the pressure of necessity is equal, and that the powerful exact what they can, and the weak grant what they must." There are, in addition, similar passages in Aristophanes' *Clouds* and Xenophon's *Memorabilia* which McIlwain quotes to the same effect. But more than this, Sophist doctrines have stood the test of history extremely well. The very essence of modern democratic government rests on their notions of individualism. It was they who first developed the thesis that not only is man the measure of all things but each man is the *only* measure. Truth rested in each man's opinion of the truth, not in a system of norms or absolutes.[20] The Sophists, to conclude, deserve a better name than they are usually given.

[18] *Republic*, 339.
[19] McIlwain, *op. cit.*, pp. 13-20.
[20] For an interesting discussion of this question, especially as it concerns the contrast with Plato, see K. R. Popper, *The Open Society and Its Enemies*, rev. ed. (1950).

Socrates

The contribution to political philosophy of Socrates and of his pupil Plato must be viewed in the above light. They believed that these new and corrosive doctrines were responsible for the disintegration of Greek society, which was taking place all around them. To prevent this, society had to be pulled together again by recalling men to a belief in those great truths which made a virtuous life possible. Men had to be made to see that virtue is knowledge.[21] This was their purpose. Nothing comes closer to the center of political philosophy than this struggle between "truth" and "opinion," between the doctrines of Plato and those of the Sophists. Does the security of "truth" outweigh the unleashed energies and freedom of "opinion"? This question is far from solved, but wherever it has been present, political philosophy has had its greatest meaning. Certainly this is true of the struggle between British empiricism and German idealism during the eighteenth and nineteenth centuries, and of the present struggle between East and West.

In seeking this objective, Socrates (470-399 B.C.) led the way for those that followed. About Socrates little is actually known. Of his method and of those views described below we can speak with some certainty. But little else can be definitely ascribed to him.[22] He wrote nothing because he never believed writing to be necessary. The people and the problems in which he was interested were right at hand. He wished to promote the well-being of Athens, but this could better be done by personal exhortation than by closeting himself with books and writing paraphernalia. To understand and appreciate Socrates you must picture him talking in the market place to anyone willing to answer his questions. You can even picture him as his worst critics did, and you will still find him to be one of history's truly great figures. One such picture has been recounted by Catlin.[23] "The son of a sculptor and a professional midwife, ugly as a satyr with the waddling gait of a waterfowl, he [Socrates] was primarily a bore, even if a sincere one. Never at home looking after his family or his vocation (scandalmongers said he was a bigamist), he was, as it were, a frequenter of coffee-houses who boasted of seldom going into the country. A coffee-house politician, his habit was to buttonhole people, to whom he had scarcely been introduced, in the market place, and pertinaciously to

[21] Virtue as knowledge is discussed more fully in Chapter IV.

[22] Most of his ideas must be taken from the dialogues of his pupil, Plato. Because of this, it is hard to determine how much that is credited to Socrates really represents Socrates, rather than Plato.

[23] *Op. cit.*, pp. 30-31. By permission from *The Story of the Political Philosophers*, by George Catlin. Copyright, 1939. McGraw-Hill Book Company, Inc.

ask them inconvenient and discourteous questions. Anyone, soldier, prostitute, priest was a fit subject for his inquisitive curiosity. A heavy drinker, he could be guaranteed to drink the rest of his boon friends under the table." Even Aristophanes was hardly more complimentary. Socrates appeared in his plays as sardonic and irreverent, smart but gloomy, full of himself and of fantastic ideas.[24]

Socrates appears in truth to have been a meddlesome fellow. Yet for all this, he and those who were his pupils contributed more to our intellectual traditions than any who preceded or followed them. Impressed by the political and ethical anarchy of his day, Socrates taught that beneath the variety and confusion of laws and customs general and universal rules of morality might be found. He realized it was impossible to restore the old ideals and beliefs of the Greeks, and agreed with the Sophists that conceptions of right must be subjected to the scrutiny of individual reason and not rest upon religion or upon traditional customs. But he believed that fundamental principles of right and justice might be discovered, that man was naturally social, that the state was a necessary and desirable result of human needs, and that its laws, if based upon wisdom, would correspond to universal reason. He demanded political education, attacked the rampant democracy of his time, with its theory of equality among men and its choice of officials by lot, and proposed that the state be governed by an aristocracy of intelligence.

In teaching these doctrines he employed a method later associated with his name—the now famous Socratic method. Having gathered a group of friends about him, Socrates, after a few pleasantries, would introduce into the conversation an unresolved question. He might begin by asking if it were not better to be a great bad man than a small good man? Having posed the question, he would then plead his inability to answer it. This mock profession of ignorance led his hearers to propose views of their own. With their views now in the open, Socrates could proceed to the business at hand—questioning the *consequences* of these views. Professing not to be as sophisticated as his friends, Socrates would test these proposals with simple analogies, usually involving carpenters, shoemakers, or the like. Initial inquiries would suggest further questions, until after hours of discussion the problem would finally be circumscribed. And there would emerge from the discussion what Aristotle later called a "universal definition" or essence of the problem.[25] This keen insistence on clear definition and logical thought did much to stamp Socrates as the godfather of political philosophy and the founder of speculative ethics.

[24] *Ibid.*, p. 32.
[25] *Metaphysics,* 1078 b.

REFERENCES

BARKER, Ernest, *Greek Political Theory: Plato and His Predecessors*, 3rd ed. (London, Methuen, 1947), Chaps. 2-5.

————, *The Political Thought of Plato and Aristotle* (New York, Putnam, 1906), Introduction and Chap. 1.

BURN, A. R., *Pericles and Athens* (New York, Macmillan, 1949).

CATLIN, George, *The Story of the Political Philosophers* (New York, McGraw, 1939), Chap. 1.

CORNFORD, F. M., *Before and After Socrates* (Cambridge, Cambridge Univ. Press, 1932).

GLOTZ, Gustave, *The Greek City and Its Institutions*, trans. by N. Mallinson (London, Kegan Paul, 1929).

GROTE, G., *A History of Greece*, 12 vols. (London, Everyman's, 1934).

JAEGAR, Werner, *Paideia: The Ideals of Greek Culture*, trans. by Gilbert Highet, 3 vols. (New York, Oxford, 1939-45), Bk. II.

McILWAIN, C. H., *The Growth of Political Thought in the West* (New York, Macmillan, 1932), Chap. 1.

MYRES, J. L., *The Political Ideas of the Greeks* (New York, Abingdon, 1947).

POPPER, K. R., *The Open Society and Its Enemies*, rev. ed. (Princeton, Princeton Univ. Press, 1950).

PRENTICE, W. K., *The Ancient Greeks* (Princeton, Princeton Univ. Press, 1940), Chap. 6.

SABINE, G. H., *A History of Political Theory*, rev. ed. (New York, Holt, 1950), Chaps. 1-2.

TAYLOR, A. E., *Socrates* (New York, Appleton, 1933).

WILLOUGHBY, W. W., *Political Theories of the Ancient World* (New York, Longmans, 1903), Chaps. 4-6.

ZIMMERN, A. E., *The Greek Commonwealth*, 5th ed. (Oxford, Oxford Univ. Press, 1931).

CHAPTER IV ～

Plato

Life of Plato

Plato, who dedicated his life to recalling Athenians from the intellectual anarchism and political decay into which they were sinking,[1] was born in Athens in 427 B.C. On his mother's side he was related to Solon; his father's family was equally distinguished. Brought up in an aristocratic environment, he was probably conditioned from the beginning to support the Oligarchs against the Democrats in the many contests for power then occurring. One of Plato's letters recounts that he had in fact an ambition to enter politics as a member of the reactionary party. In his early twenties he decided to participate in the Revolt of the Thirty, which coincided with the end of the Peloponnesian War in 404 B.C.; but the immediate excesses which accompanied this reactionary upheaval so sickened him that he began to recoil from political life. When in 399 B.C. the other faction, the Democrats, condemned his friend and teacher Socrates to death, his revulsion from Athenian politics was complete.[2] He never again took an active part in the political life of Athens.

After the death of Socrates, Plato suffered an extended period of disillusionment during which he traveled abroad. He supposedly visited Persia, Egypt, Africa, Italy, and Sicily. But we know with certainty only of his visit to the latter two countries.

[1] The Cynics, who followed the Sophists, had already begun to teach an openly anti-social philosophy. They advised the virtuous man to shun political life as he would the plague and to forego the artificialities of social existence. Diogenes, the most famous of the Cynics, disavowed the state, called himself a citizen of the world, discarded most of his clothing, and lived in a tub. On one occasion, if we are to credit legends, he was visited by Alexander the Great who solicitously asked what he could do for the philosopher. Diogenes' only reply was that Alexander could "stand from between me and the sun." He is also reported to have thrown away the single wooden bowl he possessed on seeing a peasant boy drink from the hollow of his hands.

[2] Letter VII.

48

In Italy he came into contact with the Pythagorean colony at Tarentum. His contact with this group shaped his views on the importance of mathematics. Plato was especially impressed by the certainty of the proofs of geometry, which was then being systematized. If truth could be demonstrated in geometry, why not in politics?

It was on this same trip that he had his famous encounter with Dionysius I, the tyrant of Syracuse. This ruler held a special fascination for Plato. He was so all-powerful that his every wish was law. Yet he had done much to encourage letters in Syracuse, and he was himself something of a playwright. Such a person might be the philosopher-king Plato sought. Plato consequently undertook to inform him of his obligations and duties as a just ruler. But he had only begun when Dionysius tired of Plato and had him sold into slavery. Fortunately he was soon ransomed [3] and returned to Athens to found the Academy,[4] where most of his later life was spent.

This was not the end of Plato's Sicilian adventure, however. He had also become acquainted while in Syracuse with Dion, brother-in-law to Dionysius I. On the death of the latter, Dion became regent for Dionysius II. Young Dionysius had much impressed Plato, and he had hoped great things might come out of his rule. Consequently, when requested by Dion, Plato again set out for Syracuse in 367 B.C. to aid in the education of the young king. On his arrival, however, he found his expectations had run away with him. Dionysius II would neither take advice nor apply himself to serious study. Politics at court also proved too much for Plato, and he was forced to admit failure. He returned to Athens once again, saddened but not without a lingering hope.

In spite of his previous failures, Plato was led by this hope to correspond over many years with his friend Dion and to return five years later for one last try. But in the end Plato could only say of this adventure that he had done his best to meet his obligations. A philosopher, he had not proved unwilling to face the challenge of uniting in one person political power and a love of truth. He had proved to be more than "a man of words." [5]

Plato died in 347 at the age of eighty. During the later years of his life

[3] An interesting sidelight is afforded by the value placed on Plato. Diogenes Laertius mentions the fact that the ransom was set at twenty minae. As an Attic mina was worth $16, the sum demanded for Plato's release equaled $320. Diogenes Laertius, iii. 19-21.

[4] The Academy was founded in 386 B.C. It was located in an olive grove in one of the outlying sections of Athens called Academe, from which it drew its name. The first of the schools which maintained the fame of Athens after her military decline, it served as a model for other great schools that followed.

[5] Letter VII, 328 c.

he had enjoyed widespread personal recognition, and his Academy had become the foremost school of Athens. As he had succeeded Socrates, so he was to be succeeded in this great tradition by Aristotle, to whom we will turn presently. But first we may consider with profit the dialogues of Plato and the political philosophy they contain.

Dialogues

Political theory crops out in most of Plato's dialogues, but three of them are more concerned with this subject than are the others. These are the *Republic*, the *Statesman*, and the *Laws*.[6]

Of the three, the *Republic* is the best known and most highly regarded. It was written when Plato was at the height of his mental powers and represents his conception of the ideally best form of government. It is the dialogue with which we will be primarily concerned. The *Statesman* [7] is a short, not widely read treatise coming between the *Republic* and the *Laws*. It represents a transition in thought from the *Republic* in that Plato here argues the merits of rule by law, contrasted with the personal rule of the guardians in the *Republic*. Plato concludes that conditions being as they are, rule of law must be accepted as the most workable form of government. In the *Laws* this transition is completed. This work, written at the end of Plato's career and after his experiences in Syracuse, accepts the limitations practically imposed by an imperfect society and undertakes to prescribe for the best practical form of government. The ideal of the *Republic* is never repudiated. But it is laid aside in favor of a society not more perfect than the men who live in it.

First Principles of the *Republic*

The first principles or fundamental ideas contained in the *Republic* never appear in simple form. In fact, on first reading they tend to become lost in the intricacies of the argument and in the various analogies. But the *Republic*, like most good things, improves on better acquaintance. After a little reflection it will be seen that the major tenets of the *Republic* arrange themselves very neatly around a few basic assumptions. If these are understood, it becomes a relatively easy process to trace out the other ideas deduced from them.

[6] Of the other dialogues, the *Apology* and the *Gorgias* will prove interesting to students of political thought. The *Apology* is a defense of Socrates, written shortly after his death. It pleads for respect for freedom of conscience. The *Gorgias* is an extended attack on the skepticism of the Sophists. It argues the existence of higher laws and absolute right.

[7] The *Statesman* is also referred to as the *Politicus*.

The foremost assumption of the *Republic* is that virtue is knowledge. This means that absolute truth exists and can be known. Or put differently, it means that "good" [8] has an objective existence and can be known by those of the keenest intelligence. Consequently, virtue (good) is knowledge (can be known).

On this assertion everything else hangs. But this itself is an outgrowth of a larger problem. This is the problem of nature versus circumstance which had been troubling Greek philosophers for a hundred years prior to the appearance of the *Republic*. The question, simply put, is this: Does value or worth depend on circumstances, or are there things which have a universal value not dependent on surrounding conditions which may vary? Is true knowledge possible in solving man's problems, or must we rely only on the subjective judgments of individuals? Here Plato differs with the Sophists and all those whom he thought were undermining Greek civilization. There are, he asserted, absolute truths [9] which can be known, if only by the selected few who are capable of greater insight than their contemporaries.

This brings us to the second major proposition of Plato's political philosophy, which is that men are essentially unequal. They vary in their capacities for temperance, courage, wisdom, and justice—the four cardinal virtues listed by Plato. As some are better suited by their courage to protect the city from invasion, so others by their capacity for wisdom are better suited to rule. Democracy, consequently, is both a sham and a delusion. It assumes an equality which does not exist and results in mistaking mere opinion for true knowledge.

Nothing upset Plato more than the Athenian belief in "happy versatility," expressed by Pericles in the Funeral Oration. Statecraft, Plato stated, is not only a science, but the most difficult of all sciences. No one proposes to make every man a physician, yet democracy assumes something even more impossible. It assumes that every man can equally well govern other men. It assumes that insight into the intricacies of the state is shared by all. More than this, democracy is the cause of faction and revolt. So often had Athens been thrown into turmoil by struggle for control of its government that Plato came to dread revolution and violence as he dreaded nothing else. This perhaps explains his emphasis on harmony and a controlled life. He wanted to find a stability which he believed to be vitally lacking in Athens. He pictures the democratic man as "drunk one hour, an abstainer the next; veering from violent athletics to no athletics at all, and from both to the study of philosophy; today a politician, who jumps to his feet and talks unpremeditated nonsense, and

[8] Here equated with truth.
[9] Plato refers to these truths collectively as the Idea of the Good.

tomorrow a warrior." [10] Such a person can never remain constant to anything and can consequently never find real happiness. Happiness depends upon a "higher order" of life in which every man plays the one role he can play best.

An Aristocracy of Intelligence

The type of government prescribed by this higher order, Plato tells us, can be deduced from the first principles already mentioned. If virtue is knowledge, if truth can be known, but if only the few are possessed of such wisdom; then government ought to be placed in the hands of an aristocracy of intelligence. Or put more directly, philosophers ought to be kings.

Plato proposed that members of a ruling class of guardians, as they are called, be allowed to govern with complete power [11] and according to an all-wise discretion, unencumbered by laws. He suggested that they consider each case on its merits, as a doctor might prescribe differently for each patient. Laws, he argued, are by their very nature general and so geared only for the average or usual case. But the problems of people are not average or usual at all. Every problem is different, if only in detail, and demands a specific remedy.

Laws by their very definition are *general* rules: their generality is at once their essence and their main defect, because generality implies an average, and such rules can never meet the exceptions that are always arising, as can the unfettered discretion of an all-wise ruler. At best these rigid rules are a rough make-shift far inferior to the flexibility of that wisdom which alone meets the test of true justice, by rendering unerringly to *every* man *his* due, not the due of some "average man" who never existed nor can exist. For Plato, therefore, discretion if it is wise discretion is higher than the straight-jacket of the law.[12]

While the guardians are to have the broadest range of powers, Plato does not intend that they live extravagantly or have other privileges. The guardians exist for just one purpose, to promote the well-being of the

[10] Ernest Barker, *The Political Thought of Plato and Aristotle* (1906), p. 88.

[11] By placing all power in the hands of the Guardians, Plato was able to solve one of political theory's most pressing problems. He identified or brought together reason and authority. Democratic countries are subject to the criticism that the "reasonable" element is scarcely speaking to the "authoritative" element. The President of the United States, who has great authority, is seldom chosen for his brilliance. We accept this as a condition of democratic government. But Plato was unwilling to do so. It remained his unshaken conviction through life that power and a love of truth ought to be united in the same hands. If reason and authority could be so joined, nothing was beyond expectation.

[12] C. H. McIlwain, *The Growth of Political Thought in the West* (1932), p. 27. By permission of The Macmillan Company.

state, and Plato expects them to specialize in this to the exclusion of all else.

Specialization of Classes

This keynote of the ruling class, specialization, provides Plato with the basis for constructing the other classes in this ideal society. As the guardians are specialists, so must the whole state adhere to this principle if justice is to be achieved.

Societies, Plato observes, arise out of the mutual needs of their members. Men have a variety of wants which they satisfy by exchanging those things they can best produce for other things they need. As this process of specialization becomes increasingly complicated, a high degree of interdependence is built up.[13] It is (or more properly ought to be) an interdependence of classes—one with the others. These classes, of which there are naturally three, come into being because there are three sorts or categories of men. First, there is a group motivated wholly by appetite or desire. These can be called artisans. They will be happiest when specializing in material pursuits. Secondly, there is a group motivated by spirit or courage which can be called warriors or auxiliaries. Their special function is to serve as the protectors of society. And thirdly, there is the class, already mentioned, composed of men outstanding for their wisdom. This is the guardian class [14] whose duty it is to govern. When each of these classes is performing its appropriate function, states Plato, and when each is complementing the others to produce a perfect whole, then justice will be achieved.[15]

Justice

Plato viewed justice, the climax of his political philosophy, as not merely the harmonious relationship of these groups, but as an arrangement so inherently right that all would accept it, were they only possessed of sufficient reason.[16] Plato believed, in fact, that even the artisans or

[13] For an interesting distinction between Plato's analysis of this process and laissez-faire notions concerning division of labor, see G. H. Sabine, A History of Political Theory, rev. ed. (1950), p. 49.

[14] Plato refers first in the Republic to the guardians as both the warriors and the rulers, but he concludes that only the latter group ought properly to be called guardians. 414.

[15] Ibid., 435.

[16] To guarantee the coöperation of the artisans, who were considered beyond reason, Plato suggested that a "needful falsehood" be created. A myth was to be invented, using the analogy of metals. Gold would represent the guardians, silver the warriors, and brass and iron the workers. As brass and iron were baser metals than gold, so must the working class be on a lower plane than the ruling class. Much drumming on this point might be necessary, but in the end the masses would succumb to this apparent logic. Ibid., 414-415.

workers would have willed their own stations in life, had they understood the universal justice of his proposals.

For Plato, justice meant more than giving to each man his due. He
anticipated Jesus in proposing a larger conception of justice in which
good was returnable for evil. Moreover, each person, in doing the thing
he could do best, was expected to find a happiness which would guarantee
the fullest growth of his own soul. This concept of the moral perfection of
the soul is at the heart of the *Republic,* and it has led many commentators
to conclude that Plato was not writing about politics at all. He was, they
believe, merely using the state to "write in large letters" about the human
soul. But such a distinction makes little sense. Plato was never concerned,
as we are, with this dualism or split between things private and public.
Assertions which held true for one held true for both. When, consequently,
he compared justice to a state of health and injustice to a disease, he was
talking about both the individual and the state. Health was achieved in
the individual when appetite and spirit were controlled by reason, as it
was in the state when these factors were similarly ordered.

This view of justice is opposed in the *Republic* by two competing
theories. In the middle of Book I, Thrasymachus, a Sophist, enters the
conversation to assert that justice can be nothing more nor less than the
interest of the stronger. Might alone makes right. Government, in short,
exists for the good of the governors, not the governed. And if Socrates
wishes to call this unjust, then, declares Thrasymachus, injustice is better
than justice.

To this Plato answers that as the function of a doctor is to heal his pa-
tients and of the shepherd to protect his sheep, so the true governor must
unselfishly concern himself with the welfare of his people. As to injustice
being better than justice, Plato replies that the just person will be a
happier and better man in the long run that the unjust man because
of the inherent contradictions in the course of the latter.

The third view of justice encountered is supported by Glaucon. He is
inclined to be conciliatory, but still believes justice to be a convention,
rather than a law of nature. Glaucon argues that every person would like
to practice injustice, if he were the only one allowed to do so. But to his
consternation others are practicing it, too, and at his expense. The only
solution is for each to contract with all to guarantee that none will practice injustice nor suffer it to be done by others.[17] This contract thus becomes the basis of government, but it still remains only a convention
drawn up by the people, not a condition of nature as Plato believed.

[17] It is surprising how little is or can be new in political philosophy. Hobbes marks
a turning point in later developments, but he actually added little to this fundamental
notion.

To answer Glaucon is more difficult. Plato must prove that justice is a universal principle and is everywhere the necessary condition for a good life. This leads Plato to consider the nature of justice through considering in detail the nature of the ideal state, a task which largely occupies the remainder of the *Republic*. If justice in the state can be discovered and turns out to be universally good, then Glaucon will have been in error.

The two problems are thus to discover justice and then to demonstrate its absolute value. The method of discovery used by Plato is technically called the method of residues, which means to isolate or identify a factor by eliminating all others. This Plato does by first enumerating all of the virtues of the state. These are temperance, courage, wisdom, and justice, as previously mentioned. He then assigns each of the first three its proper place, leaving justice to fulfill the remaining role.

Its role differs from the others because where each of the first three are specific forms of virtue,[18] justice has a different character. It is the "ultimate cause and condition" [19] of the others, being common to all. It is specifically the will to concentrate on one's own sphere of duty and not to meddle with the sphere of another.[20]

That justice, now discovered, is also universally good, follows from the foregoing. Meddlesomeness, the opposite of justice, can lead only to strife and ruin.[21] And other virtues, Plato concludes, can flourish only where they are "preserved" by justice.

This completes the reconstruction of Plato's basic philosophy as it applies to the state. It now remains to consider some of the more interesting ramifications of these doctrines.

Life of the Guardians

The life to be led by the guardians is of particular interest. Their education, family relationships, and property rights, or more properly the lack of property rights, are fully discussed in the *Republic*.

---

[18] Specific in the sense of adhering to a particular class. The guardian's virtue is wisdom, the warrior's courage, and the worker's temperance, though Plato goes on to say that temperance is, in addition, a sort of harmony of all. To this extent it, like justice, is a general rather than a specific virtue.

[19] *Republic*, 433.

[20] Barker, *op. cit.*, p. 116.

[21] *Republic*, 433. "When the cobbler or any other man whom nature designed to be a trader, having his heart lifted up by wealth or strength or the number of his followers, or any like advantage, attempts to force his way into the class of warriors, or a warrior into that of legislators and guardians, for which he is unfitted, and either to take the implements or the duties of the other; or when one man is trader, legislator, and warrior all in one, then I think you will agree with me in saying that this interchange and this meddling of one with another is the ruin of the State."

The education of the guardians is so carefully considered that the *Republic* is often regarded as a treatise on this subject. Rousseau, himself one of the noted contributors to the theory of education, believed the *Republic* to be the greatest of all treatises in this field. Certainly, Plato places the fullest possible emphasis on education. He believed that it was the one weapon which held hope for remodeling an imperfect society. Where all else failed, education, given enough time, might succeed.

As to the sort of education required, Plato prescribed compulsory public education for everyone, for the children of the artisans as well as those of the guardian class. The training was to be divided into two parts. The first concerned the mind and came under the heading of "music." It included the reading of poetry and other forms of literature and the singing and playing of music. In order that nothing detrimental might be included, the selections used were to be heavily censored. The second concerned the body and came under the heading of "gymnastics." It included the teaching of self-discipline and other manly virtues. This dual form of education was to continue until early manhood, when those who had shown the greatest aptitude would be selected to continue their training, the others turning to lives as members of the working or artisan class.

The next period of training was to cover the years from twenty to thirty. Women as well as men were to be eligible, and there was to be a noticeable upgrading of the curriculum. The staples of this higher education were to be logic, astronomy, and mathematics. From thirty to thirty-five (after further thinning of the ranks) attention was to be turned to philosophy and training in dialectical thinking. Then for a period of fifteen years those who had proved their superiority were to be tested by actual experience in government and war. Finally, at the age of fifty, those who had met every test were to assume at last the mantle of guardians. "The time has now arrived at which they must raise the eye of the soul to the universal light" and assume the full burden of bringing justice and order to the state.[22] As guardians they were to be allowed time for reflection and pure mediation. But when their turns came, they were also to toil at politics, ruling for the public good

not as though they were performing some heroic action, but simply as a matter of duty; and when they have brought up in each generation others like themselves and left them in their place to be governors of the State, then they will depart to the Islands of the Blest and dwell there; and the city will give them public memorials and sacrifices and honour them.[23]

[22] *Ibid.*, 540.
[23] *Ibid.*

Concerning family relationships, Plato was willing that the artisans continue to have private families and monogamous marriages, but such practices were not acceptable for the guardians. Plato reasoned that members of the guardian class [24] must be entirely unselfish if they were to successfully discharge their duties. They could not even be allowed the privilege of being partial to their own children.[25] Such partiality might take precedence over their duties to the state. The remedy lay in communizing family relationships. Wives, husbands, and children must be held in common and shared by all. This would lead to other advantages. Women would be freed from the routines of family life, allowing them to take their proper place in the guardian class. And parenthood could be more easily planned to develop the best possible offspring. This latter notion appealed to Plato very much. He believed that proper breeding might revolutionize this already select group, resulting in men vastly superior in intelligence and manliness.

Plato really was objecting to more than the institution of marriage. He was objecting to the principle of private property. Monogamous marriage and families were, after all, only forms of private property, and they would result, as did all private property, in stirring up greed and envy. The guardians had only one reason for existing—to promote the well-being of the state. If private property interfered with this purpose, it should be abolished. Plato proposed therefore that the guardians be prohibited from owning property of any sort. They were to live in barracks and eat common meals. Any requirements that they might have were to be supplied by artisans. Plato precedes Rousseau in admiring the virtues of the unrefined, less artificial life.[26]

Forms of Government

Plato was also the first to arrange an imaginary cycle through which governments pass in degeneration from the best to the worst form. At the top he placed a perfect aristocracy, in which the wise rule, animated by the idea of justice. This was followed by timocracy, in which the ruling class is influenced by love of glory or honor, rather than justice. Next came oligarchy, when the rise of private property placed political

[24] In discussing family relationships and property rights, Plato included the warriors with the rulers.

[25] Plato intended not only that members of the artisan class might rise to the top, but that children of the guardian class be sent into the lowest class if they were not suited to rule.

[26] This section of the Republic shows clearly the influence of Sparta on Plato's thinking. The common tables, barracks life, and absence of economic concern are all patterned after Spartan institutions.

power in the hands of those possessing wealth. The gradual rise of the masses led to democracy, which abused liberty and resulted in anarchy. At the bottom of the scale, farthest removed from justice, was tyranny, which arose when dissension among the masses necessitated a strong ruler. Like all Greeks, Plato considered tyranny the worst form of government.

The *Statesman* and the *Laws*

In the *Statesman* Plato is concerned not only with the *ideal* state, but with the best *possible* state as well. He aims to distinguish the ideal ruler and the abstract science of the state from the politician and the methods of actual administration. He develops in a more definite and logical way his ideas, set forth in the *Republic*, that the true statesman is the all-wise philosopher and that the aim of politics is education in virtue and justice. If an ideal ruler could be found, there would be no need for laws, since such a man should be free from all restraint; but since omniscient individuals are not available, written laws and customs are important. They are the expressions of practical wisdom and of experience; hence conformity to law is essential in the imperfect systems of government that are in existence.

On the basis of these conceptions, Plato makes a new classification of governments from the point of view of the number of persons exercising authority and the degree to which these persons are subject to legal restraint. If the government is subject to law, monarchy is best, democracy worst, and aristocracy holds an intermediate position. If it is unrestrained by law, democracy is best, tyranny worst, with oligarchy between. The rule of one may thus be the best or the worst form of government. Aristocracy and oligarchy occupy a middle position with regard to their possibilities for good or evil. Democracy is the worst form of government subject to law, but because of its essential weakness and inefficiency is least oppressive if the restraints of law are absent.

In the *Laws* Plato traverses still further the field of practical politics. Since the ideal form of government is not possible among imperfect human beings, and since laws are therefore indispensable, he proposes a legal system which will accomplish the best results under existing conditions. He modifies somewhat his earlier doctrines, and permits private property and domestic life, although under strict governmental supervision. Education, though less rigidly controlled by the magistrates, is still given primary consideration, and a strict censorship is established over the intellectual and artistic interests of the citizens. Governing authority is based not on intellect alone, but on a division of the population into classes on the basis of wealth in land, the state placing a limit on the amount any individual may possess. Plato proposes a governmental system which aims to avoid the extremes of monarchy and of democracy. Checks must be placed upon tyrannic authority, and at the same time the freedom of a democracy must not be allowed to degenerate into anarchy. While every citizen may have some share in government, the proportion of his share will depend upon his ability. The details of an elaborate system of administration are then set forth, combining aristocratic and democratic elements and providing for extensive checks and balances. This insistence on a balanced, well-ordered state provided the starting point for Aristotle's *Politics,* to which we now turn.

REFERENCES

BARKER, Ernest, *Greek Political Theory: Plato and his Predecessors,* 3rd ed. (London, Methuen, 1947).

——, *The Political Thought of Plato and Aristotle* (New York, Putnam, 1906).

BLUCK, R. S., *Plato's Life and Thought* (London, Routledge, 1949).

CORNFORD, F. M., *Before and After Socrates* (Cambridge, Cambridge Univ. Press, 1932).

CROSSMAN, R. H. S., *Plato Today* (New York, Oxford, 1939).

GRUBE, G. M. A., *Plato's Thought* (London, Methuen, 1935).

McILWAIN, C. H., *The Growth of Political Thought in the West* (New York, Macmillan, 1932), Chap. 2.

NETTLESHIP, R. L., *Lectures on the Republic of Plato* (London, Macmillan, 1937).

PATER, Walter, *Plato and Platonism* (London, Macmillan, 1910).

POPPER, K. R., *The Open Society and Its Enemies,* rev. ed. (Princeton, Princeton Univ. Press, 1950).

ROBIN, Léon, *Greek Thought* (New York, Knopf, 1928).

SABINE, G. H., *A History of Political Theory,* rev. ed. (New York, Holt, 1950), Chaps. 3-4.

TAYLOR, A. E., *Plato: The Man and His Works,* 5th ed. (New York, Dial Press, 1948).

CHAPTER V ~~~

Aristotle and the Decline of Greece

The Philosopher

Aristotle (384-322 B.C.) [1] holds an enviable place in the annals of political philosophy. During the Middle Ages he was referred to as simply *the philosopher*. As an authority in argument he ranked with the Bible. The recovery of his manuscripts in the thirteenth century marks a turning point in the history of civilization. [2] Through St. Thomas Aquinas, who incorporated much of Aristotle into the *Summa Theologica*, medieval thought was given a new breadth and purpose. [3] Aristotle is also responsible for the basic categories into which modern scholarship is divided, [4] as well as many of the terms and definitions now commonplace.

Aristotle was born in Stagira in Thrace. His father was court physician to Amyntas II, father of Philip of Macedon. As this calling was traditional in his family, it can be supposed that Aristotle was indebted to his early environment for his later interest in biology and the scientific method. Little, however, is actually known of his youth. Not until 367 do his

---

[1] The political thought of Aristotle is found mainly in the *Politics*. Some discussion that is indirectly political occurs in the *Nicomachean Ethics*. A work called *The Constitutions*, in which more than one hundred and fifty types of government were analyzed, is referred to in ancient literature. Only fragments of this work survive, the most important of which is the *Constitution of Athens*. The *Politics* was an unfinished work, containing frequent repetitions, omissions, and inconsistencies. Errors and accidents in the transmission and editing of the manuscripts through the centuries increase the difficulties of the modern student.

[2] While it was not until the thirteenth century that most of Aristotle's treatises found their way west from the Arabic world, parts of the *Organon* were known and studied much earlier in Western Europe.

[3] See A. J. and R. W. Carlyle, *A History of Medieval Political Theory in the West* (1928), Vol. V, pp. 10-14.

[4] Aristotle's categories included logic, metaphysics or "first philosophy," physics, psychology, biology, politics, ethics, and literature.

movements become clear. In that year Aristotle, seventeen, journeyed to Athens to study with Plato at the Academy.

In the ensuing twenty years, until Plato's death in 347, a strong connection developed between master and student. Plato regarded Aristotle as the most gifted of his "sons." And in his turn Aristotle wrote of Plato that "'he was a man whom the bad have not even the right to praise—the only man, or the first, to show clearly by his own life, and by the reasonings of his discourses, that to be happy is to be good.'"[5] During the latter part of this discipleship, Aristotle tried his hand at several dialogues, modeled after those of Plato.[6] But unfortunately, these have all been lost.

Aristotle had expected to succeed Plato as head of the Academy, but in this he was disappointed. On the death of the latter, this honor went to Plato's nephew Speusippus, leading to Aristotle's departure from Athens. During the years that followed, from 347 to 335, Aristotle pursued his varied interests first under the aegis of Hermias, tyrant of Atarneus, whose niece he married, and later at the court of Philip of Macedon, where he was employed as tutor to Alexander.

This relationship between two of history's most famous figures lasted for six years, but it had no apparent effect on either. Aristotle, for his part, was unable or unwilling to go beyond the city-state in his thinking. Whereas Alexander, in his search for empire, was oblivious to the admonitions of his tutor.[7]

The last period of Aristotle's life dates from 335. In that year he returned to Athens to found his own school, the Lyceum. Here he lectured and wrote for twelve years. During this period the Lyceum prospered. Aristotle's lectures met with great success and the investigations of the school were pushed farther than had heretofore been possible. Through scientists and philosophers who accompanied Alexander on his eastern adventures, the Lyceum was supplied with a variety of information previously lacking.

Aristotle's success, however, was short-lived. The report of Alexander's death, reaching Athens in 323, caused war to flare again, this time against Macedonian hegemony. And Aristotle, supposed to be a friend of Alexander, was forced to flee. He died a year later in Chalcis, a city on the island of Euboea.

[5] Ernest Barker, *The Politics of Aristotle* (1946), p. xiv.
[6] One, entitled *On Justice*, would have made interesting comparative reading with the *Republic*.
[7] Barker, *op. cit.*, pp. xxii, note.

Character and Method of Writings

While our interest in Aristotle rests chiefly in his *Politics*, this is only one of the many treatises which have secured his reputation. Aristotle had an equal understanding of logic, ethics, metaphysics, and the natural sciences. So vast was this understanding that it is doubtful if the catholicity of his mind has ever been equaled. The method pursued in these studies is inductive,[8] or "scientific" if you prefer. This method is now commonly said to have five stages. First, a hypothesis is advanced concerning probable causes of an existing situation. Secondly, this is followed by extensive investigation and collection of information. Thirdly, the information collected is classified, which is to say that it is organized according to any cause and effect relationships which appear. Fourthly, generalizations or laws are formulated on the basis of these causal relationships. And lastly, predictions are attempted concerning the working of these laws. In following this method Aristotle placed himself in sharp contrast with Plato. Plato held facts up to a preconceived yardstick, his concept of the perfect or absolute, and judged them accordingly. Aristotle on the other hand always tested his premises or preconceived notions by comparing them with existing circumstances or previous experience.

Aristotle thus reasoned inductively from a comparative and scientific study of actual governmental systems. His discussions, based on history and observation, are clear and precise, with relatively little poetic or allegorical embellishment. He separated political and ethical concepts, and thus made possible an independent science of politics. He realized that no one form of government is best under all conditions, but that constitutions must be adapted to the peculiar needs of each people.

Respect for Tradition

"This inductive habit of mind," to quote Barker, "was naturally accompanied by what may be termed an historic temper, a respect for tradition and a readiness to accept the verdict of general opinion." [9]

Plato had expressed little faith in tradition or general opinion. He had put his faith in invention and all-wise guardians. But Aristotle differs fundamentally in this respect from his master. He criticizes the more

[8] It is true, however, that Aristotle never completely escaped from the idea of politics as an abstract science concerned with the absolute good of man. Books II, III, VII, and VIII of the *Politics* attest to this fact. But as he grew older and moved farther from Plato in his thinking, he turned from such studies to an analysis of the actual workings of government and the political forces behind them. In this he discovered his real genius.

[9] Barker, *op. cit.*, p. xxviii.

novel of Plato's ideas as wanting in the stored sense of mankind. "Let us remember," he admonishes, "that we should not disregard the experience of ages; in the multitude of years these things [Plato's innovations], if they were good, would certainly not have been unknown. ..." [10] He is also less dependent than Plato on a guardian class or an aristocracy of intelligence, because if intelligence can be stored in the customs, experiences, and laws of mankind then it need not be sought elsewhere.[11]

Aristotle, moreover, "holds it clearly impossible that the knowledge of the wisest ruler can be better than [this] customary law." [12] Where Plato would rely on *rule of men,* Aristotle relied on *rule of law* or what we would now call constitutional government. He conceded that laws might not be able to provide perfect justice in every case because of their generality. But this very generality resulted in an impartiality of treatment, unaffected by personal ambition or desire, which was the essence of good government.[13]

This belief in the supremacy of law and in the desirability of constitutional government is one of the concepts for which Aristotle is best remembered and for which later generations are most in his debt. For centuries we have taken pride in the fact that ours is a "government of laws and not of men." And in our own age we have been made increasingly aware of the value of constitutional government by observing the results of government by edict or decree.

The Nature and Origin of the State

Aristotle believed, in keeping with his predecessors, that the individual could find his fullest expression only in the state. Man, he argued, is destined by his inherent nature to lead a political life. The state in consequence can be described as a natural and necessary institution for the development of the powers and for the satisfaction of the needs and desires with which men are by nature endowed. And the best state can be described as that in which all citizens are able to lead as complete a political life as possible.

The origin of the state Aristotle finds in the efforts of men to satisfy their individual needs and desires. The association of male and female for the perpetuation of the race, and of master and slave for the produc-

[10] *Politics,* 1264 a.
[11] G. H. Sabine, *A History of Political Theory,* rev. ed. (1950), pp. 95-96.
[12] *Ibid.*
[13] In a characteristic passage Aristotle adds that "he who bids the law rule may be deemed to bid ... Reason alone rule, but he who bids man rule adds an element of the beast; for desire is a wild beast, and passion perverts the minds of rulers, even when they are the best of men." *Politics,* 1287 a 28-32.

tion of subsistence, gave rise to the family or household. As long as men were satisfied with a bare existence and the satisfaction of their elementary wants, this sufficed. When urged by their nature to seek a fuller life, households were combined into a city or state, of such size and nature as to be self-sufficing. This is the perfect form of association; and man, naturally a political animal, can attain the true end for which he is intended only in the life of the state. Without social life man would be a brute. In this sense the state, as an idea, is prior to man. What made man a rational being, distinguished from the lower forms of animal life, was the power of speech and organized association with his fellows. The state thus precedes the individual, for only in the state can the human being rise above the brute and become a man.

The state, therefore, exists to satisfy the higher moral and intellectual needs of man; the household, within the state, to provide for the physical needs of life. The state may thus be justified on utilitarian grounds also, and upon this basis slavery is upheld as right and natural. Since men differ in intellectual capacity and in physical strength, some are intended by nature for masters, others for slaves. Men who are highly endowed intellectually are intended to command; those with slight endowment of reason, but with strength of body, are fitted only to carry out orders. Under such conditions, if the authority of the master is not abused, slavery is mutually advantageous. The enslavement of prisoners of war is justified only when success in war indicates the superior intelligence of the victors, not when men of ability are subject to the misfortunes of war. Aristotle shared the universal belief of the Greeks in their intellectual superiority over their neighbors. Greeks therefore can never rightfully be made slaves.

Like the other Greeks, Aristotle placed a low estimate on all occupations connected with the production of wealth. It was a necessary function of the household, but the lowest of its functions, suited only to slaves and aliens. The citizen, who engaged in public affairs, should be free from the care and the debasing influence of economic concerns. Agriculture, cattle raising, hunting and fishing, as natural occupations, were placed higher in the scale than trade and commerce; and the lending of money at interest was considered wholly unjustified. Aristotle was the first to give attention to the economic basis of political institutions; and, in spite of some confusion of thought, he worked out the fundamental principle that the character and distribution of wealth is a determining factor in fixing the form of government, that the occupations of a people influence their political attitude and ability, and that revolutions are usually contests between those who have much and those who have little property.

Aristotle gave considerable attention to criticizing some of Plato's ideas, especially his emphasis on unity within the state and his communistic schemes for achieving it. Aristotle believed that desirable unity in the state was to be accomplished, not by crushing out differences among individuals through a strict disciplinary régime, but by a proper organization of individuals of diverse types. Accordingly, while he favored public and compulsory training and education, he believed that the abolition of family ties and of private property interests, which Plato favored, would narrow men's lives and prevent the establishment of valuable social bonds.

The limitations upon state action which Aristotle favored were not based on any idea of rights possessed by individuals with which the state should not interfere. Aristotle, however, was more concerned with the welfare of citizens as individuals than with the abstract conception of the good of the social whole. He viewed the state as a means of securing the highest welfare of the aggregate of its citizens, and believed that to accomplish this a considerable degree of individual liberty should be permitted. Since men differ in abilities and needs, the best development of their powers would result from a system that left them a certain freedom in conducting their lives.

Aristotle defined the state as the collective body of citizens, and defined a citizen as one who has the right to take part in government. Basing his ideas on the facts of Hellenic life, he believed that citizenship implied participation in assemblies and in juries, in the active exercise of political rights. The qualifications for citizenship he considered to be the capacity to rule and to be ruled; and he believed that the working classes, too dependent upon the commands of others to develop ability to rule, should not be admitted to the privilege of citizenship.

A clear distinction between state and government was found in Aristotle's thought. While the state consists of the whole body of citizens, the government consists of those who order and regulate the state, hold the offices, and possess the supreme power. Accordingly, in discussing the best form of *government,* he was concerned with the proper distribution of political power among the administrative organs of the state. In discussing the best form of *state,* he considered questions of geographic situation, climate, resources, and the number and character of citizens. The principle of separation of powers was also clearly brought out, and the proper organization and duties of executive, legislative, and judicial organs were examined.

Classification of Governments

Numerous attempts to classify the forms of government had already been made. Pindar, Herodotus, Thucydides, and Plato recognized the differences among government in the hands of one, of the few, and of the many. Aristotle's classification, based upon the earlier efforts, was more exact and has remained without essential change to the present day. He analyzes governments, first according to the number of persons in whom the sovereign power is *vested;* second, according to the end to which the government is *directed.* The latter distinction separates pure from corrupt forms, depending upon whether the governing group sets before itself the perfection of all the citizens, or its own interests alone.

His classification was as follows: A state governed in the interests of all by one person is a monarchy. If the monarch governs arbitrarily for his own benefit, this type degenerates into a tyranny. A state governed for the common good by a few is an aristocracy. If the few use their power selfishly, or place wealth above intelligence and patriotism, the aristocracy becomes an oligarchy. A state governed by the whole people for the general welfare is a polity. If, however, the majority of the people, realizing their distinctions, govern in the interests of the poor alone, the polity in its corrupt form becomes a democracy. The pure forms are ideals, most desirable if perfect men existed, but in the case of monarchy and aristocracy practically impossible of realization. The corrupt forms fall in the realm of practical politics. Of these forms, tyranny and extreme democracy are the worst. Only in the case of polity is the ideal in close relation with possible government.

In deciding which form of government is best, Aristotle realized that political institutions must correspond to the character and needs of the peoples concerned. An ideal state, therefore, is possible only under ideal conditions. If men of preëminent excellence could be obtained, Aristotle believed that monarchy and aristocracy were the best forms of government. But, taking human nature as it is, he was inclined to favor a moderate democracy or polity.

The Basis of Authority

Controversy had been keen in the Greek world between those who favored placing sovereign power in the hands of the wealthy or intelligent classes and those who upheld the authority of mere numbers. Since the end of the state is to promote a good life, Aristotle held that the greater share of authority should be exercised by those who contribute most to the state. The virtue and ability of the whole people is greater than that of any part or faction; hence final authority should lie in the mass of the citizens. Through their assembly they should pass upon fundamental questions, choose the magistrates, and hold them to account for their official actions. But this should not prevent wealth from also being weighed in the balance. The propertied class should play a large role in the government, because virtue and ability tend to become associated with property. Aristotle believed, as did Edmund Burke, that those who were the most able would also become the most wealthy.[14]

Aristotle laid great emphasis upon the value of moderation and stability in the state. He realized the tendency toward extremes in the democracy of his day, and deplored the violent factional contests that were prevalent in the Hellenic cities. He believed that the best state for the Greek peoples was a city, with comparatively small territory and with a limited population, so that citizens might know one another and take an active part in political affairs. The city should lie sufficiently near the sea to secure necessary goods from abroad, but not so near as to unduly develop commerce and maritime interests. Extremes of wealth and poverty, making one class arrogant and the other slavish, were undesirable. A strong middle class, making for order and stability, would furnish the best basis for the state. The various occupations, necessary to have the state self-supporting, must be represented, but the citizen class should be limited to the administrators, warriors, and priests. They should own the land and have leisure for the duties of citizenship. The city must be fully capable of defending itself, although aggressive warfare was undesirable. Detailed provisions were made for public education along physical, intellectual, and moral lines.

The frequent changes in the government of the Greek cities led Aristotle to devote considerable attention to the subject of revolution. The general trend from monarchy through oligarchy and tyranny to democracy he explained as the result of social and economic changes. He made a masterly analysis of contemporary political evils, and found the main source of factional contests in the discrepancy between the political abilities of the different classes of citizens and the actual authority that they possessed. Since men crave equality, a feeling of injustice arises among those who see others possessing privileges which they do not share. The proper apportionment of political power is, therefore, fundamental to the security of the state. A mixed form of government combining demo-

---

[14] Aristotle adds that sovereignty ought to be exercised in the last analysis by "a majority of persons who are also the owners of a majority of property." By this he means that those who have the most property in the aggregate should prevail. This is not equivalent, it will be noted, to rule by large property owners alone. Aristotle would include the property of the mass of poorer citizens, the total of which would be considerable. See the *Politics*, vi. 3.

cratic and oligarchic elements he considered most enduring. A number
of practical suggestions were also made as to the methods by which
various types of government may be successfully maintained and revolution prevented.

Aristotle's contribution to political thought is important because of the
actual information it gives concerning the conditions of Greek constitutional life. It established a logical method of political inquiry and made
possible a distinct science of the state. While based on conditions in the
Greek world, Aristotle's work contained many profound generalizations
applicable to political life in all times and places. He also recognized the
importance of economic influences and of geographic conditions on political organization and activity. Finally, he held the high civic ideal of a
state governed by reason and aiming at a good life. He believed that the
purpose of the state was not to extend its dominion or enrich its people,
but to widen knowledge, promote virtue, and secure justice to all.

Certain limitations of thought caused by Greek conditions are obvious.
Aristotle assumed the superiority of the Greeks over other peoples, the
necessity of slavery, the city-state as the natural type of political organization, and the unsuitability of the laboring classes for the duties of
citizenship. Though he wrote at the time when the era of independent
city-states was near its end, he apparently did not appreciate this fact,
and he could not see in the Macedonian Empire any desirable qualification that a state should possess. His aim was to restore and perpetuate
the city as the proper form of political unit.

The Epicureans and Stoics

Sixteen years before Aristotle died, the free life of the Greek cities was
brought to an end. Through the conquests of Alexander, and the later
partition of his dominions among his successors, the military empire
became the typical form of political organization. For a time, under the
weakest of Alexander's successors, some of the Greek cities, united in the
Aetolian and the Achaean Leagues, maintained a considerable degree of
autonomy and made a valuable contribution to the principle of federal
government. However, these federations also fell before the conquering
power of Rome, and Greek political institutions survived merely as phases
of local government in the Roman Empire.

Greek political thought was so intimately connected with Greek institutions that the decline of one necessarily meant the decline of the other.
Plato and Aristotle represented the highest achievement of Greek political
philosophy. With their passing and with the slipping into unimportance
of Greece politically, the thinking of the third and second centuries B.C.

turned to other things, leaving political philosophy in the back wash of a new tide. The political writings of this period are consequently without much originality or positive influence.[15] What influence they had was of a negative sort. The two great schools of this period, the Stoic and Epicurean schools of Zeno and Epicurus respectively, taught men to have as little to do with politics as possible. The loss of civic independence and the disappearance of popular participation in government so weakened the patriotism of the Greeks that they found it easy to turn away from the "life of the market-place" which they had known.

Philosophy now became concerned with the means by which the individual might secure happiness, rather than with the aspects of public welfare. Attention was shifted from the state to the citizen; and it was even held that there is no connection between individual and social welfare, and that the state is not necessary to a good life. The cosmopolitan character of the age was clearly reflected in its speculative thought. Universalism and individualism replaced city patriotism. The distinctions between Greek and barbarian and between city and city were broken down, and men viewed themselves either as citizens of the world or as separate individuals engrossed in their private interests.

This concern of the individual with his private affairs and the growing insistence on universal brotherhood and equality mark a decided change in the development of political philosophy. Professor Carlyle suggests in fact that, "There is no change in political theory so startling in its completeness." [16] Public concern and a belief in inequality had been the very touchstones of Platonic and Aristotelian philosophy. Now they were repudiated.

Both the Epicureans and Stoics agreed in making individual happiness the aim of life. They differed, however, in defining happiness and the method by which it might be secured. The Epicureans advocated the temperate satisfaction of every desire, sensual and intellectual; the Stoics taught the suppression of the emotions and the subordination of immoral desires to the demands of reason.

The Epicureans based the state upon individual self-interest. They defined law as an agreement of utility entered into among individuals in order that they might be secured against violence and injustice. The social contract theory of the state was here foreshadowed. They believed

[15] Much of the literature of this period, however, has never been recovered. About these volumes we can only speculate. The tradition has been handed down that the famous library at Alexandria contained several thousand political works of this period. But this library was burned in the early part of the fifth century A.D. in the effort of Emperor Theodosius to crush out pagan learning.

[16] A. J. and R. W. Carlyle, *History of Medieval Political Theory in the West* (1903), Vol. I, p. 8.

that political life is burdensome and that the wise man will take no part in it unless his interests absolutely demand it. The Epicureans taught submission to any government that maintained peace and order. Efficient despotism was as good as democracy. The suitability of this doctrine to the situation after the conquest of Greece by Alexander and by Rome is evident.

The Stoics conceived of nature as the embodiment of universal law. Reason, as the creative source of law, was the revealer of nature. The law of nature was therefore fixed and immutable; it was the reflection of the process of nature, in harmony with human reason, the divine element in the universe. In this form the idea of natural law was handed down through Roman law and through medieval political thought.

However, human reason as the source of natural law did not mean the independent judgment of the individual, but the common judgment of mankind. Men, as rational beings, are essentially alike; they are subject to the same natural law and have equal rights. Upon this doctrine, a cosmopolitan political theory was created. All men are naturally brothers, fellow citizens in a world republic. Universal natural law and universal citizenship were Stoic ideals. The importance of these conceptions in a society based upon slavery is at once evident.

While the Stoics developed these ideals from a philosophic and humanitarian point of view, the conditions of the time soon became favorable to their political application. The empire of Alexander broke down the barriers between Greek and barbarian. Petty social and civil distinctions were swept away, and diverse peoples actually became members of one political system. With the establishment of the Roman Empire, universal law and universal citizenship became practical facts. The idea of the law of nature and of principles of justice common to all men were adopted by the Roman jurists. The conception of universal brotherhood, especially when it was taken up and expanded by Christianity, was transmitted, with the profoundest results, to modern times.

Greek Theory of International Relations

Conditions in the Hellenic world were favorable for a considerable growth of inter-municipal customs and principles. The Greeks drew a clearly marked distinction between Hellene and barbarian, and recognized the existence of a law of the Hellenes, not applicable to the world at large. The Greek cities, like the Hebrew tribes, formed an international circle, distinct from the world around them, and were bound together by a close community of interests, and by a common race, religion, and culture. The idea of city autonomy, however, was more powerful than the sense of national unity, and a scientific body of inter-municipal principles was never created.

Relations among the cities were governed, in the main, by considerations of policy and expediency. Religious leagues, such as the Delphic Amphictyony, and political confederations, such as the Delian Confederacy and the Achaean and Aetolian Leagues, were established. The military and political leadership of a single city was sometimes recognized—Sparta, Athens, and Thebes occupying such positions before the Greeks were united under Macedon. Attempts were also made to maintain a balance of power among the leading cities.

Warfare was frequent and was characterized by great severity and cruelty. Booty was divided among the victors, and prisoners were usually put to death or sold into slavery, although later Greek customs showed progress toward more humane principles. Few obligations were recognized in dealing with foreigners, and resident aliens usually possessed rights only through some Greek citizen who acted as their patron. Certain rules and customs, such as the inviolability of envoys, the right of asylum, truces for the burial of the dead, and suspension of hostilities during great religious festivals, e.g., the Olympic games, were generally observed. A frequent task of the popular assemblies was to hear and criticize the reports of returning ambassadors, to instruct envoys sent abroad, and to discuss proposals made by foreign ambassadors.

The Greeks made a decided contribution to the idea of settling disputes by arbitration. Questions of religion, commerce, and territory were referred by agreement to individuals, to other cities, or to religious oracles for decision.[17] Agreements beforehand to submit disputes to arbitration were sometimes inserted in treaties. In the field of maritime law considerable progress was made. Piracy, regarded as honorable in the early Greek period, was supplanted by legitimate and peaceful commerce; and a body of maritime law was developed as early as the third century B.C. by the commercial city of Rhodes, which acted as a sort of mandatory of all the Greek states interested in the safety of the seas. This Rhodian Sea Law[18] served as the basis for commercial codes in the Middle Ages.

In relations with peoples outside the Hellenic world, the Greeks of the later period came to recognize the obligation of certain ill-defined rules. References were made to "the laws of all mankind"[19] in the dealings between Greeks and Persians. Whatever the origin of the idea of a universal law, it was a distinctly progressive step to recognize that the inter-

---

[17] See J. H. Ralston, *International Arbitration from Athens to Locarno* (1929).

[18] R. D. Benedict, "The Historical Position of the Rhodian Sea Law," *Yale Law Review*, Vol. 18 (February, 1909), pp. 223-242.

[19] Herodotus, vii. 36; Thucydides, i. 67.

course of men, even of diverse races and religions, was not absolutely lawless.

The ancient world tried two methods of regulating international life. The first was to impose peace by force and create a world state. The Oriental empires tried this method and failed. Rome alone succeeded in creating for some centuries a general peace on this basis. The price paid, however, was heavy. It cost the stagnation of creative effort, the decadence of civilized life, and finally a bitter internal struggle. The other method, that tried by the Greeks, established a system of independent states, which aimed to maintain a balance of power. They were bound one to another by treaties and settled some of their disputes by adjudication. This method did not establish peace; on the contrary, wars were frequent. It made possible, however, a period of active political life, in which many modern international ideas had their origin.

Contributions of Greek Political Thought

The Greek civic ideal, especially as it existed in Athens, created a civilization which no city has since been able to attain. It developed an intensity of patriotism and exercised an educational influence which no modern state can equal. The city was the individual on a larger scale, an integral and essential part of his life. Its law was identified with supreme reason and covered the entire field of morality. The city was thus state, church, and school. Religious feelings were associated with civic allegiance. Education was acquired from personal experience in the assembly and in the law courts and from holding administrative office. Individuals existed as persons only as members of the state, in which they took active part, and from which they received that which made life worth living.

The chief contributions of the Greeks to political thought were the ideals of liberty and democracy. The freedom of the Greeks stood in striking contrast to conditions in the Oriental states that preceded or in the Roman Empire that followed. This love of liberty was manifest in many ways. In the first place, the Greeks insisted that each city should be an autonomous unit, independent of external control. Athens took the leading part in resisting the Persian invaders in their efforts to extend Eastern despotism to the Hellenic world. Aeschylus makes his chorus say that the Athenians "call no man their master," [20] and the "games of liberty" [21] were established at Platea to commemorate the freedom of Greece at the suggestion of the Athenian Aristides. This love of city independence prevented unity in the Hellenic world; but at a time when means of com-

[20] Aeschylus, *Persae*, 244.
[21] The celebration of the Eleutheria.

munication and transportation were undeveloped, and when the device of representation had not been thought of, democracy and individual freedom were possible only in states small in area and population.

In the second place, Athens encouraged freedom of thought and expression. A critical attitude in philosophy and in politics was to some extent tolerated. Citizens, freed from trivial cares by the labor of slaves, devoted their attention to non-materialistic interests and considered it proper that the state should foster literature, art, and science. In contrast to the Oriental world, the intellectual life of Greece was comparatively free from dogma, superstition, and external control; and the intellectual achievements of the Hellenes were their permanent contribution to history. What we call today the western spirit, in contrast to that of the Orient, is a direct legacy from the Greeks.

Finally, the Greeks made some progress toward the ideal of individual liberty. Tyranny and oligarchy they considered the worst forms of government, largely because they involved an elaborate system of espionage and of annoying interferences with the lives of individuals. Aristotle taught that a considerable amount of individual freedom was necessary for the highest development of human powers, and the Epicureans held the extreme belief that each person should place first the satisfaction of his individual desires. However, the Greeks never quite developed the true conception of the individual as a moral person whose welfare is an end in itself. They recognized the will of the state, but did not clearly separate from it the free will of the individual. The Greek citizen submitted himself to the laws of his city in much the same way that he yielded to the forces of nature around him. Both were equally natural and inevitable. A clear understanding of the nature of authority and of freedom, of the conflict between them, and yet of their essential harmony, was never worked out in the philosophy of the Greeks.

The Greek idea of the state was not, as in later theory, based upon the relationship existing between sovereign and people, but rather between the individual and the community. The notion of an independent sovereign, possessing inherent powers, can scarcely be found in Greek thought. Final authority was vested in the laws rather than in persons. An order based on natural law determined the relations among the members of the community, and types of government were merely the form through which the self-directing life of the community expressed itself. From the Middle Ages to the present time, political theory has been concerned with the question of sovereignty, justifying it and giving it legal character, and elaborating the organization of its powers. These concepts were unimportant in Greek political thought.

The conception of liberty among the Greeks did not always work successfully in practice. The right of all to mind the public business was made an excuse for each to interfere with his neighbor. Sycophants and public informers were numerous, and the independence of individuals was made an excuse for excessive egoism and jealousy. Besides, the ideas of liberty and equality led to incompetence and mediocrity. Where all had an equal voice in the state, no one would admit the superior value of any opinions, and the way was made easy for the demagogue. The Athenian democracy was suspicious of its leaders. Socrates was put to death by a public opinion hostile to any who differed from the mass, and ostracism always threatened the man who possessed conspicuous ability.

Moreover, Athens, the leading exponent of liberty, refused to extend it to large classes of her own population and to the cities she brought under her sway. In her efforts to build up an empire, she was accused by her allies and by her enemies of being a tyrant city; and her fall in 404 B.C. is explained mainly by her attempts to restrict freedom to herself. Greek liberty came down to the modern world rather as an ideal than as a practical system. Worked out by later peoples in the form of democracy and of individualism, the Greek conception of freedom was a valuable political contribution. The modern world agrees with the Greek that each citizen should have free development and should share in the business of the state.

REFERENCES

BAILEY, Cyril, *The Greek Atomists and Epicurus* (Oxford, Clarendon Press, 1928).

BARKER, Ernest, *The Politics of Aristotle* (Oxford, Clarendon Press, 1946).

CARLYLE, A. J. and R. W., *A History of Medieval Political Theory in the West*, 6 vols. (London, Blackwood, 1903-1936), Vol. I, Chap. 1.

CHERNISS, H. F., *Aristotle's Criticism of Plato and the Academy* (Baltimore, Johns Hopkins Press, 1944).

JAEGER, Werner, *Aristotle: Fundamentals of the History of His Development*, trans. by Richard Robinson (Oxford, Clarendon Press, 1934).

McILWAIN, C. H., *The Growth of Political Thought in the West* (New York, Macmillan, 1932), Chap. 3.

POPPER, K. R., *The Open Society and Its Enemies*, rev. ed. (Princeton, Princeton Univ. Press, 1950), Chap. 2.

RALSTON, J. H., *International Arbitration from Athens to Locarno* (Stanford, Stanford Univ. Press, 1929).

ROBIN, Léon, *Aristote* (Paris, Presses Universitaires de France, 1944).

———, *La Pensée Hellenique des Origines à Épicure* (Paris, Presses Universitaires de France, 1942).

SABINE, G. H., *A History of Political Theory*, rev. ed. (New York, Holt, 1950), Chaps. 5-8.

SINCLAIR, T. A., *A History of Greek Political Thought* (London, Routledge and Kegan Paul, 1952), Chaps. 11-12.

CHAPTER VI ~~~

Roman Political Thought

Roman Political Institutions

Rome contributed little to the literature of political thought. Her political institutions and legal system, however, exerted a tremendous influence on political evolution; and for many centuries after her fall the idea of the state was based upon the institutions that Rome had established. Rome first appeared as a city-state, formed by a union of tribes living on neighboring hills. Her government was monarchic, consisting of a king, an advisory senate, and an assembly, the *comitia curiata*, whose chief duty was the election of the king. At first only the patricians, a limited group of aristocratic families, had any share in political authority. Under the later kings, the remainder of the citizens, the plebeians, demanded a voice in the government, and a new assembly, the *comitia centuriata*, in which both patricians and plebeians took part, was added.

As in the Greek cities, the general tendency in early Rome was toward a more democratic form of government. About 500 B.C., with the expulsion of the last king, a republic was established; and for two centuries the patricians and plebeians carried on a contest for control of the state, the result of which was the fusion of the two classes into a common citizen body, having equal political and civil rights. In this process the government underwent decided changes. The civil and military authority of the king was vested in two consuls elected annually by the *comitia centuriata*. Other magistrates, such as the praetors and the censors, were created later to assist in the administrative and judicial functions of the consuls, and in time of emergency provision was made for the temporary establishment of a dictatorship. At first only patricians were eligible to these offices, but the plebeians worked steadily to secure admission. Meantime the plebeians created their own assembly, the *concilium plebis,* and chose

75

their own officers, chief of whom was the tribune, who had the right to intervene on behalf of the people and to veto acts of the consuls.

As the two classes were gradually amalgamated, the plebeian organs were fused into the government of the city. The plebeian assembly, with name changed to the *comitia tributa,* became the chief law-making organ. The *comitia centuriata* chose the consuls, held them responsible for their acts in office, acted as the final court in criminal cases, and decided questions of peace and war. The old patrician *comitia curiata* survived only as a formal body in control of certain religious matters. The Senate, however, retained its aristocratic character and came to be composed of those who had held high administrative office. While in theory its functions were advisory only, in practice it exercised large powers: the regulation of finances and of political and social privileges was in its hands, and through its control of foreign relations and of dealings with the allies and with subject nations, its powers increased with the growth of the empire.

After the conclusion of the contest between patricians and plebeians and the satisfactory working out of the republican government of the city, the attention of Rome was directed to foreign conquest and expansion. The Greek cities, facing east, came first in contact with older civilizations and were compelled to wage defensive wars to maintain their own existence. Their surplus of population went out as colonists to found new cities that became virtually independent. Under these conditions the city-state remained as the typical form of government in the Hellenic world until the time of Alexander. Rome, facing west, came first in contact with weaker peoples and easily conquered and absorbed them; and her colonists remained under the control of the home city and extended its dominion. As a result of this process, democratic development within the city ceased, and with the territorial expansion of Rome, an imperial system of government, reverting to the autocratic type, was gradually created.

The expansion of Rome began with the incorporation of the neighboring Italian states. Some of these were recognized as allies and allowed considerable autonomy in local government. Over others governing authority was vested in a group of colonists sent out from Rome, or in a Roman official called a prefect. The right to share in the government at Rome was limited to citizens residing in the capital, but a limited citizenship was conferred upon some of the allies; and in 90 B.C., after a serious revolt, practically all the peoples south of the Po were granted full citizenship.

In the wars with Carthage Rome destroyed her only rival in the west, became a naval power, and acquired over-seas dominions. By the middle of the second century B.C., a large part of the fragments of Alexander's

Graeco-Oriental empire had come under Roman control. And by the close of the first century B.C., Rome had extended her authority over the barbarians to the north and west, and governed from the Euphrates to the British Isles and from the Sahara to the Rhine-Danube frontier. Practically the entire western civilized world was united in a single political system. Roads leading from Rome in all directions gave trade a permanent course, kept the provinces in touch with the capital, and made it possible to maintain order.

An effective system of centralized administrative control was worked out to hold the empire together. The conquered territory was divided into provinces, over each of which was placed a Roman official, known as a proconsul or a propraetor, with full powers in civil and political affairs. The right to impeach this official at Rome on the expiration of his term was the only safe-guard which the people of the provinces possessed against arbitrary authority. Although the form of the republican city-state constitution survived at Rome, the work of Julius Caesar and Augustus, about the time of Christ, virtually set up a military despotism. This was done by securing control of the army and of the voters of Rome, and combining in the hands of one man, the emperor, the powers of the most important magistrates. The popular assemblies ceased to have any important functions, gradually losing their criminal jurisdiction, their right to elect officers, and their voice in legislation. The senate retained an important position, its resolutions being the usual form of legislation. However, the emperor exercised a dominant influence in determining the make-up of the senate, his proposals initiated new measures, and his decrees came finally to be recognized as law. The establishment of Latin as a common official language and the application of a general system of law over the empire marked the completion of the process of unification.

By the end of the second century A.D., Roman citizenship had been extended to the provinces, the city-state basis of the empire thus disappearing, and all members of the state were placed on an equality of subjection to the rule of the emperor. During this period the earlier legal theory that the emperor received his powers from the Roman people was challenged by the idea that imperial authority was of divine origin.[1] For a time the emperor was himself worshipped as a god. Later, when Christianity was adopted as the state religion, the idea survived in the belief

---

[1] A. J. Carlyle observes in his monumental study that the theory of ultimate popular sovereignty was still to be found, however, as late as the sixth century. He suggests that it was in fact never wholly lost, ultimately being incorporated in the "Teutonic theory of law and political authority, a theory which again knew nothing of any legislative authority in the State apart from the whole body of the State." *History of Medieval Political Theory in the West* (1903), Vol. I, pp. 63-70.

that the emperor ruled as the agent of God's will on earth. The administrative reforms of Diocletian and Constantine, about A.D. 300, definitely abandoned the legal fictions of republican Rome and recognized the imperial system. Thus the democratic city-state became the autocratic world-empire, emphasis shifting from the Greek ideals of democracy, liberty, and local independence, to the Roman ideals of unity, order, universal law, and cosmopolitanism.

Nature of Roman Political Thought

In general, the Romans derived their philosophical ideas from the Greeks, the doctrines of the Stoics being especially popular. Deliberate purpose played little part in the creation of Roman political institutions. Aside from the general policy of playing off her enemies one against another,[2] and of attaching each newly conquered region directly to herself, the empire resulted from the situation that confronted Rome, and not from any general plan or theory. Even after the completion of the imperial system, no effort was made by any Roman writer to formulate a system of political philosophy, as Aristotle had done for the Greek world. However, the Romans, in applying to the facts of political life some of the ideas which they borrowed from the Greeks, reduced them to more definite form, and in their system of government and law they unconsciously applied certain principles which mark an advance over Greek thought. Among these the most important was the idea of positive law. This involved the separation of politics and ethics, the formation of an abstract conception of the state, distinct from society in general, and the development of the idea of the legal personality and of the political sovereignty of the state as a maker of law.

In Roman thought the state did not absorb the individual, as in the theory of Plato, nor was the state considered non-essential as in the teachings of the Epicureans. The Romans separated state and individual, each having definite rights and duties. The state was a necessary and natural framework for social existence; but the individual, rather than the state, was made the center of legal thought, and the protection of the rights of the individual was the main purpose for which the state existed. The state was thus viewed as a legal person, exercising its authority within definite limits; and the citizen was viewed as a legal person, having rights which were to be safeguarded against other persons and against illegal encroachment by the government itself. On the basis of this conception, the elaborate system of Roman law was created.

[2] The *divide et impera* of the Romans.

The content of this law is plain. It is to be found in the works of Gaius and Ulpian and in the Justinian Code. Its source, however, is less clear. Conflicting beliefs and a divergence of practice from theory complicate the issue. A belief in divine-right absolutism was supported, as just mentioned, in some circles during the years of Roman imperialism. At the same time, however, the established view that ultimate authority resided in the people still claimed adherents. According to this view, the emperors were said to receive their authority from the citizens and were considered to be responsible to them. In practice, nevertheless, this latter group conceded that the emperor's will had the force of law. His decrees replaced popular action and he came to be considered as the sole *legis lator*.[3] The justification for this is given by Ulpian in a famous passage:

The will of the Emperor has the force of law, because by the passage of the *lex regia* the people transfers to him and vests in him all its own power and authority.[4]

Carlyle comments that "few phrases are more remarkable than this almost paradoxical description of an unlimited personal authority founded upon a purely democratic basis. The Emperor's will is law, but only because the people choose to have it so." [5]

This transfer of power was in the form of a contract, an idea which played a large part in Roman legal theory. Like the Greeks, the Romans considered the state so natural as to need no justification, and the idea of a *social* contract by which men gave up their natural rights in order to form a body politic held no place in their thought. On the other hand, they did develop the idea of a *governmental* contract, by which the authority of the people was delegated to the public officials. Once chosen, however, the power of the magistrate within his legal duties was complete, the people having no right to withdraw the powers which they had conferred. The Romans recognized no right of revolution. Their idea of the governmental contract was similar to that held by Hobbes, rather than that of Locke; and, as in the case of Hobbes, they used the doctrine to justify autocratic government.

The creation of law also took the form of a contract during Rome's earlier years. New laws were enacted in the form of an agreement between the magistrates and the people in their assemblies, being proposed by the former and ratified or rejected by the latter. Law was not a command imposed by a sovereign upon his subjects, but a contract arranged among the constituent organs of the state after negotiation. The idea of

[3] Carlyle, *op. cit.*, Vol. I, p. 70.
[4] *Digest*, l. 4. 1.
[5] Carlyle, *op. cit.*, Vol. I, p. 64.

contract was likewise important in Roman religious thought, their worship consisting largely of a bargain by which the worshipper agreed to perform certain ceremonial duties to the gods in return for certain expected benefits from them. Finally, the Romans clearly recognized the nature of a contractual relation among individuals and built up a large part of their private law upon that conception.

Roman Theory of Law

The Roman idea of law developed gradually. The first Roman laws were a mixture of religious regulations, customary rules, and popular conceptions of justice. As usual among early peoples, religion was an important element in authority, offenses against public order being regarded as injuries to the gods rather than as offenses against the state. As in Greece, a distinction gradually developed between those rules that were considered the direct commands of the gods and those principles which were held to be rationally implied in the customs of men. The idea that the state might create new law was, however, entirely lacking, and the first codification of the Roman law in the Twelve Tables (about 450 B.C.) merely put into definite form the existing customs of the Roman people.

Nevertheless, the establishment of the Twelve Tables marked the beginning of a new period in legal thought. It pushed the religious element into the background, made offenses against the law primarily crimes against the state rather than disobedience to the gods, and marked the disappearance of custom as the chief source of law. Henceforth the law was increasingly considered as the will of the state, human in origin and in the source of its authority. Politics more and more dominated religion, the laws becoming secular in nature and the priests being made the agents of the state. In theory the laws of the Twelve Tables were supposed to cover the whole field of Roman private law, and change could be made only by interpreting the Tables or by making express statutory additions to them with the formal consent of the Roman people. Thus additions were made by the legal legislative organs of the state—the patrician and the plebeian assemblies, and later the senate and the emperors. In this process the doctrine became firmly established that the body of Roman law represented the will of the state, from which it received its formulation and its sanction.

With the expansion of Rome several new ideas were introduced which widened and liberalized the Roman law, making it especially well fitted for the government of a world-empire, and enabling it, after the fall of the empire, to serve as the basis for the legal system of Europe. The body of civil law growing out of the Twelve Tables was narrow and formal. It contained many survivals of early religious ideas and of conditions peculiar to Rome, and involved many technicalities that were destructive of justice. This exclusiveness and rigidity was gradually broken down by the edicts of the praetors, the responses of the jurisconsults, and the constitutions of the emperors. By their work the law was expanded and rationalized, and in this process the important ideas of the *jus gentium* and the *jus naturale* were worked out.

When the administrative functions were subdivided under the republic, in the fourth century B.C., the civil judicial powers were bestowed upon an official known as the praetor. In applying the law, this official was compelled to interpret it, and in so doing inevitably established new principles. Besides, at the beginnings of their terms, the praetors issued edicts laying down the general principles that they intended to follow in the administration of their office. These edicts, forming precedents, were generally accepted by their successors, and, with the additions made from time to time, gradually modified and expanded Roman legal principles and practice.

With the extension of Roman rule over conquered peoples, and with the growth of foreign trade and the increasing number of aliens living in Rome, an additional praetor was set up in the third century B.C. to administer justice in suits in which foreigners were concerned. Since Roman magistrates could not apply alien law, these praetors were compelled to develop a system of law suitable to their purposes. This was done by selecting the legal principles common to Rome and to the different Italian peoples over whom Rome governed, and fusing them into a system of law known as the *jus gentium,* that is, the law common to all nations. It embodied the principles of natural equity that growing enlightenment was bringing at Rome, as well as the customs and legal ideas of subject peoples; and the praetor, in applying the law, was at liberty to modify it, subject only to his own sense of justice. Because the principles thus developed were free from technicalities, appeared to be the spontaneous creation of different peoples, and were characterized by abstract principles of justice, the *jus gentium* seemed to correspond to the perfect dictates of reason, universally valid, and contributed to the idea of a law of nature, with which it was finally identified. In this form it was gradually incorporated into the general body of Roman law, especially as the older civil law increasingly fell behind the requirements of the times.

The Roman law was further widened when the emperors bestowed upon learned jurists the right to answer legal appeals on disputed points coming from all parts of the empire, such responses finally coming to have the full force of law. Out of the enormous mass of diverse legal ideals, the jurists were expected to determine the general principles that were applicable to the entire empire. This demanded careful consideration of the ultimate nature of rights and of justice. In undertaking this work, the jurists, by their exact definition and logical classification, gradually built up a scientific system of jurisprudence, the great Code of Justinian representing their highest achievement. In their efforts to apply principles of justice and reason, they were much influenced by the Stoic doctrine of natural law. Through the influence of Greek philosophy, especially through the work of the jurists, it became an accepted principle of Roman political thought that behind the particular rules of law there lay fundamental principles of abstract right, derived from the authority of nature, as interpreted by reason. In dealing with the practical affairs of the whole civilized world, the jurists found the Stoic ideas of the brotherhood of man and of universal law particularly valuable.

Through the incorporation of the ideas of the *jus gentium* and the *jus naturale* into legal thought, Roman law ceased to be a narrow and rigid system, applicable only to a particular people in a single city, and became a broad and general system of jurisprudence suitable for the government of a world-state, and liberal enough to serve as the basis for the jurisprudence of diverse types of states for many centuries. From Roman jurisprudence the idea of natural law passed into the literature of the Middle Ages, identified often with the Christian conception of the universal divine law implanted by God in the hearts of men. The organization of the Roman Catholic church and its system of canon law were based upon Roman legal ideas. When the study of Roman law was revived toward the close of the Middle Ages, the Roman dictum that the will of the prince is the source of law,[6] separated from the Roman idea that the prince is the agent of the people, was used as the basis for the theory of the sovereignty of the national king. The Stoic doctrines of the jurists that by natural law all men are born free [7] and that all men are equal in natural rights [8] were revived by the opponents of royal authority in building up the theory of social contract and natural rights that served as the basis for revolution and democracy. Finally, the concepts of *jus gentium* and *jus naturale* played an important part in the creation of the theory of international law as finally worked out by Grotius.

[6] *Institutes of Justinian*, i. 2. 6.
[7] *Ibid.*, i. 2. 2.
[8] Ulpian, *Digest*, l. 17. 32.

Polybius

No discussion of the principles of Roman government was attempted until after Rome had become the greatest state in the world, and a beginning was then made by a Greek. Polybius (204-122 B.C.) [9] was one of the statesmen who directed the policy of the Achaean League at the time when Macedonian power was destroyed and Greece brought under Roman control. He favored a negative attitude toward Rome, in contrast to the pro-Roman leanings of the leaders of the League; and after the conquest he was taken to Italy as a hostage. There he became acquainted with the Roman constitution and the statesmen of the day, was sent by the Roman government on several missions to Greece, and spent most of his time in traveling and collecting materials for his *History of Rome.*

When Polybius wrote, the republican constitution had reached the height of its development and had not yet given way under the strain imposed by the expanding area and interests of Rome. The motive of his *History* was to explain the greatness of Rome, to trace the steps by which Rome had become the ruling power in the world, and to describe the manner in which control over her vast dominions was exercised. In doing this, he presented a theory of the origin of the state and described the various types of government and the natural cycle of political change. He then analyzed the constitution of Rome, showing that, by combining elements of the various forms of government and establishing a system of checks and balances among the different organs, Rome was safeguarded against the decay that inevitably destroyed the simple type of state.

Polybius adopted the Greek classification of government into monarchy, aristocracy, and democracy, and held that each of these types might exist in a pure or a corrupt form. He believed that these forms followed one another in a natural sequence, each type containing within itself the germs of its own decay. The earliest form of authority was a monarchy, based on force, established over a group of people bound together by natural instinct. As reason and experience gradually taught the value and necessity of government, and ideas of justice and morality appeared, the people obeyed the monarch willingly, and government proper was established in the form of royalty. However, as the monarch assumed arbitrary power and ruled unjustly, this type tended to degenerate into its corrupt form, tyranny. Conspiracies, headed by distinguished and virtuous leaders, overthrew the tyrant and established aristocracy. Aristocracy, in turn, developed its inherent defect, oppressed the people, and became an

[9] The political theory of Polybius is found in his *History of Rome,* especially Bk. VI. Of the forty books composing the *History,* the first five survive entire; the other thirty-five, only in fragments.

oligarchy. The people, rising against their oppressors, established themselves in power and for a time governed in the interest of the whole as a democracy. But dissensions soon arose, the wealthy corrupted the ignorant masses, injustice and discontent increased, and mob rule resulted. The excesses of the mob brought some bold leader into prominence, who secured for himself autocratic power and gained popular support; and the cycle began its course anew.

Polybius believed that to insure stability and prevent these successive transformations, it was essential to combine the better elements of all these forms. This had been partially accomplished by Lycurgus for Sparta, and it had been even better worked out gradually by experience in the Roman system. In the Roman constitution the consuls represented the monarchic principle, the senate was essentially aristocratic, and the popular assemblies were democratic. Moreover, each of these organs exercised some restraint on the powers of the others, no one being able to act effectively without the consent of all. Thus an elaborate system of checks and balances was created. While the writings of Plato and Aristotle contained some conception of the value of this principle, the Greek writers preferred a simple form of government, somewhat modified by traces of the other types. Polybius was the first writer to make a clear statement of the advantages of a mixed form of government, and of the principle of checks and balances in constitutional organization. These conceptions were recognized in theory and in practice in later periods, and in a slightly changed form remain valid in modern political thought.

Polybius viewed the Roman state as an impartial spectator, and in his point of view was detached and rationalistic. He believed that the motive to action is self-interest, that statesmen must treat interests as natural political forces, that political life results in an equilibrium of such interests among different classes, and that individuals and classes must be controlled by a system of mutual restraints. His attitude bears some resemblance to that later taken by Machiavelli.

Cicero

Scarcely had the work of Polybius, praising the Roman constitution, been completed before the period of agitation and civil war began which destroyed the republic. The system of checks and balances, valuable as long as opposing interests made mutual concessions, became unworkable when factional hostility led to deadlock and revolution. The economic changes that accompanied the growth of the Roman Empire created a sharp division between the wealthy nobles, who composed the senate, and the proletariat represented in the assemblies; and the hostility between these bodies resulted in civil war, in which leaders such as the Gracchi, Marius, Sulla, Pompey, and Caesar brought the individual into prominence and prepared the way for the empire. During this period political speculation did not flourish. But in the effort of Cicero (106-43 B.C.) [10] to prevent these changes and to recall the Roman citizens to the former methods of working their government, clear and eloquent statements were made of the best Roman and Greek views concerning the nature of the state and of law. By adopting, in an eclectic fashion, the ideas of other men and working them into the dialogue form used by Plato,[11] Cicero was able to sum up the political philosophy of his time in a manner not approached by his contemporaries.

The body of Cicero's political philosophy is composed of three related elements. They are a belief in natural law, natural equality, and the state as natural to man.

Cicero is perhaps best known for his restatement of the idea of natural law. Following the teachings of Plato that the principles of right and justice are eternal, and of the Stoics that a supreme universal law exists in nature, Cicero brought the concepts of abstract reason and natural law into immediate relation with the activity of human reason and the legislation of the state. He believed that moral principles are as applicable to political matters as they are to private affairs, and that "true law is right reason in agreement with nature; it is of universal application, unchanging and everlasting." [12] There exists, in short, behind all laws and customs of men, a supreme and permanent law to which all else must conform if there is to be justice in the state.[13]

Cicero's commentary on natural law became a classic because of the clarity with which he was able to express himself. For the same reason his views on natural equality were only slightly less well known. Here he agreed with the Stoics, but disagreed with Plato and Aristotle, that men are much more alike than they are different.[14] Men do not differ in kind, though they may vary in degree, because nature has given reason to all men. "In fact, there is no human being of any race who, if he finds a guide, cannot attain to virtue." [15] This emphasis on natural equality also

---

[10] Cicero's political thought is found mainly in the De Republica, the De Legibus, and the De Officiis.

[11] There are other striking similarities between Plato and Cicero. Cicero's best known work, De Republica, is in many ways an imitation of Plato's Republic. It also is based on a search for justice in the state. The counterpart of Socrates is Scipio Africanus the Younger.

[12] De Republica, iii. 22.

[13] Carlyle, op. cit., Vol. I, p. 17.

[14] De Legibus, i. 10. 28.

[15] Ibid., i. 10. 32.

leads to a repudiation of slavery. Slaves are not to be considered as merely property. They have a right to just treatment and to an independent personality.[16]

As for the state, Cicero believed that it was the natural result of the social instincts of man. Moreover, participation in the business of the state was the highest function to which men could aspire. "For there is really no other occupation in which human virtue approaches more closely the August function of the Gods." [17] Cicero thus followed the earlier Greek and later Stoic [18] idea of the state as a rational and desirable institution rather than viewing the state as an artificial creation resulting from self-interest.

Cicero also undertook to classify governments and to consider their respective merits. Here he followed Polybius. The three simple forms of government are monarchy, aristocracy, and democracy. Each is possessed of certain advantages, but each is subject to decay that results in a corrupt form and leads to a cycle of revolutions. Of these forms, Cicero considered monarchy best, aristocracy next, with democracy least desirable. He preferred, however, a mixed form of government, combining the excellences of each, and represented the republican system of Rome as a perfect example of the checks and balances needed for stability and good government.[19]

Cicero followed the *De Republica*, containing most of the ideas discussed above, with the *De Legibus*. As in the *De Republica*, he was again obviously influenced by Plato. But in contrast to the *Laws* of Plato, which modified and made more practical the earlier ideals of Plato's *Republic*, Cicero in his *De Legibus* developed further the same line of thought that appeared in his *De Republica*. He insisted that all civil law must be

---

[16] *De Officiis*, i. 13. 41.

[17] *De Republica*, i. 7. 12.

[18] Stoicism had undergone an extensive revision by Cicero's time. The philosophy of Zeno and Chrysippus had lost much of its negative quality in being restated by succeeding generations of philosopher's such as Panaetius of Rhodes. "The great work of Panaetius," Sabine tells us, "was to restate Stoicism in a form such that it could be assimilated by Romans of the aristocratic class, who knew nothing of philosophy and who yet were fired by enthusiasm for the learning of Greece, so different from anything that Rome could produce for herself . . . . In place of self-sufficiency he set up an ideal of public service, humanity, sympathy, and kindness." G. H. Sabine, *A History of Political Theory*, rev. ed. (1950), p. 153.

[19] To this prescription Cicero added a warning. A distinction must always be made, he insisted, between the government in power and the state itself. Ultimate authority must remain with the people of the state in their corporate capacity, with the government acting merely as their agent. Only in this way would constitutional government be safe from tyranny.

founded upon the principles of natural reason, and that an enactment that contravened the law of nature had no force as law. Fifteen centuries later this idea was still effective in European political life. He urged upon Roman citizens high ideals of patriotism and of justice. Holding that all men are subject to the same natural principles of right, he taught a cos· mopolitanism similar to that of the Stoics. Guided by these principles, Cicero, like Plato, designed a detailed constitutional and civil code that would conform to the principles of the law of nature. Only fragments of this code survive.

There was little that was original in the political thought of Cicero. His chief work was to transmit Greek ideas to Roman thought, but in this process a distinct change of emphasis took place. The Stoic cosmopolitanism, which among the Greeks reflected the decadence of their political importance, became at Rome the theory of an actual world-empire and represented a proud self-consciousness of an historical mission. Cicero made the law of nature the basis for a system of law consciously framed to be of world-wide application. All men, possessing equal rights, were destined by nature [20] to be ruled by universal principles. Hence a satisfactory basis for the empire was established, the Roman power seeming providentially destined to carry out the work of divine reason. Although Cicero's writings exerted only a mild influence upon the politics of his day, when factional strife was bitter and patriotism was declining, his ideas of justice and natural law sank deeply into Roman legal thought and profoundly influenced the later imperial jurists and the early Christian writers. And his idea of world unity and of universal law and authority remained the central principle of political thought throughout the whole medieval period.

Roman Theory of International Relations

Roman theory of international relations was more primitive and elementary than that of the Greeks. Rome returned to the earlier idea of war as the natural relation among states. In her treaties of peace, however, she was not content with merely bringing war to an end, but established some permanent relationship of alliance with the former enemy. At first

[20] Cicero was not always consistent in his use of the term *nature*. He generally used it to mean the true and rational order of things. Occasionally he seems to mean by it the primitive, undeveloped order. (Cf. *De Officiis*, l. 7. 12.) The conception of a state of nature, as a condition of primitive innocence before the organized political life of man began, was worked out by Seneca. (Cf. Carlyle, *op. cit.*, Vol. I, Chap. 2.) This idea became important later in the social-contract theory of Hobbes, Locke, and Rousseau.

Rome dealt with neighboring states on the basis of equality, but by clauses added to later treaties some form of vassalage was created in which the superior position of Rome was recognized. Foreigners were treated more liberally at Rome than in the Greek cities, and Roman foreign policy was guided by shrewder considerations of self-interest. In estimating the justice and legality of international acts, Rome always applied her own standards. A just war was one declared with due regard to Roman religious ceremonies and legal formalities.

The expansion of Rome into an empire was accomplished almost as much by diplomacy and statecraft as by force. Rome's policy was to sow discord among different nations, to aid the weaker in overthrowing the stronger, and finally to bring both under her own control. She carefully husbanded her own resources and used those of her allies whenever possible, and she frequently evaded treaties by subterfuge and practiced injustice under the guise of equity. Even after the establishment of her world-empire, Rome had to deal with her neighbors in war and peace. Embassies were received from India, Scythia, and from the kings of the Medes and the Iberians. Wars were waged with the Germans along the northern frontier. However, Rome never treated these peoples as her equals. The Roman theory considered the empire as the only legal state, and from the point of view of international law other states did not exist. The *jus gentium* applied only to the peoples who were the allies of Rome. With others no legal relations whatever were recognized.

The establishment of the Roman Empire, while making international relations of any importance impossible by bringing practically the whole civilized world into one political system, nevertheless prepared the way for the later growth of international law. The creation of a common citizenship, the maintenance of the *Pax Romana,* and the impartial administration of justice over many nations broke down the earlier isolation of states and the idea that foreigners were naturally inferiors and enemies. Men became accustomed to the idea of a common superior and a universal law, and these conceptions, especially prominent in the Middle Ages, were essential to the creation of a law among nations. Equally important in this direction was the idea of a *jus gentium,* a body of rules and usages common to diverse peoples. In the minds of the later Roman jurists the general principles of the *jus gentium* were identified with the law of nature, and were thus considered to be universal principles applicable to all nations. These ideas were appropriated by the founders of international law toward the close of the Middle Ages, were applied in international practice, and gradually prepared the way for the modern conception of a family of nations carrying on their relations according to definite legal principles.

Contributions of Roman Political Thought

The political ideals of the Greeks and of the Romans were complementary, each being strong where the other was weak. In contrast to the Greek ideas of liberty and democracy, Rome placed chief emphasis on the ideas of law, order, and unity. The weakness of the Greeks was in their failure to unite, factional strife within the cities and constant wars among the cities costing them their political independence. Rome, unifying her population at home and bringing the western world under her control, crushed individual liberty and transformed the republican city into the autocratic empire. In working out her contribution of order and unity, and in establishing peace and world law, Rome was compelled to destroy the Greek conception of freedom and democracy, and to make the state highly centralized and all-powerful. As liberty degenerated into anarchy in Greece, so order became tyranny in the Roman Empire. Natural growth was checked, anything novel was looked upon with suspicion and dislike,[21] and the maintenance of the *status quo* became an obsession.

However, the Greek ideal of freedom and popular government was workable only in small and homogeneous units. It was always exclusive and essentially aristocratic. Before the modern democratic national state could develop, the work of Rome was necessary. Local jealousies and petty class distinctions had to be broken down, and the ideals of human brotherhood and of the equality of men before the law had to be put into political practice. The exclusiveness of early peoples, implied in such words as "barbarian" and "chosen people," and the universal system of slavery had to be destroyed before democracy and freedom could be established on a comprehensive and satisfactory basis. The cosmopolitan power of Rome and the Stoic-Christian conception of the brotherhood of man laid the foundation for the modern point of view. These ideals survived the fall of Rome, were given new impetus by the Renaissance, and worked themselves out into political institutions during the period of Revolution.

Rome also contributed valuable principles of colonial and municipal administration; the degree of self-government permitted to the provinces made the *pax Romana* something more than military imperialism. Even the subject peoples in the empire recognized the value of Roman order, and felt that they had lost something of value when the Roman world went to pieces. No people over whom Rome extended her control ever entirely lost the conception of civilized life, and the provinces continued

---

[21] A revolution was a *res novae;* a man of no position was a *homo novus.*

to flourish long after the capital itself was disorderly and corrupt. Rome remained a name of much power when the actual city was a ruin. Her language and law had overspread the world; the barbarians who conquered the empire considered it their highest glory to deck themselves in some shreds of the Roman purple; the church built up its organization and its authority on the model of the Roman Empire; and the Roman words *Caesar* and *Imperium* were long powerful in political thought. Roman ideals fixed themselves so strongly in the minds of men that the theory of world unity and of a single, all-powerful authority, enforcing a universal law over the western world, survived for centuries in spite of actual conditions decidedly contradictory to it.

REFERENCES

BOWLE, John, *Western Political Thought* (New York, Oxford, 1948), Bk. I, Chap. 6.

CAIRNS, Huntington, *Legal Philosophy from Plato to Hegel* (Baltimore, Johns Hopkins Press, 1949), Chap. 4.

CARLYLE, A. J. and R. W., *A History of Medieval Political Theory in the West*, 6 vols. (London, Blackwood, 1903-1936), Vol. I, Parts I and II.

COWELL, F. R., *Cicero and the Roman Republic* (London, Pitman, 1948).

GLOVER, T. R., *Springs of Hellas* (New York, Macmillan, 1946), Chap. 6.

HASKELL, H. J., *This Was Cicero* (New York, Knopf, 1942).

MAYER, J. P., *Political Thought* (New York, Viking, 1939), Chap. 2.

McILWAIN, C. H., *The Growth of Political Thought in the West* (New York, Macmillan, 1932), Chap. 4.

RAND, E. K., *The Building of Eternal Rome* (Cambridge, Harvard Univ. Press, 1943).

SABINE, G. H., *A History of Political Theory*, rev. ed. (New York, Holt, 1950), Chap. 9.

SCHULZ, Fritz, *History of Roman Legal Science* (Oxford, Clarendon Press, 1946).

SYME, Ronald, *The Roman Revolution* (Oxford, Clarendon Press, 1939).

PART III

Medieval Political Thought

CHAPTER VII ~~~~

Beginnings of Medieval Political Thought

Christianity in the Roman Empire

Two new elements were added to political life at the beginning of the Middle Ages. These were the doctrines of Christianity, as they developed in contact with Roman philosophy and institutions, and the political ideas of the Teutonic barbarians who overthrew the Roman Empire. The ideas of the Teutons worked themselves out mainly in the form of institutions, and did not affect political philosophy until the close of the medieval period. On the other hand, the establishment of the Christian religion and the development of the Christian church became cardinal influences on medieval political thought.

Christianity, with its Stoic doctrine of the equality of men in the sight of God and its emphasis on the supreme value of the individual, appeared just after the Roman world was reorganized under a monarchy. It originated among a despised people in an obscure part of the empire; and as long as the Roman power was strong, it grew slowly, appealing in the main to the lowest ranks of society. As the empire declined, it spread more rapidly, until, in the early part of the fourth century, it was the religion of the dominant classes in the Roman world, and was on an equal legal footing with paganism. When Constantine made it the official worship of the state, it rapidly triumphed over the dying pagan beliefs, and by the close of the fourth century it was the only legal religion in the Roman world. Through the zeal of its adherents it also made considerable headway among the Teutonic barbarians who were soon to destroy the empire. The sanction of the Christian church was thus added to the authority of the emperor, and the belief became firmly established that

93

the Roman authority was divinely ordained to rule the world and that it was to last forever. These ideas remained fundamental in medieval political thought.

At first the church was organized on a democratic and local basis, but the churches located in the important cities and those that were founded by the apostles enjoyed a certain preëminence. The Roman church and its bishop were especially prominent. After Christianity became the official religion of the Roman Empire, it was immediately drawn into politics. The emperor exercised ultimate authority in religious matters and the organization of the church followed that of the government. During the last century of the empire, however, the ecclesiastical authorities gained power at the expense of the political ones. Most of the emperors were weak, the church had able men in its chief positions, and the doctrines of the church were especially attractive during this period of turmoil and social decadence.

With the fall of the Western Empire, the political institutions of Rome were destroyed or seriously modified, though the organization of the church remained untouched. Accordingly, the church represented the Roman tradition, emphasized the principle of unity during the period of anarchy following the invasions, and was compelled to take over an increasing amount of temporal authority in its effort to maintain order and peace. The bishops became recognized officials of government in the barbarian kingdoms and virtually controlled some of the most important cities. The burden of secular work thus thrown upon the church further centralized authority in the organization that centered around the bishop of Rome. In the Eastern Empire, which survived the invasions, the church remained subordinate to the state. Its energies were devoted to philosophical speculations concerning obscure questions in theology rather than to the practical problems of converting and controlling barbarians in a world whose political system had gone to pieces.

The Rise of the Papacy

At the time of the conversion of Constantine the process of transforming the church into a hierarchical organization had already begun. The clergy were separating from the laity as a body with distinct rights and privileges, divided within itself into different grades of rank and power. The leading church official in a city became the bishop. The bishops of the more important cities exercised some power over the other bishops of their province. The final step was taken when the bishop of the capital city founded an ecclesiastical monarchy. When Christianity became the official religion of the empire, the bishop at Rome was made the legal adviser of the emperor in church affairs, and it often fell to him to settle ecclesiastical questions submitted to the emperor's decision. The belief that the church at Rome had been founded by St. Peter, recognized as the chief apostle, gave a theoretical basis for the preëminence of the Roman bishop, who was considered to be his apostolic successor. Besides, the provincial churches in the west had been established under the auspices of the Roman church, had received financial aid from it, and owed allegiance to the Roman bishop. Missionaries sent out by the Roman church were active in converting the barbarians, and it was natural that the barbarians would recognize the headship of the church from which their teachers had come.

The formation of a powerful, centralized church organization was hastened by changes that took place in the doctrines and practices of the church. In its first two centuries Christianity remained a simple, spiritual religion. But when Christianity became fashionable, after its adoption by the state, many pagan ideas were introduced by those who became nominal Christians but had no conception of its spiritual truths. In the process of converting the Teutonic barbarians further changes in church practices and beliefs came in. Finally, the interest in speculative philosophy, especially in the Eastern Church, gave rise to many differences in doctrine that compelled some decision between orthodoxy and heresy. It became necessary, therefore, to guard and regulate the doctrines and ceremonies of the church, and for that purpose an ecclesiastical government was gradually formed, and an elaborate system of canon law, modeled upon the Roman law, was created. When the Arian heresy convulsed the church in the fourth century, a general church council gave to the Roman bishop appellate jurisdiction over the decrees of the other bishops. And in the following century, the western emperor declared the supremacy of the Roman bishop and made him the legal court of appeal in ecclesiastical cases.

The group of influences and ideas that grew out of the historical position of Rome were the chief causes in elevating the Roman bishop to the papacy. Since Rome was the capital of the political world, it seemed logical that it should also be considered the center of the religious world. As the church built up its system of organization, it was natural that it should follow Roman imperial models; and after the barbarian conquest, when there was no longer an opportunity for Roman political and legal genius in actual government, the ablest minds in the Roman world turned to the church and found a new field of activity in the creation of an ecclesiastical empire under the papacy. The belief that the empire of Rome was divinely founded and eternal was also useful and, with the added Christian idea that the kingdom of Christ was to rule the whole world, led to a spiritual conception of the world-empire which was embodied in the organized church and the papacy.

When the imperial court was moved from Rome to Constantinople, the bishop at Rome was left with no overshadowing authority beside him. As a result, the Roman bishop was able to act more independently than was his chief rival, the bishop at Constantinople, and was also able to maintain a more consistent theology and thus gain a reputation for orthodoxy, while the eastern bishop was subject to the ideas and demands of a court frequently in revolution. In the absence of the emperor from Rome, the bishop became the most important official in the city, and considerable power of local political administration passed into his hands. In this way there was added to the large ecclesiastical power of the Roman bishop the practically independent political government of a little state.

From the beginning of the seventh century the political affairs, first of Rome and finally of Italy, became a definite part of the pope's duties. The attacks of the Mohammedans on the Eastern Empire prevented the emperor at Constantinople from giving serious attention to affairs in the west, and the pope became virtually independent of any superior political authority. The final separation of the Eastern and Western churches also occurred about this time. When the empire was divided the close connection between the government and the church led the church to group itself about the two main centers, Rome and Constantinople. This division was accentuated by the differences in language and civilization between the Graeco-Oriental world and the Roman world. Differences in doctrine also separated the churches, and the great controversy over image worship in the eighth century finally brought to a crisis all the divergent tendencies of Greek and Roman Christianity. The churches separated, and in spite of numerous efforts to unite them, remained apart. The Roman pope thus became independent of the East in ecclesiastical as well as in political affairs, and was recognized without opposition as the supreme head of the Western Church.

When the Lombard kings tried to incorporate the city of Rome within their dominions, the pope resolutely opposed them, and when his efforts seemed hopeless, he appealed for aid, in the name of St. Peter, to the warlike Franks, who had adopted Roman Christianity and with whom the pope had long had an understanding. The powerful *major domus* of the Franks, Charles Martel, and later his son Pepin, responded to this appeal, drove the Lombards from the lands they had occupied, conquered the territory formerly held by the eastern emperor in Italy, and bestowed it upon the pope. The papacy thus became in law as it had long been in practice the holder of political authority. In return the pope sanctioned Pepin's usurpation of royal power among the Franks, confirmed his position by crowning him king, and after the Frankish kingdom had expanded over a large part of western Europe, crowned Pepin's son Charlemagne Roman emperor. Thus, in A.D. 800 the medieval empire was established and the connection was begun between church and state that furnished the main issues in political thought for centuries.

The chief defect in the early position of the pope was the method by which he was chosen. Selected at first by the clergy and people of Rome, the choice of a new bishop was frequently accompanied by popular rioting and bloodshed. After the fall of the empire, the office fell into the control of the powerful families who dominated the city. As the office gained in political importance, contests among these families became bitter, and rival feudal factions at Rome set up and deposed popes at will. Through such influences persons of scandalous life were, through violence and bribery, elevated to the papal office. This source of weakness was removed in the eleventh century, when a church council vested the selection of the pope in a college of cardinals, made up at first of the leading clergy around Rome, later extended to include a wider field. The pope was thus made more independent of local politics, and the way was prepared for the great popes who elevated the office to a position of highest dignity and power.

Political Theory in the Early Church

The founder of Christianity had little interest in political doctrines. In appealing to the lowly and oppressed, the importance of the rich and the powerful was disparaged. In emphasizing the principle of the Golden Rule, the morality of the individual was appealed to, and the authority of government was thereby minimized. Jesus carefully distinguished the spiritual kingdom, which he aimed to establish, from the kingdoms of this world, and evaded every attempt to entangle him with the Roman authorities by insisting that he was not concerned with temporal affairs. This same spirit pervaded the writings of the Apostles. Passive obedience to the powers that be was enjoined, government was conceived as a means of carrying out God's will on earth, and meekness and humility were insisted upon. Only when the state interfered with the teachings of the church was disobedience permitted. Then the injunction to obey God rather than man led to the passive resistance of the martyrs.

At the same time there were certain elements of political theory which the early Christian writers drew from the ideas current in their times, and which increased in importance as Christianity spread to the upper classes and was more influenced by Stoic philosophy. The New Testament contains important statements concerning the doctrines of natural law, of human equality, and of the nature of government.

St. Paul, in referring to the Gentiles, who "do by nature the things of law," [1] implies a conception of natural law, written in men's hearts and revealed by reason, distinct from the law of the state. This Stoic idea of the law of nature was taken up by the Church Fathers and became an important element in medieval political thought.

The Apostles also adopted the cosmopolitan ideas of the later Greek philosophers concerning the equality of men. The universal fatherhood of God, and the teaching that all classes and peoples are one in Christ Jesus, led to a conception of the identity of human nature in all parts of the world, and to a belief in human equality. On the question of slavery, however, the attitude of the early Christians, like that of the Stoic philosophers, was not altogether consistent. In the sight of God there was no distinction between bond and free. Slavery might control men's bodies, but it could not control their spirits. St. Paul wrote that "there can be neither bond nor free, . . . for ye are all one in Christ Jesus." [2] Yet as a human institution, slavery was recognized and was not considered unlawful. Slaves were advised in fact to serve their masters faithfully and "to obey them in all things." [3]

Finally the New Testament taught a definite theory of the nature of government [4] which was of the greatest importance in the later history of political thought. Civil government was viewed as a divine institution, deriving its authority from God. Obedience to the state was demanded as a religious obligation as well as a political necessity. The state existed to maintain justice. It therefore had a sacred character, its ruler was God's servant, and obedience was essential. These ideas were stated by the Apostles, not only because of the necessity of adjusting the relations of the early church to the Roman government, but also because of the desire to counteract the anarchical tendencies in the early Christian societies. The Christian theory of the state was essentially based upon that of the later Stoics, that government is necessary to proper human development. The Christian writers, in adopting the Stoic rather than the Epicurean attitude [5] toward the state, and in adding the Christian conception of the divine order in human society, laid the foundation for the political thought of the following thousand years.

[1] Romans 2:12-14.
[2] Gal. 3:28.
[3] Col. 3:22.
[4] See Romans 13:1-7; Titus 3:1-2; I Peter 2:13-17.
[5] In the early church there were distinct traces of the unpatriotic and disintegrating Epicurean doctrine that the state was unnecessary to a good life.

The early Church Fathers, who followed the Apostles, furthered these ideas. They adopted the conception of natural law as worked out by Cicero and suggested by St. Paul, and they taught that men are by nature free and equal. This did not prevent them, however, from also recognizing slavery as a legal and even necessary institution. It was necessary, they suggested, as a punishment for sin, due to the fall of man from the state of nature when all men were equal. At the same time the church held masters responsible for the treatment of their slaves and aimed to mitigate the worst evils of the system. The Fathers likewise accepted the state as a divine institution. They taught that ultimate authority for government must be sought in God [6] as the creator of all things, and that the authority of the ruler was to be held sacred. The Fathers added, however, that while government was divinely ordained, it, too, was the consequence of sin, resulting from the fall of man from original innocence to the depraved condition that made coercive authority necessary. It was, in short, a divine remedy for human wickedness.[7] This change in attitude, considering coercion as a necessary evil, tended to diminish the importance of government and to increase the relative position of the church.

As Christianity became the official religion of the Roman Empire, gradually developed its semi-political organization, acquired property and power, and built up its system of theology, a new attitude began to appear in its political ideas. The church began to assume rights and dignities equal to those of the empire. The Roman bishops began to exercise authority in spiritual and moral affairs over even the emperors, and the Church Fathers claimed that there were rights possessed by the church with which the imperial authority could not interfere. While the civil ruler was considered the "vicar of God," and a clear statement of the theory of the divine right of kings may be found in the writings of the Church Fathers,[8] a line of separation began to be drawn between ecclesiastical and secular authority. The church became more self-conscious and claimed greater independence within its own sphere; and the tendency developed to depreciate the importance of political authority and to exalt by comparison the spiritual authority of the church. The writings

[6] The church doctrine that the ruler derived his power from God was the chief point of difference between the Fathers and Roman legal writers who traced all authority to its ultimate source in the people. Later medieval political thought gave considerable attention to the contrast between these two principles.

[7] See A. J. and R. W. Carlyle, A History of Medieval Political Theory in the West (1903), Vol. I, Chap. 11 for a more complete discussion of this subject.

[8] See Gregory the Great, Regulae Pastoralis, iii. 4; Libri Moralium in Job, xxii. 24. "It was from the doctrines of Gregory the Great that the religious theory of the absolute and irresponsible authority of the ruler continually drew its strongest arguments, both in the Middle Ages and later." Carlyle, op. cit., Vol. I, p. 153.

of Ambrose of Milan, of St. Augustine, and of Gregory the Great [9] illustrate these lines of development.

St. Augustine

While the writings of St. Augustine (A.D. 354-430) belong to the period of the Church Fathers just considered, and represent in the main the same point of view, they contained several ideas that demand special attention. The work of Augustine embodies the transition from the classical world, about to pass away, to the world of Christendom; from the period of hostility between the church and a pagan state to the period of unity in a Christian church-state.

When the city of Rome was sacked by the Goths in A.D. 410, those who adhered to the pagan beliefs attributed the fall of Rome to the fact that the government had abandoned the old worship and adopted Christianity. In order to answer this accusation, Augustine, Bishop of Hippo in North Africa, spent thirteen years in preparing his *City of God* [10] the most influential book written in the fifth century. He attacked paganism, traced Roman history to show that the old gods had not saved Rome from misfortune, and argued that Christianity, if adopted generally by people and rulers, would save the state. The tone of this part of the work is aggressively apologetic. He then turned from the earthly to the spiritual city. By this he meant not only Heaven, to which the Christians looked forward as their eternal home, but also its counterpart on earth composed of the body of true believers. The church was, thus, the City of God.

Augustine deliberately imitated Plato in working out his ideal city, [11] and combined the philosophy of Plato with the doctrines of Cicero and with the theology of the Christian religion. He justified slavery as the result of the fall of man, which made necessary the conventional institutions of society. Accordingly, slavery was both a remedy and a divine punishment for sin. He criticized Cicero's conception of the state as an embodiment of justice, holding that justice could not exist in non-Christian states. Justice, therefore, was not created by the civil authority but by the ecclesiastical, which existed as a principle of authority, independent of the state. In this respect Augustine broke away from the earlier Church

---

[9] The writings of the Church Fathers may be found in English translation in the sets of volumes called *The Ante-Nicene Fathers* and the *Nicene and Post-Nicene Fathers*.

[10] The best current edition of this work is to be found in the Modern Library series.

[11] The conception of the state as a city shows the Greek influence. Augustine believed that the world would be most happily governed if it consisted of a society of small states, but in his conception of the church he was imperialistic, believing in a world-wide organization under a single leader.

Fathers and eliminated the elements of law and justice which the Roman writers had considered the fundamental basis of the state. Augustine considered the state partly as a punitive, partly as a remedial, institution. Men by their nature were impelled to form social relations. They were originally equal, and freely obeyed rules of wisdom and justice, but as a consequence of sin some men had to be subjected to the authority of others. Augustine believed in the divine origin of the state, and bitterly opposed the Donatists, who claimed freedom from civil obligations and considered the state a diabolical institution. The ruler was the representative of God on earth and as such was entitled to the obedience of his subjects, but the real kingdom of God was not of this nature. Holding these ideas of the state, it was quite natural that Augustine should consider the earthly state inferior to the eternal state of the spirit and of the hereafter. The fundamental distinction in Augustine's thought, however, was not between church and state, but between two societies, one composed of the wicked, the other of the godly. On earth these groups were always mixed, and it was by symbol, rather than by identification, that the City of God was represented by the church. Augustine conceived of the City of God as a "Christianized Church-State, from which unbelievers are excluded, and claimed the supreme power in that state for the leaders of the ecclesiastical hierarchy." [12]

Augustine's *City of God* dominated Christian thought for centuries. It "set over against the declining world of ancient Rome the eternal commonwealth of God's elect, and sketched in fervid rhetoric the ideals and interests of that church here on earth which strives toward the kingdom of heaven." [13] Thomas Aquinas, Dante, Wyclif, and Grotius drew largely from the *City of God* for their writings. It was a favorite book of Charlemagne, who in establishing his empire aimed to make a state in which God's will should rule; and Bryce says that it is hardly too much to say that the Holy Roman Empire was built upon the foundation of the *City of God*.[14] The work of Augustine gave to the church at a critical period of its history a crystallized body of thought, and put into definite statement the ideal which gave it distinctive existence and self-conscious purpose. As it developed its administrative machinery and concentrated more on earthly activities, it was well-started on its way to the position of church-power represented by the papacy at its height.

[12] J. N. Figgis, *Political Aspects of St. Augustine's City of God* (1921), p. 79.
[13] L. Thorndike, *History of Medieval Europe*, rev. ed. (1928), p. 416.
[14] James Bryce, *The Holy Roman Empire*, rev. ed. (1932), p. 94, note.

Political Ideas of the Teutons

The Teutonic invaders who overthrew the empire not only added a young, vigorous, and healthy population to the decadent Roman peoples, but brought with them certain political ideas and institutions quite different from those prevalent in the Roman world. They placed a high value on personal independence and emphasized the importance of the individual man as compared with the state. This was manifest in the proud spirit of the individual warrior. It was also illustrated in their idea of criminal justice. The wrong-doer was not punished by the public authority; the injured person took the punishment into his own hands. Even when the Teutonic states began to punish crime, they did not interfere with the liberty of the freeman. They imposed a money fine, part of which went to the injured person to satisfy his rights in the case. Moreover, all their early governments contained decidedly democratic elements. The unit of public life was the individual, not the state.

These ideas combined readily with the teachings of Christianity, which also emphasized the independence and supreme worth of the individual. Although in economic and religious organization this idea largely disappeared in the Middle Ages, when the individual was absorbed in the corporation, guild, commune, or order to which he belonged, it survived to some extent in the political organization of feudalism; and by the intellectual changes brought about during the Renaissance and Reformation, and by the gradual working out of Teutonic institutions into modern governments, the ideas of individual liberty and individual rights were transmitted to the modern world. In England, as early as the thirteenth century, ideas of civil liberty were crystallized in Magna Carta, which served as the model for numerous later bills of rights.

The political principles tacitly underlying the democratic institutions of the Teutons were especially important. While the influence of Roman law and government, and the military necessity of maintaining their power over a large conquered population, soon compelled the Teutonic leaders to centralize their government and establish a more autocratic authority, many traces of their earlier political methods survived and contributed to the democratic and individualistic spirit of the eighteenth and nineteenth centuries.

The early Teutons possessed popular assemblies of two types. A national assembly, composed of all the freemen of the tribe, chose the chieftains, decided for or against important proposals submitted to it, and occasionally acted as a judicial tribunal to hear important disputes. This assembly, however, early disappeared, as the Teutonic peoples were centralized into monarchies. In addition there were local representative assemblies, in the hundreds or the cantons, which decided local issues and served especially as judicial bodies. These survived on the continent until the end of the Middle Ages, when the revival of Roman law introduced a new judicial system. In England they furnished the model for the House of Commons, the local representative principle being transferred to the national legislature. Thus was introduced a device of government that combined central control with local self-government and made possible popular control over large areas. With the possible exception of federal government, which is similar in principle, no more valuable contribution to the machinery of government has been made in historic times.

In the early Teutonic tribes the freemen possessed the right of electing their king. There was, however, a general tendency toward the principle of heredity, especially when the kings gained power after the conquest. In Germany the elective principle was kept alive, the emperor, for centuries, being chosen by a body of electors. The fact that the medieval German emperor seldom possessed real governing power made the elective principle of little importance. In England, while the monarchy became hereditary, the idea that the king ultimately owed his authority to the people survived, and the right to depose an unsatisfactory king was actually exercised. Finally, in the Revolution of 1688 and in the accession of the House of Hanover, the principle of the right of the people's representatives to bestow the throne was clearly established, and a nominal monarchy became virtually a republic. The Teutonic principle of elective monarchy thus contributed to the modern theory of constitutional government.

The invaders' idea of law also differed from that of Rome. The Teutonic peoples thought of legal rights as belonging to individuals, not because they were members of the state, but because they were persons. Their law was a part of themselves, which they took with them wherever they went, and which they could not change or abandon. In contrast to the territorial basis of Roman law, which applied to all persons in the empire, Teutonic law had a personal basis, each man having the right to be tried according to his own law. Accordingly, after the conquest, the Roman population continued to be governed by the legal system of Rome, with which the Teutonic rulers and judges were compelled to make themselves familiar. In this process Teutonic legal principles were influenced by Roman ideas, and within a few generations, written codes of Teutonic laws,[15] prepared in the Latin language by Roman scholars, appeared.

[15] These were the *Leges Barbarorum,* of which the most important were the *Lex Salica,* the *Lex Ripuariorum,* the *Lex Wisigothorum,* the *Lex Burgundium,* and the *Lex Saxonum.*

In the Roman empire, the law had become crystallized into an elaborate and scientific code, which was supposed to make provision for all possible cases, but which made further growth difficult. Teutonic law, while often crude and unscientific, was declared by the public assemblies, acting as courts. These bodies, in declaring tribal customs to have the force of law and in applying the popular sense of justice to new cases, established precedents and built up, by a natural process, a constantly expanding body of unwritten or common law. This system of jurisprudence was practically destroyed on the continent of Europe by the adoption of Roman law toward the close of the Middle Ages. Influenced by Roman legal theory, the control of the people over law ceased, and law-making power was centered in the royal sovereign. In England, however, while influenced somewhat by Roman legal principles, the common law continued to develop, the legal system remained flexible, and the courts maintained their independence of the legislative and executive branches of government. From England, the common law system was transferred to the United States and to the self-governing colonies of the British Empire.

The idea of personal allegiance, emphasized in the Teutonic *comitatus*, in which a band of young warriors attached themselves to a leader, were maintained by him, and followed him to war, also contributed important elements to the feudal system in the Middle Ages. While the Teutonic peoples gradually adopted, in the main, the ideas of the peoples they conquered, in a vague way recognized the continuance of the eternal empire after they had overthrown it, and finally accepted the theory of the permanence of the Holy Roman Empire, their peculiar contributions to political thought were not entirely lost. They survived, especially in England, and contributed much to the later rise of distinctively modern ideas.

Feudalism

From the point of view of political institutions, the early medieval period was characterized, not only by the formation of a powerful ecclesiastical organization which exercised extensive political authority, but also by a contest between two forms of society, the patriarchal, clan type, as represented by the Teutonic barbarians, and the imperial state type, as represented by the Roman Empire. The compromise form of organization that resulted from this contest was called feudalism. In its earlier stages it seemed to have more of the personal clan than of the territorial state in its composition, but by the tenth and eleventh centuries the state idea was revived, and by the close of the medieval period it was completely successful, both the clan and the church having failed in their efforts to retain political power.

The Teutonic invaders were warriors, organized under a military leader. They were held together by ties of kinship and by vows of personal allegiance. Their organization was decentralized, emphasizing local independence. They were in a low stage of economic development, caring little for industry or commerce, but eager to secure land. During the period of the conquest and break-up of the Western Empire, the barbarian bands had organized into armies of considerable size, whose leaders had attempted to rule over large fragments of the empire. In this process the Frankish rulers had been most successful. Having upheld the cause of Christianity against both Pagan and Saracen, and having become the actual possessor of imperial authority over a large part of the ancient empire, the Frankish king Charlemagne was formally recognized by the pope as the successor of the Roman emperor. However, these early attempts at state-forming were too ambitious, and even Charlemagne's empire fell to pieces shortly after his death. Local officials and great landowners became a law unto themselves, and in the anarchy that followed, bonds other than political had to be found to hold society together and to maintain order and protection.

Such bonds, in addition to those furnished by the church, were found in personal relations among men and in a system of dependent land tenure, with which governing authority was associated. The peasants on the land needed protection, which the lords who held the land could furnish, but which bound the peasants to the soil and compelled certain obligations. Men unable to make an independent living "commended" themselves to some great man on the understanding that he would support them and they would serve him. Warriors attached themselves as personal friends and followers of some powerful chief. Land grants were made by the kings and the great nobles to their followers, with the understanding that certain services, especially military, would be required. The church was also drawn into this system, and a complex set of personal, local relationships based on landholding was built up.

Feudalism was essentially personal, private, and non-political. Any one who was able waged war, coined money, and held courts of justice. In it, men paid feudal aids, not taxes; they owed knight service instead of forming standing armies; they gave court attendance instead of creating a parliament; they were vassals, not citizens. Personal lordship and dependent land tenure took the place of modern nationality and territorial sovereignty. The power of the feudal lords was distinctly limited. A contract, expressed or understood, defined the relations between lord and vassal. Feudal territories were small and scattered, although efforts were made to unite adjacent holdings and to follow geographic and racial lines. By its very nature, feudalism prevented the idea of an absolute authority ruling within a definite area. Its theory required a succession of lordships within lordships, no one having complete sovereignty. The modern conceptions of sovereignty and of law were entirely foreign to the Middle Ages. Law was primarily custom, and existed as a part of local or national life; it was not the command of a lawmaker nor the will of a community. Legislation was merely the promulgation of what was already recognized as binding upon men.

Although certain valuable elements were contributed by feudalism to modern institutions, and although modern national states were finally formed by combining these feudal fragments and centralizing authority within them, real political progress was impossible as long as feudal ideas held sway. At the same time, feudal theory was not entirely anarchic. The personal relations of feudalism were based upon definite ideas of loyalty and of contract, and lord and vassal were equally obliged to obey and maintain the law which prescribed their mutual rights and duties. Besides, the idea grew steadily that beyond the obligation to his immediate overlord, every freeman owed direct allegiance to the king, and this principle hastened the growth of national states. In these the feudal theory taught that ruler as well as subject was bound to obey the law. The conception that the landowner is bound to render service, in war and in peace, to the community was also a valuable contribution.

The Holy Roman Empire

Throughout the whole period of feudal anarchy, the ideal of an empire, and of an emperor whose authority must be confirmed by a papal coronation at Rome, survived. This idea was upheld by the popes who sought the support of a strong temporal ruler in their contests with the Italian princes. It was also kept alive by the ambitions of those German rulers who governed a part of Charlemagne's empire and who hoped to regain the whole. In the tenth century, the German king Otto added Italy to his dominions and was declared emperor by the pope. With his coronation, the Holy Roman Empire began.

The Roman world in its demise bequeathed to the medieval period the ideals of world empire and of a world church. Roman rule, with its common law and language, had created political unity. Christianity, with its belief in one God before whom all men are equal, had established spiritual unity. The coincidence of the boundaries of the Roman Empire and the

Christian church made them appear parts of a universal movement toward world unity. The rise of the pope to the position of monarch in the church and the reëstablishment of an emperor in the west seemed the final steps in this process. The theory of a time when the only conception of civil or religious order was submission to authority required that both the church and the state should be governed as monarchies. The Holy Roman Church and the Holy Roman Empire were thus the same thing in two aspects, uniting church and state, and representing the dual divine and human nature of the founder of Christianity. The pope, as its spiritual head, ruled men's souls. The emperor, as its temporal head, governed men's actions. Opposition or conflict between pope and emperor was at first inconceivable, mutual coöperation being essential for perfect unity.

In theory, the emperors claimed a wider jurisdiction than the German duchies and the Italian provinces over which they actually exercised some authority. They regarded themselves as successors of the old Roman emperors and as feudal suzerains of the other European kings. In practice, they could not develop this imperial ideal and feudal overlordship into actual sovereignty. On the contrary, the attempt to combine Germany and Italy increased the prevalence of feudalism and local division in both. The feudal conception of the emperor's power prevented him from exercising real authority. The Italians despised the Germans as barbarians and were constantly in revolt against their foreign rulers. The popes, who wished the emperors to be their allies but not their masters, and who wished to rule independently in their own territory, always opposed imperial efforts to unify Germany and Italy, and finally became the chief rivals of the emperor for supreme headship in the empire. By the latter part of the eleventh century, the imperial authority had become little more than a name in Italy, and the increased secular authority of the pope brought about the struggle between political and spiritual authority with which medieval political philosophy is chiefly concerned.

Political theory in the Middle Ages was not based on an observation of the actual conditions that existed in political institutions, nor was it derived by induction from the past. It was partly inherited from the Greek and Roman world and partly deduced from the principles of metaphysical theology that were crystallizing into scholasticism. No two systems could be more unlike than the ideal Holy Roman Empire which dominated men's minds and the actual feudal régime in which these same men lived: "the one centralized, the other local; the one resting on a sublime theory, the other the rude offspring of anarchy; the one gathering all power into the hands of an irresponsible monarch, the other limiting his rights and authorizing resistance to his commands; the one demanding the equality

of all citizens as creatures equal before Heaven, the other bound up with
an aristocracy the proudest, and in its gradations of rank the most exact
that Europe had ever seen." [16]

REFERENCES

BARKER, Ernest, "Medieval Political Thought," in F. J. C. Hearnshaw, ed., *The
Social and Political Ideas of Some Great Medieval Thinkers* (London, Harrap,
1923), Chap. 1.

BRYCE, James, *The Holy Roman Empire,* rev. ed. (New York, Macmillan, 1932).

BURLEIGH, John, *The City of God: A Study of St. Augustine's Philosophy*
(London, Nisbet, 1949).

CARLYLE, A. J. and R. W., *A History of Medieval Political Theory in the West,*
6 vols. (London, Blackwood, 1903-1936), Vol. I, Part III.

COCHRANE, C. N., *Christianity and Classical Culture* (Oxford, Clarendon Press,
1940).

COULTON, G. G., *Studies in Medieval Thought* (London, Nelson, 1940),
Chaps. 1-3.

FIGGIS, J. N., *The Political Aspects of St. Augustine's City of God* (London,
Longmans, 1921).

GIERKE, Otto, *Political Theories of the Middle Ages,* trans. by F. W. Maitland
(Cambridge, Cambridge Univ. Press, 1900), pp. 1-7.

LA MONTE, J. L., *The World of the Middle Ages* (New York, Appleton-Century-
Crofts, 1949), Bk. I.

McILWAIN, C. H., *The Growth of Political Thought in the West* (New York,
Macmillan, 1932), Chap. 5.

SABINE, G. H., *A History of Political Theory,* rev. ed. (New York, Holt, 1950),
Chaps. 10-11.

THORNDIKE, Lynn, *History of Medieval Europe,* rev. ed. (Boston, Houghton,
1928).

TROELTSCH, Ernst, *Augustin, die christliche Antike, und das Mittelalter* (Berlin,
Oldenbourg, 1915).

————, *The Social Teachings of the Christian Churches,* trans. by Olive Wyon,
2 vols. (New York, Macmillan, 1931), Chap. 1.

[16] Bryce, *op. cit.,* p. 127.

CHAPTER VIII ～

The Conflict Between
Church and State

The Relation of Spiritual to Secular Authority

In the early days of Roman Christianity, the emperor had been recognized as head of both state and church. The right of the church to impose spiritual penalties for immoral acts was acknowledged, however, and was exercised even upon the emperors. As the church grew in power and its authority gravitated into the hands of the pope, the right to excommunicate disobedient members became a valuable weapon. The consequences of this penalty were extended into temporal affairs, and the doctrine was developed that an excommunicated ruler was no longer entitled to the allegiance of his subjects. The feudal theory of the state proved useful to the church on this point. As early as the ninth century, the pope excommunicated the King of Lorraine, who had divorced his wife and married his mistress. In spite of the fact that the king was supported by his brother, the emperor, and by many powerful bishops, the pope prevailed, mainly because the moral issue involved was clear. In this contest, the pope not only strengthened his position in the church, but also put forward claims to authority that encroached seriously on temporal jurisdiction.

When the alliance of church and state was consummated under Charlemagne, and even when the Holy Roman Empire was established under Otto, no attempt was made to define the respective powers of emperor and of pope. They were expected to rule jointly and harmoniously in a universal church-state. The feudal political conditions of the period, however, made it impossible for the emperor to exercise real headship, while the organization of the church on the Roman imperial model tended to concentrate authority in the hands of the pope. The increasing wealth of the church, especially in land, made it necessary for church officials to take an active part in politics. Accordingly, the temptation to extend their activities into the secular field was too strong to be resisted by the able men who governed the church. The ruler who was strong enough to bring others under his control turned to the popes to get a sanction for claiming universal power. In forming the empire, therefore, the papal claims to universal power were also fostered. Ultimately two authorities, emperor and pope, were left face to face.

In the eleventh century the rival powers of the emperor and the pope were brought to a distinct clash. In order to prevent the corrupt practice of purchasing church offices, and with the deliberate purpose of increasing his authority and independence, Pope Gregory VII decreed that no ecclesiastic should be invested with the symbols of office by a secular ruler, under penalty of excommunication. This decree transferred to the pope the selection of men for important church offices formerly exercised by the temporal rulers; and, because of the large landed estates of the church, diverted valuable feudal privileges from the secular to the ecclesiastical powers. The emperor, Henry IV, refusing to obey this decree, called a council of subservient church officials and declared the pope deposed. The pope in turn excommunicated the emperor and absolved his subjects from their oaths of allegiance. Thus began a contest which lasted, with numerous compromises and fluctuations of power, for two centuries. Out of this struggle, the pope ultimately emerged victorious as the unquestioned head of western Christendom, while the empire fell into feudal fragments and free cities. The office of emperor became merely a name.

The contest which the emperors had failed to win was taken up later by the kings of the rising national states. The papacy reached the height of its temporal power in the thirteenth century, under Innocent III. He was strong enough to decide disputed successions to the empire, to compel the French king to take back his divorced wife, to require the English king to acknowledge himself a vassal of the pope, and to hold the Christian kingdoms in Spain as papal dependencies. By the fourteenth century, however, the kings had consolidated their royal power, and the feudal independence and authority of the nobles, upon whom the popes had largely depended in their contests, had been decidedly reduced. The process of royal centralization was particularly successful in France, so that when Pope Boniface tried to prevent the French king from taxing ecclesiastical property, the king was able to defy the pope, and later to transfer the papacy from Rome to Avignon and bring it under French control. The Great Schism, which followed, further weakened the position of the pope, who found it increasingly difficult to exercise any important temporal powers in the growing national states of France, Spain, and England. In the German and Italian fragments of the empire, a show of political authority was retained. The rise and decline of the secular power of the popes, and their contests with emperors and kings were the issues about which medieval political theory revolved.

The Nature of Medieval Political Thought

During the greater part of the medieval period, political life was influenced but little by conscious purpose or by deliberately formulated theory. Certain ideas, surviving from the Roman tradition, or resulting from the teachings of Christianity, or growing out of the relations of feudalism were generally held, but they exerted little practical influence upon political institutions. From the decline of the Greek city-state to the rise of modern national states, except for the influence of Roman jurisprudence, philosophy was essentially non-political. Ideals of cosmopolitanism or of a life of religious mysticism sufficed for the individual, apart from a determinate human society. The individualized state, with its strenuous life of war and politics, disappeared. The ideal of world unity and of a single imperial authority was far removed from the actual facts of decentralization and anarchy in the western world. This discrepancy between theory and institutions in the Middle Ages is to be explained by the general nature and method of medieval thought.

Thought in the Middle Ages was unhistorical, unscientific, and uncritical. It reasoned by deduction from general dogmas based upon belief, rather than by induction from observation, investigation, and experiment. Learning was controlled by the clergy, especially by the monastic element, and speculation centered about questions of theology. The whole body of faith, developed and handed down by the organized church, was the basis of all knowledge; and this material was turned over and over by the narrow intellectual processes of scholasticism or accepted without rational demonstration by the contemplative introspection of mysticism. Thought was enchained by a rigid orthodoxy, and dissenting ideas were considered heresies to be ruthlessly hunted down.

The relation of ecclesiastical to secular power was the issue in medieval political thought. At different periods the controversy centered around concrete, and sometimes local, phases of the question; but the general tendency from the ninth to the thirteenth century was toward the development of a well-rounded theory of ecclesiastical and papal supremacy in world politics. In building up this doctrine, most of the ancient Greek and Roman writers were discarded as profane and, except for a slight uncritical appeal to history, the source of all knowledge was found by the monkish writers in the Bible and the works of the Church Fathers, especially St. Augustine and Gregory the Great.

As the conflict between church and state grew more intense, increasing use was made of the Old Testament, whose aggressive, theocratic point of view was more useful for church purposes than the submissive tone and indifferent political attitude of the New Testament. It was assumed that the history of Israel foreshadowed the life of the church, and the medieval theory of politics was decisively influenced by the Old Testament picture of the Israelitish state. The idea that law was the direct will of God, the important governmental authority of the priesthood, and the theocratic traditions that limited the powers of the king were all used by church writers to support their claims. And since the Old Testament ascribed greatest success to those kings who were most subservient to the prophets, the church writers argued that the subordination of secular to spiritual authority represented the divine plan of government.

Medieval political theory was based upon certain ideas on which all parties were agreed. The ghost of ancient Rome haunted men's minds, and the ideal of unity was firmly established. It was generally believed that there should be in Europe one state and one church, that authority in each should be concentrated in a single head, that church and state should be fused into a single system, and that the ultimate source of all authority was divine. Men lived in a universal society, which was at once a continuation of the Roman Empire and an incarnation of Christ in a visible church. The universal political empire of Rome had been established under God's will in order that within it might be formed the universal church.

Although church and state formed one society, nevertheless that society had two governments. The existence of two systems, and the strong contrast drawn by Christian writers between things of the world and things of the spirit, led to the famous doctrine of the two swords, providing for a twofold, harmonious division of authority between pope and emperor. This principle was stated at the close of the fifth century in a letter written by Pope Gelasius I to the emperor:

The true and perfect king and priest was Christ himself. . . . But Christ, knowing the weakness of human nature, and careful for the welfare of His people, separated the two offices, giving to each its peculiar functions and duties. Thus the Christian emperor needs the ecclesiastic for the attainment of eternal life, and the ecclesiastic depends upon the government of the emperor in temporal things.[1]

---

[1] A. J. and R. W. Carlyle, *A History of Medieval Political Theory in the West* (1903), Vol. I, p. 190.

This text was quoted frequently by the Church Fathers, and was supported by the symbolism of the two swords—one of the spirit, the other of the flesh—from which the doctrine drew its name.

At first, this perfect harmony between secular and spiritual authority in a unified church-state was conceived to be the divinely ordained system for ruling the earth. Each power was to rule in its own sphere, and neither was to interfere in the affairs of the other. But unhappily, this theory of dual authority was unworkable in practice. It proved impossible to separate secular from spiritual matters under the conditions of medieval life. Each authority charged that the other encroached upon its own domain, and each tried to build up a system of doctrine that would justify the extension of its own powers. Each could appeal to historical facts and biblical passages to support the widest claims and to justify the submission of its rival.

Arguments for Ecclesiastical Supremacy

During the period from the ninth to the fourteenth century, the leading exponents of the doctrine of ecclesiastical supremacy were Agobard, Bishop of Lyons; Hincmar, Archbishop of Rheims; Pope Nicholas I; Pope Gregory VII; Manegold of Lutterbach; St. Bernard; John of Salisbury; St. Thomas Aquinas; and Pope Innocent III.[2] Pope Gregory and his school emphasized *justitia* as the key-note of their policy. *Justitia* included papal sovereignty over the church, liberation of the clergy from lay control, and the right of the pope to correct even kings if they disobeyed the law of Christ. In the famous compilation known as the Decretum of Gratian (twelfth century), the church authorities were collected and edited and the theory of papal supremacy and of the church hierarchy was worked out in terms of a legal system.[3] The famous document known as the Donation of Constantine, in which the seat of imperial authority was transferred from Rome to Byzantium, and a grant of authority in the west was made to the pope, appeared as early as the ninth century; although it was not interpreted by the church writers to signify that Constantine had granted complete temporal power in the west to the pope until a later period. On the basis of this document, which was incorporated into Gratian's compilation, the popes traced their claim to temporal sovereignty back to the fourth century. This document was attacked as a forgery as early as the twelfth century, but was not generally

---

[2] The writings of most of the supporters of the church may be found in Migne, *Patrologia Latina*.

[3] Gratian, member of a monkish order, was a professor at the University of Bologna, in which a marked revival of Roman Law had centered.

recognized as spurious until the close of the medieval period. The ablest supporters of papal supremacy avoided the argument based upon Constantine's grant, since by its papal power was derived from man and not from God.

In tracing the arguments that supported the doctrine of ecclesiastical supremacy, it is difficult to separate clearly those whose chief purpose was to elevate the pope to supremacy within the church and those which supported his claim to superiority over the secular authority. The Petrine theory and the Pseudo-Isidorean Decretals aimed mainly at the former, but indirectly aided the latter, purpose. According to the Petrine theory, St. Peter was the rock upon which the church was built and was given the keys of heaven, with the power to decide on earth who should be bound and loosed in heaven.[4] The pope, as the successor of St. Peter, who was supposed to have founded the church at Rome and suffered martyrdom there, laid claim to these powers, which were far broader than any that the secular authority could claim. The Pseudo-Isidorean Decretals were forgeries made in France about the middle of the ninth century, purporting to be documents of the early popes. They aimed to free the bishops from the control of their archbishops by increasing the authority of the papacy, which the bishops hoped would be less inclined to interfere with them. These documents, with their theory of papal absolutism, were generally accepted and were largely responsible for the establishment of the centralized ecclesiastical monarchy that gave the church such a decided advantage over the decentralized, feudal political system.

The arguments that aimed primarily to justify the supremacy of spiritual over temporal authority followed two main lines. The first was based upon the belief that spiritual authority is by its nature of greater importance and of higher dignity than the secular power. Pope Sylvester urged bishops to remember that the crowns of kings are in comparison with the mitres of bishops as lead compared to gold,[5] and Peter Damian described the pope as king of kings and prince of emperors, who excels all men in honor and dignity.[6] This belief followed naturally from the teachings of the church regarding the relative value of this world and of the world to come, and of the things of the flesh and the things of the spirit. Many Scriptural texts were cited to prove the supremacy of the priesthood; and characteristic medieval analogies, such as that of soul and body and of sun and moon, were used as arguments to justify the primacy of ecclesiastical rule over temporal authority.

The second type of argument asserted that God had conferred upon

---

[4] Matthew 16:18-19.
[5] Sylvester II, *De Informatione Episcoporum.*
[6] Peter Damian, *Opusc,* xxiii. 1.

the church the right to control the actions of secular rulers whenever a question of morals was involved. As the distinction between clerical and lay elements in the church became clearly drawn, secular rulers, as laymen, were excluded from all ecclesiastical functions. Because of their exalted position, they were especially likely to sin, and the church did not hesitate to apply priestly reproof or censure when the high standard of conduct which it set up for rulers was disregarded. In the Old Testament were found numerous occasions on which the prophets had called down divine wrath upon the kings. From the New Testament the Petrine theory was interpreted to mean that final authority in disputes among brethren had been conferred upon the pope; and the command of Jesus to Peter, "Feed my sheep," was held to be a general power of pastoral supervision which included rulers as well as subjects.

In enforcing a penalty against secular rulers for offenses against the church, anathema and excommunication were first tried, in accordance with the idea that the church, as the bearer of the sword of the spirit, should impose spiritual penalties. When impious rulers sometimes ignored these decrees, the popes claimed the right to depose the offender and release his subjects from their oaths of allegiance. The religious nature of the feudal oath gave the church an interest in that obligation. Numerous Scriptural precedents could be found that seemed to justify this action, especially God's placing of Jeremiah over nations and kingdoms, with authority to root out, to pull down, and to destroy.[7] Also, the coronation of Charlemagne by the pope was claimed by the church to involve a grant of authority from pope to emperor, with the corresponding assertion that the pope could withdraw the power he had conferred.

"With a wide basis in custom and public sentiment for the exercise of jurisdiction over many classes of legal controversies; with an exclusive control of such as could be shown to be spiritual in character; with the facility for extending this control that inhered in the doctrine that it embraced whatever actions were in any way tainted with sin; and with the power to enforce its interpretation of its authority by the deposition of secular rulers from power—the medieval church was in fact, if not in theory, a most potent political institution."[8]

Arguments for Secular Supremacy

The secular rulers opposed the theory of ecclesiastical supremacy on the grounds that political society was as divine in origin as the church, and that kings, as agents of divine purpose, were responsible to God

[7] Jeremiah 1:11.
[8] W. A. Dunning, *Political Theories, Ancient and Medieval* (1902), p. 176.

alone. In spite of St. Augustine's dissent, most medieval writers, both secular and ecclesiastical, believed that the purpose of the state was ethical, that is, the maintenance of justice and right. It was the means of restraining the sinful passions of men, and in that sense the authority of secular rulers was considered sacred. The generally accepted theory held that kings ruled by divine right only so far as they carried out this divine purpose of righteousness and justice. The customary law of the Middle Ages was supposed to represent the natural principles of reason, and kings were expected to govern according to the law. The relation of king and people depended upon a mutual agreement, based largely on feudal ideals, to observe the law and to administer and maintain justice. Many medieval writers, however, including some churchmen,[9] taught that kings, responsible to God alone, should be obeyed regardless of whether their conduct was just and lawful.

Scriptural authority was also quoted to support the claim of secular independence. In the Old Testament kings were found to have received the direct sanction of God and to have been instruments in carrying out the divine will. In the New Testament, a text of especial value to the temporal authority was found in the declaration of Paul that "the powers that be are ordained of God. Whosoever therefore resisteth the power resisteth the ordinance of God." [10] But the fact that the Biblical writings in general show a distinctly anti-royal bias, and that the historical records and current traditions were the work of priests and monks, placed the supporters of secular authority at a distinct disadvantage in this regard.

Further arguments for the secular authority were made in the eleventh century by German bishops [11] who were under the control of the emperor and who wished to maintain their independence of papal supremacy. The best support of the imperial claims came, however, with the revived study of Roman law. Although the knowledge of Roman civil law was never lost in western Europe, and many of its principles were embodied in feudal customs and in the barbarian codes, there had been for centuries no systematic interest in jurisprudence, mainly because of the medieval tendency to treat law as a mass of traditions, imbedded so firmly in popular consciousness that codification or study was unnecessary. But in the later part of the eleventh century, largely because of the needs of the rising Italian cities, the written code of Justinian was revived, and the systematic study of Roman law was begun at the University of Bologna, spreading thence to France and Spain. The leading legal writers of the period were Irnerius Accursius, Bartolus, and Baldus. Bartolus, the "prince

---

[9] Especially Gregory the Great.
[10] Romans 13:1-7.
[11] Especially Theodoric of Verdun and Waltram of Naumburg.

of jurists," affirmed that the emperor was *Deu in terris,* that his sovereignty was inalienable and that to dispute him was sacrilege. He made a large contribution to the theory of sovereignty as developed later by Bodin and Grotius. In his distinction between states that recognized a superior and those that did not, he laid the foundation for the conception of a family of independent nations and of international law. He was frequently referred to by later writers on sovereignty and on international affairs.

An avenue of intellectual life was thus provided for many men who formerly had no opportunity except in theology; and laymen, educated in the law, took the place of the former clerical advisers of kings and princes. Men began to think about the principles of legal and political rights. The struggle of kings against their feudal vassals and the efforts of cities to become independent of feudal restrictions were decisively aided by the principles of Roman jurisprudence. The Roman law was the outgrowth of a highly centralized state and assumed the legislative absolutism of the emperor. Hence imperial claims could be supported by arguments quite different from those of the early medieval period. In the twelfth century, the lawyers, with the support of Frederick Barbarossa, put forward the claim that the emperors possessed the unbroken imperial power of the Caesars. The authority that the servile Roman jurists had ascribed to their despotic rulers was transferred to the medieval emperor, and was fervently acclaimed by his German and Italian partisans. The old maxim that what the emperor wills has the force of law was revived and utilized to offset the papal claims. The Roman law taught that the emperor governed the whole civilized world; hence the German emperors claimed independence from ecclesiastical control and superiority over secular rulers.

The culmination of imperial glory was reached in the first half of the thirteenth century under Frederick II, the most remarkable man of his age. He not only maintained the independence of the empire, but aimed to make himself supreme in spiritual as well as temporal affairs. He ignored papal censures and called himself the vicar of God on earth. In spite of the hostile activities of papal agents in all parts of his empire, and of the opposition, fostered by the pope, of selfish German princes and of the Italian cities, Frederick fought to maintain the dignity of the imperial power.

After his death, though, his accomplishments were undone by a series of incompetent successors, and his fame was darkened by the church, who accused him of heresies. He had committed the unpardonable crime of making a treaty on just and equal terms with the Sultan of Egypt; and even Dante, who sympathized with his struggle to maintain political independence, felt it necessary to place Frederick II among the faithless in his *Inferno*.

The kings of the rising national states, France, England, and Spain, also welcomed the aid of the jurists in so far as it strengthened royal authority against the church and the feudal nobles. They opposed, however, the argument that the German emperor, heir of Roman power, possessed any authority over their domains. They were willing in most cases to concede a figurative exaltedness to the emperor, but reserved political power to themselves. This concern for actual power marks one of the beginnings of modern thought.

While the immediate result of the revived Roman theory of the state strengthened the authority of rulers and helped to establish the absolute monarch, the study of Roman law was not wholly unfavorable to the progress of political liberty. Roman jurisprudence taught that the people are the ultimate source of political authority, and this doctrine coincided with the normal conception of the Teutonic peoples that law proceeded from the nation as a whole. Many of the jurists maintained that the people might at any time resume the authority which they had bestowed upon the emperor, that his legislative functions could be exercised only with the advice of a senate, and that he possessed no unlimited power over the property of his subjects. These ideas reappeared in the democratic doctrines at the close of the medieval period.

St. Bernard and John of Salisbury

Two of the leading writers of the twelfth century who dealt with the relations of church and state were St. Bernard of Clairvaux (1091-1153) [12] and John of Salisbury (1115(?)-1180).[13] St. Bernard was the most influential churchman of the period, although he declined all ecclesiastical honors and never became pope. He put faith above reason, and tried to revive the ascetic and mystical spirit of the Church Fathers. He had little sympathy with the secular learning that was beginning to appear in the west, and he attacked the tendency in the church to devote attention to wordly affairs. St. Bernard protested against the interference of the pope in administrative and non-spiritual affairs, believing that it was not in harmony with the lofty office of the pope to devote so much time and energy to worldly matters. Such duties, degrading in their nature, should be performed by the political authority.

[12] The political ideas of St. Bernard are found in his work *On Reflection* addressed to the pope. See John Mabillon, *Life and Works of St. Bernard, Abbot of Clairvaux* (1889-96).

[13] The political ideas of John of Salisbury are found in his *Policraticus*.

St. Bernard believed uncompromisingly in the supremacy of ecclesiastical power, but he wished it to limit its activities to those of a spiritual nature. In connection with an attempt of the pope to defend his territorial interests by force, St. Bernard interpreted the dogma of the two swords to mean that while the church possessed both the sword of the spirit and the sword of the flesh, the former alone should be used by the priest, the latter by the soldier, at the suggestion of the priest and under the command of the emperor. The venality and intrigue in the papal court, which was actively engaged in administering church property and organizing crusades, were scathingly rebuked by this reforming monk, who said that it was the law of Justinian and not that of the Lord that resounded through the papal palace.

John of Salisbury's writings were also marked by a refreshing candor. While he supported the supremacy of the church as did St. Bernard, he freely accused the church at the same time of abusing its office through love of money and other sins.

John was an Englishman by birth, though he was educated in Paris. Paris was at this time the center of a revived interest in Greek and Roman culture. John consequently received the broad training evident in his later works. On leaving Paris he returned to England where he served as secretary to Thomas Becket, then Archbishop of Canterbury. In this capacity he was closely connected with Becket's struggle against Henry II. Later he became Bishop of Chartres, where he passed the remainder of his life.

In his *Policraticus*, completed in 1159, John advanced a general philosophy of politics. Broader in scope than other works of this period, this treatise presented in a style reminiscent of Cicero a comprehensive picture of what was generally believed about political philosophy during this period.[14]

John argued, as did St. Thomas later, that a well-ordered society consists in a proper allotment of functions to the members of the commonwealth and in the right composition and strength of each organ. After attacking the obstacles that interfere with the healthy life of the state, he made the first effort since St. Augustine to frame an ideal system of government, on the basis of the necessary subordination of the secular

[14] This work is of special interest because it was written prior to the recovery of Aristotle's writings early in the thirteenth century. This recovery has often been considered a turning point in medieval history. (C. M. McIlwain, *The Growth of Political Thought in the West* [1932], pp. 338 f.) In the long run this was undeniably the case. But a comparison of the *Policraticus* with the writings of Thomas Aquinas in the next century demonstrates that the reappearance of Aristotle produced no startling break in the growth of political thought, as has sometimes been thought. See G. H. Sabine, *A History of Political Theory*, rev. ed. (1950), pp. 244-246 for additional comment.

to the religious authority. Monarchy was the only form of government with which he was concerned, and he viewed the state in terms of the Roman Empire and the Old Testament theocracies. He emphasized the ancient idea that law is really the ruler of men, viewing law as the eternal and immutable principle of divine will. The true basis of political life, therefore, he found in righteousness. The church, as the embodiment of righteousness, was the supreme ruler of man; the prince, as the embodiment of law, occupied the second place.

In defending the church against the state John declared emphatically that "Every censure imposed by law is vain if it does not bear the stamp of divine law; and a statute or ordinance of the prince is a thing of nought if not in conformity with the teachings of the Church." [15]

John was led from this to his famous doctrine of tyrannicide.[16] If the prince acted unrighteously he became a tyrant who ought to be put to death. The death of the tyrant must, however, be accomplished decently and without offense to religion; poison was not to be used, as having no scriptural authority. The safest way of getting rid of the tyrant was by prayer, but if this failed the people could have recourse to the sword.

In teaching that princes must further justice and righteousness under divine law, John of Salisbury helped to perpetuate the traditions of Rome and the early Fathers. He also aided the growth of constitutional government from the twelfth century onward by providing its adherents with a logical basis for disposing tyrannical rulers.

St. Thomas Aquinas

The thirteenth century was marked by the culmination of papal power and by an extensive interest in speculative philosophy. The ablest of the scholastic writers of the period was St. Thomas Aquinas (1227-1274).[17] He aimed to harmonize reason and revelation, to reconcile the doctrines of the church and the rational pagan philosophy which the revived study of classic learning had made known. He best represented the desire of his age for a complete unification of knowledge based on divine revelation

---

[15] *Policraticus,* iv. 6.

[16] John was the first medieval writer to make tyrannicide an integral part of his philosophy. Others, however, had suggested it by implication. See McIlwain, *op. cit.,* p. 322.

[17] The political ideas of St. Thomas Aquinas are found in his *De Regimine Principum,* of which only the first book and the first six chapters of the second are by Aquinas, the remainder being the work of his disciple, Ptolemy of Lucca. Aquinas also wrote *Commentaries on the Politics of Aristotle,* which contains little of his own theory of the state. His treatment of law and justice is found in his *Summa Theologica,* Vols. II-III.

and on the principle of final causes. In his work, politics again became a science, although, with true medieval method, it was the politics of Aristotle and Cicero as modified by St. Augustine and the Bible. Aquinas marked the beginning of the later medieval, rationalizing political thought, which combined with the old theocratic and Scriptural arguments general considerations derived from the nature of political societies and founded on the *Politics* of Aristotle. He exhibited the historical spirit and drew material from contemporary political institutions. In many respects his views were singularly advanced and moderate.

St. Thomas defined law as "an ordinance of reason for the common good, promulgated by him who has the care of a community." [18] In contrast to the Greek conception of law as existing in nature and reason, he emphasized the volitional element, and thus introduced the idea of positive law, that is, of rules actually formulated by a sovereign power in the state. Essentially, however, he viewed law as something universal, immutable, and natural; and positive law, made by man, was only a corruption of law if it conflicted with the fundamental principles of justice. The revived study of Roman law had renewed the reverence for a law of nature, which neither emperor nor pope could ignore. The development of this notion became of great importance, not only in placing limits on authority within the state, but also in creating the conception of rules of equity which control the relations among states.

St. Thomas also considered the various forms of law. There are, he states in a now famous section of the *Summa Theologica*, four types of law. On the lowest level is human law. This is composed of custom and other laws which have a human origin. Human law is followed by divine law which consists of the revealed codes, such as the laws of Moses, by which men are expected to live. Divine law in turn is followed by natural law which concerns God's reason in created things. Examples of things held to be part of natural law include self-preservation, sexual intercourse, education of offspring, and life in society with other men.[19] Finally, there is an eternal law which stands as the ultimate reality of the universe. This is God's "Divine Wisdom, directing all actions and movements." [20] It is truth itself.[21]

St. Thomas based political authority on the Aristotelian conception of the social nature of man, adding to it the doctrine of the divine origin of the state, based on St. Paul's dictum that "there is no power but of God." In contrast to the Greek ideal, Aquinas believed that the city was too

[18] *Summa Theologica*, ii. i. 90. 4.
[19] *Ibid.*, ii. i. 94. 2.
[20] *Ibid.*, ii. i. 93. 1.
[21] *Ibid.*

small and weak for defense and preferred the larger kingdom as the proper type of state. With the medieval love of unity, he preferred monarchy to democracy, believing that democracy breeds dissensions, and arguing that the ruler must be one, as the heart rules the body and God rules the universe. The widespread turbulence and anarchy of the Middle Ages made the idea of permanence and unity in political organization seem doubly excellent. St. Thomas recognized the anarchic element in the doctrines of tyrannicide and rejected them. He held, however, that a tyrannical ruler might be deposed, at least in an elective monarchy; and suggested a relation of ruler to subject which approached the later theories of constitutional monarchy and election. By elaborate scholastic reasoning, based on Greek and Roman thought and upon Scriptural quotations, he argued that the state should keep up its population, protect and care for its roads, establish a system of coinage, weights, and measures, and provide for the poor.

In spite of St. Thomas' respect for reason, he felt that the greatest truths were still obtainable only through faith. He held, as a result, that the church, the final authority on matters of belief, should be given precedence over any secular power. It was the duty of the political ruler to administer secular affairs in such a way as to further God's will, and to this extent the officials of the state must be subject to the priests and to the divine law of the church. If a ruler ignored the decrees of the church he should be excommunicated and his subjects absolved from all necessity of obedience. The authority of the priest was temporal as well as spiritual; the pope was to be obeyed above all rulers, in matters of civil welfare as well as in those which relate to salvation.

The unfinished system of St. Thomas Aquinas was worked out more fully by his follower, Egidius Colonna.[22] His treatise, intended as a text book for the French prince, was arranged with systematic clearness and precision. No important original contribution was added. The work of St. Thomas and of Egidius coördinated the doctrines of the church that had developed during the preceding centuries, and worked out what was considered to be a perfect and permanent system. Natural law was identified with the will of God; monarchic government and the supremacy of ecclesiastical authority were assumed and explained rather than justified. Believing that controversy was ended, because of the weakness of the imperial power, dogmatic finality was impressed upon political concepts. In actual fact, a new period was about to begin, in which the scholastic method and the ecclesiastical point of view were to be completely overthrown. The theories of Aquinas, however, were later made the basis

[22] In his *De Regimine Principum*.

of the Jesuit system, and exerted an influence through their political activities.

The Fourteenth Century Controversies

The controversy between ecclesiastical and secular authority at the opening of the fourteenth century centered around the dispute between Pope Boniface and Philip the Fair, king of France. Unmindful of the growth of national states and of the popular support of royal power, the pope tried unsuccessfully to extend the ideals of ecclesiastical supremacy. After the death of Boniface, his successors, Clement V and John XXII, made peace with the powerful French kings and from 1309 to 1376 resided at Avignon under their protection and influence. During this period they engaged in hot disputes with the German emperors, Henry VII and Lewis of Bavaria. On the papal side, the leading controversalists were Pope Boniface; [23] Egidius Colonna, who had been the tutor of the French king, but who abandoned him at the time of his quarrel with the pope; the friar Augustinius Triumphus; [24] and Pope John XXII. On the side of the secular rulers appeared John of Paris,[25] Pierre Dubois,[26] Dante, Marsilius of Padua, and William of Ockam.[27]

During this period a decided change of attitude appeared in political thought. The French king was the strongest ruler in Christendom. He made no claim, however, to imperial power, and to that extent was able to assert the independence of secular authority without becoming involved in the traditions of the empire. So weak, indeed, had the emperor become that the church no longer feared him. The pope, in his effort to weaken the position of the French ruler, even supported the imperial argument that all kings owed allegiance to the emperor. A growing spirit of national unity and the establishment of a centralized government had created a strong political system in France, and the claims of the French king were supported by practically all classes in the kingdom. The state was at last becoming more powerful than the church. Uncritical appeals to history were made to prove that there had been a king of the Franks before the rise of the church. And the more modern argument was put

[23] The famous bull *Unom Sanctam* (1302) was the official statement of the papal position.

[24] In his *Summa de Potestate Ecclesiastica*.

[25] In his *De Potestate Regia et Papali*.

[26] He is supposed to have been the author of the *De Recuperatione Terre Sancte*, and the *Questione de Potestate Papali*. These pamphlets are full of ideas that appeared later during the Reformation period. They propose the disendowment of the church, the absolute authority of the secular state, women's enfranchisement, mixed education, and international arbitration.

[27] On Dante, Marsilius, and Ockam, see sections following.

forward that the French king should exercise independent authority because he controlled the actual physical force to carry out his commands.
Elaborate plans to recover the Holy Land and to establish peace in
Europe under French hegemony were drawn up, with the accusation
that the popes had failed to accomplish these ends because of their
feebleness and because of the disunity of Christendom.

The fact that the controversy between the French king and the pope
arose over a question of taxation, an issue distinctly secular in nature,
strengthened the position of the royal supporters. It led to an extended
discussion of the nature of property rights, in which the church party,
putting forth the most extreme claims of papal supremacy, argued that
the ultimate ownership of all temporal goods is in the church, and therefore subject to the pope. The king's followers argued that the property of
laymen was individual, and that the property of the clergy belonged to
the church as a body. Of the church property the pope was steward, not
owner. Elaborate legal analysis was made of the distinction between
ownership and jurisdiction, and the right of the French king to jurisdiction over church property in his own territory was successfully advocated.

The supporters of secular authority, for centuries on the defensive,
began to show growing self-confidence. While fantastic analogies and
scholastic appeals to authority remained the basis of their reasoning, the
emphasis placed upon "the philosopher," Aristotle, and upon the Roman
law, both of which were anti-ecclesiastical in spirit, had decided results.
In France especially, where the jurisdiction of the royal courts was extended over both feudal vassals and the church, the influence of the
juristic advisers of the king was powerful. Pierre Du Bois even argued
that the temporal power of the papacy should be transferred to the
French king, and that by a series of marriages, alliances, and conquests
France should rule the earth. The lawyers gave a marked stimulus to the
consolidation of feudal Europe into national monarchies and to the destruction of the temporal power of the church.

The jurists supporting the French king brought forward another line
of argument which became important in the following century. They
asserted that if the pope failed to exercise his stewardship for the good of
the church, he, like any tyrant, might be deposed. Having no theoretical
basis to justify the placing of this power in the hands of the French king,
they argued that the ultimate depository of ecclesiastical authority was a
general church council, and that such a body might remove the pope. In
the controversy later between Pope John and the German emperor, this
doctrine was again asserted. The opponents of the pope argued that final
authority in the church rested in the whole body of believers, and that
a heretical or tyrannical pope might be removed by a church council.

This idea had more weight with the empire as a background than it had twenty years earlier in the French monarchy, since the history of the early church contained records of church councils in which the emperor was the dominant figure.

The controversy between Pope John and the Emperor Lewis was complicated by several side issues that weakened the papal position. The pope had taken advantage of a disputed succession to enlarge his claims to interfere in German affairs. Behind the policy of the pope, then resident at Avignon, French influence was clearly evident, and the claims of papal authority were put forward to justify the extension of French dominion at the expense of Germany. In the same way the pope was involved in the internal politics of the Italian cities, supporting the Guelf party because he was no longer inclined to recognize the imperial power in Italy. The free cities were more interested in maintaining their independence than they were in the controversy between emperor and pope, and they played off their stronger neighbors, one against the other. Besides, the Italian cities looked upon the pope with dislike because of his removal from Rome, with the resultant loss of the profitable stream of clergy and pilgrims, and of important church offices for the great Italian families.

A controversy within the church, caused by the pope's decree attacking the doctrine of poverty of the Franciscan friars, turned a number of the ablest ecclesiastical writers into papal critics. These men took refuge in the court of the emperor and employed all their controversial skill in attacking the papacy. They strengthened the position of the secular as against the ecclesiastical system and argued for the church council rather than the pope as the final authority in ecclesiastical matters. In England, the belief that the Pope was favoring the French strengthened the supporters of the king and led to the repudiation of John's tribute, to the statutes of Provisors and Praemunire, and to the hostility toward the clergy manifested in the Peasants' Revolt. It was even proposed in Parliament that church property should be confiscated for political needs. All believers who held that Rome was the true capital of Christendom were scandalized by the "Babylonish Captivity" at Avignon and the Great Schism that followed, and the papacy lost prestige which it was never able to recover.

Dante

The most logical and systematic statement of the imperial theory was that of Dante Alighieri (1265-1321).[28] Dante had considerable experience

[28] In his *De Monarchia* (about 1310). An English translation is bound with *Dante, An Essay*, by R. W. Church. See also *Dante: De Monarchia*, with an introduction on the political theory of Dante, by W. H. Reade (1916).

in the politics of his own city (Florence); and in his wanderings from city to city and from court to court during his long exile he gained valuable knowledge and experience. He was interested chiefly in the restoration of peace and unity to Italy, and his *De Monarchia* was a Ghibelline pamphlet directed against the pro-papal Guelfs. Like other medieval writers, Dante believed that man must live under universal control, either imperial or papal; and he believed that imperial control was preferable in secular affairs. Although his ideals of a secular world-empire and his method of reasoning and of combining classic philosophy, history, civil and canon law, theological dogma, and mythical analogies were distinctly medieval, he revealed traces of the modern idea that the state should exist for the sake of the individual and that the individual should have a share in its management.

In the first part of his work, Dante argued that monarchy is the rightful form of government, because man's best interests demand peace, and peace is possible only under a single ruler, the human counterpart of God. "Cities, nations, and kingdoms, should be governed by a ruler common to them all, with a view to their peace." [29] However, Dante's emperor was not a universal despot, but a sort of international overseer, whose duty it was to decide contentions among the rulers of the various principalities and cities, and to keep the peace among them. National independence and individual freedom were to be maintained as far as possible within the limits of the universal state. Dante believed that a single monarch, having no rival to dread, and no further ambition to satisfy, could have no motive to rule otherwise than justly. His monarch was Plato's heaven-born statesman transferred from the Greek city to the European empire.

In the second part of the *De Monarchia*, Dante cited the Psalmist, Aristotle, Cicero, Vergil, and Aquinas to prove that the Roman victories were considered formal trials by battle in which the judgment of God was manifest; and the fact that Christ was condemned to death by a Roman official was used to justify the righteousness of Roman world rule, otherwise the doctrine of the atonement would be based on an illegal penalty. Dante argued that perfect peace existed only under the Roman emperors, that the destruction of Roman world unity was followed by anarchy and confusion, and that the restoration of a universal authority was therefore essential.

In the third part of the pamphlet Dante considered whether imperial authority is derived immediately from God, or indirectly from God through his vicar, the pope. He attacked in true medieval fashion the

[29] *De Monarchia,* i. 16.

arguments upon which the advocates of papal supremacy depended, many of his minute refutations being scarcely less grotesque than the arguments themselves. Dante held that man's nature, being twofold, demands two guides, emperor and pope. Both received their authority from God, but the emperor is supreme in all that pertains to the secular world. The two species of authority are distinct and the pope has no right to share in the imperial power.

Aside from his clear and condensed statement of the theory of medieval empire, the chief interest in Dante's work is the proof it offers that peace was considered the vital need of the age. The quarrels of petty princes and the turbulence of the Italian cities had become unendurable. The growth of trade also demanded security. Henceforth political literature emphasized the reasonableness of peace. This idea underlay the later work of Marsilius and stimulated the efforts of the group of jurists whose ideas concerning international regulation were finally crystallized by Grotius.

Marsilius and William of Ockam

The greatest and most original political treatise of the Middle Ages was the work of Marsilius of Padua (1270-1340).[30] Marsilius, trained in medicine, was made rector of the University of Paris, where William of Ockam, the famous English Franciscan and the leader of the new Nominalist movement,[31] held undisputed mental sway. Each no doubt influenced the ideas of the other; both went beyond the limits of speculation permitted by the university; and both were excommunicated and joined the group of Franciscans who gathered around the enlightened but feeble German emperor, Lewis of Bavaria. Neither Marsilius nor Ockam was really impressed with the imperial idea, but both desired to establish the state as a consolidated authority, independent of, and in its own sphere, superior to, that of the church. Marsilius, indeed, suggested that peoples with separate languages should form separate states, and that wars among states were a wise provision of nature. Internal peace was what he desired.

The first book of Marsilius' work was devoted to a discussion of the principles of the state; the second to an examination of the origin and growth of the church, its organization under the papal system, and its relation to the civil authority; the third was a summary of conclusions. Terms were carefully defined and Aristotelian formulas frequently used.

[30] The *Defensor Pacis* was written about 1324 by Marsilius with the aid of his friend John of Jandun. The most available translation is by Alan Gewirth (1952).

[31] For the nature of medieval philosophy and the controversy between Nominalism and Realism, see D. J. B. Hawkins, *A Sketch of Medieval Philosophy* (1947), especially pp. 42-44.

The state was viewed as a living organism, intended to secure to men guarantees of order and free development of capacity, leading to general welfare. The right of the state to a life of its own independent of any outside control was the basic principle in Marsilius' thought.

Marsilius stated far-reaching principles concerning the popular basis of government in state and church, and the subordination of church to state. Influenced by the Greek concepts of democracy and by the Roman doctrine of popular sovereignty, he held that the aim of the state is the welfare of its people, that the essence of the state is in the making of law, that the source of law is in the whole body of citizens, and that the administration of government should be in the hands of persons chosen by the people and responsible to them. He taught that the people should have the right to punish their rulers for exceeding their authority or for disobeying the law, and should even be able to depose them if necessary. He made a clear distinction between the ultimate source of sovereignty in the state, which he located in the people, and the form of government chosen to execute the laws. For this purpose he decided that perhaps an elective monarch was best. The duty of the king, however, was to interpret and apply the law, not to make it; and the royal power was limited in all directions.

Marsilius believed that the church should also be organized on a democratic basis, final authority residing in a general church council, which should include secular as well as ecclesiastical delegates. The pope should be chosen by the people as represented in the council, and this body should also have the right to depose the pope. The church, moreover, should limit its activities to purely spiritual affairs; and the power to convoke the church council and to enforce even spiritual penalties should rest with the political authority. The clergy, as members of the state, should be treated in the same way as other citizens, and should have no exemption from political obedience because of their religious character. Marsilius placed the pope on a plane of equality with other bishops, except for a certain preëminence in dignity, and reduced the ecclesiastical organization to a humble position in the state.

Like Dante, Marsilius lamented the turbulence and lawlessness of the times, and supported the emperor because of the necessity for order and security. He believed that the immunity of the clergy and the paramount claims of the papacy were the chief factors that prevented peace and good government. He also attacked the corrupting influence of wealth, and upheld the Franciscan friars in their doctrine of poverty. Aside from these medieval touches, the point of view of Marsilius was distinctly modern. In his theory of political and ecclesiastical organization, he brought forward in the fourteenth century ideas that were not generally accepted until the Protestant Reformation in the sixteenth and the political revolutions in the seventeenth and eighteenth centuries. The significance both of the Reformation in substituting the congregation of believers for the hierarchy of clergy and of the later political revolutions in recognizing the people as the source of sovereign power in the state was clearly stated.

William of Ockam (1280-1347),[32] though influenced by the political ideas of Marsilius, remained primarily a scholastic theologian. He discussed the nature of secular and ecclesiastical power in the form of questions and dialogues in which both sides of the controversy were stated and subtly analyzed. This enabled him to raise questions and throw out suggestions without formulating answers, and makes it difficult for the modern reader to get a clear idea of his theory. Ockam's writings, growing out of his active resistance to the pope, maintain, more than those of Marsilius, the orderly sequence and method of medieval thought. While Marsilius was confident of the wisdom and justice of the people of Christendom as the final authority in matters secular and ecclesiastical, Ockam was less confident on this point. He was inclined to believe that no human institution is absolute and final; and he was more disposed to emphasize the law of nature, from which neither pope nor emperor could be exempt. He was less impressed with the idea of universal empire, and he suggested that it might be better to have several popes and several sovereigns. His English birth and French training no doubt made the idea of universal empire seem less real and less desirable than it was to the Italian Marsilius.

In placing limitations upon the emperor's power, Ockam held that the emperor is bound to conform to the laws common to all nations, and therein he presented conceptions which appeared later in the growth of international law. Both Marsilius and Ockam denied the absolute nature of sovereign power, viewing it as distinctly limited by considerations of justice and expediency. In dealing with political organization, Marsilius was influenced by the Greek idea that the people must either act directly or make a general delegation of their power. In outlining a plan of organization for the church council, however, he suggested a system of representation, in which each province should have delegates according to the "number and quality" of its inhabitants. Ockam worked out this idea of a general representative church council in more detail. For a century the ideas of Marsilius and Ockam concerning the location of authority and the system of representation in the church were subject to violent debate in the ecclesiastical world. They were incorporated by the jurists into the

[32] His political works include the *Octo Quaestiones* and the *Dialogus*, both found in Melchior Goldast, *Monarchia*, Vol. II.

civil and canon law, and their application to issues of purely political significance gained great importance.

During the fourteenth and fifteenth centuries, liberal ideas throve best in France. The great French poem, the *Roman de la Rose*, introduced ideas of a state of nature in which men lived in freedom and equality, without property and without fear or strife. In the reign of Charles VI, the king's chancellor stated to the people that monarchs rule by popular consent and that royal splendor flows from the sweat of the subjects. The ideas of Marsilius and Ockam were vigorously stated, for French rather than for imperial ends, in the French dialogue, modeled on the *Dialogus* of Ockam, known as the *Songe du Verger*.[33] Ideas of popular sovereignty, handed down from Greek and Roman times, and strengthened by Christianity, never entirely disappeared. Traces of the doctrine of freedom and equality under the absolute law of nature survived. The clergy frequently supported the belief that kings derived their power from the people, since a theory of monarchy limited by popular control helped to support a theory of monarchy limited by the church. The growth of the church hierarchy and the establishment of feudalism, however, crushed freedom of thought and divided society into sharply separated classes. Custom and tradition prevented individualism, and men occupied a fixed status. Not until the Renaissance and Reformation made men self-conscious individuals could they become free.

REFERENCES

ALLEN, J. W., "Marsilio of Padua and Medieval Secularism" in F. J. C. Hearnshaw, ed., *The Social and Political Ideas of Some Great Medieval Thinkers* (London, Harrap, 1923), Chap. 7.

CARLYLE, A. J. and R. W., *A History of Medieval Political Theory in the West*, 6 vols. (London, Blackwood, 1903-1936), Vols. IV-V.

CHESTERTON, G. K., *St. Thomas Aquinas* (New York, Sheed and Ward, 1933).

COSMO, Umberto, *Handbook to Dante Studies* (Oxford, Blackwell, 1950).

D'ENTRÈVES, A. P., *Dante* (Oxford, Clarendon Press, 1952).

———, *The Medieval Contribution to Political Thought* (Oxford, Oxford Univ. Press, 1939).

DUNNING, W. A., *Political Theories, Ancient and Medieval* (New York, Macmillan, 1902), Chaps. 7-9.

GIERKE, Otto, *Political Theories of the Middle Ages*, trans. by F. W. Maitland (Cambridge, Cambridge Univ. Press, 1900), pp. 7-87.

GILSON, Étienne, *Dante the Philosopher* (New York, Sheed and Ward, 1949).

HAWKINS, D. J. B., *A Sketch of Medieval Philosophy* (New York, Sheed and Ward, 1947).

LEWIS, Ewart, "Organic Tendencies in Medieval Political Thought," *American Political Science Review*, Vol. 32 (October, 1938).

[33] The author is supposed to have been Philippe de Mézières.

McILWAIN, C. H., *The Growth of Political Thought in the West* (New York, Macmillan, 1932), Chap. 6.

RUSSELL, Bertrand, *A History of Western Philosophy* (New York, Simon & Schuster, 1945), pp. 428-490.

SABINE, G. H., *A History of Political Theory*, rev. ed. (New York, Holt, 1950), Chaps. 12-15.

TROELTSCH, Ernst, *The Social Teachings of the Christian Churches,* trans. by Olive Wyon, 2 vols. (New York, Macmillan, 1931), pp. 201-328.

ULLMAN, Walter, "The Influence of John of Salisbury on Medieval Italian Jurists," *English Historical Review,* Vol. 59 (September, 1944).

CHAPTER IX ~

The Close of the Middle Ages

General Tendencies during the Middle Ages

The political thought of the last hundred and fifty years of the medieval period is to be found in the principles tacitly underlying actual changes in institutions, rather than in the writings of political philosophers. The period was one of transition. The issues of the Middle Ages were ceasing to be of importance, and a new spirit was beginning to appear in intellectual methods. A critical and historical point of view was gradually destroying the medieval scholastic dogmas and myths; and political theory, for centuries divorced from practice, was about to be brought again into close relation with the facts of political existence.

The most important developments of the period were the decline of feudalism and the rise of national monarchies, the growth of commerce and of cities, and the decline of the papacy and the appearance of church councils. The medieval ideals of world unity and of a church-state were no longer possible. The political importance of the feudal nobles and of the clergy was diminishing; that of the king and of the common people was increasing, preparing the way for the later controversies between royal and popular authority within the national states, and for keen international rivalries in warfare, commerce, and diplomacy among them.

The internal organization of the new national states showed wide variation. In the fourteenth century the power of the feudal nobles had been considerably extended. By the close of the fifteenth century, much of their power had been destroyed. The Hundred Years' War, the Wars of the Roses, the use of gunpowder, and the rise of national taxation and of standing armies strengthened the royal power at the expense of the great nobles, especially in England, France, and Spain.

In England the effects of feudalism, never firmly established, were gradually obliterated. The privileged classes, joining with the common people against the king, restricted royal power and extended liberty to the masses. As early as the thirteenth century, the liberties of the people were guaranteed in Magna Carta, and a representative parliament acted as a check upon the royal power. In many feudal states of western Europe, tax-granting and legislative bodies representing the three estates—the clergy, the landed nobility, and the townsmen—grew out of the feudal courts of the great lords. Most of these medieval states were small and were later absorbed into larger states, and in the process the medieval representative assemblies disappeared. In England alone did the medieval parliament maintain a continuous existence into modern times. England was also the only large state to emerge from the Middle Ages with a unified national law.

In France, where the feudal nobles were especially strong, the king created a strong national government only with the aid of the cities and of the people. The revival of Roman law and of the Justinian doctrine that "what the king wills has the force of law" helped the French kings to establish a royal despotism. However, the French nobles, while losing their political power, retained their feudal privileges in economic and social affairs until the French Revolution. The Spanish kingdoms, after centuries of warfare with one another and with the Mohammedan invaders, succeeded at the close of the fifteenth century in finally expelling the Moors and in forming a united kingdom with a centralized government and a strong royal power. Italy and Germany were driven farther apart by the growing national spirit in each, making impossible the unity of the former Holy Roman Empire. But neither Italy nor Germany was able to establish a strong national government. The strength of the papacy, of the German nobles, and of the free cities in both Italy and Germany were serious obstacles, and the situation was further complicated by foreign interference on the part of their more powerful neighbors.

Commerce, given a severe blow by the barbarian invasions, was not entirely destroyed in the Middle Ages and was given a decided stimulus by the Crusades. Water transportation was developed, connections were made with new peoples and with wider areas, and new commodities of trade were introduced. From the East came spices, incense, perfumery, precious stones, and rich cloths. These were secured from India through the Mohammedan states of western Asia; and since Europe furnished little that the East desired, large quantities of precious metals had to be exported to pay the balance. From the North came food supplies, such as grain and fish, and raw materials, such as wool, hides, flax, timber, furs, and tin. This trade centered in the cities that grew up around the Baltic and North Seas and that finally formed the compact commercial organization of the Hanseatic League.

As middlemen, carrying on the bulk of the transportation and marketing of the goods of the Orient and of North Europe, arose the commercial cities of Italy, especially Venice and Genoa. These maintained several routes to the East, and had both land and water connections with the North. By the fifteenth century commerce had become diversified, problems of international exchange had arisen, and men had begun to discuss the relation of the supply of gold and silver to national wealth, and the desirability of governmental restrictions upon foreign competition. These theories, upon which the mercantile system was based, were put into definite shape in the sixteenth century. At the very end of the Middle Ages, in the search for a new route to India and in the ambitions of the new states of western Europe to share in the profitable eastern trade, America was discovered and the way prepared for the important commercial and colonial activities of the sixteenth century. The center of world power was thus shifted from the Mediterranean to the Atlantic.

With the growth of commerce, old cities again became active and new cities appeared. With interests quite different from those of the agricultural villages, these cities were hostile to the feudal system and showed a natural tendency to strive for local independence and self-government. In Germany and Italy, where the central authority was weak, they became independent city-states. In England, France, and Spain, where strong national unity was achieved, they aided the kings in overthrowing the nobles, but were finally brought under the royal authority. The increased use of money and the rise of a class of wealthy merchants made land no longer the only source of wealth, and struck a powerful blow at the position formerly held by the landed nobility and the clergy in the state. The accumulation of capital and the extension of commerce also demanded peace, security, and uniformity of law, which the royal power alone could give, besides making possible a system of national taxation which relieved the central government of its dependence upon feudal military service.

The growth of commerce and of cities increased also the influence of the third estate. Wealth brought power to a new class, the merchant princes. Besides, the men of the cities, through the universities established there, secured intellectual training, formerly the monopoly of the church. Possessed of wealth and knowledge, the burghers forced the nobility and the clergy to recognize them as a factor in the management of public affairs. As the influence of the city spread into the surrounding country, and the results of the economic changes worked themselves out, the peasant laborers in the country also benefited and the slow rise from serfdom to freedom began. Forms of land tenure were modified, indefinite personal services were changed into definite and limited services, and money payments of rent and wages replaced the earlier feudal arrangements. Peasant revolts in France, England, and Bohemia demanded better conditions of life and a greater degree of human equality.

The changes that most directly influenced political philosophy occurred in the ecclesiastical system. The long residence of the popes at Avignon under French influence led to the election of a rival pope; and the Great Schism that followed involved political as well as religious issues. France, the Spanish kingdoms, Scotland, Flanders, and some of the German and Italian principalities supported the French pope. The greater part of Italy and Germany, with Poland, Hungary, Scandinavia, Portugal, and England, favored the Italian pope. In order to retain the support of these states, the rival popes made concessions to them, and the former position of the pope as the universal head of Europe disappeared. Besides, the extravagant expenditures at Avignon and the added expense of two papal courts increased the burden of papal taxation and led to new devices to raise money, which excited opposition, leading to the adoption of prohibitory legislation in some states and finally to the Protestant Revolt.

Grave discontent began to arise within the church against the papal policy. The religious life of the people suffered, and writers, especially at the University of Paris, suggested methods of ending the Schism and reforming the church. The idea of calling a general church council, used at first as an isolated weapon in special contests with the papacy, grew into a strong demand of all Europe which could not be ignored. Several church councils were assembled, and for fifty years a bitter contest was waged between those that supported the monarchical organization of the church under the papacy and those that supported the representative assembly system of the church council. Although the papal party was finally victorious, the prestige and power of the pope had suffered severely, and his influence in European affairs was seriously diminished. Henceforth, the popes devoted themselves in the main to Italian affairs, some taking active part in local politics, since the pope remained the temporal sovereign of a little Italian state, others acting as patrons of the Renaissance. They gave no further attention to church reform, however, until the Protestant Revolt forced the matter upon their attention.

Wyclif and Huss

The tendencies of the later part of the medieval period were reflected in the doctrines of John Wyclif (1320-1384) [1] in England, of John Huss (1369-1415) [2] in Bohemia, and in the national, anti-papal, and democratic movements for which their teachings were held responsible. While both Wyclif and Huss devoted themselves mainly to theological questions, they were undoubtedly influenced by the popular sovereignty ideas of Marsilius and Ockam. Wyclif, a professor at Oxford, became a popular religious reformer. His political pamphlets were written to refute the arguments of a monk, probably William Wadford, who argued that the pope possessed feudal suzerainty over England, and that the English king had forfeited his title to the throne because he had ceased to pay the papal tribute.

Wyclif's chief contribution to political theory was his doctrine of lordship, [3] (dominium) an ideal scheme of polity modeled closely on the organization of feudalism. Lordship and service were held to be the two ends of the chain that links man to God. The lordship of God is the highest, and is exercised directly upon men, not through a series of subordinate vassals. This doctrine attacked the distinction between priest and layman, and gave every man an equal place in the eyes of God.

Civil lordship is of human origin, and was necessary because of sin. The righteous man is lord of all things; sinners can possess nothing. [4] Hence only the faithful can exercise lordship and possess property. In Wyclif's view every Christian man ideally possesses everything. He probably had no intention of making practical application of this scholastic conception. His peasant followers, however, enthusiastically accepted the idea; and communistic ideals, partly religious, partly economic, appeared in various parts of Europe down to the sixteenth century.

Wyclif associated governing authority with property rights in true medieval fashion, and illustrated the relation of divine to civil lordship by that of feudal lord to vassal. Each authority, however, was held to be paramount in its own field, neither having the competence to interfere with the other. Wyclif's veneration for the spiritual dignity of the church led him to feel that it should not take part in the business of the external

---

[1] In his De dominio divino and his De civili dominio, both edited by R. L. Poole. See also his De Officio Regis.

[2] In his Determinatio de ablatione temporalium a clericis. See M. Goldast, Monarchia, Vol. I, pp. 232 ff.

[3] Previously suggested by Richard Fitz-Ralph, archbishop of Armagh, in his De Pauperie salvatoris.

[4] Based upon the text "The faithful man hath the whole world of riches, but the unfaithful hath not even a farthing." Proverbs XVII, 6, in the Septuagint.

world. He held that when the church became involved in transactions about territorial jurisdiction and money, the state should interfere and assume control over its own affairs. The practical effect of this doctrine, as applied in England and elsewhere, aided the kings in their contest with the papacy.

Wyclif's scholastic theories of divine and civil lordship led him to question the doctrine of papal supremacy. He held that the state as well as the church was directly authorized by God, and that the pope and the clergy had no right to exercise political power. He also foreshadowed the later Protestants in making the Bible the sole standard of religious belief and practice, and in attacking the doctrines of the medieval church for which no Scriptural sanction could be found. The theory of Wyclif was, in general, decidedly nationalistic. It represented the English dislike of a pope controlled by the French king. It proposed a national state with a national church subordinate to it, such as Henry VIII later established. In its exaltation of the state, it foreshadowed the doctrines of Bodin and Hobbes.

In discussing forms of government, Wyclif held that an aristocracy, which he conceived as a combination of the rule of Plato's philosophers and the Old Testament judges, is best in theory, since it is least connected with civil ordinances. Rule by priests he considered the worst form. Because of the sinful nature of man, monarchy is on the whole the most beneficial form, since it is the strongest and best able to restrain the excesses of evil doers. Wyclif gave arguments for and against the principles of heredity and election without definitely reaching a conclusion. Because of his pessimistic view of sinful man, he had a low opinion of the value of the popular vote.

The problem of private property and public poverty was of great interest during the transition from the old agriculture to the new grazing, and from the democratic craft guilds to the aristocratic merchant guilds. In England Wyclif met this problem by demanding the unification of society. He held that the best organization was a secular monarchy with large powers. This unification of authority he based upon a unification of interests among the people, to be secured by the abolition of clerical ownership of property and by a direct relation of the individual to God. John Ball and Jack Cade tried to put these ideas into practice, but failed.

The doctrines of Wyclif were adopted by John Huss, rector of the University of Prague. Though Huss added nothing of importance, he was a preacher of much popular influence, and he carried forward the reaction against the claims of the papacy and the clergy. He emphasized the idea that the property of the church was not necessary to its existence, and that secular rulers had the right to deprive the church of its possessions in case of abuse. Like Wyclif, he held that the whole body of believers composed the real church and that the pope and the clerical hierarchy were not essential or divinely ordained.

The religious teachings of both Wyclif and Huss were followed by agitations for reform in the church. Their economic and political ideas led to popular uprisings. The movement died out in England; and Wyclif's followers, the Lollards, were apparently exterminated. On the continent, partly for political reasons, a compromise was effected, the church giving way on some points to the Hussites. In the attempt of Wyclif and Huss to return to primitive Christianity, to view the Scriptures as the sole source of authority, and to permit every individual to study the Bible and reach his own conclusions, they gave evidence of the attitude of mind which led to the Protestant Reformation. Their political ideas, though scholastic in form, were modern in spirit. They asserted the divine right of the king to disendow the church, they opposed the political claims of the clergy, and they recognized the dignity of the individual as a member of the community. Their doctrine of the sovereignty of God and the equality of man led logically to democracy; and this doctrine, combined with the economic tendencies of the period, had ultimate results unforeseen in the fifteenth century.

The Conciliar Movement

In the controversies of the conciliar period, the church was viewed as a human society, similar in nature and organization to other human societies. Accordingly, in the effort to replace the authority of the pope by that of a representative church council, general principles were worked out which served equally well in the later effort to replace the power of kings by that of representative parliaments. The decree of the Council of Constance (1414-1417), asserting its superiority to the pope, has been called the most revolutionary official document in the history of the world.[5] It marked the culmination of the medieval effort to replace the Roman ideal of authority vested in a single, divinely ordained head by that of a popularly-based representative assembly. It foreshadowed the later political contest between autocracy and constitutional principles in the state. Taking advantage of the opportunity of the Great Schism, liberal churchmen tried to borrow from the rising states of Europe and from the doctrines of Marsilius and Ockam a theory of limited monarchy and a plan of representative government for the church. In its organization, the Council of Constance represented also the growing national spirit making provision that the votes of the clergy should be cast by "nations'

[5] J. N. Figgis, *From Gerson to Grotius* (1907), p. 35.

The leadership of the conciliar party centered mainly in the universities, and the new methods of the Renaissance were manifested in the critical attitude toward formerly unquestioned canons of belief. Many supported the conciliar movement because of a pious desire to heal the Schism, but when that was accomplished they lost interest, and the academic nature of the movement became a source of weakness. Resisted by the powerful vested interests which it attacked, it was doomed to failure when it opposed the Hussite movement and thus alienated popular support. The failure of the conciliar movement marked the beginning of the modern world. When it proved impossible to maintain democratic principles and to reorganize and reform the church from within, the way was prepared for the establishment of divine-right monarchies which adopted the doctrines of Machiavelli, for the work of Luther and his followers in establishing independent Protestant sects over a large part of Christendom, and for the ultramontane reaction and the efforts of Loyola and the Jesuits in behalf of the Catholic Church.

The chief writers of the period were John Gerson (1363-1429),[6] chancellor of the University of Paris; Cardinal Nicholas of Cues [7] (1401-1464); and Aeneas Sylvius [8] (1405-1464), afterward Pope Pius II.[9] Gerson favored a system of limited monarchy in church organization, and believed that a mingling of monarchic, aristocratic, and democratic elements was best in both church and state. He opposed the theory of papal supremacy and adopted some of the principles of Marsilius, although he refused to accept the democratic conception of the church as the entire body of believers. He held to the more aristocratic doctrine of the church as the hierarchy of clergy, with final authority vested in the general council. Gerson viewed the pope as the administrative agent of the church, and upheld the supremacy of the church council because of the necessity of healing the Schism. The utilitarian doctrine of necessity played a large part in his theory, and he justified resistance to pope and king when general welfare demanded it. He also held that the temporal ruler might call a church council to depose the pope if he did not fulfil his duties or if he refused to obey the laws of nature and of God, which were superior to human authority. Gerson's ideas, put forth in the decrees of the Council of Constance, spread the doctrine of constitutional government throughout Europe, and paved the way for later reformers. He aimed to preserve

[6] The most important of Gerson's political writings may be found in Goldast, op. cit., Vol. II, pp. 1384 ff.

[7] In his De Concordantia Catholica.

[8] In his De Ortu et Autoritate Imperii Romani. See Goldast, op. cit., Vol. II, pp. 1558 ff.

[9] Other writers were Cardinal Peter of Ailly, Dietrich of Niem, Gregory of Heimburg, Cardinal Francesco Zabarella, and Andrea of Randulf.

the rights of pope and king, within definite limits, and at the same time secure the liberties of the people.

Nicholas of Cues put forward, at the time of the Council of Basel (1431-1449), more radical and democratic theories. He conceived the universe as an organism or harmony of closely interrelated parts. Similarly, church and state were composed of various organs, each having definite functions; and the same principles could be applied to both ecclesiastical and political organizations. He considered a representative council to be the central organ in both church and state, and he found the source of its authority in the consent of the whole body. Holding that all men are by nature free and equal, he found the source of law and of authority in the people. Kings and bishops were chosen as administrators of popular rule, and they, with the people, formed the natural organization or corporation of society. Nicholas taught that rulers hold their position by the choice of their subjects, and that they, like their subjects, are bound by law. Law, based upon the consent of all, is ultimately divine, since man himself comes originally from God.

Aeneas Sylvius furnished a historical survey of the rise of man from an original state of nature. Man, expelled from Paradise, lived like the beasts, but discovering the value of association, he deliberately created bodies politic. When oppressors arose and rights were infringed upon, men agreed to delegate their authority to someone of outstanding strength or virtue. Thus kingship arose. When, however, the king became tyrannical, he might be driven out by those who had created him. Similar reasoning was used to justify the deposition of the pope. In the writings of Nicholas of Cues and of Aeneas Sylvius appeared the concepts of the state of nature, of natural rights, and of social contract that became familiar in the revolutionary theory of the seventeenth and eighteenth centuries.

From one point of view the theory of the conciliar party was destructive. It attacked the autocracy of the pope and appealed from the theological dogmas of the church to the general considerations of natural law and popular welfare. On the other hand, the theory was constructive. It aimed to establish a definite constitution for the church, broadly based upon popular consent. As a whole, the conciliar theory was nationalistic, representative, and moderately democratic. "The union of political principles with utilitarian notions, heightened by their religious significance, considered with reference to a body which might be a model for all smaller states, and decided upon universal grounds, was the work of the conciliar party and their opponents." [10]

---

[10] Figgis, *op. cit.*, p. 51.

The Jurists of the Fifteenth Century

The interest in legal analysis and speculation created by the study of Roman law was especially marked during the conciliar controversy of the fifteenth century. Roman law was familiar with the concept of a corporation, and its principles were applied in explaining collective ecclesiastical and political organizations, such as the church, the church council, the state, and the free city. Political theorists who desired to attack the concentration of authority in the hands of a single individual in church or state were attracted by the idea of a body corporate, recognized as a person in the legal sense. This idea served for a time as an intermediate stage between the single individual and the whole body of individuals. Those who saw the necessity of reform, yet shrank from the idea of vesting power in the whole body of citizens or the whole congregation of believers, found the theory of corporation especially useful.

Supporters of the view that the authority of rulers was delegated to them by the people and that the ultimate powers of the church resided in the general body of believers found legal arguments useful to support the new conception of the whole people as a legal personality. The church council, acting as the corporate representative of the church, was exhaustively analyzed according to the principles of Roman jurisprudence. Questions of the relation of the pope to the council, the method of summoning the council, and the mode of its procedure as to quorum and voting were all worked out by applying to it the Roman legal concepts of the corporation. The method of electing emperor and pope was also discussed in accordance with the principles of Roman corporation law.

While the concept of the corporation was applied especially to the smaller groups,[11] such as the church synods and councils, the various estates in the social order, the universities, and the free cities and communes in Italy, Germany, and France, it nevertheless prepared the way for the larger concept of the legal personality of the church and the state as a whole. Medieval theory believed that unity in church and state could be accomplished only by subordinating the members of each to a common imperial ruler. The theory of the corporation laid the basis for the idea of the legal entity of the whole body of individuals, and made possible the later concept of sovereignty residing in the people of the state, and not in the monarch. Medieval theory was thoroughly familiar with the con-

---

[11] "The federalistic character of medieval groups gave rise to many elaborate schemes for securing a certain amount of unity and independence to those smaller bodies that were components of a larger body, for example, the faculties and nations within a university." O. F. Gierke, *Political Theories of the Middle Age* (1900), p. 167.

ception of the state as an organism.[12] To this the idea of corporate personality was now added; and with the aid of the conciliar theory of representation, a clear distinction was made between state and government, between the ultimate source of authority and the organs to which the authority was delegated.

The doctrine of the corporate personality of various organizations within the state, first put forward during this period, has contributed in recent years to the pluralistic theory of sovereignty, to the doctrine of guild socialism, and to the emphasis laid upon function as the proper basis of political organization. This tendency has come down partly through the study of church institutions and history; partly through the growing importance and political activity of economic groups, such as labor unions, industrial combinations, and the like; and partly through juristic doctrines of the social nature of law and its relation to the state.

The jurists of the fifteenth century also made a clear distinction between jurisdiction and ownership, maintaining the rights of the owner of private property against the holder of political authority. This doctrine struck a blow at the feudal theory of the king as the ultimate owner of the territory of the state and tended to dissociate the ideas of landholding and governing authority. It also tended to shift the ultimate source of sovereign power from the monarch to the people of the state as a whole.

During the entire period the Roman doctrine of natural law furnished the starting point of all legal theory. The principles of the law of nature were considered superior to the commands of any ruler or to any human enactment. Whatever contradicted the eternal principles of natural law was void and could bind no one. Beside the law of nature (*jus naturale*), implanted by God in natural reason, was placed the divine law (*jus divinum*) communicated by God to man in a supernatural way, and the law of nations (*jus gentium*), consisting of the rules which all nations recognized as flowing from the law of nature. Medieval writers based the state upon moral or natural necessity. Its aim was the promotion of welfare, and for this purpose the realization of the natural law was the appropriate means. From the time of Aquinas it was held that the welfare of the whole was more important than that of any part; and this utilitarian doctrine of general welfare was one of the main arguments of the conciliar party in demanding representation of the entire church. This theory also attacked the idea that church and state were perfect and unchangeable institutions, and justified changes and reforms when necessity demanded them.

The Renaissance study of the classics revived interest in the democracy of the Greek cities and in the Roman law of contract, as well as of cor-

[12] On medieval theory of the organic nature of society, see *ibid.*, pp. 22-30.

porations. Both attacked the medieval idea of authority vested in a single head, and laid emphasis upon the importance of the many. While the application of the popular sovereignty ideas inherent in these concepts was checked by the victory of the pope over the councils and by the theory of divine right revived by the Protestant Reformation, the ideas reappeared in the latter part of the sixteenth century and finally worked themselves out in the revolutions of the seventeenth and eighteenth centuries. Modern democracy owes much to the theological controversies of the fifteenth century. And the Renaissance jurists, while they temporarily strengthened the monarchs, introduced concepts that ultimately supported democratic principles.

Machiavelli

By the end of the fifteenth century, the democratic tendencies of the conciliar period had disappeared in both church and state. The pope, no longer able to claim supremacy in secular affairs, had regained his position in the ecclesiastical organization; and church councils, seldom assembled, were brought under his control. In the political world, the tendencies toward nationality and monarchy were finally successful. The former idea of a united Europe under an imperial ruler had lost all significance. National distinctions were clearly marked, and separate states, secular in nature, stood forth under strong monarchs, who reduced the feudal assemblies to positions of unimportance. The tendency toward consolidation made least progress in Italy. By the close of the Middle Ages the numerous feudal principalities and free cities had been combined into five larger units, the republics of Venice and Florence, the kingdom of Naples, the duchy of Milan, and the territory of the Roman church. Further unification was prevented by jealousies among these states, by the absence of any single state or ruler able to control the others, by the policy of the pope, who opposed unification in order to retain control over the papal states, and by the interference of outside powers, who played one Italian state against another in their ambitions to gain power in the peninsula.

In the later Middle Ages the Italian cities lost much of their political independence and communal institutions. Factional strife within the cities and wars among them led to the rise of despots who deprived the citizens of the freedom they had abused, to the aggrandizement of a few cities at the expense of others, and to the employment of mercenary troops and leaders moved by self-interest rather than by patriotism. Political morality and public spirit reached a low ebb. The rulers of the Italian cities, although sometimes cruel and violent, were usually able and resourceful men. They encouraged the Renaissance and often improved the condition of the people as a whole. They were compelled, however, to be constantly on the alert against ambitious rivals and against the influential noble families. Conspiracies flourished, and assassinations, imprisonments, and banishments were common. Cold-blooded personal and political considerations were necessarily dominant factors in retaining power.

In the conditions existing in Italy, and in the rivalries of France, Spain, and Germany that turned Italy into the battleground of the stronger monarchies, the little Italian states, unable to maintain themselves by force, became skilled in the use of craft and diplomacy. Niccolo Machiavelli (1469-1527) [13] took an active part in the complex life of Italian politics, and his acute observations of the actual workings of government in Italy, and in other parts of Europe to which his missions took him, are reflected in the nature and method of his political philosophy. He was primarily concerned with the maintenance of Italian independence and the restoration of prosperity in the Italian cities. He was also thoroughly imbued with the spirit of the classical Renaissance, with its emphasis on intellectual freedom, its attack on the methods and dogmas of scholasticism, and its pagan attitude toward morals and religion.

Machiavelli paid no attention to the issues of church versus state or of pope versus council, nor to the teachings of the Scriptures, nor to the opinions of Church Fathers, nor to the principles of natural law. He believed that the historical method, by which present and future problems might find solution in the light of the past, was the only true approach to politics. In practice, he was chiefly interested in the questions of his own time. He observed them closely, analyzed them carefully, drew his deductions, and then called upon history to support the conclusions that he had reached. His concern was with practical policies, rather than with political philosophy, with the machinery of government and the forces that work it, rather than with the fundamental nature of the state itself. He was the first modern realist; he believed that the state should exist for its own sake, should aim at its own preservation and advantage, and should not be bound by the obligations that determine the actions of private individuals.

The chief difference between Machiavelli and the writers who preceded him was in his attitude toward religion and morality. He separated politics and ethics, even to the point of paradox and scandal. For centuries political thought had been a by-product of theology, and political issues had

[13] The political ideas of Machiavelli are found mainly in the *Prince* (1513), and in the *Discourses on Livy*. These are available in a Modern Library edition.

been confused with issues primarily religious in nature. Machiavelli frankly subordinated moral principles to the necessities of political existence and welfare. He viewed the state as a distinctly human institution, and the church as one of the factors which a statesman must take into consideration in shaping his policy. The safety and success of the state were made paramount; all other considerations were subordinate.

In his desire to get at the actual facts of political existence, Machiavelli found that the precepts of Christianity played little part in the practical politics of the Italian cities. In his desire to unify Italy, he naturally opposed the papacy, which was one of the chief obstacles to union. In his zeal to deliver Italy from the invaders who despoiled it, he felt that any political means was justified. His doctrine was a theory of the preservation of the state, rather than a theory of the state itself.

Savonarola had tried to govern Florence by moral influence, but his experiment had proved a failure. Machiavelli saw in Savonarola's attempt nothing but an abstract idealism inapplicable to the real world, and drew from it the conclusion that the essence of successful government is force and craft. He believed that the art of politics depended on motives of human self-interest, as taught by history and by experience. Having a pessimistic and cynical view of human nature, he explained the love of independence and self-government by a materialistic individualism, and made material prosperity the chief motive of political action. He did not approve of fraud and treachery, but he pointed out that power obtained in certain ways must be maintained by similar means. Machiavelli admired the strong and efficient ruler and despised a vacillating or scrupulous policy that endangered the independence of the state or the position of its governing head.

Machiavelli clearly realized the close connection between the distribution of wealth within a state and the location of actual governing authority. Accordingly, he recognized that different conditions require different forms of political organization. For men among whom economic equality prevails, he held that a democratic government is advisable, and he had a high appreciation of the value of popular government under proper conditions. A republic of the type exemplified in Sparta, Rome, and Venice, he admired; but it presupposed an intelligent and public-spirited citizen body. An aristocracy, especially if based on landholding, he disliked, believing it to be conducive to factional contests. He believed that a mixed form of government is best, and was inclined to favor an elective monarchy as best suited to the conditions of his age.

Machiavelli's interest in the unification of Italy led him to place great emphasis on the value of extending the dominion of the state. In the *Prince* he considered the theory and practice of extending monarchic dominion; in the *Discourses,* the theme was the expansion of republics. Machiavelli believed that a state must expand or perish, and he held up the Roman policy as one worthy of imitation. In his discussion of the methods by which authority may be extended and maintained over large areas, he exhibited both his acute observation of actual political conditions and his indifference to moral principles. Physical force and craft, especially the latter, were the essential bases for political greatness.

Two of Machiavelli's suggestions will illustrate this approach to politics. In the *Prince* he discusses whether it is better for a ruler to be loved or feared. "A prince," he says, "must not mind incurring the charge of cruelty for the purpose of keeping his subjects united and faithful; for ... he will be more merciful than those who, from excess of tenderness, allow disorders to arise, from whence spring bloodshed and rapine; for these as a rule injure the whole community, while executions carried out by the prince injure only individuals." [14] It is also, he concludes, better to be feared than loved, because "men love at their own free will, but fear at the will of the prince, and ... a wise prince must rely on what is in his power and not on what is in the power of others." [15] The second illustration is to be found in the *Discourses.* Here he advises prudent men to ostensibly do out of generosity what they are forced to do out of necessity.[16]

While the ideas of Machiavelli were bitterly criticized, and a distorted understanding of his doctrines brought his name into reproach, lasting to the present day, the importance of his contribution to political thought can scarcely be overemphasized. He brought political theory again in touch with practice. The medieval method of building up a system of speculative philosophy, entirely dissociated from actual conditions, was gradually destroyed by the appeal to observation and experience which was the foundation of Machiavelli's method. He abandoned the generally accepted idea of natural law, and conceived of law as a positive rule, created by the sovereign in the state and maintained by physical force. He made the distinction between public and private morality an issue which survives to this day in practical politics and in international relations. His argument in favor of conquest and expansion had far-reaching results in the international contests and colonial ambitions of the European states; and his maxims of practical politics were exemplified in the policies of the European monarchs and in the practices of diplomacy.

[14] Chap. 17.
[15] *Ibid.*
[16] i. 51.

Medieval Theory of International Relations

In the Middle Ages local dominion took the place of world dominion, and the principles of universal law were pushed into the background. The medieval period has been called an age of organized anarchy. The wager of battle was a recognized form of judicial trial, private warfare was common, and trade was hindered by pirates at sea, by robbers on land, and by numerous feudal tolls and exactions. While the church tried to maintain peace and to ameliorate the conditions of warfare, and while the ideals of chivalry tended somewhat to humanize the conduct of the nobles, it was not until the power of the kings had established royal justice over their dominions that life and property were safe and order was established. The spirit of provincialism was deeply ingrained.

At the same time, the theory of world dominion survived as an ideal, and the Holy Roman Empire made pretensions to world supremacy as pompous as they were impossible. The spirit of localism, gradually developing into sovereign national monarchies, prepared the way for international relations; the survival of the imperial concept impeded this process. The church, more powerful than the state during the greater part of the medieval period, treated each rising nation as a separate unit and recognized the national spirit. At the same time, in its world organization, in its emphasis on a common Christian brotherhood, and in its uniform doctrine for all Europe, it expounded the principles of internationalism. The Roman Empire had extended its sway over so large a part of the world of its day that it recognized the existence of no other legal state, and could not, therefore, work out a system of international law. The church was not able to maintain its claim to world dominion, nor to prevent the rise of independent states, too nearly equal for any one to exercise supreme authority. Within this society an international law could develop. Besides, the efforts of the church to curb private warfare and to apply the principle of arbitration in settling disputes furthered the idea of international regulation. Kings, eminent jurists, and cities also acted as arbitrators during the Middle Ages; and feudal principles predisposed vassals to accept their overlords as judges. During the thirteenth century there were said to have been one hundred cases of arbitration in Italy alone. During the fourteenth and fifteenth centuries arbitration declined and by the seventeenth century had practically disappeared. The use of the Latin language as the common tongue of education and of the church was a bond of unity; and the papal legates sent from Rome on various duties and the permanent ambassadors maintained by the papacy at certain courts contributed to the practice of diplomacy.

As early as the seventh century, a Spanish churchman, St. Isadore of

Seville,[17] made a clear distinction between the Roman *jus naturale* and *jus gentium*, and applied the latter to what we now consider international law. This distinction was incorporated later into Gratian's code of canon law and became an accepted truism of ecclesiastical jurisprudence. The revived study of Roman law by the jurists of the twelfth century furnished a necessary foundation for the growth of royal power that created independent sovereign states, and for the development of the principles of international jurisprudence. The idea of territorial sovereignty, inherent in the feudal system, also bore fruit, after the idea of universal empire disappeared, and the study of Roman law made it natural to look upon the kings as the owners of their territories with full sovereignty over them.

The crusades of the twelfth and thirteenth centuries exerted an important influence on international relations. They brought peoples of various countries together in a common undertaking, stimulated the exchange of ideas, and strengthened the concept of the unity of Christendom. By weakening the resources of the nobles, they helped to destroy feudalism, thus aiding the kings and the free cities. They also gave a decided stimulus to trade and to the formation of codes of maritime law [18] which influenced later international jurisprudence. As early as the twelfth century, consuls represented the interests of the merchants of the Italian cities in Mohammedan countries; and as early as the thirteenth century, Venice established a diplomatic service and laid down rules for the guidance of its ambassadors. At the close of the Middle Ages, the kings of the rising national states, eager to consolidate and to expand their kingdoms, adopted many of the diplomatic methods and ideals of the Italian cities.

The conditions of the early medieval world made international law, in the modern sense of the term, impossible. The rival claims of church and state, the complicated but unorganized political system of feudalism, the ideal of world unity, and the local independence of principalities and cities prevented the conception of sovereign states, independent and legally equal, with a balance of power maintained among them. The influence of the church prevented international relations, not only by emphasizing the unity of Christendom, but also by discouraging legal relations with the Mohammedan world. The just treaty which the forward-looking emperor, Frederick II, negotiated with the Sultan of Egypt was an unforgivable offense from the papal point of view. But medieval ideas were dispelled by the Renaissance and the Reformation. Local disor-

---

[17] In his encyclopedic work popularly called *The Etymologies*.

[18] The most important was the *Consolato del Mare,* published at Barcelona in 1494. The *Laws of Oleron* for western Europe and the *Laws of Wisby* for the Baltic nations appeared in the twelfth and thirteenth centuries.

ganization was overcome by the rise of national monarchies, and in the fifteenth century the idea of the balance of power was applied in the relations of the leading Italian cities. The concepts of international law were worked out by the group of jurists that culminated in Grotius; international wars, political and religious, led, in time, to the calling of the first great international conferences and to the framing of the international treaties of Westphalia.

REFERENCES

ALLEN, J. W., *A History of Political Thought in the Sixteenth Century* (New York, MacVeagh, 1928), Part IV, Chaps. 1-2.

BETT, Henry, *Nicholas of Cusa* (London, Methuen, 1932).

BINNS, L. E., *The Decline and Fall of the Medieval Papacy* (London, Methuen, 1934).

BUTTERFIELD, Herbert, *The Statecraft of Machiavelli* (London, G. Bell, 1940).

CASSIRER, Ernst, *The Myth of the State* (New Haven, Yale Univ. Press, 1946), Chap. 10.

CARLYLE, A. J. and R. W., *A History of Medieval Political Theory in the West*, 6 vols. (London, Blackwood, 1903-1936), Vol. VI, Part II.

FIGGIS, J. N., *From Gerson to Grotius* (Cambridge, Cambridge Univ. Press, 1907), pp. 1-62.

FLICK, A. C., *The Decline of the Medieval Church*, 2 vols. (London, Kegan Paul, 1930).

GIERKE, Otto, *Political Theories of the Middle Ages*, trans. by F. W. Maitland (Cambridge, Cambridge Univ. Press, 1900).

JACOB, E. F., "Nicolas of Cusa," in F. J. C. Hearnshaw, ed., *The Social and Political Ideas of Some Great Thinkers of the Renaissance and the Reformation* (London, Harrap, 1925), Chap. 2.

LASKI, Harold J., *The Dangers of Obedience and Other Essays* (New York, Harper, 1930), Chap. 9.

McILWAIN, C. H., *Constitutionalism, Ancient and Modern*, rev. ed. (Ithaca, Cornell Univ. Press, 1947).

POOLE, R. L., *Wycliffe and Movements for Reform* (London, Longmans, 1896).

RUSSELL, Bertrand, *A History of Western Philosophy* (New York, Simon & Schuster, 1945), pp. 476-487.

SABINE, G. H., *A History of Political Theory*, rev. ed. (New York, Holt, 1950), Chaps. 16-17.

TROELTSCH, Ernst, *The Social Teachings of the Christian Churches*, trans. by Olive Wyon, 2 vols. (New York, Macmillan, 1931), pp. 328-382.

WHITFIELD, John H., *Machiavelli* (Oxford, Blackwell, 1947).

ganization was overcome by the rise of railroad, telephones, and in the
after nth century the rise of the bureaucratic power was applied to the
problems of the teeming Italian cities. The concept of bureaucratic law
never worked for the polity. Control that culminated in 1840-50, and
institutional, was political and religious. In fact the conclusion on the
and great institutional differences and do the hegemony of the administration practice is regularized.

REFERENCES

Allen, J. W., *A History of Political Thought in the Sixteenth Century* (New
    York, Macmillan, 1928), Part IV, Chaps. I-4.

Betts, Henry (Mountague), ? vols (London, Methuen, 1923).

Baker, E. R., *The Decline and Fall of the Medieval Papacy* (London, Methuen,
    1932).

Bainbridge, Herbert, *The Structure of Absolutism* (London, G. Bell, 1967).

Andrews, Kered, *The Right of the State* (New Haven, Yale Univ. Press, 1909),
    Chap. 2.

Carlyle, A. J., and R. W., *A History of Medieval Political Theory in the West*,
    6 vols. (London, Blackwood, 1903-1936), Vol. VI, Part II.

Deane, E. S., *Political Theory of Dante* (Cambridge, Cambridge Univ. Press,
    1963), pp. 1-82.

Elton, A. G., *The Practice of the Medieval Church*, 2 vols. (London, Kegan
    Paul, 1930).

Figgis, J. N., *Political Thought of the Middle Ages*, trans. F. P. Maitland
    (Cambridge, Cambridge Univ. Press, 1900).

Jones, E. T., "Nominals of Government," in J. C. Rushbrooke, ed., *Essays in the
    History of Some Political Ideas in honor of the administration expense
    ment* (London, Harrap, 1934), Chap. 4.

Lewis, Gerald J., *The Medieval Communities and Other Essays* (New York,
    Harper, 1950), Chaps. 1-3.

Ridgeway, C. H., *Communication, Interest and Analysis*, vol. 4 (London,
    Oxford Univ. Press, 1971).

Pool, T. E., *Political and Mass Ideas in Modern London* (London, Longmans, 1958).

Strauss, Reynard, *A History of Western Federalism* (New York, Simon &
    Schuster, 1944), pp. 178-85.

Sabine, G. H., *A History of Political Theory*, rev. ed. (New York, Holt, 1950),
    Chaps. 14-15.

Thorndike, Lynn, "The social teaching of the Christian Churches, trans. by
    Olive Wyon, 2 vols. (New York, Macmillan, 1931), pp. 328-354.

Woolf, Cecil John H., *Whitehead* (Oxford, Blackwell, 1946).

PART IV

The Beginnings of Modern Political Thought

CHAPTER X ~~~

Political Theory of the Reformation

Influence of the Reformation on Political Thought

The effort of Machiavelli to separate politics and religion was temporarily checked by the Protestant Reformation. This movement, in rejecting papal supremacy in the church and in dividing ecclesiastical jurisdiction among various communities, signified the completion of the same process in the church that had already been accomplished in the empire. It consolidated the various elements of national patriotism and made the Holy Roman Empire a tradition. It thus aided in destroying the idea of unity in church and empire, and in reorganizing Europe territorially into distinct national states. At the same time, being mainly an ecclesiastical movement, it brought back the medieval alliance between theology and politics. The doctrines of the reformers were, in many ways, medieval and scholastic; their methods were those of Aquinas, rather than those of Machiavelli. The relation of church to state was again made the main problem of political philosophy. While the contest was no longer between emperor and pope, the principle involved was the same. Political authority was viewed as coming ultimately from the will of God, so that the ruler to whom obedience was due ruled by divine right.

During the contest between emperor and pope, both claimed to rule by divine authority as direct agents of God. In the later contests between the kings of the national states and the pope, the authority of the king was exalted in order to repudiate the right of the pope to absolve subjects from their allegiance to heretical rulers. The king, as champion of the sovereignty and independence of the new state, was compelled to assert equally authoritative power, which could be derived only from God. The Protestant Reformation exploited this theory in the interest of the Protestant princes, and prepared the way for the final contest between king

153

and people. If the king ruled by divine right and was responsible to God alone, he became as independent of his subjects as he was of the pope or of other sovereigns. Unquestioned obedience could be demanded, and revolution became a sin against God as well as a political offense. The theory of divine right was thus applied to uphold monarchy as a form of government and to maintain particular dynasties and individuals in royal positions. The medieval mind conceived of a universal church-state, with ultimate power in the spiritual head; by the sixteenth century emphasis had shifted from world empire to territorial state, and from ecclesiastical to civil predominance.

The reformers attacked the wealth of the church and its interest in secular projects. They also opposed the authority of the pope and the clerical hierarchy, and taught that the individual should have direct relationship with God and should interpret the Scriptures according to his own conscience. In the theological aspects of these questions the secular governments took little interest, but an issue of far-reaching political importance was involved in each. The church possessed valuable property, especially land, in all parts of Christendom. It also levied heavy financial exactions upon its subjects. The desire to acquire church possessions and to escape financial exploitation was unquestionably a powerful motive in inducing secular rulers, especially in England and Germany, to favor the Protestant Revolt. Church property, appropriated by the state or assigned by it to an ecclesiastical system under its control, increased enormously the wealth of the state and restored a large population to the jurisdiction of the secular authority. And the position of the ruler as head or protector of the new religious system strengthened his claim to rule by divine right.

The diversities of doctrine and the rise of radical sects, accompanied by peasant revolts and communistic agitations, which resulted from the Protestant teaching of individual belief, led the moderate reformers to appeal to the political authority to protect the movement against excesses and fanatical vagaries. Accordingly, the state assumed the power of defining creeds and punishing heresies, and the power of the government was in this way farther extended. All the great reformers enjoined passive obedience to the state, and taught that "the powers that be are ordained of God."

While the immediate effect of the Reformation was to strengthen the authority of the state, the ultimate effect was to further individual liberty and democracy. The individualism both of Christianity and of the Teutonic spirit experienced a revival during the Reformation period. The reformers declared, crudely enough, the essential equality of man. In attacking the hierarchy of the church, they taught the right of man to be answerable only to God. They opposed the principle of authority and demanded freedom of conscience. The idea of personal worth, which was the chief permanent contribution of sixteenth century theory, contained the essence of the philosophy of freedom and of self-government. In this respect the reformers continued the work of the Humanists of the Renaissance in viewing man as an individual rather than as a member of a group, and in enabling him to think his own thoughts and form his own judgments instead of being bound by dogmas and authorities. While the reformers broke with the Humanists, formed their own creeds and became intolerant of heresy, they never entirely abandoned the liberal outlook of the Renaissance. There was considerable truth in the accusation of their opponents that "Erasmus laid the egg and Luther hatched it."

The reformers also placed great emphasis upon the importance of those whom God had chosen to be his elect. Believing that they were divinely inspired and foreordained to salvation, the chosen of God asserted their dignity and independence, and their right to individual judgment and to freedom of conscience. These ideas as worked out by the Protestants in France, Netherlands, Scotland, England, and America, were among the most important contributions to the establishment of freedom and popular government.

The theory of the Reformation represented two distinct and contradictory tendencies. "So far as the Reformation helped to produce the compact, omni-competent, territorial, bureaucratic state, so far as directly or indirectly it tended to individual liberty, it must be regarded as modern in its results. But so far as it tended to revive theocratic ideals, theological politics, and appeals to Scripture in regard to the form of government, it was a reversion to the ideals of the earlier Middle Ages, which were largely disappearing under the combined influence of Aristotle and the Renaissance." [1]

By the middle of the sixteenth century, northern Germany, the Scandinavian states, England, Scotland, and a considerable part of Switzerland had come under the influence of Protestantism, and had more or less completely broken away from the papacy. Protestant ideas, though not legally recognized, had also made considerable headway in France and The Netherlands. The other western European states retained the Roman Catholic faith. Within the church, the Counter Reformation had strengthened the position of the pope and unified religious doctrine. The order of Jesuits had also been established and their aggressive work had begun. The way was thus cleared for the bitter contests between Protestant and Catholic states and between Protestant and Catholic parties within the states. In this process the theological aspects of Reformation theory be-

[1] J. N. Figgis, *From Gerson to Grotius* (1907), p. 24.

came less important and the political principles involved were brought into prominence.

Luther

It was natural that the Reformation, which was a revolt in favor of a more inward and spiritual worship, should begin in Germany, where the Teutonic love of personal independence and a contemplative and mystical attitude of mind were most pronounced. While most of Europe was interested in the new geographical discoveries and in the quest of wealth and empire, a German monk started a theological controversy which followed out relentlessly the logic of the Humanists, applied successfully the methods attempted by Wyclif and Huss, and finally split Europe into rival religious camps, with far-reaching results on political and international issues.

The chief contributions of Martin Luther (1483-1546) [2] to political thought were the clear distinction he made between political and spiritual authority, the emphasis he laid upon the secular as against the ecclesiastical power, and the importance he placed upon passive obedience to the established order in state and society. Luther followed Wyclif and Dante in placing civil power above the ecclesiastical system; he followed Marsilius and Ockam in finding the ultimate source of church authority in a general council rather than in the pope. He attacked the clerical hierarchy and the system of canon law as unscriptural devices of the church to gain temporal importance and wealth. In his contest with the papacy he appealed to German national sentiment against the Italians and to German opposition to the financial exactions of Rome.

His ideas were not always consistent. He was at first interested in correcting specific abuses in the church and had no plans for a general reconstruction. The logic of events made him the central figure in the Reformation movement and forced him to expand and modify his philosophy. Similarly, his doctrine of passive obedience encountered practical difficulties when the contest broke out between the Protestant German princes and the emperor, Charles V.; and Luther then taught that self-defense was permissible to Christians, especially in case of tyranny. If, therefore, the emperor disregarded the laws, his subjects were no longer under obligation to obey him. This phase of Luther's doctrine came into prominence in the later revolutions in opposition to the theory of divine right.

[2] The political ideas of Luther are found chiefly in *Liberty of a Christian Man; Letter to the German Nobility; Of Secular Authority: How Far is Obedience Due It?;* and in his *Table Talk.*

When some of his writings, criticizing the wrongdoings of secular rulers, fired the insubordination of the peasants who, for social and economic reasons, were in tumult from Switzerland to the Baltic Sea, Luther, frightened by their excesses, at first counseled moderation, but finally threw in his lot with the German princes and urged the suppression of popular revolt. While he sympathized with the grievances of the peasants, he did not believe in resistance to governmental authority, nor did he wish his doctrines to be associated with a decision based on force. He had no sympathy with the idea of equality. On the contrary, he asserted the necessity of inequality of rank in the civil state.

On the other hand, the excesses of some of the fanatical sects that arose on the fringe of the Reformation movement led Luther to modify his original doctrine that the state should not interfere in matters of belief, and forced him to permit the political authorities to fix the limits of toleration and to use force in putting down heresies. Luther's dislike of the monastic ideal helped to usher in the contempt for poverty and the placing of emphasis on material success, so distinctive of the modern in contrast with the medieval world. It also helped to explain his belief that no social groups should exist apart from the state. The feudal idea of a community of communities was replaced by the modern conception of centralized sovereign states.

Being essentially practical, and interested in German independence and in the success of the Reformation movement, Luther associated himself with the German princes, the only power that could accomplish his purpose; and while he had a real interest in individual freedom, by this process he assisted in promoting despotism. He viewed the state as sacred. Its ruler was responsible to God alone. By applying these doctrines in practical politics, the Reformation substituted once for all in men's minds the authority of the state for the authority of the church. The supremacy of the law of the land over every one within its borders, including the clergy, now triumphed universally. By transferring the idea of non-resistance from the imperial to the royal and princely authorities, and from the ecclesiastical to the political systems, Luther gave to the doctrine of the divine right of kings enduring prevalence. By his emphasis on the literal interpretation of the Scriptures, he made the texts concerning non-resistance to temporal authority the chief dependence of royalist writers for several centuries. To Luther, the state was essentially holy. Accordingly, he paved the way for the exalted theory of the state held later by Hegel and by recent German theorists. The purely secular theory of the state came down through the followers of Calvin and through the utilitarian doctrines of the Jesuits.

Melanchthon

Philip Melanchthon (1497-1560),[3] the disciple of Luther, agreed with his master on the main points of Reformation doctrine, but differed in his temperament and in his mental outlook. Melanchthon was retiring and scholarly, not practical and aggressive. He represented the influence of the liberal, humanistic spirit and was interested in classical learning. He drew largely upon the Aristotelian philosophy and the common law, both of which Luther condemned. Melanchthon attempted to create a universal system of moral and political philosophy, taking as a basis the teachings of the Bible. His chief contribution to the political thought of the period was the emphasis he laid upon the law of nature, thus giving to the Protestant world the same criterion for judging government and law that had been applied by earlier pagan and Catholic writers.

Melanchthon taught that natural law included certain principles implanted in the human mind as direct revelations of God's will, and certain principles resulting from the nature of man himself. Whatever institutions and laws could be deduced from either of these sources were considered natural and right. The state was justified as representing God's will, revealed in Scriptural texts, and as a result of man's social nature. Accordingly, the state was considered divine in nature and was given large powers. Melanchthon believed that it was the duty of the state to promote true religion; hence it should prohibit false worship and put down heresies. He justified the confiscation of church property by the argument that the state had the right to take property that was misused by its owner. He upheld slavery and had no sympathy with the peasant revolt.

Melanchthon, like Luther, opposed the monastic ideal, as incompatible with the unity and equality of believers in a Christian commonwealth. He also denied all coercive authority to ecclesiastical rule, saying that the power to make law did not belong to the spiritual sword. He believed that the true communal life is that of the state, and made the church distinctly subordinate to the political power. Melanchthon upheld the national idea. He rejected the theory of universal empire, and argued that the world should be organized into separate and independent states. He supported monarchic government, believed in the divine authority of rulers, and taught the doctrine of passive obedience. As in the case of Luther, his ideas show certain inconsistencies, due to the unsettled condition of thought during the period of revolution. Some of his writings show that he realized the danger of oppression resulting from the doctrines of divine right and passive obedience, and that, when rulers were tyrannical

[3] The political ideas of Melanchthon are found in his *Opera*, Vol. XVI, ed. by C. G. Bretschneider and H. E. Bindseil.

or when Protestant subjects were ruled by Catholic princes, he was inclined to support the right of resistance. In his later years, Melanchthon was much impressed with the organization of the free cities, and was inclined to favor aristocracy rather than monarchy as the best form of government.

Zwingli

Through the service of their mercenary troops in Italy, the Swiss had become acquainted with the absorption of the papacy in luxury and in political ambitions. During the fifteenth century, the Swiss had gradually limited the authority of the church and had brought the clergy under the jurisdiction of the secular courts. The need for ecclesiastical reform was generally recognized. The Swiss revolt from Rome, centering in the German-speaking cantons, was carried on under Ulrich Zwingli (1484-1531),[4] simultaneously with that of Luther in Germany. Zwingli was more of a humanist and more radical than Luther. Luther, indeed, called him a pagan because of his fondness for the classics and his liberal attitude on the doctrine of original sin. He was also more interested in politics and less in theology than Luther. Indeed, his zeal in the Reformation was intimately connected with his interest in the welfare of his native land.

The Swiss Reformation involved a contest between the reforming party, which favored democracy in government and which wished to prevent the corruption of morals and patriotism that resulted from foreign influence, and an oligarchy which clung to the system of mercenary service and the papal pensions they derived from it. The party of Zwingli was contending for a national reform on a religious foundation.

The Reformation in Switzerland was effected through the agency of the established governmental assemblies, and by their actions the ideas of Zwingli were put into legal form. Accordingly, Zwingli upheld the right of the community to regulate its religious as well as its civil life. In this way church and state were merged into a single system, controlled by its political agencies. The necessity of obedience to the established authority and the right of the state to put down heresies were insisted upon. Zwingli's own city, Zurich, persecuted the Anabaptists for interpreting the Scriptures according to their ideas. On the other hand, Zwingli opposed the efforts of those cantons that retained the old faith from exercising similar authority, and lost his life in attempting to prevent the Catholic cantons from enforcing their religious views upon his followers.

The democratic political atmosphere of Switzerland and the ideas of the ancient classic writers led Zwingli to adopt different ideas of political or-

---

[4] See his *Selected Works*, ed. by S. M. Jackson.

ganization from those of Luther and Melanchthon. Instead of a divine-right monarchy, receiving passive obedience from his subjects, Zwingli conceived of a Christian commonwealth in which the faithful should coöperate in establishing and administering the civil authority. A democratic state imbued with the social spirit of primitive Christianity was Zwingli's political ideal.

Calvin

The greatest of the reformers, from the point of view of contribution to political thought, was John Calvin (1509-1564).[5] Trained as a lawyer, Calvin gave to the reformed religion a comprehensive and logical system of doctrine, characteristically French in its clarity and detachment, comparable to that worked out by St. Thomas Aquinas for the Roman Catholic Church. Calvin disapproved of the individual interpretation of the Scriptures and he feared the revolutionary social doctrines that accompanied the Reformation. He aimed to give a complete and harmonious exposition of the Christian faith, based upon a legal conception of order and authority. He tried to bring thought and will, his own life and the lives of others, church and state, into subjection to law. The Mosaic code exerted a strong influence on Calvin's conception of a well-ordered commonwealth, both in its general theocratic character and in the details of its provisions.

Calvin rejected the Zwinglian idea that church and state should be united in a single system. Calvin taught that the secular and spiritual spheres of government were wholly distinct. He believed that the church should be organized in accordance with its peculiar needs, with final authority in each congregation vested in a body of elders, and that it should limit its activities to spiritual concerns. The state, he held, was equally essential, and should care for the bodily needs of its members, should preserve order and property, and should especially promote piety and religion.

Since the primary function of the state was to promote public worship and further the interests of religion, Calvin held that every Christian was bound to support the state in these purposes. It became a religious duty to obey the government, and no private individual had the right to resist the state. At the same time, Calvin taught that recognized governmental bodies, such as the representative assemblies of the estates, might restrain tyrannical kings, and that Christians might lawfully take up arms, under authorized leaders, to overthrow usurpation. Besides, subjects

[5] The political ideas of Calvin are contained in his *Institutes of the Christian Religion* (1535), Bk. IV. See trans. by H. Beveridge, Vol. III.

were permitted to disregard the will of the king if his laws were contrary to the commands of God. In these teachings were found some basis for the resistance to established government which the followers of Calvin later exerted.

In general, however, Calvin taught that government should be obeyed. The emphasis which Luther had placed upon the individual conscience had proved to be a more radical factor of disintegration than had been expected, and Calvin found it necessary to lay stress upon the necessity of civil government, the authority of law, and the degree to which obedience to magistrates was required of Christians. Calvin favored an authoritative attitude and disbelieved in freedom. He had a great contempt for the mob, and preferred an aristocratic form of government. His point of view was that of a strong ruler who dislikes obstacles to a uniform and regulated system.

At Geneva, where Calvin settled after his expulsion from France, and where he was given virtually dictatorial powers of government, he attempted to put into practice his theocratic and aristocratic ideas of government. He found it impracticable, however, within the small limits of the city, to separate ecclesiastical and political authority in accordance with his doctrines. The moral code was made the basis of law, an ascetic form of life was enjoined by severe penalties, and the secular authority was made the instrument of the ecclesiastical council. A self-perpetuating oligarchy controlled both church and state, the minutest details of life were regulated under a rigorous system of Puritanism, and dissenting ideas were crushed out, even to the extent of the death penalty for heresy.

The ideas of Calvin were accepted more widely than those of the other reformers. Protestantism in France, Holland, Scotland, and England followed Calvinistic models. In the work of these followers, and mainly because of conditions in the countries concerned, authority was resisted and the doctrines of Calvin became associated with the growth of liberty. It is interesting to note that while Luther had a real love of freedom, his work promoted despotism. Frightened by the peasants' revolt and by the excesses of the Anabaptists, Luther fell back upon the temporal princes, and became associated with the state religion of an all-powerful secular authority. Calvin, whose own motives were those of authority and order, and whose principles were not based upon any ideal of individual liberty, became associated, through his followers, with modern democracy and freedom.

The chief reason for this fact was that the doctrines of Calvin were adopted by those who formed persecuted minorities in their states and who, accordingly, offered resistance to their oppressors. In the Netherlands and in France, Calvinism was involved in a struggle against tyranny and needed a theoretical basis for its opposition. In England, Calvinism was the doctrine of a minority whose determination not to be suppressed kept liberty alive. It was the struggle for existence of the Calvinistic sects that compelled them to put forward a theory of government that placed limits upon absolute authority. Opposed in theory to secular interference in religious matters, the Calvinists became the champions of modern liberty when their doctrines were attacked by the monarchs under whom they lived. In France, the Netherlands, Scotland, and England, they worked out theories by which God's elect should be secure in their rights and privileges, definite limits should be placed upon royal authority, and both ruler and subject should be controlled by a higher law.

While Luther and Zwingli tended to subordinate church to state, permitted the civil rulers to decide questions of doctrine and ceremony, and made their religion the official worship of the state, Calvin drew a clear boundary line between church and state, and would not surrender the peculiar functions of the church to the civil authority. Wherever Calvinism was planted, therefore, it had no scruples about resisting civil rulers who attempted to interfere in matters of religion and conscience. This distinction led ultimately to both civil and religious freedom. It prevented the state from extending its powers into religious matters and from acting as the executor of ecclesiastical laws. It authorized Calvinistic minorities to resist the efforts of the civil authorities to compel them to conform to a uniform state worship.

Calvinism also promoted political liberty because of the republican character of its church organization. The body of the congregation took responsible part in the selection of the clergy, and laymen shared power with the ministers. Especially in countries where Calvinism encountered the hostility of the state, the democratic tendencies of the system developed. Men, accustomed to self-government in church affairs, claimed similar privileges in political affairs. In the New England colonies this idea became especially important.

Communistic Religious Associations

Christianity from its beginning was connected with socialistic ideas. It taught the equality of all men in the sight of God, and it placed high value upon voluntary poverty. In the Middle Ages it taught that private property came into existence as a result of the fall of man, and it set up community of possessions as an ideal. Various ascetic orders attempted to put this ideal into practice, but without success. Several heretical sects included community of property as a part of their creeds.[6] The Waldenses

[6] See Bede Jarrett, *Medieval Socialism* (1935).

in the twelfth century and the Apostolicans in the thirteenth century were examples of such brotherhoods. In both cases they claimed to be applying the principles of the early church. The doctrines of Wyclif and Huss were easily assimilated by the classes discontented with their social and economic status and already inclined toward communism; and the peasant revolts of the fourteenth century in England and in Bohemia were markedly democratic and socialistic. It has been pointed out that the communistic sects from the twelfth century onwards were composed mainly of weavers, and that the character of that occupation seems to have had a direct influence in fostering the idea of a union of workers possessing common property.

The communistic movement spread from Bohemia into Germany, where the peasants were heavily burdened by feudal exactions and by ecclesiastical extortions, and where the workers of the towns were exploited by the powerful guilds and capitalistic corporations.[7] This economic discontent, already manifesting itself in sporadic revolts, was brought to a head by Luther's doctrines, and resulted in the Peasants' War. Lacking arms and organization, the peasants were defeated by the trained soldiers of the princes. The communistic idea, with a strong religious background, survived in the tenets of the sect known as Anabaptists. The sect was especially numerous in the Netherlands. Their doctrines were considered heretical and they were accused of licentious practices. As a result, they were bitterly persecuted.

About 1526 Anabaptists migrated in large numbers into Moravia where they maintained an elaborate communistic organization for about a century. They despised learning, but held manual labor in high respect. Property was held in common, and private family life was abolished. The community was organized into large households consisting of several hundreds of persons. Marriages were usually arranged by the heads of the community, and children were taken from their parents at an early age and brought up under a strict system of common instruction. The community was democratically organized, a council of elders acting in the name of the members as a whole. Economically, the experiment was a success, and the society was prosperous until it was destroyed by force of arms. In its organization it showed marked similarities to the schemes proposed in Plato's *Republic* and in More's *Utopia*.

The Anabaptists considered the state a necessary evil, to be obeyed in so far as its laws did not conflict with the dictates of conscience. They refused to take an oath in the courts or to hold public office, believing

---

[7] About 1437 a remarkable book, called *The Reformation of Emperor Sigismund*, sketched a scheme of reform. It demanded the abolition of serfdom and the destruction of the capitalists. Wages and prices were to be fixed by the workers.

that active participation in political life was in conflict with Christian equality and brotherhood. They opposed war and frequently refused to bear arms. Groups of Anabaptists, gradually abandoning the most untenable elements of their belief, survived persecution in various parts of Europe. Some migrated from Holland into Eastern England, and in the seventeenth century their ideas were revived by the English Quakers and Independents.

REFERENCES

ALLEN, J. W., *A History of Political Thought in the Sixteenth Century* (New York, MacVeagh, 1928), Part I.

BARKER, Ernest, *Traditions of Civility* (Cambridge, Cambridge Univ. Press, 1948), Chap. 4.

BOEHMER, Heinrich, *The Road to Reformation*, trans. by J. W. Doberstein and T. G. Tappert (Philadelphia, Muhlenberg, 1946).

D'ENTRÈVES, A. P., *The Medieval Contribution to Political Thought* (Oxford, Oxford Univ. Press, 1939), Chap. 5.

FIGGIS, J. N., *From Gerson to Grotius* (Cambridge, Cambridge Univ. Press, 1907), pp. 62-107.

JARRETT, Bede, *Medieval Socialism* (London, Burns, 1935).

MACKINNON, James, *Calvin and the Reformation* (London, Longmans, 1936).

MURRAY, R. H., *The Political Consequences of the Reformation* (London, Benn, 1926).

SABINE, G. H., *A History of Political Theory*, rev. ed. (New York, Holt, 1950), Chap. 18.

SMITH, Preserved, *The Age of the Reformation* (New York, Holt, 1936).

TAWNEY, R. H., *Religion and the Rise of Capitalism* (London, J. Murray, 1926).

TROELTSCH, Ernst, *The Social Teachings of the Christian Churches*, trans. by Olive Wyon, 2 vols. (New York, Macmillan, 1931), pp. 461-655.

WARING, L. H., *The Political Theories of Martin Luther* (New York, Putnam, 1910).

WEBER, Max, *The Protestant Ethic and the Spirit of Capitalism*, trans. by Talcott Parsons (London, G. Allen, 1930).

CHAPTER XI ⟿

Political Thought in the Second Half of the Sixteenth Century

Heretics and Papists

The second half of the sixteenth century was marked by civil and international warfare in which differences in religious belief, as well as political issues, separated the combatants. Because of the contest between Protestant and Catholic, and the establishment of national religions, loyalty to God and to the king were identical. The "heretic" was an enemy to a Catholic ruler and the "papist" was a traitor to a Protestant ruler. As a result of this confusion of religious and political ideas, the bitter hostility between the rival faiths increased the likelihood of civil disturbance and of international conflict.

In Spain and England the royal authority was strong enough during this period to prevent civil war. Under Philip II the Spanish Hapsburg empire reached the height of its power. Its navy controlled the sea and its infantry was the finest soldiery in Europe. It practically monopolized the New World, and each year the fleet of treasure ships filled its coffers with apparently exhaustless wealth. In 1580 Portugal and its East Indian empire fell to Spain, and the boast that the sun never set upon Spanish dominions became literal fact. Reformation ideas made little headway in Spain and heresies were crushed by a relentless inquisition. Spain stood forth as the unquestioned leader of the Catholic faith. Through national pride in his greatness, the Spanish monarch ruled with autocratic power over a centralized and religiously unified state.

England under Elizabeth was the chief rival of Spain. A strong national spirit and fear of Spanish power enabled the English queen to exercise large powers and to rule without resistance. While opposing the extreme

165

sects, England was the mainstay of Protestantism; and the contest between England and Spain involved a religious conflict as well as a rivalry for supremacy at sea and for American treasure. The Armada was sent out in the spirit of a religious crusade. Because of absolutism in government in both Spain and England, political theory received little attention, although Spanish writers made large contribution to the science of jurisprudence.

In France, Scotland, and the Netherlands, where Calvinistic doctrines had made considerable progress, civil wars, involving political and religious motives, were frequent during the second half of the sixteenth century. In the course of these conflicts, valuable contributions to political thought appeared. In France a contest for the throne between rival noble families was combined with a conflict between the Catholics and the Protestant Huguenots, with Spain and England supporting their respective creeds. In Scotland, the Presbyterian followers of John Knox carried on a constant feud with the Catholic nobles who supported Queen Mary. In the Netherlands, the persecution of Protestants, together with interference in local government and the levying of financial burdens, led to a revolt by which the northern provinces broke away from Spain and, aided by the Protestant powers of Europe, established an independent republic.

In spite of the teachings of the reformers that subjects should render passive obedience to the powers that be, Protestantism became militant and aggressive during these controversies. A new theory was needed to support the resistance of the Calvinists in France, Scotland, and the Netherlands to their Catholic rulers. For this purpose, ideas that had appeared in the conciliar period were revived. The persistent doctrine of a law of nature was identified with the will of God, as interpreted through human reason and the dictates of conscience; and it was held that rulers as well as subjects must conform to this law. The idea that the authority of the king rested upon a contract between him and his people was also restated; and it was held that if the ruler set himself above the law his subjects were no longer bound to obey him, but might remove him from authority or even declare their independence and set up a new state. The religious contests of the sixteenth century thus prepared the way for the revolutions of the seventeenth and eighteenth centuries; and anti-monarchic doctrines of social contract and of natural rights began to appear.

The success of the Dutch revolt was especially important in its influence on political thought. It gathered up the various tendencies against absolutism and made them practically effective. It aimed at national, religious, and individual liberty. The leaders of thought in the Netherlands emphasized the principle of national independence as well as of resistance to tyranny. They began again to untangle political and theological arguments. They gave deliberate expression to ideas of religious toleration. They insisted on local autonomy and paved the way for the federal principle in government. Living in a small state, interested in commerce and desirous of peace, they developed the conception of rules of law to control the relations among states and of the equality of all states before such law.

In a world rapidly tending toward absolutism, the Dutch kept alive liberty and enlightenment. It was through their efforts in the main that the extension of the Spanish system over Europe was checked. They offered a place of refuge for persecuted minorities. They exerted an especially important influence on England, to whom they passed on the torch of freedom in the seventeenth century. In an age when statesmen like Richelieu and churchmen like Bossuet and Laud glorified divine-right monarchy, the Dutch in theory and in practice upheld advanced ideals of self-government and of individual liberty.

The Effect of European Expansion on Political Thought

The Middle Ages looked upon the world and upon knowledge as things complete and finished. The Roman Empire had been a state with no rival. The Ptolemaic astronomy conceived the universe as a great circle enveloping other circles, with the earth at its center. The system of Thomas Aquinas was supposed to be all-comprehensive and perfect. The world of nature and the world of thought were viewed as perfect unities, and new ideas were regarded with suspicion. One of the influences that broke down this point of view and that transformed the medieval into the modern world was the geographic expansion of Europe.

This process began with the crusades, which stimulated pilgrimage, trade, travel, and missionary activity. The imagination of Europe was stirred by stories of returning crusaders concerning the riches and wonders of the East; and merchants, travelers, and missionaries began to make journeys into far-off lands. As early as the thirteenth century, papal emissaries were sent to the Tartar Khan of central Asia; and the Polos, merchants of Venice, traversed by land the whole length of Asia, skirted its southern coasts by sea, and returned to their home city. When the eastern Mediterranean was closed by the Turks, the search for a water route to the East was intensified. Portuguese sailors reached India by rounding Africa. Columbus, in seeking for a western water route to the Orient, discovered America. Finally, Magellan circumnavigated the earth. The way was thus prepared for the expansion of European ideas and institutions into all parts of the earth, and for the reaction upon European life and thought which such contacts inevitably produced.

Important economic results followed the discoveries. The caravan was supplanted by the caravel, and new commercial routes became important. The Mediterranean ceased to be the center of commercial Europe, and the importance of the Italian cities declined. The new national states of western Europe bordering the Atlantic became the world powers, and new seaports came into prominence. Precious metals, formerly drained off into Asia in payment for Oriental products, became more abundant, Spain alone taking more than five billion dollars in gold and silver from the countries she conquered. The volume and variety of commerce increased enormously and great commercial companies were formed, with monopolistic privileges and governmental powers. Capitalism and city life came into prominence, a vast dislocation of social organization was begun, and new social and economic values appeared. The industrial revolution of the eighteenth century had its beginnings in the commercial revolution of the sixteenth century.

Religious ideas were considerably modified by the new geographical knowledge. The medieval conception of the earth as a disc surrounded by circling heavenly bodies was shattered; Ptolemy gave way to Copernicus; and religious beliefs based upon the idea that the earth was the center of the universe were gradually replaced by a wider and freer outlook. The growth of city life and of secular city culture, and the revival of the classic pagan spirit, also opposed the rigid ecclesiastical culture of the medieval period. The new world offered an asylum for dissenting religious groups as well as a field for missionary activity. Colonies were founded as experiments in religious and social organization. And thus the traditional belief in the immutability of religious ideas and institutions was further weakened.

The discoveries also had important political results. It was the new nations of western Europe that were active in distant lands, and the medieval empire and the idea of world unity became more than ever obsolete. Spain and Portugal at first monopolized the new lands, but they did not use their opportunities wisely. By repressing freedom of thought, by expelling the Moors and Jews in the effort to secure religious uniformity, by depending upon American treasure, and by long-continued military activity, they became backward in intelligence and contemptuous of industry, and were finally exhausted. Holland, France, and England became the great colonial powers and reaped the benefits of the discoveries.

Most of the international struggles since the sixteenth century have arisen out of commercial and colonial rivalry, resentment over inequitable distribution of territorial dependencies and of access to world markets, and unwillingness to permit any nation to dominate the world's highways. As a result, national consciousness was stimulated and broadened into a spirit of aggressive imperialism. The expansion of Europe created world politics with all its consequences for good and evil.

The changes brought about by opening up the world also helped to transform the feudal monarchies of medieval times into modern national states. The shift from agriculture to industry and the rise of a money economy, made possible by the influx of precious metals, enabled the kings to levy taxes, to maintain standing armies, and to employ paid officials, instead of depending upon the feudal nobles whose power was enormous as long as land was the only form of wealth. The royal power was thus increased at the expense of the nobility and clergy. Activities overseas and the national pride and unity that a vigorous and successful foreign policy aroused also added to the prestige of the monarch and aided him in establishing absolutism. On the other hand, the growing wealth and power of the towns and of the commercial classes created a force in the state interested in local independence and in placing limits upon royal interference. The use of money in the form of wages and rent also aided in the rise of the serfs to freedom and in preparing the way for a broad popular basis for authority.

The opening up of new lands did much to widen the intellectual as well as the physical horizon of the sixteenth century; and the states that took the leadership in overseas activities also became the leaders in political thought. The expansion of Europe stimulated the imagination and helped to turn men's interest from the study of antiquity to the opportunities of the future. Anything was possible in the new world, as the belief in an El Dorado and in a fountain of youth illustrated. Experiments in political as well as in religious ideals could be tried in the new lands. The discovery of America inspired Sir Thomas More to write his *Utopia*. The discoveries thus aided the process already at work in breaking down the medieval system of political thought. New ideas were in the air and change seemed less abhorrent.

The discoveries and the results that followed from them gradually introduced new problems and new concepts into political thought. Questions of the relation of advanced to backward peoples, of the right to seize the lands of natives and to subject their persons to slavery, of forms of colonial administration, and of the desirability and methods of imperialistic expansion received attention. Questions of the just cause and conduct of war, of the freedom of the seas, and of the distribution of colonial possessions stimulated the rise of international law and of international diplomacy. Questions of monopoly, of mercantilism, of protection and free trade, became important in political as well as in economic thought.

The immediate growth of national monarchy, the ultimate rise of democracy and freedom, the development of international law, the appearance of imperialistic ideas and rival colonial policies, and the beginnings of the important connection between economic doctrine and political principles, in both the internal and international policies of states, were influenced to a large degree by the expansion of European interests into the Orient and into the New World. The far-reaching importance of these developments could not be foreseen by the thinkers of the sixteenth century.

The Politiques

One of the most notable movements in political thought toward the close of the sixteenth century was the rise of a party in France known as the Politiques. This group carried to the fullest extent the doctrine of Luther that subjects should render passive obedience to their rulers, and the doctrine of Machiavelli that the state is an end in itself, superior to all rules of morality and law when these conflict with public policy. They believed that unity in religion should give way to unity in the state; that religion was an individual matter, whereas the state had a paramount claim upon the allegiance of its members. Accordingly, they urged toleration in religion, at the same time insisting upon the loyalty of subjects to rulers, even when they differed in religious belief.

The writings of this group, most of whom were Catholics, included the *Apologia Catholica* of Du Bellay, the *Vindiciæ* of Servins, the *De Regno* of William Barclay, the *De Republica* of Pierre Grégoire, and the *Six Livres de la République* of Jean Bodin.[1] These writings grew out of the controversy between the rival factions in the French civil wars, the Politiques supporting the claims of Henry of Navarre to the French throne in spite of the fact that he was a Huguenot. They opposed the effort of the pope to interfere in French affairs and attempted to meet the arguments of the anti-monarchic writers of the period.

Realizing that the Civil Wars with their persecutions, massacres, and assassinations were ruining French civilization and French national strength, the Politiques tried to remove religion from the sphere of political controversy. They based their theory upon legalistic arguments,[2] holding that the authority of the king grew out of the natural right of the state; and that the unity of the state must be preserved, even if it required

[1] See below, Chapter XII.

[2] It is interesting to note that, in the main, the lawyers in France supported the king, while in England most of the lawyers were found on the parliamentary side.

religious toleration. They opposed the view that loyalty must be identified
with orthodoxy, and that the duty of the state is to promote the national
worship and destroy heresies. They were therefore out of harmony with
the prevalent theory of their day, since Luther and Calvin, as well as the
Catholic Church, insisted upon religious unity under state enforcement.
The Politiques argued for toleration, not as a religious principle, but as a
policy of expediency in politics. They believed that religion should be
subservient to public policy. For this reason they were nicknamed
Machiavellists.

The Politiques thus became the upholders of the theory of the absolute right of kings in its modern legalistic form. They asserted that the
monarch ruled by indefeasible hereditary right. Scriptural, legal, philosophical, and utilitarian arguments were used to support the doctrine
that kings must be obeyed, that revolution and sedition were not to be
tolerated, and that all ecclesiastical interference in political affairs must
be removed. In actual politics, the adoption of the Catholic faith by
Henry of Navarre after he became king, the ecclesiastical changes of
William the Silent and his policy of religious toleration in Holland, and
the general attitude of Queen Elizabeth in England represented in many
respects the practical point of view of the Politiques.

Anti-Monarchic Theories of the Sixteenth Century

While the general tendency toward royal absolutism was upheld by
the divine-right doctrines of the leading reformers, by the teachings of
the national churches, established under the control and protection of the
royal power, and by the legalistic arguments of the Politiques, a number
of influences were leading in the opposite direction toward ideals of
limited monarchy and individual liberty. Humanism extolled the freedom
of the classic world. Erasmus wrote on the folly of hereditary monarchy
and the value of representative institutions. Even Luther suggested a
contract between prince and subjects, with the right of the people to
resist oppression under certain conditions; and Calvin referred cautiously
to the possibility of opposing a godless ruler.

During the civil wars in France, Scotland, and the Netherlands, an
extensive body of anti-monarchic political thought appeared, mainly the
work of the Calvinistic groups that were resisting Catholic rulers. However, when the Protestant Henry of Navarre became heir-presumptive to
the French throne and the Guises were assassinated, Catholic writers [3]
championed the doctrines of resistance and tyrannicide, and outdid their

[3] For example, Boucher, *De justa Henrici III Abdicatione,* and Rossaeus, *De justa
reipublicæ Christianæ in Reges impios et hæreticos auctoritate.*

rivals in the democratic tendencies of their writings. Besides, the Catholic Church was forced to fight for its independence in Protestant countries, and a fundamental principle of the Counter Reformation was a denial of the right of kings to do what they will with their own states in religious matters. It is interesting to note that the two religious bodies, Roman Catholic and Calvinistic, which cared least about individual liberty and which established the most autocratic systems when they were in power, did most to secure the rights of man. In their constant struggle to maintain their own independence, they placed a perpetual check upon the absolutism of the civil authority, and they developed a theory of resistance that led ultimately to democracy and freedom.

In France, especially after the massacre of Saint Bartholomew's Day, a mass of pamphlets appeared, dealing with the relation of ruler to subjects. Étienne de la Boétie (1530-1563) [4] protested boldly against the monarchical theory, holding that all men are free by nature. Budé [5] and Claude de Seysell [6] emphasized the importance of the estates-general and urged limits upon royal authority. François Hotman (1524-1590) [7] attempted to prove by history that from the earliest times a general assembly of the nation had exercised high political powers and that the monarchy was limited by the people, by the estates, and by a definite body of constitutional law. Hotman held that ruler and subjects were bound together by a contract, and that the people were justified in rebelling whenever the tyranny of the ruler violated this agreement. The author showed a marked reverence for precedent and law, and contributed to the historical method of dealing with political questions.

By far the most important work of the period was the *Vindiciæ contra Tyrannos*.[8] This pamphlet was somewhat medieval in tone. Its author was influenced largely by the doctrines of the conciliar period and confirmed his deductions by Scriptural quotations as well as by precedents in history and law. Its arguments, expressed with force and eloquence, served as a basis for attempts at political reform down to the French Revolution. The discussion was presented in the form of answers to four questions, as follows: (1) Whether subjects must obey a ruler who commands what is contrary to the law of God. To this a negative answer was given, based upon Scriptural injunctions and upon the feudal principle of obedience to a superior rather than an inferior lord. (2) Whether it is lawful to resist

[4] In his *Discours de la servitude volontaire.*
[5] In his *Institution de Prince.*
[6] In his *La grande monarchie de France.*
[7] In his *Franco-Gallia* (1573).
[8] This tract appeared first in 1579 under the pseudonym *Stephanus Junius Brutus.* Its authorship is in dispute between Hubert Languet (1518-1581) and Philippe du Plessis-Mornay (1549-1623).

a ruler who violates the law of God. Drawing upon Old Testament history and Roman law, the author based the relation between king and people upon two contracts, first, the covenant in which king and people agree with God to maintain his worship, second, the compact between the king, who agrees to rule justly and the people, who agree to obey him. If the king fails to keep his covenant with God, the people are justified in resistance. Such resistance, however, must not be offered by private citizens, but must be undertaken by assemblies or magistrates. (3) Whether it is lawful to resist a ruler who is oppressing or destroying the state. In answering this question, the author discussed the origin of the state and supported popular sovereignty upon the hypothesis that the natural state of mankind was one of complete freedom and that men later voluntarily created political institutions. This point of view was elaborated by later social-contract theorists. The author argued that kings who rule tyrannically have broken their agreement to maintain justice and may be deposed by the assembly of the estates. (4) Whether rulers should give aid to neighboring peoples who are oppressed for religious reasons, or by obvious tyranny. Arguing man's duty to God and to his neighbor, the reply was in the affirmative. The *Vindiciæ* was a propagandist pamphlet, the first three questions being intended to justify the resistance of the Huguenots to the French kings; the last question, to justify the aid given to the Huguenots by Elizabeth of England and by some of the Protestant German princes.

The Scotch Reformation produced a complete expression of the duty of rebellion against monarchs who interfered with the religious worship of God's elect. John Knox, in preaching to Mary Stuart, referred to the contract between her and her subjects, saying that if she denied her duty to them, she could not demand full obedience from them.[9] John Poynet,[10] Bishop of Winchester, declared that kings derive their authority from their people, and that the people may withdraw the authority they have delegated if it is abused.

The most important treatise of the Scotch movement was written by George Buchanan (1506-1582) [11] to justify the deposition of Queen Mary. It contained two main arguments: the one, based upon history and precedent, that checks on the royal power were ancient and customary; the other, based upon the principle of a contract between sovereign and subject. Buchanan believed that men lived originally like beasts, but that the instinct of association and a sense of self-interest compelled them to

[9] See J. W. Allen, *History of Political Thought in the Sixteenth Century* (1928), pp. 106-116.
[10] In *A Short Treatise of Political Power* (1558).
[11] In his *On the Sovereign Power Among the Scots* (1579).

form government and law. The people, acting through their assembly, possessed ultimate authority and were the source of law; the king, receiving his hereditary power from an original contract with the people, agreed to rule justly. If he obtained his power without popular consent or if he ruled unjustly, he was a tyrant and might be deposed, or in last resort, put to death.

The most scientific and systematic political treatise of the anti-monarchists was the work of Johannes Althusius (1557-1638),[12] a German jurist, who lived on the frontier of the new Dutch Republic, and who was in thorough sympathy with its political and religious ideals. Althusius had also studied at Geneva and was imbued with the Calvinistic spirit. He found the origin of the state in a gradual unification of smaller into larger groups. These groups arose through necessity and were based upon contract. Ultimate authority came from the people, the state resting upon the consent of its members, and having as its purpose their common good. Althusius gave an elaborate analysis of the contract theory as the basis of social and political organization, and added the idea of contract among the political units that form the state, thus giving it a federal basis.

Althusius worked out a clear conception of sovereignty as the supreme authority of the state, and found its source in the aggregate of the state's members. He made a distinction between the chief magistrate and the various assemblies and orders [13] that represent the people and serve as a check upon the head of the state. The authority of the chief magistrate was derived from the consent of his subjects, and the exercise of unjust or tyrannical power released the people from their pledge of obedience and justified resistance or the deposition of the ruler. Private individuals might resist passively; the public assemblies might depose the tyrant or put him to death; the political members of the confederation might withdraw from the union and join other states. Breach of contract thus justified secession as well as internal resistance. The influence of Calvin was shown in the belief of Althusius that the state should supervise religion and morals under a state church, should prescribe rules of social conduct, and should carry on a wide range of activities to promote general welfare.

The concepts of this group of thinkers—the original state of nature, the existence of natural law and of natural rights, the contractual origin of the state and of government, the ultimate sovereignty of the people—dominated political thought until the nineteenth century. These ideas, drawn from Hebrew history, from classic literature, from Roman law, and from the churchmen of the later Middle Ages, were now put into definite

[12] The *Systematic Politics, Confirmed by Examples from Sacred and Profane History* (1603). The work was dedicated to one of the Dutch provinces.
[13] Called by him the "ephors."

form and applied to the practical problems of the time. The idea of a contract between sovereign and subject was valuable in that it emphasized the idea that the obligations of government and protection are mutual, and thus made it easy to protest against tyranny. In a world dominated by the idea of a law of nature and familiar with the numerous contractual relations of feudalism, the concept of a contract between king and people seemed logical and could easily be popularized.

The anti-monarchist doctrines of the later sixteenth century elaborated the principles of Gerson and the conciliar party of the fifteenth century and applied them to political issues. The conciliar party aimed to destroy the autocracy of the pope and to place his power in an assembly of ecclesiastical prelates. The anti-monarchist party aimed to destroy the absolutism of the king and to place his power in an assembly of nobles. In both cases the point of view was aristocratic, and the sovereignty of the people was to be exercised through the upper classes. This was a main reason for the failure to check absolute monarchy at this time, since the mass of the people feared the nobles as much as the king. The latter indeed was viewed as the symbol of the new national unity and prosperity, and often received decided popular support. Not until the popular-sovereignty theory received a more democratic statement did it become widely effective. In one respect an important advance was made by the anti-monarchists. They taught that the king derived his power from a human source, and did not rule by immediate divine right. By this doctrine they helped to rectify the backward step taken by Luther and Calvin in strengthening the connection between political and ecclesiastical ideas and interests.

Catholic Political Writings of the Sixteenth Century

The spread of Protestantism led the Catholics to call a general church council which held numerous sessions at Trent between 1542 and 1563. The chief aims of the Council of Trent were to remedy the evils in the church that had been so severely condemned by the reformers, and to adopt authoritative doctrines on many disputed points of theology. The old questions of the relation of the council to the pope and the respective powers of spiritual and secular authorities were also bound to reappear. The pope succeeded in securing the adoption of decrees that recognized his preëminence in the church. The council declared most of the new religious ideas heretical and agreed upon a systematic code of belief. It also adopted rules of discipline that gave increased strength and unity to the church and provided higher standards of ability and morality for the clergy.

The establishment at about the same time of the Society of Jesus by Ignatius Loyola was an important factor in the Counter Reformation movement. The Jesuits, as members of this organization were called, played a leading part in checking the further spread of Protestantism in Europe and in carrying on the missionary activities of the church in new lands. The Jesuits were especially active in the field of political philosophy. They were led by a group of able Spanish writers who were interested not only in furthering the cause of the church, but also in promoting Spanish national interests and the Spanish monarchy. Since Spain was a new state, without a medieval tradition, they opposed the theory of universal empire and asserted the complete equality of sovereign states.

In general, the Jesuit writers revived scholasticism, and their discussions of political theory often took the form of commentaries on the ideas of St. Thomas Aquinas concerning the origin and nature of law and the authority of the lawgiver. The Jesuits opposed the claim that kings ruled by divine right, and were regarded in Protestant countries as the main supporters of those who believed in the right of subjects to resist their rulers. They held that the king, as a mere earthly agent, received his power from his people, that he was the delegate of popular choice. A cardinal principle with them was the original sovereignty of the people. They desired to contrast ecclesiastical jurisdiction, which comes from above, with civil jurisdiction, which springs from below. Accordingly, they made a clear distinction between religious and political organization, and viewed the state as a purely human institution directed toward worldly ends. The change from the medieval conception of church and state as one community to the modern conception of church and state as two separate societies was of great importance. The same idea was worked out by the Calvinists in Scotland and England.

While the Jesuits believed that there was no universal dominion but the church, they revived the idea of the unity of Christendom in the sense that, in spite of the independence of states, there is in existence a law higher than the national law. The law of nature, embodying fundamental principles of justice derived ultimately from the will of God, and often identified with the Roman *jus gentium,* was considered universal and binding upon all nations. With church and state viewed as distinct societies, and with states recognized as nationally independent, some theory of the relations among these bodies was necessary. The Jesuits, by their frank recognition of sovereign, independent states, by their belief in the law of nature as the basis of all law, and by their inheritance of the civil and canon law as a universal code of ideal rules, prepared the way for the conception of international law. They combined the new recognition of political facts with ancient ideals of unity.

The Spanish character of the early Jesuits was illustrated by the work of Juan Mariana (1536-1624).[14] His book was dedicated to the prince who was later Philip III, and contained practical, tutorial precepts for the guidance of a ruler. He held that the state arose by agreement among the people, when the golden age that preceded the state was made impossible because of the need for protection. A ruler was chosen, but with limited powers, the people reserving the rights of lawmaking and of taxation. A ruler who usurped power, or a properly chosen ruler who ruled tyrannically, might, after being officially warned by the people's assembly, be assassinated by a private citizen, either openly or by craft, but with as little public disturbance as possible.[15] Mariana discussed practical questions of administration, such as taxation, poor relief, and military policy; and gave sound advice as to how a ruler may retain the good will of his subjects. The general tone of the book is distinctly Machiavellian. War was held to be inevitable, and foreign expansion necessary. Self-interest was considered to be the primary human motive; dissimulation must be practiced by rulers. These ideas represented the typical Jesuit point of view that the state was a distinct and lower order of association than the church and was not primarily concerned with questions of morality. They manifested the tendency which came later to be known as Jesuitical.

The most influential Catholic writer of the period was Robert Bellarmine (1542-1621),[16] a French Jesuit cardinal. In upholding the divine sanction of papal monarchy in the church, he was led to consider the value of various forms of government. He attacked Calvin's preference for aristocracy and argued that Plato's aristocracy might be desirable in a city but was not suitable to a large national state. He believed that absolute monarchy was the ideal form of government, but that because of the corruption of human nature, it was desirable to limit the power of the civil ruler by organs representing the estates of the people. Final political authority resided by natural right in the people, and was delegated by them to their rulers. In discussing the relation of church to state, Bellarmine distinctly separated the two systems, and argued that the pope had no direct power in temporal affairs. For this statement his work was placed on the Index. He did, however, allow the pope an indirect power of interference to prevent laws being passed against ecclesiastical rights,

[14] In his *De Rege et Regis Institutione* (1599).

[15] Mariana objected to poison if the victim ate or drank it, since this involved suicide. He permitted poisoning through clothes or cushions. This distinction goes back to the earliest medieval apology for tyrannicide, John of Salisbury's *Policraticus*.

[16] In his *Disputations* (1581, 1582, 1593), and the *Tractatus de Potestate Summi Pontificis in Rebus Temporalibus* (1610).

and to depose a monarch if he attacked the immunities of the church. This argument was bitterly resented by the French jurists.

In a later work, Bellarmine argued for the unlimited temporal authority of the papacy. This claim was brought forward in opposition to the writings of William Barclay (1546-1608),[17] a Scotch Catholic who had taken refuge in France. Barclay opposed both the anti-monarchic doctrines of the Calvinists and the pro-papal doctrines of the Jesuits, with their belief that secular authority rested upon popular sovereignty. He asserted the independent nature of the state, upheld the divine right of kings, and opposed especially the justification of tyrannicide. The Gunpowder Plot and the assassination of Henry IV were attributed to the teachings of the Jesuits. Barclay believed that the doctrines of the anti-monarchists led to anarchy, and that the absolute authority of the king, based upon the theory of divine right, was the only safe foundation for social and political stability and order.

Adam Blackwood (1539-1581) [18] was another Scotch Catholic who opposed the attempt of the Presbyterian leaders to dominate Scotch politics, and who migrated to France. He also attacked the anti-monarchic doctrine of Buchanan and upheld the divine right of kings, the doctrine of non-resistance, and the duty of states to put down heretical beliefs. The connection between Scotland and France was close during this period, and Scotchmen living in France could not remain unaffected by the strong French monarchy and by the theories of the Politiques who supported Henry IV. Barclay's *De Potestate Papae* was translated into English in 1611, and the writings of both Barclay and Blackwood had an indubitable effect upon the mind of James I. The French and English views of divine right were closely connected, and Filmer [19] later referred to Barclay and Blackwood as his forerunners.

The religious zeal which centered in the activity of the Jesuits, and the intellectual stimulus that resulted from the discoveries and conquests in the new world, gave rise in Spain to another able school composed of theological jurists. These writers were interested in reconciling law and morality, and in developing the concept of a supreme and immutable law of nature as the basis for relations among men and among states. They contemplated the universe as subject to the reign of law, and combined divine, civil, and ecclesiastical jurisprudence into a single system. The ablest of these was Francisco Suarez (1548-1617),[20] a Jesuit professor of

[17] In his *De Regno et Regali Potestate adversus Buchananum, Brutum, Boucherium et reliquos Monarchomachos* (1600) and his *De Potestate Papae* (1609).

[18] His chief works were the *De Vinculo Religionis et Imperii*, and the *Apologia pro Regibus* (1581).

[19] See below, Chapter XIII.

[20] His chief work was his *Tractatus de Legibus ac Deo Legislatore* (1612).

theology at the University of Coimbra. He adopted the characteristic scholastic method and followed Aquinas closely. He gave chief attention to the law of nature, which he defined as the law implanted by God in the human soul, by which right is distinguished from wrong. Its principles were unchangeable, in all times and places, and for all men.

While the rational jurists combined the *jus naturale* and the *jus gentium*, and based morality on the common experience and judgment of mankind, Suarez made a clear distinction between the law of nature, which contains fundamental concepts of justice and conforms to the moral code, and the *jus gentium*, or law of nations, which contains principles of expediency. The law of nature was divine in origin; the *jus gentium* was composed of the human judgments of all peoples. To the latter he assigned principles that could not be fitted into the former system. Thus private property and slavery, difficult to reconcile with moral justice, he assigned to the *jus gentium*. The regulation of war and peace, treaties, and commercial codes were also placed under the *jus gentium*. Suarez was an important contributor to the rising science of international law.

Suarez followed Roman jurisprudence in holding that men are by nature free and equal, and that the depository of political power is the entire community. He taught, however, that the people, transferring their power by contract to the king, were thereafter bound to obedience, except in case of tyranny and injustice. Kings were, however, subject to the laws of God and of nature. Like Bellarmine, Suarez denied to the pope any direct power in political affairs except when religious issues were involved. Like Mariana, he was interested in the question of taxation, which was now becoming an issue in Europe. While Mariana held that the people reserved control over money grants, Suarez claimed that this power was transferred to the king. The ideal of Suarez was the absolute monarchy of Spain, and, like most of the Catholic jurists, he put forward the theory of popular sovereignty in order to subordinate the king to the moral dominion of the spiritual power, rather than to promote democratic institutions.

A unique contribution to the political thought of the period was made by the Italian friar, Thomas Campanella (1568-1639).[21] His ideas were a peculiar combination of humanistic paganism, Machiavellian materialism, and a narrow Christian theology. Campanella combined Platonic and monkish ideals of social organization. He believed that the phenomena of nature and history could be explained by the three principles of power, intelligence, and love; and he viewed the papal autocracy as the ideal form of political organization. In his utopian work, he described,

[21] In his *Civitatis Solis* (1623), trans. in *Ideal Commonwealths* in Morley's Universal Library.

in the form of a dialogue, an unknown commonwealth, discovered by a Genoese sailor.[22] It was ruled by an absolute monarch, Sol, chosen, like the pope, by a college of magistrates. Political and religious functions were combined. The chief ministers of Sol were Potentia, in charge of war and diplomacy; Prudentia, in charge of education, art, and public works; and Amor, in charge of the perpetuation and physical improvement of the population. Two assemblies, one composed of the priest-magistrates, and another including all the people, were provided. Citizens, divided into three classes, lived in common, possessed no private property or individual family life, and were under strict state supervision. Campanella's work is supposed to have inspired the Jesuits to undertake their communistic experiments in Paraguay.

REFERENCES

ALLEN, J. W., *A History of Political Thought in the Sixteenth Century* (New York, MacVeagh, 1928), Part III.

ARNOLD, F. X., *Die Staatslehre des Kardinals Bellarmin* (Munich, Hueber, 1934).

BARKER, Ernest, *Church, State, and Study* (London, Methuen, 1930), Chap. 3.

CARLYLE, A. J. and R. W., *A History of Medieval Political Theory in the West*, 6 vols. (London, Blackwood, 1903-1936), Vol. VI, Part IV.

CHURCH, W. F., *Constitutional Thought in Sixteenth Century France* (Cambridge, Harvard Univ. Press, 1941).

DODGE, G. H., *The Political Theory of the Huguenots of the Dispersion* (New York, Columbia Univ. Press, 1947).

FIGGIS, J. N., *From Gerson to Grotius* (Cambridge, Cambridge Univ. Press, 1907), Chaps. 4-6.

——, *The Divine Right of Kings*, 2nd ed. (Cambridge, Cambridge Univ. Press, 1914).

SABINE, G. H., *A History of Political Theory*, rev. ed. (New York, Holt, 1950), Chap. 19.

SHEPARD, W. R., "The Expansion of Europe," *Political Science Quarterly*, Vol. 34 (March, June, September, 1919).

[22] Note the influence of the new discoveries on the utopia of Campanella, as well as on those of More and of Francis Bacon. See below, Chapter XIII.

CHAPTER XII ⚬

Bodin and Grotius

Rise of the Modern Theory of Sovereignty

By the close of the sixteenth century, political thought had reached a fairly clear conception of the sovereignty of the state, that is, of a single, supreme authority within each state, and of the independence of each state from other states in a family of nations. To these ideas many thinkers contributed, but their work was systematized and put into clear statement by two great publicists. The internal aspect of sovereignty, in the relation of the state to its citizens, was worked out by Jean Bodin. The external aspect of sovereignty, that of the relation of a state to other states, occupied the attention of Hugo Grotius.

The beginnings of the theory of sovereignty were suggested in the *Politics* of Aristotle and in Roman law. Aristotle recognized the existence of a supreme power in the state, and held that this power may be in the hands of one, or of a few, or of many. Roman theory developed the doctrine that the ultimate authority of the state rested in the whole body of citizens, but that the people delegated this power to the emperor, whose will, therefore, had the force of law.

The revived study of Roman law and of Aristotle's *Politics,* in the twelfth and thirteenth centuries, furnished the basis for the theory of sovereignty which grew out of the controversy between church and state. The empire, claiming the inheritance of Rome, and demanding for its head the authority of the Roman emperor, was compelled to accept the Roman theory that final authority rested in the people, the civil ruler acting as their agent. The early church, under Augustine and Gregory VII, considered the state the work of the evil one, as the result of man's fall. Later, under the influence of Aristotle, Aquinas taught that the authority of the state came from the people, and contrasted the human origin of civil power with the divine origin of ecclesiastical authority. During the

181

conciliar controversy, the popular-sovereignty argument spread from the state to the church, and was urged against the supremacy of the pope and in favor of a representative ecclesiastical body. That government rested upon the consent of the governed was a familiar conception during the Middle Ages.

The theory that the civil ruler also ruled by divine right, put forward in opposition to the temporal claims of the pope, was strengthened by the growing royal power and by the establishment in some countries of Protestantism as a state worship under the headship of the national ruler. Against the argument that the power of the king was absolute and that his subjects owed passive obedience appeared the argument that the king derived his authority from his people in the form of a mutual contract, which might be dissolved if he failed to rule justly. Luther and Calvin, the Politiques, the Scotch Catholic writers, such as Barclay and Blackwood, and Filmer and James I in England upheld the divine right of kings. The Calvinist anti-monarchists in France, Scotland, England, and the Netherlands, and the Jesuit opponents of secular power in the interests of ecclesiastical supremacy, argued for popular sovereignty and a limited royal power based on contract. The way was thus prepared for the seventeenth and eighteenth century controversies between king and people, between the doctrine of divine right and that of popular sovereignty and social contract.

A number of influences prevented a clear conception of sovereignty, as a single, supreme, and ultimate source of authority and law in the state, during the ancient and medieval periods. The self-sufficiency which Aristotle considered the distinguishing mark of the state was an ethical rather than a legal conception. The Roman theory of sovereignty presupposed the existence of a universal law and a universal empire. After the fall of Rome, the prevalent belief in a law of nature, existing outside man in fundamental axioms of justice, and the belief in a divine law as the revealed will of God, made impossible the modern idea of human, positive law, made and enforced by the authority of the state. The identification of church and state as a single society, and the conflict for supremacy between secular and spiritual authorities, each having its own organization and legal system, prevented unity in the state or agreement upon a final source of power. The institutions of feudalism, with their local independence and their complicated system of overlords, and with their conception of limited authority and of contractual rights, also prevented political unity and centralized authority. Besides, the Roman theory that a mixed form of government is best was generally held, and numerous corporate bodies, especially the cities, put forth claims of virtual independence.

Not until the national state appeared, with its centralized monarchy, supreme over the feudal nobles and the clergy, independent of the papacy, and recognized as the creator of law, could the modern theory of sovereignty be stated. Provinces had to be joined into kingdoms, and the confused medley of feudal and ecclesiastical rights and exemptions reduced to a unified political system. This was the work of the absolute national monarchs. The people were willing to give their kings any rights they claimed in order to be free from the perpetual contests of the local nobles. It was the king of France who in the sixteenth century had best consolidated his state and unified his own authority; and it was a French writer, Jean Bodin, who first made sovereign power the essential characteristic of the state and located this power in the king.

In reaching the theory of the external independence and legal equality of states in their international relations, similar difficulties were found. The Roman state claimed universal sway and recognized no other political system. The idea of world unity, strengthened by the rise of the papacy and by the establishment of the Holy Roman Empire, became so firmly fixed that the conception of independent, sovereign states made its way with difficulty. Besides, the relations of feudalism were so local, personal, and private that their international nature was entirely obscured. The conception of a group of independent states carrying on international relations under a body of international law could not appear until centralized states, independent of external control, were recognized. The international wars and the commercial and colonial rivalries of the sixteenth century hastened this process. The recognition of the secular basis of the state, or at least of the multi-religious nature of the European state system, and the acceptance of the principle of territorial sovereignty, emphasized the disappearance of European unity. On the other hand, the ancient ideals of the brotherhood of man and the prevalent belief in the universal authority of natural law prevented the view that states had no duties one to another. Questions of international ethics assumed paramount interest.

By the close of the sixteenth century, the political development of Europe had reached the point where both the internal unity and the external legal equality of states demanded a new theoretical basis. It was from the Netherlands, a small state, interested in peace and unrestricted commerce, desirous of maintaining its independence against stronger neighbors, and of placing legal limits upon warfare, that the best statement of international sovereignty and of international law was made, in the work of Grotius. The idea that each state should have free development on its own lines, that each state should enter into equal relations with others under recognized rules, and that no state should be powerful enough to threaten the independence of any other, became the recognized basis of European politics. Nationalism began to replace cosmopolitanism; and the family of nations and the balance of power replaced the unity of the Medieval Empire.

Bodin

The work of Jean Bodin (1530-1596) [1] marked a distinct advance in the theory of politics. Trained in the law and experienced in public service, Bodin combined the scholarly and the practical point of view. He belonged to the group of Politiques,[2] who desired the restoration of peace and order, and who believed that the success of France demanded the suppression of political factions and religious controversies, and the establishment of a strong monarchy. Accordingly, he favored toleration in religion and the unquestioned supremacy of the king. He aimed to construct a theory of the state to support the national and territorial sovereignty that was coming into full strength in France, and in particular to secure the crown to Henry of Navarre.

In method, however, Bodin was not the controversial pamphleteer but the political philosopher, whose conclusions were derived from careful study and observation. He was the first modern writer to set forth a philosophy of history. He asserted the theory of human progress as opposed to the prevalent dogma of man's degeneration from a previous golden age. He also applied the historical and comparative method to the study of jurisprudence. He believed that political theory must be based on historical observation, that political institutions must be studied in their development, and that political and legal systems of various types and periods must be analyzed and compared. Bodin thus anticipated the analytical method of Hobbes and the historical method of Montesquieu, both of whom studied and profited by his work.

The *Politics* of Aristotle furnished the framework for Bodin's political theory. In method of treatment, Bodin was as systematic as the scholastics, and his fundamental concepts are stated in clear definitions. He carried further the work of Machiavelli in returning to a rational science of politics. However, Bodin was interested in the general principles of political philosophy as well as in the workings of politics in actual practice. Like Machiavelli, he distinguished between law and ethics, without, however, making the separation complete. Justice and the moral law he considered essential in political science. He accepted without question the

---

[1] Bodin's philospohy of history is contained in the essay, *Methodus ad facilem Historiarum Cognitionem* (1566). His political theory is found in his *Six Livres de la République* (1576). There is an English translation of this work by R. Knolles.

[2] See above, Chapter XI.

idea of a law of nature conditioning all human relations; and this law of nature he identified with moral law. Even the all-powerful sovereign was bound by its principles, and government was conditioned by a moral end. The welfare of the state, as well as that of the individual, was conceived in accordance with moral and rational purposes.

Bodin believed that the origin of the state, both in history and in logical development, was through the family. Accordingly, he gave little attention to the liberty of the individual or to the theory of social contract that played so large a part in the anti-monarchic doctrines. Family groups and other forms of association, economic and religious, arose because of the social instincts of man. The state was created by wars among these groups, during which the conquered became slaves, and the victorious military leaders established themselves as rulers. The union of lesser groups formed the state, which was, accordingly, the final and supreme form of organization. In discussing both the family and the other types of association, Bodin drew largely upon the principles of Roman law. The authority of the father in the family was based upon the Roman *patria potestas;* other forms of civil association were based upon the Roman law of corporations. However, Bodin, interested in subordinating the various trading companies, estates, and communes to the French monarchy, denied that these associations possessed any inherent rights of their own,[3] and held that they were completely subordinated to the final organization, the state, which alone possessed ultimate authority.

Viewing the family as the primary element in the state, the heads of the families formed the citizen body. Unlike the Greeks, Bodin did not consider active participation in public life essential to citizenship. Citizens might be of different ranks and might possess different rights and privileges. They were, however, alike in one respect, that is, in their common subordination to the political power which controlled the entire state. Subjection to the state was the test of citizenship, and the recognition of a common and supreme authority was the essential characteristic of statehood.

Bodin thus arrived at the central conception of his theory, the doctrine of sovereignty, which he defined as "supreme power over citizens and subjects, unrestrained by the laws." [4] The chief function of sovereignty was the creation of law. As the creator of law, the sovereign was not bound by the law. Sovereignty was supreme and perpetual legal omnip-

---

[3] In his theory of corporations, Bodin continued the work of the fifteenth century jurists. It was from Bodin that Althusius took his theory of the group, although Althusius, like the French anti-monarchists, made the local associations the primary political units and endowed them with natural rights.

[4] *Six Livres de la République,* i. 2.

otence. While the sovereign of Bodin was legally supreme, he was, nevertheless, limited by moral obligations found in the law of God and the law of nature, and by the moral duty to observe treaties with other sovereigns and contracts with his own subjects. Bodin also referred vaguely to certain fundamental political principles so well established that the lawmaking sovereign cannot change them,[5] but he did not develop this conception of what has now come to be considered the constitutional basis of the state. He did, however, distinguish carefully between law and custom, holding that the command of the sovereign was essential to law. He held that in some cases the sovereign should be bound by the promises of his predecessors, though if he desired, he might legally change such promises, since no law can be perpetual or unalterable against the sovereign power. Rulers who refused to obey the laws of God and nature were tyrants. The tyrant, however, remained sovereign, the distinction between tyranny and proper royalty being a moral one. Bodin thus distinguished legal obligation from moral duty, and made an important contribution to the separation of legal and ethical concepts.

Like Machiavelli who preceded him and Hobbes who followed him, Bodin leaned toward monarchy as the most desirable form of government. He tended to identify the theoretical sovereign with the actual king, especially in France, England, and Spain, where the power of the crown had reached its height. The authority of the king was asserted to come from God, and the usual texts were quoted to inculcate the duty of passive obedience. Bodin did, however, distinguish carefully between state and government, holding that the possession of sovereignty was the characteristic of the state, but that the system through which sovereignty was exercised determined the form of government. States were monarchic, aristocratic, or democratic, depending upon whether the sovereign power was vested in one person, in a minority of the citizens, or in a majority of the citizens. Forms of government, that is, the arrangements through which the sovereign will of the state was administered, might be mixed; but the idea of a mixed state, such as the Roman writers praised, Bodin could not endure. He was especially opposed to the claims put forward by the parliaments and estates-general of his day, and held that these bodies possessed no share of sovereign power, but should be limited to a purely advisory capacity. He prepared elaborate analyses of the governments of the existing states of Europe and made shrewd observations concerning their points of strength and weakness. All things considered, he believed that a hereditary monarchy, excluding women from the throne, was the most satisfactory type, since it was most free from factional quar-

[5] He cites the Salic Law in France as an example.

rels, best adapted to deal with emergencies, and best organized for extensive dominion.

Like Aristotle, Bodin discussed the cycle of changes or revolutions through which various forms of the state appear, distinguishing between changes in institutions and laws that do not affect the sovereign power and those in which a change in the location of sovereignty takes place. Monarchy he considered most stable; democracy, most liable to revolution. In discussing the causes of revolution, Bodin combined a queer mixture of astrological and occult superstition with clear and profound insight into the nature of political development. He believed that the institutions of each people should be adapted to their characteristics and conditions. Among these he gave great attention to the influence of geography and climate,[6] distinguishing between northern and southern peoples, and between dwellers in the mountains and those in the plains. He showed also that the form of government and the nature of law might influence national character.

Bodin gave considerable attention to the practical problems of the state. He condemned slavery and advocated religious toleration. On economic questions he was far in advance of his time. He recognized the close connection between the distribution of wealth in the state and the source of actual political power. While he realized the dangers of great inequalities of wealth, he opposed the communistic doctrine of equality. He distinguished between jurisdiction and ownership, and held that the ruler had no right to interfere with the private property of his subjects. In an age of bureaucracy and paternalism, he leaned toward free trade, and believed that a revenue derived from foreign commerce was undignified for a sovereign. He taught that it was unwise for kings to exercise judicial power, and that special magistrates should supervise the moral life of the people, since the authority of the father and of the priesthood had so largely disappeared. Bodin also gave attention to agreements among sovereigns, and outlined the body of principles and practices that were soon to be worked out in the international law of Grotius. The concept of sovereignty did much to strengthen the idea of the legal personality of the state, and of the equality and independence of states. Bodin distinguished between the law of nature and the *jus gentium*, holding that the sovereign was bound by the former, but not by the latter. Unlike Machiavelli, he taught that agreements among sovereigns should be observed, especially if their terms were fair and just.

Bodin's work exerted a considerable influence upon contemporary thought in France and in England, and through his concept of sover-

---

[6] Note the reappearance of this point of view in Montesquieu.

eignty, affected political thought to the present day. English sympathy was drawn to the side of those who were defending the French monarchy from papal aggression and Spanish intrigue. In several places Bodin expressed a strong opinion that sovereignty in England was vested in the king. His treatise was translated into English and made a text-book at Cambridge. Without doubt, it influenced the writings of Hobbes and Filmer. It served to place the king above the restraints of positive law and to oppose the claim of parliament that it could exert a legal check upon the sovereign.

The Forerunners of Grotius

Centuries before Grotius, attempts were made to find a rational basis for relations among peoples, especially to restrict the excesses of war. In these efforts two conceptions of Roman jurisprudence were used, the law of nature and the *jus gentium*. The Roman *jus gentium*, a body of rules discovered to be common to the juristic practice of many peoples, which grew up in contrast to the rigid *jus civile*, and which, while dealing in the main with questions of private law, dealt also with war and treaty relations and with commercial practices, has already been discussed.[7] The prevalence of similar principles among all peoples who came into contact with Rome led to the conception of the *jus gentium* as cognate to the universal law of nature. This identification exerted a far-reaching influence upon medieval thinkers, who sought for a system of law clothed with authority superior to human enactment. As theological and ethical writers attempted to develop rules of right conduct in international affairs, appeal was made to the ancient Roman *jus gentium*, which was supposed to possess the quality of universal obligation.

The Church Fathers early brought the Roman conceptions of moral and legal obligation under review in the light of Christianity. St. Augustine, in the fourth century, discussed the occasions that might render war just and that might require a Christian to take up arms. In the seventh century, Isadore of Seville laid down some of the chief divisions of the *jus gentium*, as found in Ulpian's *Institutes*. In the twelfth century, Gratian, in his *Decretals*, adopted a classification of the law of nations, together with a law of war. St. Thomas Aquinas not only distinguished between the law of nature and the law of nations, but gave considerable attention to the moral problems connected with the subject of war. In the fourteenth and fifteenth centuries, theologians and jurists alike wrote pamphlets dealing with the legitimacy of war and reprisals, the obligation of keeping faith with an enemy, and the binding quality of truces.

[7] See above, Chapter VI.

From the thirteenth century onward, political philosophers, such as William of Ockam, Marsilius, and Dante, in attacking or defending the rival claims of emperor and pope, prepared the way for a better understanding of the nature of sovereignty and of relations among political units. Machiavelli considered the policy of rulers with regard to war, treaties, and expansion in the light of the peculiar situation in the Italian cities. Sir Thomas More, in his *Utopia*, satirized methods of waging warfare, denounced war as unnecessary, and recommended certain mitigations of its worst practices. Bodin, as stated above, gave considerable attention to international questions. He discussed citizenship and allegiance, alliances and confederations, the rights of neutrals and of maritime states. In addition to his definite theory of the nature of state sovereignty, he threw much light, in his frequent examples, on contemporary international practice.

The moral theologians of Spain, at the time of the Reformation, embarked upon extended discussions of practical international questions. They denied the universal sovereignty of the emperor and the temporal authority of the pope, and accepted the Roman idea of a universal law of nature. They were influenced by the new discoveries and by the territorial expansion of Europe. They viewed Christendom as a society of independent princes and free commonwealths, with rights among themselves defined by the law of nature and of nations. In dealing with practical questions of human conduct, they were frequently compelled to take up problems of international interest, and in the process they built up a body of recognized international principles. Among these, Francisco a Victoria (1480-1549),[8] a Dominican professor of theology at Salamanca, was important. He inquired into the just causes for waging war, and discussed at length the foundation and extent of Spanish authority in the newly discovered western lands, especially the relations between the Spaniards and the Indians, and the rights acquired by discovery and conquest.

By the middle of the sixteenth century, systematic treatises on the laws regulating the relations among states began to appear. Conrad Braun (1491-1563)[9] discussed the rights and duties of a papal legate, and laid down many of the principles of diplomatic intercourse. Ferdinand Vasquez (1509-1566)[10] asserted the territorial sovereignty of the Spanish kingdom, and recognized a composite law of nature and *jus gentium* as governing the relations among independent states. He also challenged the right of the Italian cities to close the Adriatic and Ligurian Seas to for-

[8] In his *Relectiones Theologicae* (1557).
[9] In his *De Legationibus* (1548).
[10] In his *Illustrum Controversarium aliorumque usu frequentium Libri tres* (1564).

eigners, and argued for the freedom of the seas. Balthazar Ayala (1548-1584),[11] judge advocate of the Spanish army in the Netherlands, wrote an elaborate treatise on the nature and rights of war, the customs of reprisal and booty, the treatment of prisoners, the duty of keeping faith, and the qualities and duties of a military commander. Ayala drew upon Roman military precedent and the decisions of Roman law, as well as upon Spanish municipal legislation. He also referred to the canon law and to the principles of the *jus naturae,* the *jus divinum,* and the *jus gentium.* Francisco Suarez (1548-1617) [12] advanced a complete philosophic theory of international law. He made a clear distinction between the law of nature and the *jus gentium,* recognized the independence and the interdependence of states, conceived of a real society of states, and insisted upon the necessary existence of a law which all nations ought to obey. As soon as the conceptions of Suarez were applied in the field of practical politics, a body of international law could be formed.

With Alberico Gentili (1552-1608) the development of international law reached an advanced stage. An Italian refugee, Gentili found his way to Oxford. While lecturing there, he was consulted by the Spanish Council concerning the case of an ambassador. This led to his first treatise,[13] in which he gave a classification and a historical sketch of diplomatic missions. He discussed the rights and immunities of ambassadors and their relations to the states that sent and received them. He wrote his best known work after having been appointed Regius Professor of Civil Law at Oxford.[14] In it he discussed the nature of war, who may wage it, and its just causes. He classified wars, and considered the methods of carrying on hostilities and the effects of war on persons and property. He also gave attention to the nature and binding force of treaties. Toward the close of his life, Gentili was appointed to represent the interests of the Spanish crown in English prize cases, and prepared his final work,[15] which was not published until after his death. In it he made a considerable advance toward the definition of the respective rights and duties of belligerent and neutral, and clearly recognized the territorial basis of sovereignty. Gentili thus applied the growing theory of international law to the practical problems of his day. While he did not weld his ideas into a complete system, he was the chief contributor to the theory of Grotius, and, in his doctrine of neutrality, was even in advance of his more illustrious successor.

[11] In his *De Jure et officiis bellicis et disciplina militari* (1582).
[12] In his *Tractatus de Legibus ac Deo Legislatore* (1613). See above, Chapter XI.
[13] The *De Legationibus* (1585).
[14] The *De Jure Belli* (1588).
[15] His *Hispanicae Advocationis Libri Duo* (1613).

Grotius

Through the work of the Dutch Jurist, Hugo Grotius (1583-1645), the principles of international law finally achieved general acceptance. Making use of the works of his predecessors, Grotius framed a complete system of international law in his famous *De Jure Belli ac Pacis,* published in 1625.[16] The extensive influence of this work arose partly from the reputation of the author, partly from the comprehensive scope and systematic analysis of his discussion and the separation of international law from ethics and from jurisprudence.

Grotius belonged to a distinguished family, was well versed in the humanistic learning of his day, was especially trained as a lawyer, held prominent positions in the municipal and provincial governments of the Netherlands, and served on special missions to France and England. He lived during the time of the civil wars in France, the religious and civil disturbances in England and in Holland, the latter part of the war of the United Provinces against Spain, and the first part of the Thirty Years' War. Moved by these events, and eager to restore peace and to safeguard his native land, he wrote his *De Jure Belli ac Pacis* to prove that there is among nations a common law in force with respect to war and in war. For this purpose he made an elaborate analysis of the law of nature and of the *jus gentium,* as embodying legal rules of universal validity. He was also led to investigate the nature and location of sovereignty in the state in order to determine who could properly be a party to a public war. His political theory, therefore, fell under three main heads: the law of nature, the law of nations, and sovereignty.

In opposition to the doctrine, of which Hobbes was soon to become champion, that there is no universal standard of justice and that the only test of law is its utility or expediency, Grotius maintained that there is an essential justice and morality founded in the nature of things, and that this rule should prevail among nations as among men. He distinguished between *natural* and *voluntary* law. *Natural* law is the dictate of right reason, agreeing with rational nature and therefore with God. It is permanent and unchangeable. He considered it natural for men to associate, and introduced the principle of social instinct as one of the sources of natural law. Rational conformity to the needs of a social existence was the test of morality and justice. Grotius also adopted the scholastic distinction between the pure law of nature, which characterized the primitive state of man before political association existed; and the law of nature

---

[16] Grotius' other well-known work is the *Mare Liberum* (1609), which resulted from the dispute between the United Provinces and Portugal over control of trade with the Orient.

peculiar to certain circumstances, which characterized the period of later development. He was thus able to bring different ideas and customs into his system. War he considered natural, under the principle of self-preservation.

The law of nations was included by Grotius in what he called *voluntary* law. Laws of this sort originated either through human will or through the commands of God. Human voluntary law included civil law, which proceeded from the sovereign authority of the state; the law of less extent, such as the commands of fathers and masters, which were dependent upon the civil law; and the law of larger extent, which was the *jus gentium* or law of nations. Divine voluntary law was given by God to mankind after the creation, after the Flood, and in the teachings of Christ. Grotius thus separated the law of nature from divine law and gave a stimulus to the rationalizing tendency of his times. He also, like Suarez, separated the law of nature from the *jus gentium*, though believing that the fundamental principles of natural law should apply to the relations among states.

Grotius developed more fully than his predecessors the principles and extent of the *jus gentium*, and did much to change its meaning from the rules common to nations to the rules governing the intercourse of nations. Drawing upon what had been accepted by constant usage and upon the opinions of the learned, especially his predecessor Gentili, Grotius covered fairly well the field of international law as applicable to the conditions of his day. In deciding upon practical principles, he largely ignored his distinction between the law of nature and the *jus gentium*, selecting such practices as seemed to him to conform to natural justice, and tending again to combine the rules of international conduct with the principles of reason and morality that accorded with his personal judgment. Among other questions, he discussed the nature and just causes of war, the methods of carrying on hostilities, the effects of war on persons and property, the right of expansion, the relation of advanced to uncivilized peoples, slavery, and similar topics.

While Grotius was interested chiefly in the law of nature and of nations, he was compelled to consider incidentally the nature of the state and of sovereignty in order to secure a basis for his theory. He gave no attention, however, to the practical problems of governmental organization or policy. He defined the state as the perfect union of free men for the purpose of enjoying the protection of the law and promoting the common welfare. In discussing its origin, he combined the Greek doctrine that the state resulted from the natural social instinct of man and the Roman doctrine of a contract formed for reasons of utility among those living in a state of nature. While emphasizing the individual rather than the state, and believing in the rights of man under the law of nature, Grotius did not stress the conception of social contract as did the anti-monarchists who preceded him and Hobbes and Locke who followed him.

Grotius drew his theory of sovereignty largely from Suarez and Bodin, although his conception was less definite and logical. He defined sovereignty as supreme political power, vested in him whose acts cannot be rendered void by any other human will. He was not consistent, however, in his application of this concept to the actual states of Europe, acknowledging the possibility of divided and limited sovereignty. The desirability of bringing the wars waged by the semi-feudal princes of his day under the regulation of his system of international principles probably led to this point of view. Grotius was interested in determining what political bodies possessed the right to wage war. He was also concerned, for the sake of maintaining peace and order, in combating the doctrines of popular sovereignty, which he held responsible for much of the turbulence and factional strife of the period. He held that the people had the right to choose their form of government, but having chosen, were bound to obedience. The right of resistance was specifically denied. His doctrine of royal authority made his work especially popular with the ruling monarchs of the time, and helps to explain the influence it exerted at the Peace of Westphalia, the first great European international conference. Absolute monarchy, territorial sovereignty, and the equality of states were cardinal points of his theory.

The great work of Grotius was to create a scheme of rights and duties applicable to the relations among states, and to support it by the sanction of the law of nature, at a time when the unity of Europe and the religious sanction for international morality had largely disappeared. The sovereign state in a family of nations was made the unit of internationalism, in contrast to the individual brotherhood of man in the medieval theory of cosmopolitan world unity. In his theory of sovereignty, Grotius strengthened the position of the absolute monarchs, especially by his treatment of sovereign power as a private right, partaking of the nature of property owned by the king.

At the same time, Grotius advanced the cause of individual liberty by his implied doctrines of the origin of the state as a result of contract and of the contractual relations of sovereigns one to another under natural law. On the continent of Europe, the conditions of the time made the doctrines of Grotius concerning international relations and absolute monarchy particularly applicable. In England, however, the anti-monarchic doctrines were about to be put into practical application.

REFERENCES

ALLEN, J. W., *A History of Political Thought in the Sixteenth Century* (New York, MacVeagh, 1928), pp. 394-444.

CARLYLE, A. J. and R. W., *A History of Medieval Political Theory in the West*, 6 vols. (London, Blackwood, 1903-1936), Vol. VI, Part IV, Chap. 3.

GERBRANDY, P. S., *National and International Stability: Althusius, Grotius, van Vollenhoven* (London, Oxford Univ. Press, 1944).

KALTENBORN, Carl, *Kritik des Völkerrechts* (Leipzig, Mayer, 1847).

———, *Die Vorläufer des Hugo Grotius* (Leipzig, Mayer, 1848).

KNIGHT, W. S. M., *The Life and Work of Hugo Grotius* (London, Sweet, 1925).

MARITAIN, Jacques, "The Concept of Sovereignty," *American Political Science Review*, Vol. 44 (June, 1950).

NUSSBAUM, Arthur, *A Concise History of the Law of Nations* (New York, Macmillan, 1947), Chaps. 3-4.

SABINE, G. H., *A History of Political Theory*, rev. ed. (New York, Holt, 1950), Chaps. 20-21.

SHEPARD, Max, "Sovereignty at the Crossroads: A Study of Bodin," *Political Science Quarterly*, Vol. 45 (December, 1930).

VAN DER MOLEN, Gezina, *Alberico Gentili* (Amsterdam, H. J. Paris, 1937).

CHAPTER XIII ⟞

The Puritan Revolution in England

English Political Thought Before the Revolution

The striking analogy between the political development of Rome and that of England has frequently been pointed out.[1] In both cases the constitutional system was built up gradually, as a result of practical experience, by a people that showed marked ability in government. In both cases also, political institutions reached an advanced stage before political speculation of any importance appeared. Political life in England during the medieval period was strenuous, but even during the times of hottest controversies, abstract political philosophy was missing. Appeal was made to law and to custom, but not to general principles. Similarly, the controversy between the English kings and the papacy involved little political theory. Political expediency and the customary or written law of the land were considered sufficient bases for resistance.

Both Rome and England finally evolved a system of philosophy, and each pictured its own institutions as attaining abstract perfection. The praise of the Roman constitution by Polybius, a Greek, and Cicero, a Roman, was matched by the praise of the English constitution by Montesquieu, a Frenchman, and Blackstone and Burke, Englishmen. Both states created a remarkable system of law, and both extended their legal systems, over a large part of the earth. In contrast to the Roman law, which was crystallized into a systematic code, English law, except as it existed in a few great documents, was found mainly in the decisions of the royal courts. Precedent and custom played a large part in English law; and this "common law," elastic and constantly growing, became the characteristic feature of the English legal system, and one in which from early times great pride was manifested.

[1] See W. A. Dunning, *Political Theories, from Luther to Montesquieu* (1905), pp. 192-193; James Bryce, *Studies in History and Jurisprudence* (1901), pp. 1-3, 14-16.

In several respects the political development of England was different from that of the continent. England was early unified by the Norman conquest, and a strong and centralized national government was created. The governmental aspects of feudalism were never firmly established. The national parliament, representing the estates, but combining barons and clergy in a single chamber, remained continuously in existence from the thirteenth century onward, while the representative bodies of the continent disappeared under the absolute monarchies. The connection between the nobility and the masses was closer in England than elsewhere, and definite limitations were early placed upon the royal power. Coronation oaths, charters, and pledges, of which Magna Carta was the best example, guaranteed the rights of the subjects against the crown. Besides, the jury system and a fairly independent judiciary further restricted the arbitrary power of the king.

Not until the Puritan Revolution of the seventeenth century did political theory become prominent in England. During the medieval period, John of Salisbury and William of Ockam contributed to political philosophy, but the questions in which they were interested were continental rather than English. The only outstanding figure in medieval English political thought was John Wyclif with his theory of social unity and his attempt to apply natural law to everyday questions of economics and ethics. The revival of Roman law on the continent did lead English jurists to describe their legal practices. But Roman principles influenced merely the arrangement, not the content, of their work. Of these early English jurists, the most outstanding were Ranulf de Glanville [2] and Bracton.[3] They put into systematic form the principles of the common law, and insisted that the law was superior to the will of the king.

In the fifteenth and sixteenth centuries, several writers appeared who foreshadowed the main lines that English political thought was to take. Sir John Fortescue (1394-1476) [4] analyzed and eulogized the English system of law in contrast to the Roman jurisprudence. He also praised the excellence of the English system of government, which combined royal and "political" rule, in that the consent of parliament was necessary to legislation and money grants, and the law applied by the judges was superior to the royal command. Like his predecessors, he denied that the will of the prince is the source of law. The rights of Englishmen, which

---

[2] In his *Tractatus de Legibus et Consuetudinibus Angliae* (about 1190).

[3] In his *De Legibus et Consuetudinibus Angliae* (about 1250). The real name of the author was probably Henry of Bratton. For a detailed discussion of Bracton and this period in English history, see C. H. McIlwain, *Constitutionalism, Ancient and Modern*, rev. ed. (1947).

[4] In his *On the Nature of the Law of Nature; On the Excellence of the Laws of England;* and *On the Governance of England.*

he enumerated in contrasting English and French ideas of government, contained many of the items incorporated into later bills of rights.

Fortescue conceived of a state of nature, existing before the establishment of government, and found the ultimate source of authority in natural law, established by God and containing the principles of absolute justice. The authority of the king was derived from this natural law, and was conditioned by it. The king served as head of the state, but must act according to its constitution with the appropriate organs. Fortescue suggested that royal power was derived from popular consent, but did not develop this idea. Through Sir Edward Coke, the ideas of Fortescue were handed down; and they were frequently referred to by the opponents of the king in the later revolution.

The period of the strong Tudor monarchy, during the sixteenth century, was not conducive to political speculation. The fear of Spain, the strong national spirit which centered in the monarchy, the weakening, during the War of the Roses, of the nobles, who had been the chief opponents of the king, the material prosperity of the kingdom, and the establishment of a national church under royal leadership all tended toward absolutism and arbitrary interference with the liberties that Fortescue had praised. The dominant political theory was that of divine-right monarchy and the passive obedience of subjects. Tyndall's *The Obedience of a Christian Man,* Latimer's sermons on *An Exhortation concerning Order and Obedience,* and Heywood's play, *Royal King and Loyal Subject* were typical of Tudor thought. The theory of the divine right of the secular government arose in the main to oppose the theory of papal supremacy, but was strengthened by the course of political events in England, which seemed to demand a strong central authority.

The most noteworthy political treatise of the period was that of Richard Hooker (1553-1600).[5] His work was primarily theological, the outgrowth of a controversy on church government, and aimed to refute the attacks of the Presbyterians on the polity of the Anglican church. Hooker believed, however, that the same principles applied to both secular and ecclesiastical governments, and his work exerted an important influence on later political thought. He made an examination of the origin, nature, and obligation of law in general. Following a rationalistic interpretation of natural law, he held that civil and ecclesiastical laws must be shaped by the reason of men, and are changeable, unlike the immutable law of nature. Civil law he based upon public approbation, which might be expressed through representatives.

Hooker believed that men originally lived in a state of nature, without

[5] *The Laws of Ecclesiastical Polity* (1594). See Morley's edition.

organized authority and government. This condition was full of contention and violence. Men were also instinctively social. Accordingly by formal consent, they established political organization and authority. The compact by which this was done he considered perpetually binding and not to be broken except by universal consent. Hooker thus applied his theory to the support of the monarchy, and advised passive obedience; but his doctrine of government based on popular consent was found far more useful by later theorists of democratic tendency. Hooker also touched on the law of nations, and said that if it is good for the individual to avoid anarchy and adopt civil society, it cannot be good for nations to live in anarchy and avoid civil composition. In short, his work contained, either explicitly or in germ, most of the leading ideas of the eighteenth century. He avoided the scholastic method of relying upon tradition and quotations; he gave a comprehensive exposition of natural law thirty years before the work of Grotius appeared; and he clearly stated the theories of social contract, popular sovereignty, and separation of powers.[6]

More and Bacon

The work of two writers of the Tudor and early Stuart period, Sir Thomas More (1478-1535) and Francis Bacon (1561-1626), lay somewhat outside the general current of English political thought. Both were imbued with the humanist spirit of the Renaissance, were influenced by the discoveries of new lands, and portrayed ideal commonwealths after the Platonic fashion. More had no sympathy with the materialism and absolutism of his day. He satirized [7] the evils of English social and economic life, and described a fictitious country in which these evils had been remedied. More disparaged war and favored religious toleration. He was especially affected by the economic distress that was ravaging the peasant classes, in connection with the enclosure of the old farming lands and the growth of sheep-raising. He found the chief evil in society to be the institution of private property; and he pictured a new régime of peace and plenty under a system of communism. In government, his utopia was a national state, organized democratically, with large powers of self-government permitted to the local subdivisions. The Platonism of the Humanists, joined to the earlier English religious communism, is represented in More's work. On one hand, he looked back to the ecclesiastical socialism of Wyclif and of medieval group life; on the other, he looked

[6] See A. P. D'Entrèves, *The Medieval Contribution to Political Thought* (1939), Chap. 6.

[7] In his *Utopia* (nowhere). This book was published in Latin on the continent (1516), and remained for a long time untranslated into English.

forward to the administrative unity and secular powers of Tudor nationalism.

The utopia of Bacon [8] differed radically from that of More. It rested upon a basis of scientific discovery and of material prosperity, not upon an ethical communism. The idea of equality was destroyed by the vigorous and aggressive period of expansion and commercial exploitation, and Bacon favored strong monarchy and an orderly and well-graded society. In addition to his unfinished utopia, Bacon was the author of many political pamphlets and speeches,[9] in which he adopted the characteristic attitude of the Tudor period. He was a strong supporter of war and expansion, of a nationalist policy in foreign trade, and of a paternalistic government. He foreshadowed the mercantile theory, about to appear; but passed by in disdain the ideas of international law worked out by his contemporary, Grotius. His theory was distinctly reactionary. He held that submission to monarchs was as natural as the obedience of a child to its parents, and he was especially bitter against the lawyers who were upholding the prerogatives of parliament. While in science Bacon looked to the future, in political thought he had no insight into the newer currents that were moving in the direction of liberty.

Political Theory of James I

By the close of the sixteenth century the influence of the Reformation began to make itself manifest in English political thought, and the main lines of controversy began to take the same form that had already appeared on the continent. On the one hand stood the defenders of the established order, upholding absolute monarchy and the Anglican church, and supporting the king, as head of the church, by the argument of divine right. On the other hand, the English lawyers upheld the ancient rights of the courts and of parliament, especially against the claims of a Scotch king; and the Puritans began to attack the supports of the Anglican ecclesiastical system. In this contest the English Calvinists turned to the political philosophy of their religious compatriots in Scotland, Holland, and France; and the anti-monarchic doctrines of Buchanan, Althusius, and the *Vindiciae contra Tyrannos*,[10] with their basis in natural rights and social contract, began to emerge.

If the sixteenth century was the era of theological controversy, the

---

[8] *The New Atlantis* (1629). Bacon intended to expand this into an ideal commonwealth, but his greater interest in natural science prevented it.

[9] For example, his *Advice to Queen Elizabeth; Of the True Greatness of Kingdoms and Estates; of Seditions; The Art of Empire or Civil Government.*

[10] See above, Chapter XI.

seventeenth was the age of political discussion. Ethical and economic considerations became of less importance, while legal and political doctrines came into prominence. In the sixteenth century the chief problem in England was that of restoring order and safeguarding national interests. The Tudor monarchs, as champions of national unity and aspirations, were able to govern autocratically; but with the defeat of the Armada, the need for a strong authority was diminished, and with the death of Queen Elizabeth, the personal devotion to the ruler came to an end. As a result of Tudor policy, political power had passed from the nobles to the country gentry and the mercantile classes, and declining prosperity began to alienate their support. The judiciary was insisting upon its independence and upon the supremacy of the common law over the royal mandate. The contest between the crown and the judges, who claimed to be the interpreters of the common law and therefore the real sovereigns, was the forerunner of the greater contest between king and parliament. Parliament was beginning to insist upon its right to share in levying taxes and in determining general questions of policy. The Puritan sects, and especially the Independents, were convinced that autocracy was incompatible with the religious freedom they desired for themselves. Opposition to the position of the king was brought to a head by the accession of James I, with his high notions of royal prerogative and his tactless personality.

The political philosophy of James I (1566-1625) [11] arose largely from his early experiences in Scotland. His teacher, Buchanan, declared that kings derived their power from the people, and should be removed if they governed badly. His father had been murdered, his mother driven from the throne and executed, and the Presbyterian leaders had scoffed at royal power and asserted the right of subjects to control their rulers. The opposition of James to the Puritan doctrines was, therefore, natural. James' title to the English throne rested purely on the principle of heredity, and was disputed by the Roman controversialists, who desired a Catholic king. This led him to oppose the anti-monarchic theory of the Jesuits. James was also influenced by the theory of divine right that had been developed by Barclay, Blackwood, and the Politiques in France. [12] When he became king of England he found, in the Tudor theory of monarchy and in the established church, support for his ideas of royalty; and his aphorism, "No bishop, no king," expressed his views on the proper con-

---

[11] The political theory of James I is found in his *Basilicon Doron*, prepared for the guidance of his son, in his *True Law of Free Monarchies* (1598), in his *Remonstrance for the Right of Kings*, and in speeches delivered on various occasions. See *The Political Works of James I* (1918), ed. by C. H. McIlwain.

[12] See above, Chapter XI.

nection between ecclesiastical and political organization. The Anglican clergy, in turn, proclaimed the divine right of kings and the doctrine of unconditional obedience. To exalt the crown was to strengthen the established church; and the theologians of the Anglican church supported the royal prerogative as the most effective weapon against the papacy on the one hand and the Puritans on the other. When the Puritans and the Jesuits adopted the theory of the sovereignty of the people, it appeared to their opponents necessary to exalt and make sacred the office and person of the king. The arguments used by Dante, Ockam, and Marsilius in defending the medieval emperor against the pope, and by Luther in magnifying the sacredness of the independent German princes, were developed into a doctrine of passionate loyalty to the crown in terms of mystical devotion.

Arguments were drawn from the Scriptures, from the ancient laws of feudalism, and from the law of nature. The danger of anarchy was held far greater than that of tyranny; and, while the contractual theory of the origin of royal power was usually denied by the supporters of the king, they held that if there had been such a contract, God alone could act as arbiter, and to Him alone, therefore, could appeal against tyranny be made. Authority from above and not from below, in both state and church, was the doctrine of the royalist party. In his speech to parliament in 1609, James said "Kings are justly called gods, for they exercise a manner of resemblance of Divine power upon earth." In his speech in the Star Chamber, in 1616, he said, "As it is atheism and blasphemy to dispute what God can do, so it is presumption and high contempt in a subject to dispute what a king can do."

In addition to the theological party, who supported absolutism by arguing that secular power was derived immediately from God, and who depended upon Scriptural quotation and scholastic argument, the preeminence of royal authority was supported from two other points of view. Filmer [13] aimed to show that absolutism was historically justified, being a natural and constant expression of human nature. Hobbes [14] supported absolutism on the basis of a utilitarian philosophy of social contract. During the period of civil war the doctrine of the divine right of kings became the watchword of the royalist party, and was supported increasingly on political rather than on religious grounds. The theory of James I aimed at the establishment of that bureaucratic absolutism that had been the usual solution for the disintegrating effects of the Reformation. The failure of his policy made England the only country, with the exception of Holland, to avoid that fate.

[13] See below.
[14] See below, Chapter XIV.

Political Theory of the Parliamentary Party

The controversy between king and parliament, which finally led to civil war, compelled the parliamentary party to develop a political philosophy to oppose the doctrine of divine right. On the one hand, they put into definite and systematic form the constitutional and legal principles that had formed the bulk of English political thinking. On the other, they took over from the continent and from Scotland the antimonarchic doctrines that had developed in ecclesiastical and political theory during the Renaissance and Reformation. The first line of argument was put forward by the lawyers; the second was worked out, in the main, by the Dissenters who opposed the religious position and policy of the king and of the Anglican church.

In the early part of the contest chief reliance was placed upon the legal arguments. The familiar doctrines of the supremacy of the common law, of the independence of the judiciary, of the sources of law in the people, as represented by king in parliament, and of the parliamentary control of money grants were strongly urged. The chief opponent of the king was Sir Edward Coke [15] who, as chief justice, upheld the sovereignty of the law and, when removed from the bench, as a member of parliament inspired the Petition of Right. It was with Coke in mind that James I said, "As for the absolute prerogative of the Crown, that is no subject for the tongue of a lawyer, nor is lawful to be disputed." Another powerful figure was John Selden,[16] the most learned man of his time. He was a consistent rationalist and utilitarian and scoffed at supernatural sanction for royal power. He viewed the monarchy as merely a constitutional form. "There is no species of kings," he said. "A king is a thing men have made for their own selves, for quietness' sake, just as in a family one man is appointed to buy the meat." [17] Selden was especially bitter against the clergy, and did much to undermine veneration for church and king, and to encourage men to judge institutions and ideas in the light of reason and common sense.

In addition, the civil liberties of Englishmen were emphasized and more clearly stated. The arguments of Eliot,[18] Pym, and Hampden, the Petition of Right, and the Bill of Rights illustrated the gradual development of the idea that every individual possessed certain "fundamental liberties," including freedom of person and of property, that should not

---

[15] See his *Institutes*.

[16] See his *Table Talk*, ed. by Frederick Pollock. In reply to Grotius' *Mare Liberum*, Selden wrote his *Mare Clausum*, and contended that the sea was private property.

[17] *Table Talk*, 40b.

[18] See his *De Jure Magistratus*, and his *The Monarchy of Man*

be arbitrarily interfered with. The identification of these with "natural rights" was an easy next step.

Natural law, as it had been known for centuries, had been characterized by two essential but different qualities. First, it had served as a pattern of right conduct for all peoples. Secondly, it had been considered the basis for certain positive assertions, such as that all men are equal.[19] In the first case it was a negative principle of obligation in that it restrained people's actions. In the second case it was a positive principle of expectation concerning popular rights. Of these two, the negative principle of obligation had traditionally been more important. Natural law had insisted more on people's duties than on their rights. Now, however, a highly important change was made. Emphasis shifted from obligation to expectation. Large numbers of people, becoming politically important again, were beginning to demand that government guarantee to them the essential liberties or natural rights with which we are now so familiar. Thus by the development of English legal principles and because of the Dissenters being forced into politics by persecution, the theory of civil liberties and limited government was greatly advanced.

The role of the Dissenters in this process was especially important. The effort of Charles I to force episcopacy upon Presbyterian Scotland led to an ecclesiastical revolution in which the Scotch people adopted a solemn Covenant (1638), pledging themselves to maintain their worship and to uphold the king only as long as he conformed to the laws of the church and of parliament. The Scotch people thus put into practice the theories of Buchanan. When war broke out between king and parliament in England, the need of Scotch aid led parliament to draw up a Solemn League and Covenant (1643), in which leading individuals of both countries formed an alliance against the king. The conceptions of popular sovereignty and social contract were thus carried over into England; and parliament soon attempted to force the Presbyterian form of organization upon the established church and to exclude the Anglican bishops from political office.

The adoption of Presbyterianism by the English parliament was hastened by the rise of numerous sects that seemed to threaten anarchy, and by the desire to prevent the revolution from going too far in the direction of democracy. The aristocratic tendencies of Presbyterianism appealed to many of the English leaders.

At the same time, the Independents in England were becoming better organized and more numerous. The Independents believed in the autonomy of each congregation and in the right of every member to share

[19] Cicero, *Republic,* iii. 22.

in church administration. Each congregation was established by a covenant and formed a miniature republic. The founder of the Independents,
Robert Brown, believed in the separation of church and state, and taught
that magistrates had no authority over the consciences of men.[20] The
Independent sects gained in strength during the Civil War and secured
control of the government under Cromwell. They gave a further democratic impetus to the movement toward civil liberties, and through their
insistence on the right of private judgment in religious matters, did much
to add the rights of freedom of worship and freedom of speech to the
rights of life, liberty, and property worked out by the lawyers. Their
doctrine that any group of believers had the right to manage its own
worship, and that the state had no authority to enforce religious uniformity, led to the principle of religious toleration and, when applied to
political affairs, strengthened the doctrine that government is based upon
the consent of the people. Many Independents migrated to America,
where conditions were especially favorable to the development of their
ideas; and when the success of Cromwell brought their party into control
in England, doctrines worked out by American leaders were reintroduced
into England.

The combination of religious and political issues in the contest between
king and parliament thus brought into prominence the anti-monarchic
doctrines of natural rights, social contract, and popular sovereignty that
were used by the Calvinists whenever they had to struggle for religious
freedom and by the Jesuits in their contest with Protestant kings.

One other important change in these doctrines was made in England.
On the continent the units who possessed natural rights and who drew up
the contract were generally conceived to be classes, representative bodies,
corporations, and the like. In England, however, emphasis was placed
upon the individual, and the conception of popular sovereignty that
resulted was, accordingly, more definite and real. The social contract and
natural-rights doctrines as developed in England were retransmitted to
the continent in the eighteenth century, where they served as the theoretical background for the French Revolution.

Political Theory of the Commonwealth

During the Civil War, parliament was controlled by the Presbyterians
and refused toleration to other religious sects; the parliamentary army
was composed largely of Independents, and leaned strongly toward the

[20] The influence of Holland on the theory of toleration held by the Independents
was very great. Many of their leaders resided there for a time, and other groups
migrated from Holland to England.

most radical sect, the Levellers. After the defeat of the royalist forces, the inevitable break between parliament and army left the latter in control of the country. It drove the Presbyterians out of parliament, and finally executed the king and established its leader, Cromwell, as dictator. As usual, the revolution ultimately brought the radical group into power. During this process the basis of political discussion was shifted from constitutional and legal grounds to a more complete consideration of the doctrines of natural rights and human equality; and these, in turn, were supported more by rational than by ecclesiastical arguments.

The English radicals taught that men are by nature free and equal, that government is based upon law which represents the popular will, that all men, as individuals, possess natural rights to life, liberty, property, freedom of conscience and expression, and political equality. They were also accused of trying to revive the communistic ideas of Wyclif and of teaching that equality in property is also a natural right. These doctrines were put forward in numerous pamphlets of which those of Lt. Col. John Lilburne [21] were most influential. He boldly asserted the sovereignty of the common people and maintained that parliament was merely the agent of the nation at large. His democratic ideas spread rapidly through the army and were largely responsible for its clash with the aristocratic Presbyterian group in control of parliament. The leader of the communist group was Gerard Winstanley,[22] who insisted that political changes were unimportant unless they were accompanied by far-reaching social and economic transformations. In the army council, Ireton and Cromwell took a more conservative stand. They opposed equality of property and universal suffrage, appealed to law rather than to natural rights, and desired moderate and constitutional government. Force of circumstances compelled, indeed, the adoption of autocracy in the Protectorate.

An important phase of the period following the removal of the king was the attempt of the army party to draw up written frameworks of government, based on the theory of social contract. The most important of these was *The Agreement of the People* (1647),[23] put forward by the radical element in the army, and intended to serve as the basis of compromise with king and parliament. This document declared itself to be an expression of popular will and required the personal signature of every individual. It provided for a popularly elected representative body of a single house, with delegated and limited powers; it contained a bill of rights;

[21] See especially his *Vox Plebis*, and his *Fundamental Liberties of England*.

[22] See his *The Law of Freedom* (1652); *The Saints' Paradise* (1658).

[23] See S. R. Gardiner, *Documents*, No. 74. Compare the plan of government here presented with that established by the Fundamental Articles of Connecticut (1639). See W. MacDonald, *Select Charters*, No. 14.

and it specifically provided that the governing body should not interfere with the fundamental liberties. The more conservative element in the army and in the Rump Parliament prevented its being put into effect. After the dismissal of the Rump Parliament brought Cromwell clearly into power, the officers of the army drew up a new constitution, the *Instrument of Government* (1654), providing for a Lord Protector and a parliament elected by those with considerable property qualifications. The powers of both Protector and parliament were carefully limited. This represented an attempt to revert to the constitutional system under Elizabeth, and was much more conservative than the *Agreement of the People*. The fear that the election of a parliament might go contrary to the commonwealth idea prevented the *Instrument of Government* from being put into effect; and Cromwell established a military dictatorship which was avowedly temporary and transitional. While the ideas of a written constitution and of a constitutional check upon the government were thus suggested, they were not put into practical operation in England.

The more moderate theory of the commonwealth period was best represented in the writings of John Milton (1608-1674). Milton supported the parliamentary party, advocated complete separation of church and state, and at first favored the substitution of the Presbyterian for the Episcopal system in church organization. Later he upheld Independency, and took active part in politics under the Commonwealth and Protectorate. When parliament in 1643 issued an ordinance for the control of printers and book-sellers, Milton [24] defended the right of free expression as a privilege of citizenship and a benefit to the state. He proceeded to defend liberty in general, arguing that it is essential to the dignity of man and to the development of his faculties of reason. He opposed governmental restriction and supervision, argued for religious toleration, and was the first prophet of the individualism that became dominant in the nineteenth century.

After the execution of Charles I, Milton [25] identified himself with the regicides. Influenced by Buchanan, to whom he frequently referred, he argued that men, born free and with natural rights, formed political associations by mutual agreement and chose kings and magistrates as their deputies. Laws, framed or consented to by all, bound rulers as well as subjects. Ultimate political power resided in the people, who have the same right to depose as to establish a king, and who are under obligation to remove tyrants.

On the appearance of the *Eikon Basilike*, a clever forgery by Gauden, a royalist divine, Milton, at the request of the Council of State, made

---

[24] In his *Areopagitica* (1644), written in the form of a speech to parliament.
[25] In his *The Tenure of Kings and Magistrates* (1649).

reply.[26] In this he attacked the institution of monarchy. At the same time, frightened by the growth of radicalism, he opposed extreme democratic ideas and indicated his naturally aristocratic point of view. When Salmasius, professor at Leyden, expressed the horror of Europe at the execution of the king and defended the monarchical principle,[27] Milton again was deputed to reply. He argued [28] against tyranny and hereditary rule as being contrary to natural law. He described the commonwealth as the best government possible under existing conditions. Milton disliked the rule of a single person; at the same time he had little confidence in representative democracy.

As dissatisfaction with the Protectorate increased, Milton tried to prevent the recall of Charles II by putting forward a plan of republican government.[29] He advocated a system consisting of a body of representatives holding office by permanent tenure and choosing an executive council from their own number. The contrast between his great expectations in the early days of the struggle and the inability of the ignorant and fanatical men of his day to properly use the liberty they had secured drove him to the despairing paradox of a perpetual senate. Milton was temperamentally undemocratic, and personally attached to the autocratic Cromwell. It was, therefore, difficult for him to represent consistently the democratic theory that underlay the Puritan effort.

Harrington

The most systematic and suggestive plan of government to replace the monarchy that had been destroyed in England was put forward, in the form of a political romance,[30] by James Harrington (1611-1677). Harrington maintained a non-partisan attitude in the civil war, and his book, which attracted much attention, aroused the suspicion of both factions. His work manifested wide reading in history and in the writings of other political theorists, as well as keen observation of contemporary events in Europe. Harrington spent some time at Venice and derived many of his political ideas from a study of its government. He said that no man can be a politician unless he is first a historian and a traveler. He prefaced his plan of a model commonwealth by a sketch of seven of the principal republican constitutions of history. He was a great admirer of Aristotle

---

[26] In his *Eikonoklastes*.
[27] In his *Defensio Regia pro Carolo I* (1649).
[28] In his *Defensio Populi Anglicani* (1651).
[29] In his *The Ready and Easy Way to Establish a Free Commonwealth* (1660).
[30] *The Commonwealth of Oceana* (1656), dedicated to Cromwell, whom Harrington hoped would put its principles into effect. See Morley's edition.

and Machiavelli, and a severe critic of Hobbes,[31] whose *Leviathan* had just appeared.

Influenced by the study of history and by conditions in England, Harrington believed that stability in government is highly desirable, and that the true principle by which governments should be judged is the balance of forces within them. He believed that all states will have either governments of laws, aiming at general welfare, or governments of men, aiming at some private interests.[32] He made a further distinction between the self-government of a nation and the government of one people by another. He then investigated the principles underlying a permanent and desirable system of government, both in their material basis and in their psychological background, holding that all power is derived either from wealth or from intellectual distinction.

Harrington argued that political authority naturally follows the distribution of wealth, and that political stability can be maintained only where sovereignty is located in the hands of those who hold the greater amount of property. Monarchy and aristocracy, accordingly, are natural only when land, which is the main form of wealth except in commercial city-states, is in the hands of one or a few. In England, where the great estates of the nobility and the monasteries had been broken up by the Tudors, a commonwealth was the proper form of government. To maintain its stability, a law preventing any person from owning more than a certain amount of land should be enacted. Harrington was thus one of the earliest interpreters of the economic basis of history and of political structure.

A detailed scheme of constitutional organization, which the author believed corresponded to the rational nature of man, was then proposed. This consisted of a senate, composed of the "natural aristocracy," whose function it was to initiate policies and laws; a council, consisting of the mass of the population or their representatives, with the function of voting upon the recommendations of the senate; and a magistracy to carry on the administrative functions of government. This system was to be strengthened by several subsidiary provisions, such as election by secret ballot and rotation in office. Freedom of religion was provided for, and a system of universal and compulsory education under the control of the state was suggested.

While Harrington's book was written in the form of a utopia, and was allowed to circulate by Cromwell on the ground that it was too impractical to be dangerous, it was in fact an earnest appeal to his countrymen. Strong efforts were made by Harrington and his friends to induce parlia-

[31] See below, Chapter XIV.

[32] Note the closing sentence in the Bill of Rights prefixed to the Massachusetts constitution of 1780, "to the end it may be a government of laws and not of men."

ment to adopt features of the plan. Harrington was less interested in liberty than was Milton, but he was more practical and gave more attention to the system of governmental organization and to the actual facts of politics. His book was eagerly read. In England interest was so keen that the Rota Club, the first known debating society, was formed to discuss its proposals. The English preferred, however, to return to their earlier institutions, and the restoration of the monarchy brought Harrington's vogue to an end. His work was more influential in America. "The constitutions of Carolina, New Jersey, and Pennsylvania reflected his thought, and a century later his authority was fully quoted in the discussions which preceded and followed the elaboration of the American constitution. His works formed the political bible of Otis and John Adams, and Jefferson's copy is preserved in the Library of Congress. Translated into French during the Revolution, they supplied Siéyès with many of his ideas. Thus Harrington's name arrests us in the three great revolutions of the modern world." [33]

Filmer

Sir Robert Filmer (? -1653) played an unimportant part during the civil war, and his chief work [34] was not published until long after his death. His *Patriarcha* was, however, important, partly because it was answered by Sydney and Locke, partly because it was the best statement of a theory of monarchy adopted by many Tories after the Restoration. Filmer agreed with Hobbes concerning the absolute nature of royal power, but attacked the social-contract basis from which Hobbes derived it. He pointed out that the state of nature and social-compact doctrine was essentially opposed to absolute monarchy, and that if the people originally possessed supreme power and were free to choose their government, only a democracy would be lawful. He denied the assumption of original equality among men, and also the principle that authority rested upon human consent. He agreed with Bodin that there must be in every state a single, absolute, and irresponsible sovereign power.

Filmer argued that government originated in an enlargement of the family, the king being the father, and the people his children. [35] The metaphor that the king was the father of his people was thus translated into an argument for absolutism. Patriarchal rule was the original form

[33] G. P. Gooch, *Political Thought in England from Bacon to Halifax* (1914), p. 121.

[34] *Patriarcha, or the Natural Power of Kings* (1680), published in Morley's edition of Locke's *Two Treatises of Civil Government*. See also his *Observations concerning the Originall of Government* (1652), a criticism of Hobbes, Milton, Grotius, and Hunton.

[35] The patriarchal theory of government had been suggested by Aquinas, and occasionally referred to by later writers.

of authority, according to the Scriptures and to history; and monarchy was both a divine institution and in accordance with the laws of nature. Paternal authority was the only inalienable natural right, and this was perpetuated in the absolute authority of the king in every monarchic state. The alternative to monarchy was anarchy or military despotism. Moreover, monarchy was the only government that could preserve true religion, the diversity of religions in Holland and the lack of religion in Venice being adduced as proof. The king was thus made the source of law, with parliament reduced to an advisory body; and the passive obedience of subjects was enjoined. Political sovereignty was derived from the original patriarchal authority, transmitted, under divine approval through hereditary succession. In the absence of an heir, a new ruler, chosen by the heads of the great families, might be considered as the choice of God.

Filmer's notions were founded partly on history and partly on a belief in natural law. What was chiefly valuable in his theory was the conception that the state is a natural and organic growth, not a mechanical organization created by contract. He shifted the main support of the divine-right theory from Scriptural texts to the teachings of nature. What was according to nature, he held to be divinely ordained. The abandonment of the theological basis of divine right really paved the way for the overthrow of the theory, since it was easier to criticize Filmer's interpretation of history, or to point out that democratic principles are also natural, than it was to meet the theological arguments on their own ground. Besides, the tendency to interpret the principles of the law of nature in anti-monarchic terms was too strong for Filmer, or even the abler thinker, Hobbes, to effectively oppose.

Puritan Ideas in America

The period of political and religious controversy in England gave a stimulus to the colonization of America. Under the early Stuarts, Independents and Puritans migrated to New England in order to carry on their worship unmolested. When Charles I was beheaded and Cromwell came into power, many Anglican royalists settled in the southern colonies. Catholics sought refuge in Maryland, and Quakers in Pennsylvania. These colonists brought with them English common law and English traditions and institutions of government; and they found in America an environment highly favorable to the growth of democracy and individualism. Although there was little systematic political speculation until the time of the American Revolution, the form of government that grew up in the colonies showed the influence of English ideas and issues.

The Puritan ideals of New England were perhaps the most important in fixing the direction of American thought. The influence of the church was dominant; and a theocratic and intolerant system, based upon Old Testament teachings and reminiscent of Calvin at Geneva, was attempted. While the Calvinistic doctrine that church and state are distinct societies was held, it was generally recognized that the civil authority should guarantee the observance of church doctrine and ceremony and punish transgressors against the moral law. The preservation of true religion was the chief duty of the state, and church membership was a requisite to full citizenship.

This doctrine was challenged by the Independents, of whom Roger Williams [36] was chief spokesman. He contended that the state is entirely distinct from the church, and that civil magistrates should have no jurisdiction in ecclesiastical affairs. He argued for freedom of conscience, first on Scriptural grounds, second, because it is socially and politically expedient. In its political aspects his doctrine taught that civil government was based on popular consent, expressed through an original contract. His ideas exerted considerable influence in England during the period of the Commonwealth.

The Puritans brought to America the undemocratic doctrines of Calvin, and in the early settlements only a small proportion were freemen and had a voice in government. There were, however, several influences, aside from the frontier conditions of the new environment and the jealously guarded civil liberties of Englishmen, that made for democracy. The use of the social contract as a method of establishing the body politic was widespread in New England. The Mayflower Compact (1620), the Fundamental Orders of Connecticut (1639) and the Newport Declaration (1641) were examples. A clear statement of the social-contract theory was made by the Connecticut preacher, Thomas Hooker.[37] The Congregational system of church organization, in which each body of worshipers was independent and chose its own minister, was generally adopted in New England. This not only strengthened the covenant idea, but also led to local self-government and the doctrine of popular sovereignty. The contract theory emphasized the importance of the individual in both church and state; both were formed by voluntary consent. Under the conditions of the new world, this individualistic idea contained a germ of democracy which rapidly replaced the theocratic and aristocratic tendencies of early New England.

The southern colonies, with their Anglican and royalist tradition, their

[36] In his *Bloudy Tenent of Persecution for Cause of Conscience* (1644); and his *Bloudy Tenent yet more Bloudy* (1652).
[37] In his *Survey of the Summe of Church Discipline* (1648).

plantation system, and their extensive employment of slave labor, were less inclined to democracy and local self-government. Nevertheless, every attempt to establish a definite aristocratic organization of society and government failed. The Quakers also brought to America the Anabaptist attitude toward taking an oath in the courts and toward military service.

Considerable progress was made toward the idea of a written constitution in the American colonies. The charters granted to the colonial-commercial companies, containing land grants and governing powers as well as commercial monopolies, were brought to America, and served as a written basis of government and a guarantee of local privileges. Two of the colonies retained their charters until the Revolution and found them satisfactory as constitutions after becoming independent states. In the proprietary colonies, frames of government were drawn up, influenced largely by the documents of the Commonwealth period and by the ideas of Harrington's *Oceana*. The Fundamental Constitutions of Carolina (1669), often attributed to John Locke, established an aristocratic system in which governing power was associated with property. William Penn prepared charters for New Jersey (1676) and Pennsylvania (1683) in which many of the devices of the *Oceana* were put into practice. These constitutions were considered models and were expected to be permanent. Pennsylvania, in particular, acquired great fame in Europe; Voltaire and Montesquieu wrote of it in terms of high admiration. The attempts were, however, failures; although the belief in property qualifications, the conception of civil and religious liberty, and the idea of a written constitution survived.

The democratic movement during the colonial period was manifest in the contest between the royal governors and the colonial assemblies. The contest represented, in the main, the same issues as that between king and parliament in England; and parties in the colonies adopted the English names, Whig and Tory. The assemblies, controlling the finances, steadily enlarged their powers, and the administrative control of the home government was narrowed. This conflict gave the colonists experience in practical politics and served as a rallying point for tendencies favorable to popular government and to independence.

REFERENCES

ALLEN, J. W., *English Political Thought, 1603-1660* (London, Methuen, 1938).
———, *A History of Political Thought in the Sixteenth Century* (New York, MacVeagh, 1928), Part II.
BARKER, Arthur, *Milton and the Puritan Dilemma, 1641-1660* (Toronto, Univ. of Toronto Press, 1942).

BRYCE, James, *Studies in History and Jurisprudence* (New York, Oxford Univ. Press, 1901), pp. 1 ff.

CAMPBELL, W. E., *More's Utopia and his Social Teaching* (London, Eyre, 1930).

D'ENTRÈVES, A. P., *A Medieval Contribution to Political Thought* (Oxford, Oxford Univ. Press, 1939), Chap. 6.

——, *Riccardo Hooker* (Turin, Univ. of Turin, 1932).

DUNNING, W. A., *Political Theories, from Luther to Montesquieu* (New York, Macmillan, 1905), Chaps. 6-7.

GOOCH, G. P., *A History of English Democratic Ideas in the Seventeenth Century*, 2nd ed. (Cambridge, Cambridge Univ. Press, 1927).

——, *Political Thought in England from Bacon to Halifax* (London, Williams & Norgate, 1914).

MCILWAIN, C. H., *Constitutionalism, Ancient and Modern*, rev. ed. (Ithaca, Cornell Univ. Press, 1947).

——, ed., *The Political Works of James I* (Cambridge, Harvard Univ. Press, 1918).

SABINE, G. H., *A History of Political Theory*, rev. ed. (New York, Holt, 1950), Chaps. 22, 24-25.

SMITH, H. F. R., *Harrington and his Oceana* (Cambridge, Cambridge Univ. Press, 1914).

TROELTSCH, Ernst, *The Social Teachings of the Christian Churches*, trans. by Olive Wyon, 2 vols. (New York, Macmillan, 1931), pp. 666-681, 706-711.

WOLFE, D. M., ed., *Leveller Manifestoes of the Puritan Revolution* (New York, Nelson, 1944).

——, *Milton in the Puritan Revolution* (New York, Nelson, 1941).

CHAPTER XIV ~

Hobbes and Locke

The State of Nature and the Social Contract

In the works of Hobbes and Locke three of the dominant ideas of political philosophy reached their culmination. These were the doctrine of natural law, the concept of a state of nature antecedent to the organization of society, and the idea of a social contract through which the state is established.

Since ancient times all of these ideas had been familiar in political thought. The Stoics considered natural law to be an unchanging guide to moral action. The Roman lawyers usually identified the law of nature with the *jus gentium,* and distinguished it from the *jus civile;* although some jurists, Ulpian for example, distinguished between the *jus naturale* and the *jus gentium* without making the distinction clear. In the Middle Ages the usual classification of law was threefold, i.e., the law of nature, the law of God, and the positive law. The law of nature was generally combined with and subordinated to the law of God, Protestants finding its main principles in the Decalogue and Catholics in the canon law. Gradually the idea that the law of nature was the embodiment of human reason rather than of authority came to the front. In the works of Hooker and of Grotius this conception was prominent, though not yet quite clear. Scriptural texts and historical precedents were still depended upon. Hobbes, however, made an unambiguous statement. To him there was no other law of nature than reason; and the provisions of the law of nature were deductions of reason from human nature.

The idea that a state of nature, in which men lived under natural law only and possessed natural rights, preceding the establishment of political society, had likewise been suggested by earlier writers,[1] but it did not

[1] For example, by Mariana and by Grotius.

become prominent until the seventeenth and eighteenth centuries. While the conception of a state of nature is an historical one, it was not investigated by the methods of history. It was regarded as a necessary postulate to natural law and natural rights. In order to support the popular basis of authority and the inalienable rights of man, it was desirable to conceive deductively of an original association of mankind previous to the establishment of the authority and law of the state. Two main conceptions of the state of nature arose. One regarded it as an idyllic condition of simplicity and virtue, which the establishment of civil authority had destroyed and which men should aim to reëstablish. The other viewed it as a condition of strife and violence, which the establishment of the state had remedied, and to which men were prone to relapse unless they were politically wise and energetic. In the Middle Ages the doctrine of the fall of man and the antagonism of church to state pictured political society as an evil and primitive anarchy as essentially blessed. The sixteenth century was an age of economic change and political expansion. The old order was decried and new ideas were welcomed. Political theorists, especially those who wished to magnify the power of the king, regarded the state of nature as utter barbarism, and considered an orderly, well-governed political society as the noblest work of civilization. This was the point of view of Hobbes. By the time of Rousseau, a romantic belief in the excellence of primitive simplicity had again arisen. The literature of the period was filled with praises of the noble savage. Accordingly, Rousseau pictured the state of nature as one of innocence and joy, and recommended a return to natural simplicity as the only cure for the evils of his day.

The idea that the state was founded by an agreement or contract was also by no means new. It was referred to and criticized by Plato and Aristotle. In the form of a covenant, it was pictured in the Old Testament, and introduced into medieval political theory through the church. The feudal obligations of lords and vassals, freely undertaken by both parties, also prepared the way for the idea that the relations between ruler and subjects had a contractual basis. In its juristic aspects, it was closely connected with the Roman law of partnerships or corporations. In the fourteenth century, the theory was suggested by William of Ockam, who based civil government and private property upon the consent of the governed. By the later part of the sixteenth century, the idea was quite familiar, and was largely used in resisting the claims of princes to absolute dominion over their subjects. It was also used by the Jesuits in order to disparage the human basis of secular authority in contrast to the divine basis of the ecclesiastical system. It took a leading place in the theories of Buchanan and Althusius, and in the *Vindiciae*. Sometimes it was viewed as a contract between God and people to uphold the true religion; sometimes it was a contract of every man with every man to establish a body politic; sometimes it was a contract between people and ruler, defining the terms upon which authority was delegated to the latter.

In England, Richard Hooker outlined the social contract as early as 1594. The importance of economic interests, the influence of the new and wealthy mercantile class, and the strong position of the lawyers made the contractual theory of society especially popular in that country. During the Civil War, the contract theory became very prominent as a support of the democratic party against the divine-right monarchy; and the documents of the Commonwealth period took the form of "agreements of the people." The doctrine thus became an accepted article in the creed of the Whig party, and a statement of it was burned at Oxford (1672) during the reaction following the Restoration. After the Revolution of 1688, it was reaffirmed, the removal of James II being justified on the ground that, by his misgovernment, he had broken the original contract between king and people.

The theory of contract, which substituted civil for natural relations, became the generally accepted doctrine of the leading thinkers during the later part of the seventeenth and the greater part of the eighteenth century. It seemed to be the only reasonable alternative to the doctrine of divine right; and it appealed to the advocates of liberty, since it suggested a method of limiting the arbitrary authority of kings. Philosophical and rational thinkers, trying to break away from the theological method of interpretation, adopted it; for it gave authority a human basis which could be discussed and criticized.

It also appealed to many because it emphasized the part played by conscious human will in the evolution of society, and viewed the individual, with his natural rights, as the unit whose interests were of prime importance. While the doctrine was unhistorical, and was destroyed later by the criticisms of Hume, Bentham, Burke, and Kant, it exercised a tremendous influence, especially in England, America, and France, where, through the work of Locke and Rousseau, it served as the basis for the revolutions that created modern democracy and individual liberty.

Hobbes

The first comprehensive work in political philosophy by an Englishman was that of Thomas Hobbes (1588-1679).[2] Hobbes is interesting not only

[2] *Leviathan* (1651). See Oakeshott's edition. Hobbes' other important political writings were the *Elements of Law* (written in 1640, published in 1650), *De Cive* (1642), and *Behemoth or a Dialogue on the Civil Wars* (1679).

as a political theorist but as a person. Indeed, his personality played a vital role in shaping his views on the "comfort" of government.

He was born prematurely near Malmesbury when his mother became frightened by reports of the Spanish Armada. This was an event from which he was never to recover, if we are to believe Hobbes himself. He tells us through his biographer, John Aubrey, that the extraordinary timorousness which marked his whole life was due to the circumstances of his birth.[3] Hobbes was also the victim of what is now called a broken home. His father, the vicar of Westport, deserted his wife and children when Hobbes was still a boy.[4] In later life, Hobbes found even less peace and quiet. During the civil wars he was forced to flee to France. Later, he was allowed to live out a very long life in England only on the condition that he stay out of political controversies. The troubles of this period fell doubly hard on Hobbes because his doctrines alienated both republicans and royalists. He had little use for the democratic ideas of the groups around Cromwell. And his utilitarian doctrines dealt the divine-right royalists, whom he professed to support, a blow from which they never recovered.

Hobbes believed that peace through stability could be achieved by neither of these groups. Peace depended on government strong enough to crush all opposition, yet so *necessarily* absolute that it would be accepted without wide opposition. But how to demonstrate the necessity of an all-powerful government? The story told by Hobbes is that he chanced upon a copy of Euclid's *Elements of Geometry* in a friend's library. The book lay open at the forty-seventh proposition. "My God," he exclaimed, "this is impossible." But on discovering that it was not only possible but inescapable Hobbes fell "in love with geometry." [5] Here was a method for demonstrating the truth of propositions he had already conceived.

These propositions he determined to include in a work based on the two realities of life, as Euclid's geometry had been based on its first propositions. These two ultimate facts were matter and motion. From their interaction all else could be explained. The work he planned was to have three parts. The first, *De Corpore*, would deal with matter and mo-

[3] O. L. Dick, ed., *John Aubrey's Brief Lives* (1949), p. 156.

[4] Hobbes' father is pictured by Aubrey as being best known for his "ignorance and clownery." He remarks that "The old vicar Hobs was a good Fellow and had been at cards all Saturday night, and at church in his sleep he cries out *Trafells is troumps,* viz. clubs. Then quoth the Clark, *Then, Master, he that have Ace doe rub.*" *Ibid.,* p. 148.

[5] *Ibid.,* p. 150. This was, of course, the great age of mathematics and of the newly developed physical sciences. Hobbes served for a time as Francis Bacon's secretary and he came in contact with Descartes while in France. Thus it is not surprising that he believed politics could be reduced to a science no less exact than physics.

tion in general. The second, *De Homine*, would deal with motivation in man. And the third, *De Cive*, would deal with man in society or with the state. All three parts of this major work were finally completed. But Hobbes, in his desire for a stronger government, wrote the third part first.

He argued in this work, as he argued later in the *Leviathan*, that man in society is governed by a fundamental principle. This is a desire to seek pleasure and avoid pain. If human behavior is analyzed, it will be seen that this pleasure-pain mechanism explains action on all levels. Through the ego the living body seeks instinctively to preserve itself, and having secured this position, to heighten its "vitality" through the acquisition of more and more power.[6]

Turning from psychology to politics, Hobbes viewed man as living originally in a state of nature without the benefits of government. Individual egoism and the goal of self-preservation controlled all actions. It was a period which Hobbes describes as "solitary, poor, nasty, brutish, and short." [7] The trouble arose from every man being the equal of every other man. "Nature has made men so equal" that one man cannot claim for himself benefits to which another might not lay equal claim.[8] Nor do men vary so much that "the weakest has not strength enough to kill the strongest." [9] Men were beset, moreover, by the sins of competition, diffidence, and glory which provoked added strife and resulted in a perpetual war of "every man against every man." [10] During this period, nothing could be just or unjust because there was no law or notion of right and wrong. There was only "force and fraud."

Such a condition might have continued indefinitely except for two factors inherent in man—reason and fear of violent death. Man's reason discovered that peace has more utility [11] than war, and fear of violent death brought man's passions into line with his reason. Men agreed to two fundamental rules which are prerequisites of peace. The first is that "every man ought to endeavor peace, as far as he has hope of obtaining it." The second is that he must "be contented with so much liberty against other men, as he would allow other men against himself." [12] On this basis it was possible for men to covenant together one with the other, to establish a sovereign force to whom all authority was trans-

---

[6] *Leviathan*, Chap. 11. Egoism was thus accepted by Hobbes as a scientifically grounded principle of human behavior and was institutionalized as a social ideal. See G. H. Sabine, *A History of Political Theory*, rev. ed. (1950), pp. 461-464.

[7] *Leviathan*, Chap. 13.

[8] *Ibid.*

[9] *Ibid.*

[10] *Ibid.*

[11] Which is to say that it promotes pleasure and decreases pain.

[12] *Leviathan*, Chap. 14.

ferred. This force might be one man or a group of men. Its only essential characteristic was that it be all-powerful. Thus in order to guarantee peace, individuals were compelled to give up their natural rights to some "common power to keep them in awe, and to direct their actions to the common benefit." [13] The person or body who received this power was not, however, a party to the contract. He was, rather, the result of the covenant and was consequently above it. This left him free to exercise an unlimited power which could not be taken from him. Indeed, while he might delegate his powers, he could not divest himself of them. The contract once made could not be broken, since any one who refused to obey returned to the original state of war and could be destroyed.

While Hobbes did not insist that sovereignty should necessarily be vested in one man, he believed that monarchy was the most desirable form of government, since it was least subject to passion or to dissolution by civil war. He insisted that sovereignty was absolute and could not be divided, and that it must be located in a simple organ. The idea of limited monarchy was especially repugnant. Neither did Hobbes emphasize the formation of the state by a social contract as an actual historical occurrence. He viewed the state of nature rather as the logical and normal condition of mankind if unrestrained by a political system.

The right of subjects to resist, even in case of tyranny, was expressly denied. The punishment of unjust rulers must be left to God alone. The liberty of the subject consisted in whatever the sovereign did not forbid, and in such natural rights as men could not surrender, such as self-preservation and freedom from self-accusation. On the other hand, since the sovereign was established to furnish protection, the obligation of subjects was due only as long as the sovereign was able to fulfil this function. If a revolution prevailed against him, he had failed to keep the peace and to carry out the contract. His legal rights, therefore, had disappeared. In this part of his doctrine Hobbes was driven to logical confusion. He did not, however, approve of paternalistic government. Although the sovereign had the right to make laws in detail, he should in practice permit whatever did not disturb the peace. Laws should be few and simple. Hobbes had no conception of the state as a promoter of social welfare. The state was a necessary evil, needed to protect men from their savage instincts.

Hobbes defined law as the formal command of the sovereign, addressed to a subject, and clearly distinguished it from morality and from policy. The sovereign alone had the power to make and to repeal laws, but was himself above the law and not subject to it. Hobbes repudiated the law

[13] *Ibid.*

of nature, as it was generally held, saying that if it existed every man could interpret it in his own way. He swept away the support which the various English factions found in the moral law, in custom, and in precedent, and made the will of the sovereign authoritative. His doctrine that law is the command of a superior and that every law must be enforceable by punishment was taken over later by Austin. Hobbes taught, however, that no one was answerable if, through no fault of his own, he was ignorant of the law.

Hobbes held that the sovereign was supreme in spiritual as well as in temporal affairs, although in practice he advised religious toleration. The claims of Puritan and Catholic in the England of his day threatened the absolute sovereignty of the state which he considered essential. His strongest accusations were made against the Catholic Church, and he repudiated the pretensions of the ecclesiastical system and the dogmas with which it controlled men's minds. He was bitterly attacked by the clergy and accused of atheism; for years, every sort of free thought was stigmatized as Hobbism.

Hobbes' political system also attracted immediate attention. His style was so lucid that he gained a much wider audience than is usually afforded philosophers. It was commonly said of him that though he was basically in error, he erred so ingeniously that "one had rather erre with him than hitt the mark with Clavius." [14] This, however, must be taken only as a reference to his literary style, because the substance of his political philosophy found few immediate friends. Sterling Lamprecht states that "Hobbes' political philosophy was greeted in his own day by a more extensive and more virulent rejection than, probably, any other philosophy in modern times. Many of the pamphlets and broadsides directed at Hobbes have doubtless perished. But we can name fifty-one hostile criticisms which were printed against Hobbes during his lifetime and the next ensuing decade, and we know of only two defenses of him (both of which were composed by continental authors)!" [15]

No writer has taken a more extreme view than Hobbes of the absolute nature of sovereignty. While Machiavelli had separated politics from religion and morals in practice, Hobbes set politics above religion and morals in philosophic theory. While Bodin limited sovereignty by divine law, natural law, and the law of nations, Hobbes made sovereignty all-powerful and unlimited. While Grotius taught that the law of nature and of nations was binding upon all states, Hobbes taught that the law of nature and of nations, and even of God, was binding upon men only through the will of their own sovereign. States, he said, lived in a state of

[14] Dick, op. cit., p. 151.
[15] S. P. Lamprecht, ed., De Cive (1949), p. xx.

nature, and the law of nations was merely the dictates of reason as to the rules best adapted to secure the desires of each. While Hobbes' theory of sovereignty resulted in absolutism, it was nevertheless based upon the doctrine that all men are naturally equal, and upon a belief in the desirability of a large degree of individual freedom. The attempt to divert the social-contract theory to the support of absolutism was a complete failure, and the main line of development in the direction of revolution and democracy was taken up by Locke.

Political Theory of the Restoration

The restoration of the English monarchy in 1660 strengthened the alliance between the crown and the established church, and gave a new impetus to the doctrine of divine right and of passive submission. The popularity of Filmer's work indicated the dominant theory of the day. The Tories, as the supporters of the king and the Anglican Church were called, resisted every attempt of their opponents, the Whigs, to limit the royal authority or to liberalize existing institutions in church and state. They repudiated the theory that the state was based upon popular contract or that the people had any right to resist, even in case of tyranny. In the tide of reaction, Harrington was sent to the Tower and Milton's works were burned by the hangman.

The Protestant sects urged religious toleration,[16] but ceased to take an active part in politics; and the radical political and economic theories which they had urged practically disappeared. Fear of the Protestant dissenters and of the Catholics prevented toleration. During this period the church party was inclined to treat the dissenters liberally, but feared the Catholics. Charles II, however, had no interest in the Protestant sects, but was inclined to favor the Catholics. The accession of James II, an avowed Catholic, united Anglican and dissenter, revived the old issue of royal prerogative, and brought the Whig party into power. The deposition of James, the accession of William and Mary by act of a revolutionary convention, and the passing of the Bill of Rights marked the final success of the parliamentary over the royalist theory of government. The Revolution of 1688, however, was the work of conservative and practical men who had little confidence in republican government or in theories of equality. While they opposed the doctrine of divine right, they desired a limited monarchy and an aristocratic control of government. This point of view, characteristic of the Whigs in English politics, was represented in the political philosophy of John Locke.

[16] See Andrew Marvell's *The Rehearsal Transposed;* and William Penn's *Great Case of Liberty of Conscience* (1671), and *England's Present Interest Discovered* (1675).

Even before Locke, the challenge thrown down by Filmer had been taken up by Algernon Sydney (1622-1683), a leader of the more advanced Whigs and a firm believer in liberty. Sydney was charged with treason and executed after the Rye House Plot, one of the accusations being the nature of the doctrines in his unpublished book.[17] He made a reasoned indictment of divine right, and restated the doctrine that authority rests upon public consent. Sydney displayed an enormous amount of historical learning and was especially attracted by the Roman commonwealth. In many ways his *Discourses* resembled Machiavelli's *Discourses on Livy*.

Sydney followed Milton in expounding the theory of limited contract, in which the people, delegating certain powers to their ruler, reserved certain liberties to themselves. He also argued that the contract bound only those who made it, or at most their descendants; and that it remained in force only so long as the ruler used his delegated authority for the public good. Sydney praised liberty, but disliked equality. He favored a moderate and constitutional system. He kept alive the flame of liberty during the dark days of the Restoration, and gave an impetus to the constitutional revolution of 1688 which finally destroyed, in England, the theory of divine right.

The most original thinker of the Restoration period, George Savile, Marquis of Halifax (1633-1695),[18] steered a middle course in the conflict between Whigs and Tories. Though he never wrote a comprehensive treatise, his pamphlets, full of wit and brilliant aphorisms, were marked by deep thought and observation. Halifax was a conservative by temperament, and favored a moderate policy of compromise. Like Hobbes, he held a pessimistic view of human nature. He opposed persecution and violence, and wished to avoid civil war. He advocated a limited monarchy and a restrained individual liberty, and supported legal and constitutional methods. He favored toleration of non-conformists and of Catholics, although he would exclude the latter from office. In foreign policy he believed that England should form an entente with Holland, and should hold the balance of power between France and Spain; and that Cromwell had made a mistake in supporting the stronger rather than the weaker state. He insisted upon the importance of a strong navy as the basis of England's security. Halifax approached politics in an empirical spirit and tested theories by their workings. He opposed both the divine-right theory of the monarchists and the natural-right theory of the republicans. In an

[17] His *Discourses Concerning Government*, prepared as a reply to Filmer's *Patriarcha*, but not published until 1698. This book was eagerly studied in both the old and new world during the eighteenth century.

[18] See his *The Character of a Trimmer* (1684), written in answer to Roger L'Estrange's attack upon him in *The Observator*. Also his *Letter to a Dissenter* (1694). His *Thoughts and Reflections* were published in 1750, long after his death.

age when most men appealed to Scripture and to precedent, or to the precepts of natural law, the modernity of his thought is most refreshing.

The theories of the Whigs, especially as they were put forward by Sydney and Locke, found many advocates in France. Sydney's *Discourses* were translated into French in 1702 and read by Rousseau. Bourdaloue, the famous preacher at the court of Louis XIV, preached his ideas in the presence of the king. In 1750 d'Argenson wrote: "The English ideas on politics and liberty have passed the sea and are being adopted here." [19] In America the Whig doctrines were accepted by the colonists and embodied in the Declaration of Independence and the Bills of Rights.

Locke

The theorist of the Revolution of 1688 was John Locke (1632-1704), whose chief political work [20] was a philosophic defense of the parliamentary party. Locke came under the liberalizing influences that were beginning to be felt in England. He was confidential secretary to Lord Shaftesbury, the founder of the Whig party, and he had some experience in practical politics. He opposed the ecclesiastical and political methods in force during the later Stuart period. He attacked both the divine-right theory of the Anglicans and of Filmer, and the theory of absolutism which Hobbes had deduced from the social contract. At the same time, he had no sympathy with the extremist doctrines held by the radical Whigs.

The first of Locke's two treatises was written to disprove the doctrine of royal prerogatives based upon divine right. It followed the method of Sydney in refuting point by point the arguments of Filmer's *Patriarcha*. His second treatise, *Of Civil Government,* was a comprehensive and systematic discussion of the origin, nature, and province of government. It was, implicitly, a reply to Hobbes, although Locke noticeably avoided a deliberate refutation of the *Leviathan.* He acknowledged his indebtedness to Hooker, from whom he derived his main ideas. He agreed with Hobbes in his individualistic point of view and in his dependence upon the social-contract theory, but he rejected almost every premise of Hobbes' philosophy.

According to Locke,[21] the original state of nature was one in which

---

[19] J. Texte, *Rousseau et les origines du cosmopolitisme littéraire* (1895), pp. 25-26.

[20] His *Two Treatises of Government* (1690). See Sherman's edition (1937). The *Letter on Toleration* (1685) gives his views on the relation of church to state.

[21] The following discussion is primarily concerned with Locke's political ideas. In the realm of philosophy Locke was instrumental in establishing the divergent philosophy of empiricism. The logical difficulties of these two positions seem not to have bothered Locke. He never faced the difficulty of proclaiming the existence of certain innate concepts, such as natural rights, on the one hand, while demonstrating on the

peace and reason prevailed. It was pre-political, but not pre-social. It was not lawless, since men lived under natural law, which Locke, following Grotius, defined as a body of rules determined by reason, for the guidance of men in their natural condition. Under the law of nature all men were equal and possessed equal natural rights. Following the Independents, Locke defined these as the rights to life, liberty, and property. Of these three, property properly came first and was the most important. Locke believed that the right of property included the right of a man to his person and that this was the basis of his rights of life and liberty. Private property came into existence through the labor a man incorporated into some object. If his efforts increased the value of a piece of land, that increased value was due solely to him and he must be allowed to profit from it. This, in simple form, was Locke's celebrated labor theory of value. Its effects were twofold and are still being felt. It advanced the cause of capitalism by justifying free enterprise and the profit system. And it was used by Karl Marx and others as a support for modern socialism. Marx argued that if a thing were given value by the labor expended in producing it, the *laborer* rather than the owning class should receive the full value of his production.

The absence in this natural state, to return to Locke, of any agreement as to what constituted the law of nature, and of any judge to settle disputes, as well as the inability of the individual to maintain his natural rights against injustice, led to uncertainties which became intolerable. Accordingly, the individuals, by means of a social contract, formed a body politic, giving up their personal right to interpret and administer the law of nature in return for a guarantee that their natural rights to life, liberty, and property would be preserved. The contract was thus specific and limited, not general as Hobbes had said. Moreover, the power given up was not vested in a single man or organ, but in the community as a whole. Even the sovereignty of the political community, or state, was not absolute, it having only the power to protect natural law. The word "sovereignty," indeed, does not occur in Locke's treatise.

Such a contract involved the necessity of majority rule. Each individual surrendered to the community his right to execute natural law; hence the minority must be bound by the will of the majority, who might use force if necessary. The consent of individuals to membership in the political community might be expressed or tacit. Tacit consent was given by remaining in the community or holding property in it. Thus the effect of

---

other that no idea is innate because all ideas have an empirical origin. This latter point of view is discussed in his *Essay concerning Human Understanding*.

the original contract was made binding upon the descendants of its founders. Locke was more inclined than Hobbes to view the contract as an historical occurrence, although he deemed its implications more important than its origin.

Locke recognized, though he did not explicitly describe, the distinction between state and government. At times he approximated a secondary contract by which government was created after the establishment of civil society. While the earlier anti-monarchists had emphasized the "governmental contract" between people and king, by which the authority of the ruler was created, both Hobbes and Locke emphasized the "social contract" among the people by which the state was formed. Locke followed the Aristotelian tradition in dividing governments into monarchies, aristocracies, and democracies, considering the location of legislative authority as the fundamental test. The executive and the judiciary he viewed as clearly dependent upon the lawmaking body. Locke did not, however, develop the theory of separation of powers implicit in his discussion. He considered a limited democracy, in the hands of delegates controlled by election, the best form of government. He was willing to have a king if the king were divested of his lawmaking power and if his right to rule were acknowledged to depend upon popular consent. The connection between his ideas and the conditions in England is obvious.

While Locke viewed the legislature as the supreme organ of government, its powers were not to be absolute. Behind it stood the community, which retained its natural rights, and which might dissolve the government if it acted contrary to its trust. When injustice became obvious, the people might resist the civil authority. There was need of rebellion, Locke stated, whenever the government endeavored to invade the property of the subject and to make itself the "arbitrary disposer of the lives, liberties, or fortunes of the people." [22] This right of revolution was qualified in only two ways. Force was not to be used except in the most serious cases. And only the majority could act to overthrow the government. Because of its influence on Jefferson and others, Locke's theory of revolt must be considered one of the most important parts of his doctrine.

In the relation of church to state, Locke denied that any theocratic government could claim political validity. He held that the state should deal only with the preservation of social order, not with the souls of men. He considered the church a voluntary society, without the right of coercion; and he favored toleration in religion. The state should suppress opinions only when they were subversive of public peace. Catholics,

[22] *Two Treatises of Government,* Chap. 19.

Mohammedans, and atheists alone were not to be tolerated. Catholics owed allegiance to a foreign power; Mohammedan morals were incompatible with English civilization; atheists lacked a sanction for good conduct.

While Locke's theory contained little that had not been worked out by previous thinkers, it added definiteness to the ideas of natural rights, popular control, and the right of resistance. It also emphasized the individualistic implications of the social-contract idea. While Hobbes aimed to make authority absolute, Locke wished to establish its limitations. He emphasized the importance of consent and, like Hobbes, considered the happiness of the individual of prime importance. He overemphasized human rationalism and the artificial nature of human society, not realizing the organic nature of the state, as Rousseau did later. Locke's theory was also more purely political than that of his predecessors. He was not concerned, like earlier anti-monarchists, in opposing a religious tyrant. He separated church and state, not to secure ecclesiastical independence, but in order to assert the preëminence of the state itself.

Locke's theory, essentially moderate and practical, lacked the clarity and logic of Hobbes, but it adhered more closely to the problems of the time. It aimed to establish governmental channels by which popular consent could make itself effective and individual liberty could be safeguarded. While Locke's propositions were guarded by practical reservations on all sides, his theory, in spite of half-truths and hesitations, corresponded to the system established by the Whig leaders in England. It justified capitalism, and it eased the burden of their action against James II.

The influence of Locke on later writers was extensive. William Molyneaux embodied his ideas in his demand for Irish freedom. French Huguenots and the Dutch adopted many of his doctrines. Montesquieu made Locke's separation of powers the main idea in his work. Locke's theories were developed by Rousseau into an even more daring form of social contract and were pushed to their logical limits in the French Revolution. In America the authors of the Declaration of Independence and of the American Constitution drew largely upon Locke's ideas. Locke reflected more faithfully than any thinker before him the forces that were making for enlightenment. He represented the modern spirit of independence, of criticism, of individualism, and of democracy, that had sought utterance in the religious Reformation and in the political revolution of the seventeenth century, and that reached its climax in the intellectual, political, and economic revolutions of the eighteenth century. No philosopher was more important in impressing his thought on the minds and institutions of men.

REFERENCES

CZAJKOWSKI, C. J., *The Theory of Private Property in John Locke's Political Philosophy* (Notre Dame, Univ. of Notre Dame, 1941).

DICK, O. L., ed., *John Aubrey's Brief Lives* (London, Secker & Warburg, 1949), pp. 147-160.

FOXCROFT, H. C., *A Character of the Trimmer: Being a Short Life of the First Marquis of Halifax* (Cambridge, Cambridge Univ. Press, 1946).

GOUGH, J. W., *John Locke's Political Philosophy* (Oxford, Clarendon Press, 1950).

KENDALL, Willmoore, *John Locke and the Doctrine of Majority Rule* (Urbana, Univ. of Illinois Press, 1941).

LAIRD, John, *Hobbes* (London, Benn, 1934).

LAMPRECHT, S. P., "Hobbes and Hobbism," *American Political Science Review*, Vol. 34 (February, 1940).

———, *The Moral and Political Philosophy of John Locke* (New York, Columbia Univ. Press, 1918).

LANDRY, Bernard, *Hobbes* (Paris, Alcan, 1930).

LARKIN, Pascal, *Property in the Eighteenth Century, with Special Reference to England and Locke* (Cork, Cork Univ. Press, 1930).

LASKI, H. J., *Political Thought in England from Locke to Bentham* (New York, Holt, 1920), Chaps. 1-2.

SABINE, G. H., *A History of Political Theory*, rev. ed. (New York, Holt, 1950), Chaps. 23, 26.

STRAUSS, Leo, *The Political Philosophy of Hobbes*, trans. by Elsa Sinclair (Oxford, Clarendon Press, 1936).

TEXTE, Joseph, *Rousseau et les origines du cosmopolitisme littéraire* (Paris, Hachette, 1895), pp. 25 ff.

CHAPTER XV ⚞

From Spinoza to Hume

Continental Politics in the Seventeenth Century

On the continent, political interest centered, during the first half of the seventeenth century, in the Thirty Years' War. This contest, which began because of religious hostilities in Germany, finally involved a number of the European powers and became increasingly political in its motives. At its close, the Peace of Westphalia (1648), formulated by the first great international conference, marked the beginnings of a new era in European politics. Differences in religious beliefs became a less important issue. The preëminence of the papacy in European diplomacy was no longer recognized. The traditional unity and importance of the Holy Roman Empire was also much weakened. Powerful new states had arisen outside its boundaries; Germany was split up into numerous independent fragments; and the emperor was practically limited to his Hapsburg domains.

The principles of Grotius exerted a strong influence on the Peace of Westphalia; and the idea of sovereign, independent states, each the property of its monarch, forming a family of European nations under international law, was generally accepted. The doctrines of the concert of powers and of the balance of power began to dominate European diplomacy. Spain, the most powerful state in the sixteenth century, was so obviously weakened that the stronger states began to scheme for the partitioning of her empire. France, through the genius of men like Richelieu and Mazarin, had become the leading power in Europe. She had also worked out, in her internal government, the most centralized and powerful national monarchy.

Political interest during the second half of the seventeenth century centered in the ambitious policies of France under Louis XIV. The period was characterized by strong rulers, absolute dynastic governments within the states, and aggressive, unscrupulous foreign policy among them. Rulers looked upon their states as their personal possessions, aimed to expand their territories, and placed their dynastic aggrandizement above the interests of their peoples. Colonial and commercial rivalries were keen, each state aiming to gain at the expense of its neighbors. Economic interests and foreign trade policies began to play an important part in political thought. The accession of William of Orange to the English throne in 1688 brought England into the full current of European politics. She helped to defend Holland against Louis XIV and became the chief rival of France. A contest which lasted until the nineteenth century was thus begun.

During the wars growing out of the ambitions of Louis XIV some progress in the development of international law was made. The rights and immunities of legations were generally recognized. Intervention to maintain the balance of power in Europe was constantly discussed in the laborious state papers of the period. The laws of maritime warfare also became more generally known and followed. Much of this was due to the survival of the earlier maritime codes, such as the *Consolato del Mare*, whose principles were commonly recognized by the leading European states. In 1681, however, the famous French Marine Ordinance [1] was issued, which extended the claims of belligerents to interfere with neutral trade. The doctrine of the freedom of the seas, in spite of Selden's arguments to the contrary,[2] was generally conceded; and some rules were laid down regarding visit and search, blockade, and contraband.

Conditions on the continent were not favorable to the development of political theory. Spain, whose writers had been important in the preceding century, became intellectually stagnant. In France the only important work was a eulogy of divine-right monarchy along theological lines. In Germany and Holland, where there was more of theological and intellectual liberalism and less of political absolutism, the rational methods of Hobbes and Grotius were continued, and the political thought of England was introduced into Europe. As usual in times of political disturbance, chief interest centered in the moral aspects of political theory, both in the relations of rulers to subjects and in the relations among states.

Political Thought in Holland

Grotius' doctrine of sovereignty and certain of Hobbes' psychological and political ideas were developed in Holland during the seventeenth

[1] See Henry Wheaton, *History of the Law of Nations* (1845), pp. 107-161.
[2] In his *Mare clausum seu de dominio maris* (1635).

century by a Portuguese Jew resident in the United Provinces, Benedict Spinoza (1632-1677).[3]

Spinoza, though best known for his work in the fields of religion and ethics, was also concerned with the political problems of his day. He agreed with Hobbes that self-interest is the chief motive of human action, but he believed in an enlightened self-interest which Hobbes did not contemplate. Spinoza viewed the state not as a necessary evil, but as a positive good. It was created not through fear, but because of the realization that it could promote general happiness. The state came into existence through a voluntary compact by which the powers of its individuals were combined, and their natural rights to do what seemed for their separate advantage were resigned in favor of a ruling power which employed the natural right of the whole community. Spinoza, however, gave little attention to the details of the contract, to its legal connotations, or to the exact nature of the sovereignty thus created. He was more detached than Hobbes from the practical politics of his time. This aided him in distinguishing the state, as the possessor of sovereignty, from the person of the ruler. While he insisted upon the unity of the state, he viewed this unity as the rational unity of the wills of all members in the state, or at least of a majority of them, rather than that of an individual personal will. He suggested the organic unity of the state, and conceived its sovereignty as resting upon the common reason or general mind of its members. These ideas later became central points in Rousseau's theory of the general will. The sovereign power was thus distinguished from the particular organ which exercised it. State and government were clearly separated. In discussing forms of government, Spinoza leaned toward an aristocratic republic. He had little sympathy with radical democracy, and he believed that a monarchy, in the sense that one man actually possessed and exercised sovereign power, was in theory indefensible and in practice impossible.

Hobbes was concerned primarily about establishing the absolute nature of sovereignty; Spinoza, on the contrary, aimed to secure the liberty of the individual. The preservation of individual liberty, so that men could live according to reason, was for him the chief end of the state. Accordingly, the power of the state was limited by the natural rights of its members to acts that made for general welfare. Efficiency was the test by which the sovereign should be judged. Its authority was coextensive with its power to afford aid against wrong doers; or, as stated later by Austin, the rights which it recognized were those for which it had provided a remedy. The right to rule lapsed if the conditions essential to a rational life could not

[3] In his *Tractatus Theologica-Politicus* (1670), his *Tractatus Politicus* (1677), and his *Ethics* (1677).

be maintained. The value of freedom of thought and of expression was especially emphasized by Spinoza, not only because it was essential to the proper development and dignity of the individual, but even more because it was essential to the security and welfare of the state. Conscious of religious intolerance, Spinoza was also a strong supporter of religious freedom. Spinoza's conception of rights marked a distinct advance upon that of Hobbes. Hobbes believed that men have natural rights apart from the state. Spinoza held that individuals have no rights except those bestowed upon them by the state. All rights must flow from the consciousness of a common interest on the part of the members of the state; every right implies recognition by the common will.

In the international field, Spinoza adopted many of the ideas of Machiavelli, for whom he expressed warm admiration. The difficulties that confronted the Netherlands in the diplomacy of Europe were similar to those of the Italian cities in the fifteenth century. Her aristocratic governmental institutions also suggested the earlier systems of Florence and Venice. Spinoza, like Machiavelli, held that the principles applicable to individuals could not always be applied to states. The duty of the state is to safeguard the interests of its individuals; it cannot therefore be bound by treaties which would interfere with its main end. War among states he believed to be inevitable, unless an organized force stronger than any one of them was established. Federation among states was a desirable means of diminishing war.

The political works of Spinoza remained practically unknown on the continent for a century, political speculation taking other directions. His pantheistic religious ideas aroused intense indignation, and he was generally viewed as an atheist. The nationality of the author and the undeserved disrepute which a prejudiced age attached to his works prevented them from affecting the practical politics of Europe. Locke, who was familiar with the writings of European philosophers, was probably influenced by the ideas of Spinoza, his treatment of individual liberty being markedly similar. And many of the ideas of Spinoza were adopted later by Rousseau, through whom they were brought into contact with the revolutionary movements in Europe.

Political Thought in Germany

The period in Germany following the Reformation, occupied by barren theological controversies and by the Thirty Years' War, was not conducive to political speculation. With the division of the country into independent principalities, the spirit of nationalism declined. Germans became ashamed of their language and of their culture, and modeled their manners and their political institutions upon the paternalistic French court. The first representative of rationalistic thought and of modern enlightenment in Germany was Samuel Pufendorf (1632-1694).[4] In a manner similar to Spinoza, Pufendorf attempted to reconcile the absolute theory of sovereignty of Hobbes and the limited, ethical sovereignty of Grotius. His method was distinctly rationalistic, avoiding both the classical references of Grotius and the Scriptural quotations of Hobbes. He was especially bitter against the obscure and mystical doctrines of the theologians of his day, who upheld the theory of divine right. The basis of Pufendorf's theory was the concept of natural law, which he developed into an elaborate system of political philosophy. He followed Grotius in defining the law of nature as the dictates of reason concerning right and wrong; at the same time he inclined toward the utilitarianism of Hobbes, viewing self-interest as the dominant motive in human conduct and judging institutions largely on the grounds of expediency.

Pufendorf began with the state of nature, which he viewed as an historical as well as a logical condition of mankind. The social instinct of men drew them together into society, in which, however, natural law alone held sway and human authority was lacking. In the state of nature men were wretched, since the majority lived by impulse rather than by reason, and were essentially selfish. Pufendorf did not agree with Hobbes that the state of nature was one of constant warfare, though he did agree that it was an intolerable condition in which right and justice could not be maintained against the ignorance and irrationality of the majority of human beings. In order to escape from the evils resulting from the imperfections of human nature, a civil society was established by means of a voluntary contract. This contract was twofold. Both the social contract of Hobbes and the governmental contract of the earlier anti-monarchists were considered essential. First, the individuals formed an agreement among themselves to establish a state, and decided by majority vote what form of government they desired. Second, a compact was made between the community as a whole and the designated holders of governing power, the former promising obedience, the latter agreeing to execute their authority so as to promote the general welfare.

The sovereignty thus established was, however, not absolute. It was supreme, in the sense that there was no higher human authority and no human law to which it was subject. It was, on the contrary, limited by the law of nature and of God, by custom and by ancient usage, and by the purpose for which it was established. States as well as individuals must conform to the law of reason as interpreted by sane and intelligent

---

[4] In his *De Jure Naturæ et Gentium* (1672), trans. by B. Kennett. The *De Officio Hominis et Civis* (1673) was an abridgement of the earlier work.

men. The sovereign possessed the highest power, but it did not possess all power. Pufendorf followed Grotius rather than Hobbes in this part of his work. He recognized an elective or limited king as a genuine sovereign, and believed that the participation of a parliament in legislation did not detract from the sovereignty of a monarch.

Pufendorf taught that the law of nations was that part of the law of nature which dealt with the relations among states. Its rules were discoverable by reason from the tendency of actions to promote general welfare. He expressly denied, however, that there was any positive or voluntary law of nations based upon general consent. On this point he agreed with Hobbes rather than with Grotius, identifying the *jus naturae* and the *jus gentium,* and denying the existence of any binding rules among states, resting upon custom or treaties, or upon the general practices of nations. Pufendorf occupied the first university chair founded for the study of the Law of Nature and Nations.[5]

The theory of Pufendorf, partly because of its moderate and somewhat contradictory nature, became widely influential. It reconciled the benevolent despotism of the German states with the spirit of individual freedom by allowing supremacy to the sovereign of the state and at the same time denying to it absolute control over the lives and actions of the members of the state. The theory of Pufendorf, with slight changes made by his followers, remained the dominant theory in Germany until the time of Kant. It was opposed by Gottfried Leibnitz, who objected to the effort of the rationalists to separate natural law from theology, and by Johann Horn, who upheld the theory of divine right.[6] The German theologians, in general, opposed it because it found a standard of social and political institutions in human reason, apart from the teachings of religion. Among the leading rationalists who followed in the footsteps of Pufendorf were Wolff and Thomasius.

Political Thought in France

During the reign of Louis XIII (1610-1643), political thought in France gradually abandoned the doctrine of Bodin that there were certain fundamental laws of the kingdom which not even the crown might transgress, and adopted the view that there were no limitations upon royal power except those found in the king's conscience. During the reign of Louis XIV (1643-1715), the dominant political theory justified absolute monarchy as the best form of government, magnified the king as the direct agent of God on earth, ruling by divine right, insisted upon the absolute

[5] Established by the Elector Palatine at Heidelberg in 1661.
[6] In his *Politicorum Pars Architectonica de Civitate* (1664).

submission of subjects, and maintained the independence of the Gallican church under the king against the claims of the pope. France was the strongest power in Europe, and the ambitious policy of her kings included extensive schemes of expansion abroad and of royal absolutism at home. In the early part of Louis XIV's reign, the Fronde tried in vain to check the growth of absolutist theory. In the later part of his reign, when the heavy expenditures caused by constant wars and by the extravagance of the court resulted in widespread economic distress, occasional criticism of the *grand monarque* was heard. Thus, Marshall Vauban,[7] famous for his skill in military engineering, proposed a revision of taxation in the interest of the people. He regarded labor, especially in agriculture, as the foundation of wealth, and was a pioneer of the single tax. Pierre Boisguilbert, in discussing the condition of the public finances,[8] questioned the wisdom of the royal policy. He argued that wealth depended upon a natural harmony of industry, not upon political polity, and urged equality in the distribution of taxes. Fénelon, in his liberal literary works,[9] questioned the desirability of personal rule over a great people and favored freedom of trade. In general, however, political thought, mainly the work of theologians, was completely subservient to the will of the king. Cardinal Richelieu,[10] the famous minister of Louis XIII, was especially influential in furthering the belief that the royal power was unlimited. He put forward the doctrine of the *raison d'État* to justify his policies.

The divine nature of kingly power was set forth with especial eloquence and ardor by the distinguished orator and theologian, Bishop Jacques Bossuet (1627-1704), whom Louis XIV chose as the preceptor of his son. Bossuet's treatise on politics [11] was written for the purpose of giving the heir to the French throne a proper idea of his lofty position and of his responsibilities. In general, Bossuet followed the scholastic method of laying down fundamental principles and supporting them by ingenious use of Scriptural quotations. At the same time, he was considerably influenced by the rationalistic methods of contemporary philosophers, especially of Hobbes, whose works had been translated into French and were popular because of their support of absolutism in government.

Bossuet justified government on the ground of the necessity of regu-

[7] In his *Project for a Royal Tythe* (1707).
[8] In his *Détail de la France sous le règne présent* (1697), *and his Factum de la France* (1707).
[9] Especially in his *Télémaque* (1699).
[10] Probably the author of the *Testament politique*.
[11] The *La Politique tirée de l'Écriture Sainte* (1709). See also his *Avertissements aux Protestants* (1689-91).

lating the evil passions of mankind. Hereditary monarchy he held to be the oldest and most natural form of government, being modeled on the authority of the father in the family. Royalty was sacred, and it was sacrilege to attack the person of the king. "Kings should be guarded as holy things." Royalty was paternal, requiring the king to care for his subjects as a father does for his children. Royalty was absolute, in that the king was obliged to render account for his conduct to no one, and that subjects must render passive obedience. At the same time, royalty was subject to reason, that is, it must not be exercised arbitrarily. The king was an embodiment of the divine majesty and must act accordingly. He must maintain religion and justice. The king was regarded, not as a private person, but as a public personage. "All the state is in him; the will of all the people is included in his." Bossuet added the characteristic of sacredness to the attributes of sovereignty already developed. At the same time, he laid great emphasis upon the moral responsibility of rulers. "Kings must exercise their power with fear and self-restraint, as a thing coming from God and of which God will demand an account." The arguments of Bossuet were echoed by a host of lesser writers; the doctrines of the Politiques were victorious, those of the anti-monarchists were for the time crushed out.

The First Half of the Eighteenth Century

The first half of the eighteenth century was marked by no work in political philosophy of first rank. Some progress was made on the continent in the development of international law. In England the critical attack on the theory of social contract was begun. In general, however, the period was one of relatively small importance in the development of political thought, in striking contrast to the active century in England which preceded it and the equally important period in France and in America which followed it.

On the continent, chief political interest centered in the series of dynastic wars that originated in the ambitions of Louis XIV and finally involved all the leading states of Europe. France and England were the chief rivals in western Europe, carrying on a contest for colonial empire in America and India, for control of the sea, and for preëminence in European diplomacy. In central Europe, Prussia and Austria stood opposed, beginning their contest for headship in Germany. Numerous alliances and treaties were concluded in the efforts of the great states to win advantages or of the smaller states to safeguard their independence or to maintain the balance of power. Wars were waged, not in the interests of the people, but for the advantage of the ruling dynasties—Hapsburg,

Bourbon, or Hohenzollern—who exercised absolute and despotic authority and looked upon their states as their personal possessions. Agriculture and industry within the states, and commerce among them, were also viewed as sources of profit to the rulers. Foreign and colonial trade were strictly regulated in the interest of the government, and mercantilist ideas flourished. The identification of the state with the monarch prevented extensive speculation concerning the nature or location of sovereignty. Locke's ideas had not yet influenced the continent; divine-right absolutism was little questioned. Continental thought during the period dealt mainly with the relations among states.

However, the foundations were being laid in France for the revolutionary doctrines of the second half of the century. After the death of Louis XIV (1715) the liberalist spirit made rapid headway. English thought, with the exception of the philosophy of Hobbes, was practically unknown in France during the reign of the *grand monarque*. In the half-century following there was scarcely a Frenchman of importance who did not either visit England or learn the English language. Among those who were especially impressed by English governmental institutions and ideas were Voltaire, Montesquieu, Gournay, and Mirabeau. The writings of Locke became widely accepted, and the rationalist and critical thought of Shaftesbury and Hume worked as a leaven in French philosophy. The study of the English Revolution and of the nature of the constitutional system that resulted from it was largely responsible for the revival of interest in political theory in France, and for the creation of a philosophical basis for the French Revolution in the work of Rousseau. In the first half of the eighteenth century French writers attacked the church; in the second half of the century the opposition turned against the state.

In England the period following the Revolution of 1688 was marked by the establishment of parliamentary and party government. The principle that the king must govern through ministers who command the confidence of the lawmaking body was definitely accepted. The effort of James II to restore Catholicism had temporarily united Whigs and Tories, but with the accession of William and Mary party lines again diverged. In general, the Tories favored the return of the Stuart line, as legitimate monarchs by divine right; the Whigs supported the Revolution of 1688 and later favored the accession of the Hanoverians. The attempt to ignore party divisions in choosing ministers proved a failure, and the monarchs were compelled increasingly to recognize party divisions in parliament in choosing their advisers.

The success of the Whig party in securing the Hanoverian succession on the death of Queen Anne in 1714 placed it securely in power, and there was not another Tory government until the middle of the century.

During this period the original issues separating the parties largely disappeared. The Tories gradually abandoned the doctrine of divine right and ceased to expect the restoration of a Stuart king. On the other hand, the Whigs, once they came into actual power, ceased to distrust royal authority and strong government. Contest for office rather than differences in policy formed the basis of party division. Both parties supported and praised the constitutional system that had been worked out; and political theory consisted mainly of an analysis of its nature and of discussions as to whether its principles were being maintained by the group controlling the government. The adjustment of the relation of church to state also led to much discussion.

The idea of natural law exerted a peculiar attraction during the eighteenth century. It was a time when the historical spirit was lacking and when men had little reverence for the past. They wished to be freed from antiquated customs and institutions. No other age had such faith in the possibility of perfection, reason being regarded as a panacea for all human ills. The simple laws of nature were regarded as preferable to the numerous and conflicting laws of the state; men were restive under the intolerable meddling of the benevolent despots. As a reaction against centralization and paternalism, they desired individual liberty, and wished to limit state interference to a minimum. The belief in inalienable natural rights led to the idea that governments which encroached upon these rights were tyrannical. The belief in the equality of men and of their natural rights was in striking contrast to the actual condition of affairs in Europe. Men were becoming dissatisfied and critical, and were beginning to inquire how the state should be organized to conform to the laws of nature. In the middle portion of the century, the benevolent despots tried to apply the principles of natural law in a paternalistic way; in the later part the people took its application into their own hands in the French Revolution.

Pufendorf's Followers in Germany

At the opening of the eighteenth century, the German principalities were absolutist in government and reactionary and obscurantist in their intellectual life. Theological influences dominated, although the followers of Pufendorf tried to maintain his rationalist point of view. The leading writers of this group were Christian Thomasius (1655-1728) [12] and Christian Wolff (1679-1754).[13] Thomasius separated the sciences of law and morals and distinguished between natural and positive law. He also

[12] In his *Fundamenta juris naturæ et gentium* (1705).
[13] In his *Die Politik* (1721), and his *Institutiones juris naturæ et gentium* (1750).

distinguished between natural rights, inherent in man, and acquired rights, resulting from human laws. Freedom, the common ownership of nature's gifts, and the rights to life and to one's own thoughts were natural rights; the possession of property and the exercise of authority were acquired rights.

Wolff, a professor at Halle, enjoyed an almost incredible reputation. In France his popularity was so great that for a time it seemed as if his works would supplant those of the English writers. He developed the political ideas of Grotius and of Pufendorf along lines similar to Locke, discussing the law of nature, the law of nations, and the theory of the state. He deduced natural law from the moral nature of man, and natural rights from the innate moral duties of man. He held that all men are equal because their rights and duties are equal, and that no man has any power over another by nature. The state came into existence through the voluntary surrender of the natural rights of individuals, each giving up only so much as was necessary to secure the common good. The purpose of the state was the realization of common safety and the promotion of individual welfare.

The work of Thomasius and Wolff was especially valuable in the development of international law. Thomasius distinguished between the perfect and the imperfect duties of states. Wolff's treatment was abstract and mathematical, but was important because of the attempt to simplify his ideas and to introduce them to men of letters and to statesmen which was undertaken by the Swiss jurist, Emeric de Vattel (1714-1767). The influence of Vattel's work [14] on the conduct of international relations was second only to that of Grotius. He followed Pufendorf in basing the law of nations upon the law of nature. He added, however, a positive law of nations, based upon general consent, expressed or tacit, which was to be observed as long as it did not violate the precepts of natural law. Vattel's work enjoyed great renown in both Europe and America, and was frequently quoted by Otis, Samuel Adams, John Adams, Hamilton, and Jefferson.

Although Thomasius and Wolff were lacking in originality, they gave a great impetus to the rational enlightenment of Germany through the common-sense presentation of their philosophy and because they used the German language. They believed that ideas should be derived from reason and from experience, and they were bitterly opposed by the German mystics and Pietists. Wolff's ideas remained the dominant system in Germany until about the middle of the eighteenth century, when English thought began to exert an influence through translations of the

[14] *Le droit des gens* (1758).

works of Locke, Hume, Shaftesbury, and Ferguson. As a result, rationalist methods and ideals transformed the prevalent absolutist political theory, and doctrines of equality and natural rights became popular even at the courts of the rulers.

In 1740 Frederick the Great assumed the throne of Prussia and threw his influence on the side of the liberals. The way was thus opened for a brilliant period of intellectual activity during the remainder of the century. Even before he came to the throne, Frederick had accepted the doctrine of natural law,[15] admiring especially the philosophy of Locke. He sympathized with the enlightened scholars of the period, restored Wolff to his university chair from which the theologians had forced him, and invited the critical and free-thinking Voltaire to make his home at Berlin. Frederick attacked the doctrine of divine right, believed that kings ruled by the consent of their subjects, and emphasized the duties rather than the privileges of monarchs. He refuted the prevalent theory that the people and territory of a state were the private possessions of the ruler, and asserted that the monarch is the first servant of the state, his rule being justified only in proportion as it secures the welfare of his subjects.

In his *Anti-Machiavel*, he criticized the doctrine that rulers should not be judged by ordinary standards of morality, and he opposed Machiavelli's favorable attitude toward "ideas of interest, of grandeur, of ambition, and of despotism." Though wielding despotic power after he came to the Prussian throne, Frederick was influenced by considerations of justice and of morality, and did not use his power for personal ends. In furthering the interests of Prussia, he was, however, compelled to adopt some of the methods which he had most severely condemned. The influence of natural law may be seen in his famous code of laws. It says: "The good of the state, and of its inhabitants in particular, is the end of civil association and the universal object of the laws. The laws and ordinances of the state may not limit the natural liberty and rights of the citizens any further than the above mentioned object requires."

An enthusiastic follower of Frederick was the "enlightened despot," Joseph II of Austria. He was schooled in the principles of natural law and tried to apply them to existing conditions. He had, indeed, a passion for reforming, and said that when he ascended the throne he "made philosophy the lawgiver in his realm." Animated by motives of justice and equity he desired a complete regeneration of conditions in his kingdom. His lack of reverence for historical development, and a growing opposition to his well-meant but sweeping plans by those whom he sought to benefit, finally led to the failure of almost all his reforms.

---

[15] In his *Anti-Machiavel* (1739), and his *Essay on Forms of Government and on The Duties of Sovereigns*. See his *Posthumous Works*, Vol. V, trans. by T. Holcroft.

Vico

Italy's contribution to the political thought of this period was made by the founder of the psychologico-historical method in political philosophy, the jurist and philosopher, Giambattista Vico (1668-1744).[16] Vico was much influenced by Francis Bacon and by Grotius, and made frequent references to Machiavelli and Bodin, with whose points of view he was in general agreement. Vico's method was in striking contrast to that of the natural-law philosophers who were dominant at the time. He had no sympathy with their doctrine of the existence of a body of law, corresponding to perfect reason, good for all times and places. He insisted upon the fact that political institutions and ideas pass through transitions in accordance with their environment and with the national character of their people. Government and law, therefore, vary according to the stage of general enlightenment and to the needs of their time. These ideas unquestionably exerted a considerable influence on the later work of Montesquieu.

Vico drew many of his ideas from his study of Roman history, and he worked out a theory of the process by which governments arise and disappear. He believed that men passed first through the theocratic stage, in which political authority was based upon the will of God as expressed through oracles. This was followed by aristocracy, in which the heads of the conspicuous families possessed supreme power. The final stage was a democratic society in which all the people became an integral part of the state. This type might be organized either as a republic or as a monarchy; in the latter case the king was delegated to act for the people. Mixed forms of government were merely the transitional stages between the types. Vico believed that this succession of divine, heroic, and human forms corresponded to human nature and to the general principles of philosophy. In this process positive law tended to approach the principle of universal or natural law. Europe, since the fall of Rome, had already passed through the theocratic and aristocratic forms, and was about to enter upon the period of popularly controlled monarchies and republics. Though Vico's attempt to place all phenomena within his threefold categories was somewhat forced, he made a valuable interpretation of political institutions and aided in creating a more scientific approach to political speculation. In his own day he was little known outside the group of jurists at Naples, and his point of view was obscured by the spread of the Kantian system over Europe.

[16] See his *De universi juris uno principio et fine uno* (1720), *De constantio jurisprudentis* (1721), *Principii d'una scienza nuova* (1725-30).

Bolingbroke and Hume

After the Revolution of 1688 England settled down to a century of self-complacency. The doctrine that rulers derive their authority from popular consent was firmly established, and the average man, weary of the constant threat of civil war, desired mainly to be let alone. It was a prosperous period, the development of agriculture, commerce, and the towns foreshadowing the industrial revolution. The theologians withdrew their attention from political affairs and composed themselves to comfortable living. The practical politicians were occupied with the corrupt system of party politics out of which Walpole, eager to avoid controversial issues, was fashioning cabinet government. Political theory, lacking the vital interest of the previous century, became academic and literary, appearing mainly in essay form. Pope's *Essay on Man*, with its neat verses and its glorification of civil society, was typical of the period. Bishop Berkeley, affected by the speculative mania which resulted in the South Sea Bubble, wrote on the decadence of England,[17] but his voice was an exception to the general eulogy of the British system as approaching perfection in its balance of monarchic, aristocratic, and democratic elements. The belief was widespread that the mixed system of government safeguarded liberty; and it was fashionable to make proud comparisons between the British government and that of ancient Rome.

The relation between church and state and between the established church and the non-conformist bodies led to some controversy. The Anglican clergy accepted with reluctance the accession of the Calvinist William of Orange; and the exaction of an oath of allegiance from the clergy created a considerable schism in the church, some of the ablest ecclesiastics being among the nonjurors. Arguments were put forward claiming that the church was independent of civil control, that it had a personality and will of its own, and that its relation to the state was federal in nature.[18] The adjustment between a national church, desirous of retaining its independent, divinely ordained position, and a sovereign state, supreme over all institutions within it, was indeed a difficult problem. The state tended to make the established church a subordinate subdivision of its government. The church desired independence, without being willing to give up its privileged position in the state or to meet the dissenting groups on terms of equality. Both the Oxford Movement of the nineteenth century and the modern pluralistic theory of sovereignty show the influence of the religious issues of this period.[19]

[17] In his *Essay towards Preventing the Ruin of Great Britain* (1721).
[18] See Bishop Warburton's *Alliance between Church and State* (1736).
[19] See H. J. Laski, *The Problem of Sovereignty* (1917).

The leading essayists dealing with political questions were Viscount Bolingbroke (1678-1751) [20] and David Hume (1711-1776). [21] Bolingbroke had held high office under Queen Anne, but upon the Hanoverian accession was succeeded by Walpole. He schemed to overthrow his successor by forming an alliance between the Tories and the discontented elements in the Whig party, and he did much to destroy the remaining Jacobitism of the Tories. His political ideas were expressed in terms of the immediate situation in England and were animated by his hatred of Walpole. He founded the *Craftsman,* the first official journal of a political party in England, and favored freedom of the press largely because he desired to fight Walpole openly without punishment. When in power Bolingbroke had favored a strict division of parties; when out of power he attacked the party system, holding that parties were moved, not by issues, but by the prospect of enjoying office and patronage. His political practices, however, frequently conflicted with his teachings, and his ideas were often inconsistent and lacked sincerity. [22]

Bolingbroke praised the mixed form of government, with its balance of powers, and attacked Walpole's system of corruption as tending to weaken the check exerted upon the monarch by an independent parliament. He followed the usual thought of his time in placing the basis of authority in the people, and in viewing the relation between sovereign and subjects as resting upon contract. He also considered the relation among the various organs of government as being somewhat vaguely contractual. Bolingbroke favored a vigorous foreign policy, argued for wider commercial freedom in colonial matters, and believed that England should play off the ambitions of France against those of Austria. He especially emphasized the value of the navy. The doctrines of Bolingbroke, especially his ideal of a patriot king at the head of a national party that would prevent factional contests, exerted considerable influence upon George III, and for a time upon Chatham and Disraeli.

The critical philosophy [23] of Hume was one of the most powerful dis-

[20] In his *Dissertation on Parties* (1734), *Letters on the Study of History* (1735), and *Idea of a Patriot King* (1738).

[21] In his *Essays, Moral, Political, and Literary* (1741-2), and his *Political Discourses* (1752).

[22] In his *Letter to Sir W. Windham,* published after his death, the cynicism of his political ideals is clearly evident.

[23] Though the discussion which follows is concerned primarily with Hume's political thought, it should be noted that his greatest contribution was made in the field of philosophy. His *Treatise of Human Nature* has had a profound effect on all modern philosophical speculation. His general philosophy is, of course, beyond our scope, but in essence Hume argued that natural law or any value system could not claim scientific validity because it could not be demonstrated that values were either true or false. See N. K. Smith, *The Philosophy of David Hume* (1941).

solvents of the century. He rejected both the theological conception of the state and the theory of social contract. In his philosophy he owed much to Locke, and also to Francis Hutcheson and others of the Scotch school, who were combining psychology with ethics, politics, and economics. Hume attacked the use of history to bolster up divine right and social contract; and he held that morality is based on general opinion as to what is expedient, and that it cannot be separated from positive law. He opposed the rationalists, with their theory of natural law, and believed that history and psychology were able to furnish the materials for a political philosophy. He foreshadowed both the historical method of Burke, on which modern conservatism is based, and the utilitarian doctrines of Bentham, through which radical opinions found a means of acceptance.

Hume attacked the theory of social contract in both its historical and its logical aspects. From the historical point of view, he pointed out that the idea of a voluntary contract was far above the intelligence of primitive man, that no example of an original contract could be found, that the consent of the original contractors could not bind their descendants, and that in most parts of the earth the idea that political authority was based upon consent would be considered absurd. He showed that states were often founded by usurpation or by conquest, and that obedience was rendered by most people because of custom and habit, men being born into the state and giving no attention to its origin or cause. Most revolutions, he held, were accomplished by a small number of persons, the majority giving little rational thought to the process. Besides, the doctrine that men voluntarily consent to obey their rulers would imply that men could withdraw from the state, which was contrary to fact.

Having showed that the idea of a voluntary contractual basis for the state was contrary to the teachings of history and to the actual facts of political life, Hume turned to the philosophic basis of the theory. He found the basis of authority in the facts of human psychology. The state existed because of its obvious utility. Hume showed that beliefs and opinions, rather than reason, determine men's actions, and that the ideas that are generally accepted are those that are conducive to men's interests. Hume agreed with Hobbes in viewing men as essentially selfish, and believed that laws and magistrates were necessary to prevent the encroachment of the strong and the unjust. The state, therefore, was justified because it was necessary; men were bound to obey authority, not because they had promised to obey it, but because otherwise human society could not exist.

Although Hume was opposed to popular government, his writings contained many acute observations on the political issues of his day. He recognized, with Harrington, that governing authority tends to accompany the distribution of property. He realized the growing democracy that was making the House of Commons the real center of power, and he saw the inevitability of parties and the necessity of a free press in a popular government. His economic ideas were in advance of his age. He opposed the mercantilist doctrines of a strictly regulated trade and of national prosperity expressed in terms of bullion. He argued for free communication and exchange, denied the necessity of any antagonism between commerce and agriculture, and believed that high wages were economically valuable. On the other hand, he held the accepted view that England must play one European power off against another in order to guarantee her own safety. Many of the later ideas of *laissez faire* were suggested in his writings.

The generation between Hume and Burke was practically barren of English writing on politics. There was, however, a general growth of democratic opinion throughout the country, and the voters were beginning to exercise more control over their representatives in parliament. While the ideas of Locke were influencing the actual development of governmental institutions in the country, the philosophic basis of his theory in natural rights and social contract was being destroyed by the relentless logic of Hume. On the continent, however, through the influence of English ideas on French writers, the theory of social contract was still to find its most eloquent exponent in Rousseau. In America also the ideas of Locke were popular, his theory that emphasized legislative supremacy and justified revolution being particularly applicable to the issues of the time. In England, the idea of natural rights took the form of individualism, on a utilitarian basis, and prepared the way for the work of Bentham, Mill, and Adam Smith.

REFERENCES

BOWLE, John, *Western Political Thought* (New York, Oxford Univ. Press, 1948), pp. 376-398.

CROCE, B., *The Philosophy of Giambattista Vico*, trans. by R. G. Collingwood (New York, Macmillan, 1913).

DUFF, R. A., *Spinoza's Political and Ethical Philosophy* (Glasgow, Maclehose, 1903).

LAING, B. M., *David Hume* (London, Benn, 1932).

LAIRD, John, *Hume's Philosophy of Human Nature* (London, Methuen, 1932).

LASKI, H. J., *Political Thought in England from Locke to Bentham* (New York, Holt, 1920), Chaps. 3-4.

——, *The Problem of Sovereignty* (New Haven, Yale Univ. Press, 1917).

RENSI, Giuseppe, *Spinoza* (Milan, Bocca, 1942).

SABINE, G. H., *A History of Political Theory*, rev. ed. (New York, Holt, 1950), pp. 597-606.

SÉE, H., *Les Idées Politiques en France au XVII siècle* (Paris, Giard, 1923).

SMITH, N. K., *The Philosophy of David Hume* (London, Macmillan, 1941).

SWINNY, S. H., "Giambattista Vico," *Sociological Review*, Vol. 7 (January, 1914).

WHEATON, Henry, *History of the Law of Nations* (New York, Gould, Banks, 1845), pp. 107-161.

CHAPTER XVI ~

Montesquieu and Rousseau

Conditions in France after Louis XIV

France in the eighteenth century was feudal in its social organization and autocratic in its government. Of a total population of about twenty-five millions, a quarter million of nobles and clergy owned half the soil, took from the peasant, in church dues and feudal payments, over a fourth of his income, and received in pensions and sinecure salaries a large part of the taxes, being themselves nearly exempt from taxation. Between the social extremes, a small middle class, the *bourgeoisie*, was becoming prosperous but possessed no social or political privileges. The government was centralized and despotic, clumsy with feudal survivals; personal liberty was at the mercy of the king and his officials. No representative parliament existed to serve as a check upon the royal power, and the judiciary was controlled by the higher nobility.

Unnecessary wars and extravagant life at the court had exhausted the treasury and created a heavy debt. Loans had been made under unfavorable conditions, and taxes were heavy and unfairly distributed. Burdensome duties prevented goods from passing from one part of the country to another, and the collection of taxes was farmed out to officials whose chief interest was the exploitation of the people. Land values were low, and mercantilist doctrines of strict regulation and of the importance of a favorable balance in foreign trade were the accepted policies of the government. By the middle of the eighteenth century a strong reaction in economico-political thought was apparent in the writings of the Physiocrats, who applied the doctrine of natural rights in the form of *laissez faire*, emphasized agriculture as the chief source of wealth, and proposed improved methods of taxation. The writings of the economists did much to widen the schism between the people and the government.

After the death of Louis XIV, a decided reaction set in against the repressive policy of the French monarchy. A spirit of scepticism in religion and a demand for rational liberty in thought began to appear. English political ideas, especially those of Locke, were introduced into French thought; and a knowledge of English political institutions, with their striking contrasts to those of France, led to comparisons decidedly hostile to the French monarchy. The liberty of the English people filled the French with admiration. The effect of the sceptical and rational philosophy that resulted was to create contempt and hatred for both church and state, to foster discontent with the established order of things, and to stir up a passionate desire for change. Criticism of social arrangements was general; even the privileged orders began to talk about their own uselessness. This attitude was in part sentimentality, in part a desire of some of the nobles to resume long-abandoned duties. In general, however, the upper classes remained selfish and scornful, and the new ideas influenced chiefly the unprivileged masses.

While the political writings of Montesquieu and Rousseau stand out conspicuously as the first comprehensive treatments of political philosophy in France since Bodin, a number of other thinkers contributed to the period. The argument for a more liberal government, put forward by Fénelon [1] in the later part of Louis XIV's reign, received serious attention after the death of the monarch. The Abbé de St. Pierre,[2] an acute but visionary critic, attacked the evils in the French governmental system with considerable freedom, proposing councils for each department of government. His *Projet de paix perpétuelle* (1713) exerted a considerable influence on the various schemes for securing universal peace that culminated in the Holy Alliance. The Marquis d'Argenson suggested a scheme of reform that aimed to transform the Bourbon despotism into a moderate and enlightened monarchy.

The most powerful critic of the period was Voltaire (1694-1778).[3] He had spent three years in England, was intimate with Bolingbroke, and had studied the writings of Bacon, Newton, and Locke. He did much to popularize English ideas in France. Voltaire attacked superstition and ecclesiastical domination, combated oppression of all kinds, and fought for intellectual, religious, and political liberty. He argued for freedom of the press, freedom of elections, and freedom of parliaments, and demanded political rights for the middle class which was growing prosperous in industry and trade. He had no faith, however, in the capacity of the lower classes for self-government. He preferred a benevolent and

---

[1] In his *Télémaque* (1699).

[2] In his *Discours sur la polysynodie* (1718).

[3] See his *Lettres sur les Anglais* (1728).

enlightened monarchy; but since kings could not be trusted to govern well, he considered the republican form of government the most tolerable. Voltaire taught that all men have equal natural rights to liberty, property, and the protection of the laws. He opposed the feudal dues and the extensive sumptuary laws of the paternalistic monarchy. At the same time, he had no intention to prepare men for a revolution; he expected reforms to be carried out by the rulers themselves.

Considerable stimulus to the process of enlightenment was also given by the Encyclopedists, of whom Diderot (1713-1784) and D'Alembert (1717-1783) were most important. They compiled an immense work in twenty-eight volumes, the aim of which was to gather up and systematize the facts of science and history in order to create a philosophy of life and of the universe which should supersede the old systems of thought and belief resting on ancient authority. In the Encyclopedia natural liberty was defined, in accordance with the doctrines of Locke, as the right of all men to dispose of person and property as they judge best, subject to natural law alone. By nature all men are equal, and after the formation of civil society all men were entitled to civil liberty.[4]

Montesquieu

The first systematic work in politics to result from the enlightened spirit of the eighteenth century in France was that of Baron de Montesquieu (1689-1755).[5] Montesquieu was a great reader of literature and of history, and was in thorough sympathy with the intellectual movement of his times. As early as 1721, in his *Persian Letters*, he had satirized the political, religious, and social institutions of France. Shortly after, he determined to travel and study the institutions of other countries. After an extensive journey through the continental states, he spent two years in England. Here he came into contact with the leading politicians and was much impressed by the English conception of liberty and by the English system of government. Montesquieu was especially interested in the history and politics of Rome, and he published an essay [6] in which he made a philosophical analysis of the rise and fall of the Roman state system. Roman history and English institutions were the sources from which, in the main, he derived his political philosophy. After long preparation, his great work on the *Spirit of the Laws* appeared in 1748.

Montesquieu's method was empirical rather than rationalistic or idealistic, political questions being treated not so much in connection with

---

[4] See article on *Liberté naturelle et civile*, in the *Encyclopédie*.

[5] The *De l'Esprit des Lois* (1748), trans. by T. Nugent.

[6] The *Considérations sur les causes de la grandeur des Romaines et de leur décadence* (1734).

abstract political ideas as with actual, concrete conditions. Like most writers of his time, Montesquieu believed that the fundamental principles of law and justice existed in nature, but he held that the teachings of nature were to be found, not in deductions from assumptions based on reason, but in the facts of history and in observations of the actual workings of political life. He did not believe in abstract justice, nor did he attempt to establish a system of perfect laws. He was a forerunner of the historical school, rather than a member of the natural-law group. His method was that of Aristotle and Bodin, not that of Plato and Locke.

Montesquieu's work stood somewhat aloof, not only from the natural-law philosophy of his time, but also from contemporary issues in France. It aimed to reform, rather than to uphold or to attack, the existing system; it dealt with practical questions of justice and governmental efficiency, rather than with doctrines concerning the rights of citizens or the prerogatives of the sovereign. There is little in Montesquieu's work concerning either the nature of sovereignty or the rights of man and natural equality. He wished to preserve the French spirit and to retain the monarchy, but to safeguard liberty by separating the legislative and the executive branches of government. His work aimed to explain the nature and the workings of political institutions in general, not those of France alone. In scope, it included all the institutions of social existence, and it considered the interrelations among such factors as physical environment, racial characteristics, social, religious, and economic customs, and governmental institutions on the one hand, and political and civil liberty on the other. It aimed to construct a comparative theory of law and politics, based on a study of actual systems in different lands and ages; likewise a comparative theory of legislation, adapted to the needs of different forms of government. The most important part of the work was that which dealt with liberty and with the value of the separation of powers as a necessary safeguard of liberty.

In contrast to the idea that law existed in nature and could be deduced from the dictates of reason, or to the idea that law was the definite command of a sovereign, Montesquieu widened the conception of law to include the general relationship of cause and effect. He believed that a body of principles was constantly operative in determining the nature of institutions and of legislation. From the relations among states arose the law of nations. In the relations between government and governed in any given state was the source of political law. In the relations among citizens was the source of civil law. The law of nations was common to all states; political and civil laws varied from state to state, depending upon the conditions in each. The natural form of government and the natural system of law was that which conformed to the numerous influences which determine the nature of a people and the circumstances in which they live. Those complicated influences constitute the "spirit of the laws"; and in their consideration, Montesquieu was led into the fields of geography, sociology, economics, and jurisprudence, as well as of politics proper.

Montesquieu endeavored to discover the principles underlying all forms of government. He classified governments as despotisms, in which an individual ruled without law; monarchies, in which an individual ruled according to law; and republics, in which the people possessed political power. This later type might be either democratic or aristocratic. Each form of government was associated with its peculiar principle. A despotism was based upon fear; a monarchy upon honor; an aristocracy, upon moderation; a democracy, upon political virtue or patriotism. Montesquieu considered the dangers that were inherent in each system and the institutions and laws that were appropriate to each form, explaining many of the most important governmental devices and political principles in the light of their relation to a particular system and to a particular set of conditions.

To Montesquieu, no form of government was essentially good in itself; its value was relative. If the spirit which characterized each form underwent change, a revolution in government necessarily followed. Democracy became impossible if political virtue and the spirit of equality disappeared. Aristocracy could not survive if moderation among the ruling classes ceased. Monarchy was impossible if honor grew weak among the rulers. Despotism by its nature was unstable. Revolutions, however, followed no regular sequence; the new form depended upon the conditions in each case.

One factor upon which Montesquieu laid emphasis was extent of territory. He held that despotism was natural in large states; monarchy in those of moderate size; and republican government in small territories. France, he thought, was too large to have a republican government. A change in the size of a state would be followed naturally by a change in its form of government. Since increasing size led to undesirable types of government, Montesquieu opposed Machiavelli's theory of the value of expansion. The difficulty which a small, republican state faced in protecting itself led Montesquieu to favor the principle of federation. The influence of his theories as to the connection between the size of a state and of its government, and as to the value of the federal form, exerted considerable influence in America at the time of the adoption of the federal constitution.

The topic to which Montesquieu gave chief attention was the nature of liberty. On this subject he drew his ideas largely from Locke, but developed them along different lines, laying little emphasis upon natural rights or individualism. He distinguished between political and civil liberty. Political liberty resulted from the relation of man to the state. It consisted in security under law to act as one desired, in accordance with the law. It was the opposite of despotism. Civil liberty grew out of the relation of man to man. It was the opposite of slavery, and was more closely associated with the law of nature. Montesquieu gave considerable attention to criticizing the prevalent theories upholding slavery and waxed eloquent in attacking the system. He proposed, although somewhat ironically, an international agreement for the prevention of the slave trade.

The chief interest of Montesquieu was to set forth the governmental organization that would best safeguard political liberty. This demanded security against individual caprice, and implied subjection to law rather than to the will of a human being. Liberty was possible only where governmental powers were subject to limitations. Montesquieu believed that the essential safeguard against tyranny, and the surest guarantee of liberty, was the separation of the executive, legislative, and judicial powers of government, such as he believed to exist in England. Each power must be exercised by a separate organ and a system of checks and balances thus established. The separation of executive and legislative power was especially important. Criminal law and procedure must also be safeguarded against abuses that led to injustice. The doctrine of separation of powers, though based on a misconception of the English constitution, since the rise of cabinet government was combining executive and legislative functions, exerted a great influence in America. It was applied in both federal and state constitutions, and was included in many of the state bills of rights. It was also included in the Declaration of the Rights of Man, drawn up by the revolutionary assembly in France.

Montesquieu followed Bodin in giving considerable attention to the influence of the physical environment upon political and social institutions, paying especial attention to climate and the fertility of the soil. He held that political liberty was natural in the colder climates; slavery, in the warmer. Mountainous regions were conducive to liberty; the fertile plains, to tyranny. The large geographical divisions of Asia favored despotism; the smaller units of Europe promoted freedom. Island peoples were more disposed to democratic government than continental peoples.

The influence of social, economic, and religious conditions upon law were also given much attention, Montesquieu holding that law should conform to prevailing standards and customs. Questions of population, poor relief, money, and commerce were discussed in a scientific spirit, with examples drawn from history and from the conditions of his own time. Montesquieu realized, with Harrington, that the balance of political power tended to follow the balance of property. Highly developed commerce he held unsuited to monarchies; monopolistic commercial companies should not be tolerated in free governments. He agreed with the Physiocrats in the value of competition and individual effort.

While Montesquieu believed in Christianity, he discussed the relation between religion and politics in a spirit almost Machiavellian. He held that Mohammedanism was adapted to despotic governments and Christianity to limited governments, and that Catholicism was best suited to monarchies and Protestantism to republics. He favored religious toleration, and held that the regulation of morals and of religious questions lay outside the proper scope of governmental authority.

Montesquieu followed the inductive and historical tradition of Aristotle, Machiavelli, and Bodin; and like them was interested in practical political activities, rather than in general theories concerning the origin and nature of the state. He widened the field of history and observation to include remote and uncivilized peoples,[7] drawing conclusions, not always accurate, from information, not always authentic, concerning the institutions of Chinese, Japanese, Africans, and South Sea Islanders. His attempt to merge politics with general social science, and to base political principles upon broad inductive generalizations was, however, outside the main current of political philosophy. The political movements of the close of the eighteenth century were based upon a development of Locke's theory of natural rights, social contract, and revolution, which found expression in the writings of Rousseau.

Rousseau

The writer whose work most truly reflected contemporary conditions in France and aimed at a solution of the social and political injustice of the period was Jean-Jacques Rousseau (1712-1778).[8] About the time that the logic of Hume was demolishing the theory of social contract in England, Rousseau was applying that theory in a view of the state quite different from the absolutism of Hobbes or the moderate constitutionalism of Locke. More dogmatic than Hobbes and more popular and eloquent than Locke, his work, in spite of its inaccuracies and inconsistencies, exerted a tremendous influence upon the period following its appearance.

---

[7] Note the influence of the discovery of America and the opening up of new lands on this tendency in European thought.

[8] In his *Contrat Social* (1762), trans. by H. J. Tozer. In two earlier essays, the *Discourse on the Progress of the Arts and Sciences* (1749), and the *Discourse on Inequality* (1754), Rousseau had put forward his ideas of the state of nature and of the evils resulting from civilization. Some political doctrines were contained in the *Émile* (1762), his work on education.

Rousseau was familiar, in a superficial way, with history and with the writings of earlier political philosophers. He admired and idealized the Greek and Roman republics. His admiration for small states and for direct democracy can also be traced partly to the influence of Geneva, where he spent his boyhood, under a system markedly different from that of France.[9] Many of his ideas were drawn from Pufendorf, Locke, and Montesquieu. His doctrine of popular sovereignty resembled in many particulars that of Althusius; [10] though it is difficult to determine to what extent Rousseau was indebted, as he mentioned by name the writers with whom he disagreed, rather than those from whom his ideas were drawn. The doctrines of Hobbes and Grotius he held in special dislike.

His ideas also reflected his own personality and upbringing. Of the latter, Rousseau had very little. He was deserted at an early age by his father,[11] his mother dying during his birth. Left to his own devices, he led the life of a vagabond, accounting perhaps for a vain, sensitive, and un-controlled temperament which led him to rebel against all conventions and restraints and to criticize authority and civilization. Conditions in France, with its divine-right monarchy, its feudal class distinctions, and its dissolute society, were especially open to such criticism. However, Rousseau had no sympathy with ideas of moderate reform, such as those of Voltaire, the Encyclopedists, and the Physiocrats, who favored an en-lightened monarchy, or of Montesquieu, who desired the adoption of English constitutional checks and balances. Rousseau desired to extend equal rights to the peasants and laborers, as well as to the middle class. He attacked the belief of the intellectuals that progress would result from enlightenment. He had no confidence in an artificial civilization based upon human achievement in arts and sciences. His ideals aimed at direct democracy and equality, demanded a radical reconstruction of the social and political order, and led logically to the Revolution.

The theory of Rousseau was based upon the conception of a pre-politi-cal state of nature, in which men were equal, self-sufficient, and con-tented. Their conduct was based, not on reason, but on emotions of self-interest and pity. With the progress of civilization, evils arose. The division of labor that followed the development of the arts and the rise of private property created distinctions between rich and poor that broke

---

[9] Rousseau's early years in Geneva and his later experiences in France and else-where are recounted in his *Confessions*. This is one of history's most revealing auto-biographies.

[10] See above, Chapter XI.

[11] An interesting parallel with Hobbes can be observed here. If it were not for the fact that figures like Locke and Kant had very orthodox beginnings, it might be sup-posed that an irresponsible father is an essential condition of greatness in political philosophy.

down the happy natural condition of mankind and necessitated the establishment of civil society. Rousseau was more inclined than Hobbes or
Locke to picture the state of nature as an actual historical condition. He
also differed in minimizing the importance of human reason. Grotius,
Hobbes, Pufendorf, and Locke had held that the rational powers of
natural man had enabled him to create social and political organization.
Rousseau taught that reason was the outgrowth of the artificial life of men
in organized society, and that the results of its development were calami-
tous. The "noble savage" was Rousseau's ideal. The state was an evil,
made necessary by the rise of inequalities among men.

The process by which political society was created was a social contract,
since only by agreement and consent could authority be justified and
liberty retained. Both Hobbes and Locke influenced this part of Rousseau's work, the method of Hobbes and the conclusions of Locke being
curiously combined. Rousseau held that each individual gave up all his
natural rights to the community as a whole. By this process a body politic,
with a life and will of its own, was established. Yet each person in the
state, possessing an equal and inalienable portion of the sovereignty of
the whole, gained back under the protection of the state the rights he had
given up. The process is summarized by Rousseau in the following famous
passage:

To find a form of association which may defend and protect with the whole
force of the community the person and property of every associate, and by
means of which each, coalescing with all, may nevertheless obey only himself,
and remain as free as before. Such is the fundamental problem of which the
social contract furnishes the solution. . . . In short, each giving himself to all,
gives himself to nobody; and as there is not one associate over whom we do
not acquire the same rights which we concede to him over ourselves, we gain
the equivalent of all that we lose, and more power to preserve what we have.[12]

Thus while the authority established was absolute, following Hobbes,
individuals still possessed equal rights, following Locke. This is difficult
to follow, but Rousseau believed that there could be no conflict between
authority vested in the people as a whole and their liberty as individuals.

According to Rousseau, the will of each individual was merged into a
general will. The general will corresponded to the common interest of
all members of the community, as contrasted with particular interests.
It was normally arrived at by asking each member to vote for what he
believed to be the common good and accepting the view of the majority.
The majority could of course be wrong,[13] but Rousseau believed that the

[12] Social Contract, Chap. 6.
[13] The general will itself, however, was never wrong because by definition it represented the best interest of the community.

majority would err less often in identifying the general will than any other group [14] because their interest in community welfare would not be as easily corrupted. As for those who voted against measures accepted by the majority, Rousseau suggested that they, too, would be benefited. They would be more free in being outvoted than if they had had their own way because their larger interest would have prevailed over a more selfish interest, mistaken by them for the general will.[15]

The acts of the general will alone were properly law. Laws, therefore, must deal with general interests and must emanate from the people. The enactment of any governmental organ was merely a device for carrying into effect the superior commands of the true lawmaking body. Rousseau's idea of law thus approached the modern concept of a fundamental law or constitution, in accordance with which all governmental powers are exercised.

The distinction between state and government was consistently pointed out by Rousseau. The state was the entire body politic, manifesting itself in the supreme and sovereign general will, the government comprised the individuals chosen by the community to apply the general will. The government was created, not by contract, as Hobbes thought, but by the act of the sovereign people. It might be changed at their pleasure, and was merely their agent. So confident was Rousseau in the indefeasible rights of the sovereign people that he was willing to delegate powers which Locke and Montesquieu thought dangerous. Viewing the executive merely as an agent of popular will, Rousseau even spoke calmly of a dictatorship. Later, when the Committee of Public Safety ruled France, this idea was acted upon.

Rousseau classified governments into monarchies, aristocracies, democracies, and mixed types; and he adopted many of the ideas of Montesquieu regarding the adjustment of governmental forms to economic and social conditions. He also followed current economic thought in holding that an increasing population was a test of good government. Believing that the sovereign people must act directly in making law, Rousseau favored direct democracy and held that representative assemblies were a sign of political decay. The tendency of government to expand its powers at the expense of popular control led to his doctrine that only in small states and under simple conditions can the general will permanently maintain its supremacy. To prevent governmental usurpation in larger and more complex states, he suggested periodical assemblies of the sovereign people, at which they should decide whether they wished to maintain the existing form of government and to retain the existing office holders. While the

14 Such as an intellectual elite.
15 The danger to democracy in this latter notion should not go unobserved.

people were thus assembled in a sovereign body, all jurisdiction of the government ceased. The periodical vote for officers and the periodical vote on the question of revising the constitution were here foreshadowed. The idea that each generation should have the right to reëxamine its constitution was adopted by Jefferson, and the device of holding constitutional conventions at stated intervals was adopted by several of the American states.

Rousseau and Democratic Institutions

The ideas and spirit of Rousseau were reflected in the governmental changes of the period following his death. His doctrines of human equality, of popular sovereignty, and of the desirability of a return to nature were especially popular. Many of his principles were applied in the political experiments of the French Revolution and were expressed in the Declaration of the Rights of Man of 1789.[16] However, the idea of a bill of individual rights was derived from America, rather than from Rousseau. His doctrine that the individual surrendered all his natural rights to the general will established a popular sovereign as absolute as the *Leviathan* of Hobbes. Against the sovereign people, the individual possessed no rights.[17] His emphasis on liberty, equality, and popular sovereignty, nevertheless, was largely responsible for the enthusiasm with which the French people hailed the American idea of a declaration of rights.

In the decade following the death of Rousseau, Frenchmen became deeply interested in the institutions of the American states that had won independence from Great Britain. Their governments seemed to realize the principles of sovereignty and of a popularly created fundamental law as put forth in the *Contrat Social*. The constitutions of these new states, dealing with fundamental questions and distinguished, by their theoretical source in the people and by their superior authority, from the governments established under them, satisfied the requirements of Rousseau for law in its proper sense. This coincidence, resulting from the fact that both Rousseau and the Americans derived their ideas from the doctrines and practices of seventeenth century England, exerted a far-reaching influence on the development of the Revolution in France.

[16] Article I reads: "Men are born and remain free and equal in rights." Article VI reads: "The law is the expression of the general will."

[17] Rousseau makes it clear, however, that a person might expect to be free to do anything which does not adversely affect others.

Rousseau and German Idealism

In Germany, Rousseau also exerted a mighty, though contrary, influence. The school of German idealism was much influenced by Rousseau's concept of the general will. Kant tells us that it was while reading Rousseau's *Émile* that he reached the basic conclusions of his philosophy. Rousseau would never have concurred with later German doctrines associated with his name, but on two counts he made himself vulnerable to the resulting interpretations.

His concept of the general will served as a basis for German notions of the "will of the people." By evolvement, this became the "real" will of the people as opposed to what they merely conceived their will to be. It was now an historic will of the state, leaving little room for individual differences of opinion.

On the second count Rousseau was even more vulnerable. He had turned sharply from Diderot and other contemporaries in his distrust of reason. To Diderot reason was everything, but Rousseau identified it with the artificialities of his age. He felt that reliance must be placed instead on the basic emotions of mankind. He argued that people could be moved politically in three ways. First, they could be coerced. Secondly, they could be reasoned into action. And lastly, they could be led by appeals to the emotions. The first course was unjust and so impossible. The second course was suspect because of artificialities to which it led and because it failed to reach the people. This left only the third course. Such fundamental emotions as compassion were to be accepted and acted upon as the wellspring of public happiness. From such a beginning, the romanticism of the nineteenth century had its start. Rousseau also provided a club which could be used to beat down the reasoned arguments of Hume. In place of Hume's reason, German philosophy produced a new reason. It was a higher form of reason which became "The reason of God's march in the universe." Value systems must either be justified or abandoned. If Hume's attack on accepted values had been allowed to stand, there could be no values which were better or worse than other values. And as a consequence, there could be no authoritarianism because such a term implies a final standard of right. With the assertion of a higher reason than Hume's, authoritarianism was thus saved, but in so doing another step was taken toward fascism and communism. It is important to note, incidentally, that the basis of both fascism and communism rests on authoritarianism combined with totalitarianism. The only fundamental difference is that fascism has relied more heavily on the emotional appeals first suggested by Rousseau, whereas the communists have combined their authoritarianism with bad economics.

Hobbes, Locke, and Rousseau

The social-contract theories of Hobbes, Locke, and Rousseau showed important variations. Hobbes viewed natural man as essentially selfish and the state of nature as a period of constant warfare. Rousseau viewed the natural man as essentially good, and the state of nature as a period of idyllic happiness. Locke occupied a middle position on these points. Hobbes and Rousseau maintained that sovereignty was absolute; Locke viewed it as limited. Hobbes held that sovereignty might be vested in one, the few, or the many; but that, once conferred by the people, it could not be recalled. Rousseau believed that sovereignty was always vested in the whole people, and that law must be a direct expression of their general will. Hobbes made no distinction between state and government. To him the *de facto* government was always *de jure*; Locke and Rousseau distinguished between state and government, and between *de facto* and *de jure* governments. Hobbes held that a change in government meant a dissolution of the state and a return to anarchy; Locke held that the people had the sovereign right to choose their government and to change it if unsatisfactory. To Rousseau the government was merely the agent which executed the popular will. Locke and Rousseau agreed in vesting sovereignty in the people and in limiting the powers of government. Locke, however, viewed the sovereignty of the people as held in reserve and exercised only in extreme cases when revolution was necessary. All acts of the government were legal unless they violated the rights of the people. Rousseau viewed popular sovereignty as constantly active, the direct participation of the people being essential to the creation of law.

After Rousseau, the theory of social contract continued to be politically important. In America, the theory exercised a profound influence. It was recognized in the Declaration of Independence and in nearly all the bills of rights in the state constitutions. The writings of Jefferson and Madison state the doctrine in its most advanced form. The fact that a theory which was historically unsound and logically fallacious could serve as the justification for the English Revolution of 1688, for the French Revolution, and for the American Revolution, and could furnish a philosophic basis for modern democracy and civil liberty, is one of the paradoxes in the history of political thought.

REFERENCES

BABBITT, Irving, *Rousseau and Romanticism* (Boston, Houghton, 1919).

BOSANQUET, Bernard, *The Philosophical Theory of the State* (London, Macmillan, 1920).

CATTELAIN, Fernand, *Étude sur l'influence de Montesquieu dans les constitutions américaines* (Besançon, Imprimerie Millot frères, 1927).

COBBAN, Alfred, "New Light on the Political Thought of Rousseau," *Political Science Quarterly*, Vol. 66 (June, 1951).

———, *Rousseau and the Modern State* (London, G. Allen, 1934).

DERATHÉ, Robert, *Jean-Jacques Rousseau et la science politique de son temps* (Paris, Univ. of Paris Press, 1950).

———, *Le Rationalisme de J.-J. Rousseau* (Paris, Univ. of Paris Press, 1948).

FLETCHER, F. T. H., *Montesquieu and English Politics (1750-1800)* (London, E. Arnold & Co., 1939).

GOUGH, J. W., *The Social Contract* (Oxford, Clarendon Press, 1936).

LEROY, Maxime, *Histoire des idées sociales en France: de Montesquieu à Robespierre* (Paris, Gallimard, 1946).

SABINE, G. H., *A History of Political Theory*, rev. ed. (New York, Holt, 1950), Chaps. 27-28.

SPINK, J. S., *Jean-Jacques Rousseau et Genève* (Paris, Boivin, 1934).

WATKINS, Frederick, *The Political Tradition of the West* (Cambridge, Harvard Univ. Press, 1948), Chap. 4.

PART V

Modern Liberal Thought

CHAPTER XVII

Economic Development and Political Thought

Political thought has been dominated in our century by three contending ideologies—liberalism, fascism,[1] and communism. All of them owe a debt to Rousseau,[2] who wittingly or unwittingly contributed as much to authoritarianism as he did to liberalism. It will consequently be convenient to turn from Rousseau to western liberalism, to be followed in later chapters by analyses of fascism and communism.

The Relation of Economic to Political Thought

Economic theory and practice have played a very significant role in the development of the political institutions of liberalism. Indeed, from the beginnings of political philosophy the ablest thinkers have understood that there is a close connection between political and economic institutions and ideas. Aristotle realized that politics cannot be divorced from economics, that the form of the state depended upon the kind and distribution of property, and that revolutions were often caused by struggles of power between economic classes. He held that a large middle class was necessary for a well-governed state; and that an agricultural population was stable, conservative, and industrious, while a commercial population was turbulent and easily led by demagogues. Machiavelli understood the importance of economic groups and gave advice as to how a prince might play one class off against another. Harrington taught that

---

[1] Unless otherwise qualified, fascism is hereafter used to describe the doctrines of Hitler, as well as Mussolini.

[2] Though communism's debt is less direct and important than is the case in regard to liberalism and fascism.

political power followed property, and held that it was the duty of the statesman to see that property was widely distributed and that a substantial landed class was maintained as the stabilizer of the state. Locke held that the preservation of property was the cause of the state's origin and the chief end for which it existed, and that the invasion of property rights by the government was just cause for revolution.

Communistic ideas concerning economic equality were associated with the doctrines of early Christianity and with the peasant revolts of the Middle Ages; and the leaders of those movements, more acute perhaps than their later counterparts, emphasized equality of property rather than political equality as the necessary basis of their reforms. On the other hand, theories were advanced to justify slavery and inequalities of wealth, in spite of their apparent contradiction to the principles of justice incorporated in the law of nature. The economic basis of politics was recognized in practice as well as in theory. For centuries the governments of the great nations were deliberately fitted into separate orders or estates— the clergy, the nobles, the burghers and the peasants—each pursuing a separate calling and having definite economic interests.

Mercantilism

However, the connection between economic and political theory did not become prominent until the sixteenth century, when the rise of modern nations, of a money economy, of taxation, and of foreign trade focused attention on the relation between the state and wealth. In the Middle Ages economics was domestic rather than political in nature. Agriculture was fostered; manufactures and commerce were despised. The idea of protection and control was universal. Custom, regulation, and monopoly, in the hands of church, manor, town, and guild, were unquestioned. The growth of commerce, especially after the discovery of the new world, and the influx of gold and silver shifted attention from agriculture and barter to foreign trade and the importance of bullion, the greatness of Spain being supposed to result from the precious metals secured from America. The growing national monarchies took over the control formerly exercised by the medieval bodies and used this control in their keen international rivalries. The royal estates and prerogatives no longer sufficed to meet the increasing expenses of government. Money was needed for standing armies; and the commercial classes, growing in wealth, became a power in the state. The establishment of colonies raised the question of their economic relation to the mother country, the accepted policy being to restrict colonial trade to the mother country alone, and to confine colonial industry to the production of raw materials which the mother country could work up and sell in the form of finished products. Commercial interests governed foreign policy, and the belief that government should actively concern itself with industry and trade was generally accepted. It was held that the commercial advantage of one country could only be obtained at the expense of another. In the hostility between the English and the Dutch in the middle of the seventeenth century, and in the later rivalry between France and England, these ideas were applied.

Out of this situation arose the point of view known as mercantilism, which was the economic aspect of the vigorous nationalism of the period. Manufactures were exalted above agriculture as a source of national wealth, and foreign trade was considered more valuable than domestic trade. A favorable balance of exports over imports was especially desired, since it brought money into the country. A large store of precious metals was considered important; a dense population was viewed as a source of strength; it was the duty of the state, by every expedient, to increase its power and wealth. Tariffs, bounties, and prohibitions were numerous. Charters were granted, monopolies were established, and the world was parceled out among privileged companies. Colonies were estates to be exploited for the benefit of the merchants in the mother country. This point of view prevailed from the sixteenth to the later part of the eighteenth century. In the earlier period the importance of bullion was especially stressed; in the later period the importance of a favorable balance of trade was considered of chief importance. Economics was merged into politics, and mercantilism was an instrument in the rise of the great powers. It aimed at the creation of strong, populous, self-supporting states.

The practice of mercantilism began when Charles V, on his accession to the throne of Spain in 1516, began retaliatory measures against the commercial monopoly of Venice. The doctrines of mercantilism were first systematically stated by an Italian writer, Serra.[3] In England, Sir William Petty[4] emphasized the importance of treasure in gold, silver, and jewels, and urged statistical investigations, improved methods of taxation, and the scientific development of natural resources. Thomas Mun,[5] a director of the East India Company, emphasized the importance of foreign trade and of a favorable balance, but attacked the doctrine that money alone is wealth. The rise of Holland and the decline of Spain provided him with examples. His writings were often reprinted during

[3] In his *Brief Treatise on the Causes which make Gold and Silver Abound in Kingdoms where there are no Mines* (1613).

[4] In his *Essays in Political Arithmetic* (1655), and his *Treatise on Taxes and Contributions* (1662).

[5] In his *England's Treasure by Foreign Trade* (written about 1630, but not published until 1664).

the seventeenth and eighteenth centuries, and were considered authoritative until they were displaced by Adam Smith's *Wealth of Nations*.

During the later part of the seventeenth century mercantilist theories were held in England, especially by the Whig party, which hated French influence and desired to restrict trade with that country. The Tories, who supported Charles II in his policy of close relations with France, opposed the protective measures of parliament. The writings of Dudley North [6] and Josiah Child [7] upheld the doctrine that the world is a commercial unit and that supply and demand, rather than state regulation, should determine prices and interest rates. This group foreshadowed the *laissez-faire* and free-trade doctrines of the next century.

The restrictive policies of mercantilism were carried furthest in practice in France under Jean Colbert (1619-1683), the able finance minister of Louis XIV, unlimited and arbitrary jurisdiction being exercised by the state over industry and trade. Colbert fostered French industries by a protective tariff, improved the system of taxation, created a navy, and labored to build up a great French colonial empire. Through his influence the French East India Company was formed in 1664. In England, the Corn Laws, the Navigation Acts, and extensive sumptuary legislation were characteristic. In Prussia, especially under the Great Elector and under Frederick the Great, many measures, usually wisely applied, were adopted to foster agriculture and industry and to control foreign trade.

In the German states, the mercantile point of view was represented in the body of learning known as kameralism.[8] It was a combination of political, juristic, technical, and economic ideas, and had to do mainly with the methods by which the royal income could be best maintained, increased, and administered. The German states, disunited and backward in their industrial development, clung to a medieval system of finance. No distinction was made between the personal income of the absolute monarch and the public treasury. The income of the state was derived from the royal domains and from the various profitable prerogatives possessed by the sovereign. When the growing expenses of government demanded increased income, there was a tendency to increase the number and scope of royal privileges, or "regalian rights."

Accordingly, the kameralists were less concerned with foreign relations and a favorable balance of trade than were the mercantilists in the maritime countries, such as Holland, France, and England. The German writers gave more attention to domestic industry, to the development of national resources, and to the efficient administration of the estates and

[6] See his *Discourses on Trade* (1691).
[7] See his *New Discoveries in Trade* (1690).
[8] The *kammer* was the place in which the royal income was stored.

prerogatives of the sovereign. They agreed with the mercantilists, however, in favoring strict governmental regulation of economic affairs, in emphasizing the importance of precious metals, and in preaching dense population, economic self-sufficiency, and national greatness. Whereas the English mercantilists were business men and pamphleteers, the German kameralists were professors of finance [9] and wrote voluminous and systematic treatises. Among the most important writers were Bechers,[10] von Hornig,[11] Justi,[12] and Daries.[13]

The Physiocrats

Although mercantilism continued well into the eighteenth century, its approaching decline was foreshadowed in the writings of Locke and others who supported an individualistic point of view. The regulations and restrictions of a paternalistic government were becoming so burdensome to the rapidly growing middle class that they turned to the doctrine of natural rights for relief. The doctrine was applied to support the principle that the individual should exercise his economic activities with the least possible interference from the state. It was held that in the absence of restraints upon industry and trade and of monopolistic privileges, enlightened self-interest, in free competition, would realize both individual and public welfare. This view, the opposite of mercantilism, was worked out by the Physiocrats [14] in France and by the school of writers that accompanied the Industrial Revolution and centered around Adam Smith in England.

In France the abuses which attended and followed Colbert's régime, with its extravagant expenditures and its high and inequitable taxes, soon brought about a decided reaction. The condition of the peasants led numerous writers to attack the government's policy of restricting markets and of fostering manufactures and trade at the expense of agriculture. Besides, the profitable nature of farming on a large scale, with more capital and with rotation of crops, was proved by the agricultural revolution in England. This fact, known to French economists, further shook the prestige of mercantilism and turned French thought toward the importance of agriculture. The criticisms of Boisguilbert, Vauban, and Fénelon all contained suggestions of tax reform, freedom of trade, and

[9] Frederick William I founded chairs of Economic and Kameralistic Sciences at several German universities in 1727.
[10] *Political Discourse* (1667).
[11] *Oesterreich über Alles* (1684).
[12] *Staatswirthschaft* (1755).
[13] *First Principles of Kameral Sciences* (1756).
[14] For the writings of the Physiocrats, see *Physiocrates,* ed. by E. Daire (1846).

development of the land. The treatise of Richard Cantillon,[15] which taught that the earth is the source from which all wealth is drawn, and which emphasized domestic rather than foreign trade, was widely circulated in France. These writers prepared the way for the Physiocrats.

The Physiocrats were deeply imbued with prevalent ideas of natural law, and applied the belief in a natural order to the relation of the state to industry and trade. Influenced by contemporary developments in the natural sciences, and by the doctrines of Descartes, Locke, and Rousseau, they held that the production and distribution of goods should be carried on according to fixed laws of nature, and should not be interfered with by governmental restrictions. They emphasized the individual and his rights, especially the right of private property; and held that the individual should be left considerable freedom in disposing of his property. They believed in a "natural order," whose arrangements were perfect and whose laws were the will of God, in contrast to the "positive order," whose laws were the human and imperfect rules of existing governments. The state should protect life, liberty, and property; the individual, knowing his own interests best, would act more in accordance with the law of nature than would the government. Hence their well-known maxim, *laissez faire, laissez passer*.

The Physiocrats believed that land was the source of wealth, and that labor applied to the raising of crops or the extracting of raw materials from the earth was the only form of labor that produced a surplus. Commerce and manufactures were regarded as non-productive. Accordingly, they favored increased application of capital to land, the abolition of the internal duties on the grain trade in France, and the introduction of a single-tax on land. In discussing their theory of taxation, they criticized the cumbersome and wasteful tax system that existed, and increased the general dissatisfaction with the policies of the French monarchy.

In their political theory the Physiocrats supported hereditary monarchy, but they believed that the monarch should be enlightened and liberal. They had no interest in suffrage rights, and detested the parliamentary system of England. They believed in an absolute and undivided sovereignty, but viewed the monarch, not as the creator of law, but as the administrator of the natural rules of justice and morality. The laws of the state should declare the essential rules of the natural social order. The state existed to safeguard the natural rights of the individual. These included primarily the right of each man to property in his person, which involved the right to labor, and the right to the property which resulted from his labor. The government, therefore, should exercise as little restraint as possible upon property and upon the efforts of men to utilize

[15] The *Essay upon the Nature of Commerce in General* (1755).

their faculties. The abolition of unnecessary laws was the most valuable service that a legislative body could render. Education, however, was a proper state function, since it was necessary that citizens should know the fundamental principles of natural law. The Physiocrats thus added support from a new standpoint, that of the production and use of wealth, to the familiar doctrine of natural rights to liberty and property. In foreign relations they favored freedom of trade, peace, and internationalism. They held that the aggressive patriotism and the international rivalries of their age were unnecessary evils.[16]

Among the leading Physiocrats were François Quesnay (1694-1774),[17] Jean de Gournay (1712-1759),[18] Mercier de la Rivière (1720-1793),[19] Jacques Turgot (1727-1781),[20] and Dupont de Nemours (1739-1817).[21] These writers were the first to grasp the conception of a unified science of society and to argue that all social facts are linked together by inevitable laws. They founded the science of economics and, in spite of their one-sided emphasis on land at the expense of manufactures and commerce, they constructed the way along which Adam Smith and the writers of the century following him advanced. The approach of the French Revolution, however, subordinated all speculation in France to questions of constitutional issues; and leadership in the development of economico-political doctrines was transferred to Great Britain.

The ideas of the Physiocrats exerted some influence outside France, although the nature of the Industrial Revolution made their views as to the relative importance of land and capital untenable, especially in England. In America, Benjamin Franklin and Thomas Jefferson were acquainted with their writings and adopted some of their ideas. Catherine II of Russia, Joseph II of Austria, and Gustavus III of Sweden admired the Physiocratic system and made some attempts to carry out its principles. In France, Turgot, as minister of finance under Louis XVI, tried to abolish some of the most burdensome restrictions, but the hostility of the clergy and the nobility prevented extensive reform.

[16] A peculiar feature of eighteenth century thought in France was the highly favorable view held of Chinese culture. The prevalence of an agricultural régime and of a pacifist policy seemed to coincide with Physiocratic ideas. The French moralists also held up China as a model. The fallacies in many ideas regarding the Chinese were exposed by Montesquieu.

[17] He wrote articles on Les Grains and Les Fermiers in the Encyclopédie; also the Tableau économique (1758), and Le Droit naturel (1765).

[18] He translated the English works of Sir Josiah Child, and influenced Turgot.

[19] See his L'Ordre naturel et essentiel des sociétés politiques (1767).

[20] See his Eulogy of Gournay (1760), also his Réflexions sur la Formation et la Distribution des Richesses (1766).

[21] See his Origine et Progrès d'une Science Nouvelle, and his Physiocratie, ou Constitution essentielle du gouvernement le plus avantageux au genre humain (1768).

Adam Smith

The eighteenth century was a period of important economic change in England, resulting in vast increase in national wealth, as well as in terrible distress for a large class of the population. The invention of machinery for spinning and weaving cotton and wool, the use of the steam engine to furnish power, the substitution of coal and coke for wood and charcoal, and improvements in the iron industry transformed the domestic manufacture of the seventeenth century into the large-scale factory system of the nineteenth century. Better methods of agriculture were also adopted. Wet lands were drained, poor lands were fertilized, the breeds of animals were improved, and new food plants were introduced. A new enclosure movement led to farming on a larger scale. The construction of roads and canals made possible cheaper and speedier transportation. As a result, the small farmers and the cottage laborers were driven to the cities, which grew rapidly as centers of factory labor. Great landowners controlled the farms; a growing capitalist class controlled manufactures. Foreign trade and shipping grew rapidly. The use of machinery threw many out of employment, and conditions of employment and of life in the factories and in the towns finally became unspeakable. Poverty and crime increased rapidly.

This Industrial Revolution took place at a time when the mercantilist ideas of the seventeenth century were being abandoned and the doctrine of *laissez faire* was leaving employers and laborers to settle affairs among themselves. In turn, the economic changes helped to break down mercantilist ideas, since the elaborate regulations applicable to the old system were obviously unsuited to the new, and the necessity of abolishing them led many to believe that the government should keep its hands off industry entirely. Besides, the need of England to import food and raw materials for her growing factory towns, and the advantage in foreign competition given by her cheaply manufactured goods, led to the idea of free trade, since England could thus buy in the cheapest markets and undersell her competitors in all parts of the earth.

Mercantilist doctrines were attacked in England by writers, such as North and Child, in the later part of the seventeenth century. In the first half of the eighteenth century, Walpole removed or lowered import and export duties on over one hundred commodities, and neglected to enforce the Navigation Acts, being opposed to the system by which England tried to monopolize colonial trade. The effort of George III to reëstablish a paternalistic system of government met opposition, not only in the colonies, but also from a large class of Englishmen who had come to realize the opportunities offered by free competition and by free trade. Besides, the dominant philosophy in England, as in France, laid emphasis on natural rights and individual liberty, and the application of these ideas in the form of economic liberalism was inevitable. While numerous books and pamphlets, often anonymous, were published on economic subjects in England during the eighteenth century, the epoch-making work in the development of economico-political thought was that of Adam Smith (1723-1790).[22]

Smith built largely upon the work of his predecessors. He represented the culmination of certain principles which were common to his time and which made the hampering system of government control seem incompatible with industrial advance. He was acquainted with the writings of the mercantilists, of the philosophers of the seventeenth and eighteenth centuries, and of the Physiocrats. His teacher at Glasgow, Francis Hutcheson, in his lectures on "natural jurisprudence," exerted a deep influence, and handed down to Smith the views of Pufendorf, Grotius, and Locke. While traveling in France, Smith met Diderot, Quesnay, and Turgot, often discussing questions of taxation and foreign trade with the last-mentioned. From his contemporaries, Josiah Tucker[23] and Adam Ferguson, he derived political, ethical, and economic ideas, especially concerning the importance of giving self-interest free play and the value of unrestricted foreign trade. Hume exerted the greatest influence upon the general philosophy of Smith, his ideas of human nature, his historical spirit, and his understanding of the interrelation of social forces being especially important. Hume also attacked the mercantilist belief in the importance of money and its restrictive attitude toward foreign commerce, holding that English trade would benefit by the commercial prosperity of her neighbors.

In his lectures at Glasgow, Smith, in addition to dealing with natural theology, ethics, and jurisprudence, "examined those political regulations which are founded, not upon the principle of justice, but that of expediency, and which are calculated to increase the riches, the power, and the property of a state. Under this view he considered the political institutions relating to commerce, to finances, to ecclesiastical and military establishments."[24] The fundamental conceptions of Adam Smith were that self-interest is the primary force in society,[25] that men possess natural rights, that the earth is ruled by a beneficent Providence, and that government

[22] *The Wealth of Nations* (1776). See also his *Lectures on Justice, Police, Revenue, and Arms.*

[23] Tucker advocated the union of England and Ireland and the recognition of the independence of the American colonies. He believed that there is a harmony of economic interests, rather than an antagonism, among nations.

[24] *Works*, Vol. X, p. 12. Dugald Stewart edition.

[25] This idea was influenced by the work of Helvetius, *De l'Esprit* (1758).

interference with industry and commerce should be reduced to a minimum. In contrast to the Physiocrats, he held that labor, rather than land, is the chief source of wealth. He agreed with the Physiocrats, however, in believing that a harmonious natural order would arise if artificial, men-made restrictions were removed. He was more practical and utilitarian than the Physiocrats, and found justification for what was useful and expedient, even if it seemed to conflict with natural law. He thus combined nature, philosophy, and a common-sense utilitarianism. The influence of Montesquieu,[26] with his emphasis on things as they are and on the importance of the environment, offset somewhat the *a priori* metaphysical and theological assumptions of the divinely established order of nature. In his belief that, in the absence of artificial interference, men will be led through self-interest, as by a divine hand, to a natural order that insures the best results to the individual and to the state, Smith's point of view was optimistic. In his doctrine that the interests of various classes clash, and that every nation must at some time reach a "stationary state," his point of view was pessimistic.

Smith held that the state should limit its activities to protection against foreign states, to the administration of law and justice, and to the maintenance of certain public works and institutions, such as roads, harbors, schools, and the church. In exceptional cases, he would permit the government to abandon the *laissez-faire* policy with regard to industry and trade. For example, he would permit government regulation of banking and of interest rates, a duty on imports, if similar goods produced at home were taxed, a duty on imports in order to make a nation self-sufficient in such things as saltpeter and shipping, and retaliatory duties in case English products were taxed in foreign countries. He would also permit a limited regulation of the relation between employer and employee.

The time was ripe for the appearance of an explanation of the new social order when Smith's work appeared, for revolutions in industry, in philosophy, and in politics were in the air. The movement for religious toleration also played a part. Arguments for liberalism could be used equally well in political, economic, and religious matters. Both the Physiocrats in France and the free-traders in England favored toleration. The landowners were churchmen; the men of commerce were largely non-conformist, and religious intolerance interfered with British trade. The non-conformists in general distrusted the government; they opposed the monopolies granted by the court to its favorites. They desired to be let

[26] In his later years Smith is said to have been preparing a commentary on the *Esprit des Lois.*

alone, and believed that business success, secured by energetic individual effort, was a sign of God's favor. Smith's book passed through five editions during his lifetime. It was translated into several languages, and influenced legislation in a decisive manner. The dominant economists in England and France soon adopted his ideas; even in Germany, though to a less degree, *Smithianism* became a decided tendency. The younger Pitt was a careful student of Smith, and modified his policies to make them accord with the principles of the *Wealth of Nations*. In spite of the conservatism of the trading classes, many of whom clung to the belief that wealth meant gold and silver and that commerce was fostered by monopolies and government regulation, Pitt was able to effect numerous economic reforms. He favored a liberal policy toward the colonies, and his union of England and Ireland was intended to break down the tariff barrier between them.

The spread of Smith's ideas was also aided by the events that followed. The Industrial Revolution, which was in its earlier stages when Smith wrote, bore out his ideas as to the value of division of labor and made it desirable that England should widen her markets. The factory owners also welcomed his principle of governmental non-interference in their desire to exploit cheap labor, and opposed the Corn Laws, which kept the price of food high and tended to increase wages. The American Revolution showed the danger in a colonial system that led to revolt; it also proved the uselessness of the protective policy, since after the independence of the colonies trade between England and America flourished as never before. As a result, a strong anti-imperialist reaction set in. The British colonial policy had been mainly commercial, justified by the doctrines of mercantilism. When these doctrines were swept away, many believed that it would be beneficial for England to abandon her colonies. Tucker and Adam Smith denied that colonies were essential to commercial prosperity. The Utilitarians, Bentham and Mill, held that colonies were a source of expense and political corruption, and a cause of war.

The ideas of Smith were carried on by the "Manchester School," a group of men, chiefly merchants and manufacturers, of whom Richard Cobden and John Bright were leaders. Although they favored factory laws to protect children, they stood for the natural freedom of the individual and believed that governmental restrictions on industry and trade were injurious. They were especially interested in the repeal of the Corn Laws. Smith's individualism was a valuable reaction against the paternalism of mercantilist doctrines and was largely responsible for the prosperity of England's manufactures and commerce. Nevertheless, its application led to a selfish and materialistic point of view and to many evils, affecting especially the laboring classes. The development of modern government regulation of business and of labor, and the rise of socialistic doctrines were protests against the practical results of his policies.[27]

The Theory of Population

Numerous writers of the seventeenth and eighteenth centuries gave attention to the question of population.[28] The mercantilists taught that dense population was desirable and that rapid growth in population meant prosperity. The Biblical injunction to be fruitful and multiply was frequently quoted, and it was observed that the wealthiest and strongest states were usually the most populous. The government and the employing classes, in particular, favored a dense population: the former because it swelled the army; the latter because it furnished cheap labor for the factories. Bounties were paid for large families; in the German cities, only married men could hold office.

The condition of the peasants in France led Montesquieu to show some concern over the question of population. The results of the Industrial Revolution in England led to a reëxamination of the whole problem. Toward the end of the eighteenth century it seemed as though there were too many people for the land to support. Food prices rose rapidly; unemployment, poverty, and disease were widespread. The agricultural prosperity of the first half of the century was followed by great distress as the population shifted from country to city. In Ireland especially, the rapid growth of population gave rise to the work of Thomas Robert Malthus (1766-1834),[29] who followed the pessimistic tendencies in the teachings of Adam Smith, and held that the increase of population brought only hardship.

The immediate cause of Malthus' essay was the publication of the *Enquiry Concerning Political Justice* by William Godwin. Arguing for a sort of enlightened anarchism, Godwin held that government, which he considered a necessary evil, was to blame for the unhappiness and misery of mankind; and he taught that there was plenty for all if it were equally distributed. About the same time Condorcet,[30] in France, expressed equally optimistic views concerning the ability of the earth to furnish sufficient subsistence. He held that science would increase the food supply or that reason would prevent excessive growth of population.

[27] This subject will be more fully considered in later chapters.

[28] For example, Davenant, Child, Hume (in his *Essay on the Populousness of Ancient Nations*, 1752), and the German economists Süssmilch and Sonnenfels.

[29] See his *Essay on Population* (published anonymously in 1798, much enlarged in later revisions).

[30] In his *Esquisse d'un Tableau historique des Progrès de l'Esprit humain* (1794).

To this Malthus replied that there was a fundamental law operating in society which would prevent poverty from ever being eradicated no matter what was done. The population, he stated, tended to increase by geometrical progression (2, 4, 8, 16, 32), while the world's food supply increased merely by arithmetical progression (2, 4, 6, 8, 10). This meant that the world's population tended constantly to outrun its food supply. It would, in fact, do so but for the incidents of poverty—starvation, disease, and misery—which held the population in check. Poverty, in consequence, was here to stay.

Malthus did mention the possible solutions of birth control, emigration, or government intervention to raise the living standard, but he rejected each of these steps as unsound. Birth control would work only if individual prudence were more widespread than he believed to be the case. Emigration might open up new lands, but the population through doubling and redoubling would soon outdistance the food supply. And governmental interference, if it eased the living standard, would only make conditions favorable for more births, which would mean more mouths to feed and less for everyone until the people were again on the lowest level of subsistence. Malthus opposed these last two solutions on principle, anyway. They called for government controls and regulations which would break down the individualism in which he believed.

In effect, Malthus condemned the great majority of people to hunger and want because he considered their plight unavoidable. In so doing, he salved the consciences of industrial leaders and politicians who might otherwise have been more troubled by the suffering around them. The essay of Malthus provoked much discussion, numerous works appearing to attack or to defend his conclusions. His doctrines influenced legislation, especially in connection with poor relief and with emigration. They were partly instrumental in leading Darwin to his theory of natural selection. They strengthened the individualism of John Stuart Mill, who was prevented in his earlier writings from advocating governmental interference on behalf of the laborers because of the theory of population growth that Malthus put forward. And they had a tremendous influence on the impending rise of socialism.

REFERENCES

BEARD, C. A., *The Economic Basis of Politics* (New York, Knopf, 1934).

BONAR, James, *Malthus and His Work* (London, Macmillan, 1885).

BRAILSFORD, H. N., *Shelley, Godwin, and Their Circle* (New York, Holt, n. d.).

BUCK, P. W., *The Politics of Mercantilism* (New York, Holt, 1942).

COLE, C. W., *French Mercantilism, 1683-1700* (New York, Columbia Univ. Press, 1943).

GINZBERG, Eli, *The House of Adam Smith* (New York, Columbia Univ. Press, 1934).

GOOCH, G. P., *Political Thought in England from Bacon to Halifax* (London, T. Butterworth, 1937), Chap. 11.

JOHNSON, E. A. J., *Predecessors of Adam Smith* (New York, Prentice-Hall, 1937).

LASKI, H. J., *Political Thought in England from Locke to Bentham* (New York, Holt, 1920), Chap. 7.

RUSSELL, Bertrand, *Freedom versus Organization* (New York, Norton, 1934).

SCHUYLER, R. L., "The Rise of Anti-Imperialism in England, 1760-1830," *Political Science Quarterly*, Vol. 37 (September, 1922).

WEULERSSE, Georges, *Les Physiocrates* (Paris, Doin, 1931).

CHAPTER XVIII ✐

Later Eighteenth Century
Moralists and Jurists

Conditions in the Later Part of the Eighteenth Century

The year 1763 marked the end of the Seven Years' War, in which England, allied with Prussia, defeated France and her ally, Austria. As a result of this war, France lost to England the empire which her colonists had been building up in the St. Lawrence and Mississippi Valleys, and was compelled to abandon her hopes of conquering India. In addition, the French monarchy was burdened with an unpopular alliance with the Austrian Hapsburgs, and had incurred a great war debt, which hastened the financial disasters and the social troubles that led to the revolution. Influenced somewhat by the separation of powers theory of Montesquieu, the French *parlements,* or higher law courts, which had frequently had difficulties with the king's ministers, pushed their claims to protect political liberty against the king. They were summarily suppressed, however, in 1771, and the French monarch ruled with despotic power until the final crash.

England emerged from the contest with enormous territorial gains. She was incontestably the mistress of the sea and the world's greatest colonial power. The accession of George III (1760) marked, however, an attempt to establish a more independent royal power and to check the growing importance of parliament and prime minister. As a result of this effort, party controversies were stimulated and doctrines regarding the nature and value of the English system were reëxamined. In colonial policy, a more vigorous effort to enforce the Navigation Acts and to compel the Americans to bear part of the expense of conquering the Canadian provinces alienated the colonists and led to the American Revolution.

Prussia was consolidated and strengthened. Her ruler, Frederick the Great, was a typical example of the "enlightened despots" of the period, among whom were Catherine II of Russia, Joseph II of Austria, and Charles III of Spain. These rulers, influenced especially by the social and economic suggestions of the Physiocrats, put into effect far-reaching internal reforms. The position of the serfs was made more tolerable, methods of taxation were improved, administrative and judicial methods were reformed, commerce and industry were relieved of many burdensome restrictions, and the privileges of the nobility and clergy were curtailed. The control of the church over intellectual life was especially attacked, and the influence of the pope and the activities of the Jesuits were reduced.

It was popular for monarchs to act as patrons for the rational philosophers of the "enlightenment." In this process, political theorists began to exert a practical influence in government. Turgot was made finance minister under Louis XV and for a time was given an opportunity to apply the principles of the Physiocrats. Voltaire was called to the court of Frederick the Great. Rousseau was applied to for suggestions on the difficult political situation in Corsica and in Poland.[1] Mercier de la Riviere was summoned by Catherine of Russia, who had read Beccaria on law, to advise as to a proposed code for her dominions. Joseph II was personally acquainted with Rousseau and Turgot. Beccaria in Milan and Filangieri in Naples were publicists who also exerted a practical influence upon government. While the principles of Montesquieu were most influential in bringing about social reforms, his political doctrine of a separation between executive and legislative functions received little consideration from the enlightened despots. They preferred to carry out their policies without a political reorganization of their kingdoms; and the movement for representative parliaments did not appear until the French Revolution.

The foreign policy of the later eighteenth century showed little trace of enlightenment or of respect for the rules of natural justice which were supposed to underlie international law. The question of neutral rights at sea, raised by the maritime pretensions of England, received some consideration,[2] but in general international law made no progress. The dynastic diplomacy of the times was unscrupulous, and any method that would bring national advantage or weaken a rival was adopted. Long and disastrous wars were undertaken on the slightest pretexts, and treaties were violated whenever the interests of the state appeared to demand it.

[1] See his *Considérations sur le gouvernement de Pologne* (1771), in *Political Writings*, ed. by C. E. Vaughn.
[2] In the Armed Neutrality of 1780.

Of all the states which guaranteed the Pragmatic Sanction of the emperor, England alone, for motives of self-interest, kept faith. The seizure of Silesia by Frederick the Great and the partition of Poland were characteristic of the Machiavellian diplomacy of the period.

The political philosophy of the later eighteenth century was marked by a generally optimistic spirit. It believed that social and political evils could be remedied by the application of human reason, that a panacea could be discovered in natural law, and that fundamental principles could be discovered and applied to all social phenomena. Elaborate legislative codes were prepared with the belief that perfect and permanent systems might be established. Simple and uncritical formulas exerted a profound influence on men's minds. The single tax of the Physiocrats, their doctrine of *laissez faire,* and the slogan of liberty, equality, and fraternity, were examples. Montesquieu stood almost alone in realizing the complexity of human affairs and the difficulty of formulating and applying universal principles. Simplicity of mind and belief in the ability of reason to reshape institutions was, perhaps, necessary for the uprooting of old abuses. But the difficult task of constructing a new system after the French Revolution was aggravated by the doctrines of the natural-law philosophers.

French Social and Moral Philosophy

Between Rousseau and the French Revolution, political theory in France was concerned largely with social, economic, and religious reform. Many of the proposals made were specific in nature. The Physiocrats found the chief difficulty in the conditions that determined the production and use of wealth. Their remedy was agricultural development, the single tax on land, the abolition of internal restrictions on trade, and a general *laissez-faire* policy that would enable natural laws to operate. Other writers, such as Morelly and the Abbé Mably, found the main evil in private property, especially in the ownership of land, and urged communistic and socialistic projects.

Morelly, concerning whose life and work little is known, marked a distinct advance in the direction of modern thought, using both the utopian medium of fiction [3] and the analytical and philosophical form of the treatise.[4] He predicted the downfall of the Bourbon monarchy and the establishment of a state free from feudal privileges. He attacked inequalities in property and favored a general division of land. His ideas exerted a profound influence on the social theories of the French Revolution.

[3] In his *Basiliade* (1753).
[4] In his *Code de la Nature* (1755). Published as by Diderot in Vol. II of his works.

Gabriel de Mably (1709-1785) [5] developed the ideas of Rousseau, believing that inequalities of wealth and the usurpation of power by those possessing property were the sources of social and political injustice. By nature men were essentially equal. If men have the same needs and the same faculties, they ought to be given the same material and the same intellectual opportunities. Inequality was the result of bad laws, especially those that sanctioned private property. The remedy was to be found in proper legislation, preferably in the form of a code prepared by a wise lawgiver, inspired by pure reason and justice. Mably admired Sparta and Rome,[6] and he illustrated his writings by the acts of Solon, Lycurgus, and Cato. Their legislative reforms and their attitude toward property, especially in land, influenced his doctrines. Mably also held advanced opinions on international questions, in opposition to the Machiavellian practices of his time. He advocated love of humanity, respect for treaties, and the immunity of private property in maritime warfare.[7] The ideas of the Encyclopedists and Rousseau in emphasizing natural rights and human equality, as developed by Morelly and Mably, led to the communistic type of French socialism.

Other French writers, such as Helvetius and Holbach, attacked the prevalent moral and religious ideas, urged toleration and freedom of the press against the ecclesiastics in influence at the court, and put forward principles of utilitarian ethics and of atheism. They opposed the sentimentalism of Rousseau and followed rather the tradition of Hobbes and Locke, carrying their doctrines to logical conclusions. Claude Helvetius (1715-1771) [8] made egoism the sole motive of human action, and enlightened self-interest, based on love of pleasure and fear of pain, the criterion of morals. The only way to make a man moral was to make him see his own welfare in the public welfare, and this could be done only by legislation, that is, by proper rewards and punishments. The science of morals became, accordingly, the science of legislation; and the best government was that which secured the happiness of the greatest number.

Helvetius held that all men are naturally equal in intellect, and urged the importance of education and culture in national development. All governments love power and are naturally despotic; the best is that in which the greatest enlightenment is displayed by those in authority.

[5] In his *Entretiens de Phocion* (1763), *De la législation* (1776).

[6] In his *Parallèle des Romaines et des François* (1740), he praised Rome and criticized France.

[7] In his *Le droit public de l'Europe* (1748).

[8] In his *De l'Ésprit* (1758), trans. by W. Mudford, and his *De l'Homme* (1772), trans. by W. Hooper. The *De l'Ésprit* was intended to rival Montesquieu's *De l'Ésprit des Lois*.

Helvetius approved of the efforts of the enlightened despots in Prussia, Russia, and Austria. Believing that the vices and virtues of a people are the necessary effect of the laws under which they live, he demanded radical reforms in the social and political system in France. His utilitarian ideas exerted an influence on the later theory of Bentham; Beccaria stated that he was largely inspired by Helvetius in his attempt to modify the penal laws.

Baron Paul d'Holbach (1723-1789),[9] a French philosopher of German origin, was intimately connected with the Encyclopedists and Rousseau, and carried still further the ideas of Helvetius and the other French followers of Locke. He attacked religion as the source of all human evils, and wished to replace it by a system of education which would develop enlightened self-interest, believing that the study of science would bring men into accord with nature. Holbach ridiculed the "noble savage" of Rousseau, but adopted his ideas of social contract and general will, holding that the state was created by agreement in order to secure the greatest good of the greatest number, and this was accomplished by guaranteeing natural rights of individual liberty, property, and security. He followed Locke in basing authority on a contract between rulers and citizens, and in holding that citizens were absolved from obedience if those in authority failed to promote the public welfare. He followed Montesquieu in the doctrine that authority should be distributed among various organs of government in order to safeguard liberty.

Holbach believed that all existing governments, even the highly praised English system, were defective, being based on violence and ignorance. He urged a return to the natural order under the guidance of intelligent opinion. Ancient institutions and antiquated laws must be replaced by institutions comformable with reason and justice. Believing that men's nature and actions were largely determined by the institutions and laws under which they lived, he held that injustice and inequality were the result of artificial and irrational social and political systems. Utility, according to sound reason, should be the test of such systems. In his bitter attack on governments in general, and in his vehement arguments for radical reform, as well as in his Lockian philosophy, Holbach suggested the idea of revolution.

The eighteenth century writers who urged reform in France fall into four main groups. The liberal school of the first half of the century, represented by Montesquieu, D'Argenson, and Voltaire, was historical in method, looked to the English government as a model, and was moderate in its aims. The second school, of which Rousseau, Diderot, Helvetius,

[9] In his Le Système de la Nature (1770), his Politique naturelle (1773), and his Système Social (1773).

and Holbach were the chief exponents, was doctrinaire and intolerant of existing institutions. It applied *a priori* methods and relied upon pure reason to construct a perfect state. The Physiocrats, of whom Quesnay and la Riviere were most influential, were monarchists, but urged economic reform. The revolutionary school, represented by Mably and Condorcet, accepted the premises of democracy and urged that revolution was necessary in order to establish the sovereignty of the people. All were agreed, however, that men possessed natural rights, and this became an unshakable precept of liberalism and the cardinal doctrine of the revolution.

The Italian Jurists

In applying the spirit and method of Montesquieu to needed social and political reform, excellent work was done by two Italian jurists in the second half of the eighteenth century. Throughout Europe criminal law was antiquated, criminal trials were scandalously unfair, and punishment was incredibly cruel. Informers were rewarded and the flimsiest evidence was considered sufficient. Torture was used to force confessions, and the death penalty was inflicted for a great variety of offenses. Even in England, where methods were better than on the continent, Blackstone found more than one hundred offenses punishable by death.

The Italian jurist, Cesare Beccaria (1735-1794), from his study of Montesquieu, found his interest turned toward economic and social questions. His first publication was a proposal for the remedy of the currency in the Milanese states. But his best-known work dealt with crime and its punishment.[10] In this he advocated public trials and denounced torture and secret accusation. He believed that punishment should be less harsh, but more certain; and he favored the abolition of the death penalty. He held that persons of all classes should be treated equally, and that confiscation of property, as a penalty, should cease, since it brought suffering on innocent members of the family. He insisted that the prevention of crime was more important than the punishment of crime, and that this could be best accomplished by making the law clear, by making punishment certain, and especially by spreading enlightenment through education.

As a general basis for his ideas, Beccaria held the familiar belief that self-interest is the chief human motive, that men, naturally independent, voluntarily united themselves into civil society, and that the aim of legislation is to secure the greatest good of the greatest number. The public welfare was the sum of individual welfares, that is, the welfare of the

[10] The *Dei Delitti e delle Pene* (1764). It was published in English, with a commentary attributed to Voltaire in 1767.

majority. Laws and punishments, therefore, were just only in so far as they were necessary to the maintenance of the state and were shaped by intelligent reason. Beccaria's little book was translated into several languages and led to reform in the penal codes in many European states. His ideas influenced the later work of John Howard [11] and of Bentham in England.

The Italian jurist and publicist Gaetano Filangieri (1752-1788) [12] was an ardent reformer, vehement in denouncing the abuses of his time. He drew most of his ideas from Montesquieu, but applied them to practical problems of reform. Montesquieu had emphasized the spirit of the laws; Filangieri aimed to work out the proper content of the laws, based upon experience and reason. He held the optimistic view that Europe had reached a condition of peace, that individual liberty was secure, and that the development of industry, commerce, and the arts would make the nations prosperous. Accordingly, the time was ripe for a comprehensive science of legislation.

The first book of his unfinished treatise dealt with rules on which legislation ought to proceed. The second book was devoted to economic questions, urging unlimited free trade and the abolition of medieval obstacles to production. The third book dealt with principles of criminal jurisprudence; the fourth book, with education and morals. Filangieri drew his ideas on criminal law and procedure from Beccaria. While following Montesquieu in his theory of government, he was somewhat more critical of the English system. The party contests under George III and the American Revolution dampened his enthusiasm for English ideas and drew his attention to the experiments in government in America, where the simplicity of life approached the state of nature of the philosophers. Filangieri was a great admirer of William Penn, comparing him to Lycurgus and Solon. He prophesied that the nature and resources of the new American nation would enable it to stand independent of Europe.

English Legal and Moral Philosophy

After the middle of the eighteenth century, English political thought began to show signs of change. The complacency of Walpole's era was less obvious, especially after the accession of George III. French influence also began to be felt, and a perspective was given on English institutions by the writings of Voltaire, Montesquieu, and Rousseau, and by comparisons between English and French methods of government. Montesquieu, in particular, by his historical method, his emphasis on legislation as a

[11] See his *The State of the Prisons in England and Wales* (1784).
[12] In his *La Scienza della Legislazione* (1780), trans. by Sir Richard Clayton.

method of social change, and his insistence on the importance of liberty, gave an impetus to the thought that led to Burke and Bentham. His praise of the British constitution and his belief that its essential principle was the separation of powers led English writers to examine their system of government, and resulted in the work of Blackstone and of the Swiss jurist, De Lolme. Rousseau's ideas, too direct for the England of that day, were bitterly attacked. Rousseau was, however, the disciple of Locke, and some of his doctrines of reform were finally put forward, in different words, by Priestley and Price. By that time the optimism of Blackstone, and the veneration for the past of Burke were on the defensive, and a new era in British thought had begun.

The growing spirit of discontent was manifest in the writings of the clergyman, John Brown (1715-1766).[13] He attacked politics, the church, and the customs and manners of his time, complaining of the prevailing luxury and effeminacy. He compared the state of England with that of Carthage and of Rome before their fall, believing that the commercial greatness of England was a symptom of decay, and prophesying destruction at the hands of France unless the simplicity of nature could be restored. The secret of English liberty he found in the foggy climate and in the temperament of the nation. He had no confidence in popular government. His political remedy was to depend upon the enlightened wisdom of a great statesman, after the fashion of Bolingbroke's *Patriot King*. For this position he believed the elder Pitt was best fitted.

Hume's ideas were carried forward at the same time by the Scotch philosophers, and resulted in the work of Adam Ferguson (1723-1816),[14] at the University of Edinburgh. There was little that was original in Ferguson's writings, but his literary skill and his ability to paraphrase the ideas of other men made his work immensely popular. Hume and Adam Smith, in addition to Montesquieu, were chiefly drawn upon. Ferguson realized the danger of easy generalizations concerning the state of nature, and of easy solutions for the problems of social and political life. He held that the course of civilization was determined by definite but complex principles, and that the various forms in which institutions appeared were equally natural. Instinct and habit, not reason, created social organization, deliberate purpose playing but a small part. Legislation, therefore, could do little to control the inevitable course of events. The state was not founded by contract though, with increasing intellectual progress, consent became more and more important.

Ferguson was especially scornful of Rousseau's doctrine that the natural

---

[13] In his *Estimates of the Manners and Principles of the Times* (1757).
[14] In his essay on the *History of Civil Society* (1767), and his *Principles of Moral and Political Science* (1792).

and desirable state of mankind is one of stability and peace. He regarded opposition and conflict as natural and beneficent. Competition in politics, industry, commerce, and even international war were inevitable. Liberty was "maintained by the continued differences and oppositions of numbers." Self-interest was the guiding motive of individuals and of nations. Ferguson believed that the authority of the state was limited by the natural rights of man; at the same time, liberty should be carefully restricted and not made to imply equality. Absolutism and popular democracy were both undesirable. Of a conservative and somewhat cynical temperament, he disliked extremes in any form and had little sympathy with the philosophy of reform or with the revolutionary movements.

The more optimistic tradition of the excellence of the British system was continued in the work of Sir William Blackstone (1723-1780).[15] His analysis of the constitution and laws of England was preceded by a general philosophy of the state, drawn largely from Pufendorf, Locke, and Montesquieu. The ideas of various thinkers were combined with little regard for consistency. Natural law, divine law, and civil law all found a place in his system, together with the new utilitarian doctrines. From its first publication, the *Commentaries* exerted a tremendous influence, not only in England, but also in France and America. French lawyers and judges were accused of following Blackstone rather than their own national law. Of an American edition, published in 1771, fourteen hundred copies were sold in advance, the name of John Adams heading the list of subscribers. Burke said that as many copies of the book were sold in America as in England; and the ideas of natural rights and individual liberty that prevailed at the outbreak of the American Revolution were largely those of Blackstone.

Blackstone found the origin of the state in the natural result of the efforts of men to secure their best interests. He rejected the idea of a state of nature and a social contract as having no basis in history. Nevertheless his book is full of contractual notions. He seemed to realize that Hume had destroyed the basic conception of Locke; at the same time he wished to follow Locke's general ideas. The result was confusion. He made no distinction between state and government, holding that the government possessed supreme and absolute sovereignty. This was vested in the lawmaking body, consisting of the king in parliament. At the same time, Blackstone believed in natural rights, the primary aim of the state being to protect individuals in their rights of personal security, personal liberty, and private property. These were either the residuum of natural liberty or the civil rights granted by the state in place of the natural liberties

---

[15] The *Commentaries on the Laws of England* (1765).

given up. As subordinate rights he mentioned the right to bear arms, to petition for redress of grievances, and to apply to the courts for justice in case of injuries.

Blackstone glorified the British constitution as a perfect mixture of monarchic, aristocratic, and democratic elements, and believed that political and civil liberty in England fell little short of perfection. He held that the English system is "so admirably tempered and compounded that nothing can endanger or hurt it, but destroying the equilibrium of powers between one branch of the legislature and the rest." Blackstone was too content with the conditions of his times to question old concepts that were no longer applicable to new conditions. There is nothing in his work on the cabinet, on the party system, or on ministerial responsibility. His idea of the royal prerogative was entirely antiquated; his theory that the House of Commons represented all men of property was absurd in view of the lack of representation of the new industrial cities.

Blackstone's work contained much real learning, and, as Bentham said, it taught jurisprudence to speak the language of the scholar and the gentleman. At the same time, it gave attention to forms rather than to the substance, and its defense of a system that did not exist acted as a barrier to legal and political progress for half a century. In the history of political theory it was important chiefly because it was the target at which Bentham directed his *Fragment on Government*. By his writings, and by those of Austin, its flimsy legal philosophy was ruthlessly shattered.

Another panegyric of the British constitution was the work of a Swiss jurist, Jean De Lolme (1740-1806) [16] who was compelled to emigrate from Switzerland because of offense given by his political pamphlets. During his exile he made a careful study of the English government; and his book, while lacking in breadth of view and in scientific spirit, made many acute observations on the causes of the excellences in the British system. With Blackstone's *Commentaries* and Hume's *History of England,* it supplied the political philosophers of the time with their ideas of the English constitution, and was largely used as a political pamphlet in the contest between George III and his opponents.

De Lolme found the secret of liberty in the constitutional equilibrium between royal and popular power. He emphasized the value of judicial independence, of the freedom of the press, of the party system, and of the supremacy of the civil over the military government. The use of the jury and the writ of *habeas corpus* he found especially admirable, in contrast to continental methods. The importance of the cabinet and the prime minister escaped his notice, and he had no confidence whatever in the

---

[16] In his *Constitution de l'Angleterre* (1771), English edition (1772).

masses. A passive share in government was all that he would entrust to the common man. From this point of view he made a severe attack on Rousseau's doctrine that liberty depended upon the direct participation of each citizen in lawmaking. De Lolme believed that the unorganized and unintelligent masses could not govern, and that the general will would be in reality the will of the politicians and the great interests. He held that liberty was best safeguarded by properly balanced political devices, being somewhat too much inclined to view government as a machine and individuals merely as inert adjuncts.

The influence of Rousseau began to appear in England about the time that popular discontent with the policies of George III became widespread. John Wilkes, in the *North Briton*, and the anonymous author of the *Junius Letters* represented the growing demands for liberty on the part of the English people. Rousseau's individualistic doctrines of natural rights and of popular sovereignty were, therefore, welcomed, especially by the nonconforming Whigs, who were naturally suspicious of governmental interference. Joseph Priestley (1733-1804) [17] taught that men are equal and possess equal natural rights, and that no man can be governed without his consent, since government was founded upon a contract by which civil liberty was given up in exchange for a power to share in making law. The people, therefore, are sovereign and may resist if their natural rights are encroached upon. Moreover the government must interfere as little as possible with men's actions, especially in trade, individual initiative being preferable to state action. Many of the ideas of Adam Smith were foreshadowed by Priestley. The happiness of the majority of members of a state was the standard by which the success of a government should be judged. It was from Priestley that Bentham derived the significance of the "greatest good of the greatest number." Priestley preceded Condorcet in believing in the perfectability of man, and glorified reason as being able to work out a future golden age.

Dr. Richard Price (1723-1791), [18] like Priestley a leading non-conformist, was stirred by the American Revolution. He avoided, however, the utilitarian arguments, and based his ideas wholly upon abstract rights, following especially Locke and Rousseau. He believed that liberty depended upon direct, popular self-government, that men are naturally free and equal, and that the people possess the right to revolt against any attempt to deprive them of liberty or property. He also held an individualistic view of government, believing that it should restrict its activities to particular and limited ends. He had less optimism than Priestley, being more

[17] In his *Essay on the First Principles of Government* (1768).
[18] In his *Observations on the Nature of Civil Liberty* (1776), and his *Additional Observations* (1777).

inclined to the doctrine of Brown that the growing luxury of England was a sign of degeneration, proved by his fallacious belief in a declining population.

While Priestley and Price represented the Whig attitude during the period that centered in the American Revolution, the Tory and Anglican point of view was put forward by Josiah Tucker, the Dean of Gloucester (1712-1799).[19] He typified the prejudice against foreigners, the hatred of metaphysics, and the sturdy, common-sense nationalism of his class. He was impatient with Rousseau's doctrines of the noble savage and the state of nature. He held that popular sovereignty meant mob rule, and that the right of the people to change their government would lead to violence and anarchy. While denying the right of the American colonies to revolt, he believed that colonies of all kinds were useless, and that England would save money and avoid political corruption by giving up all her dependencies. He favored a policy of free trade, and held that self-interest would lead the colonies to trade with England even if there was no political tie.

While liberal theory was making rapid progress in England during the period of the American Revolution, and while English opinion was inclined at first to favor the French revolutionary movement, the excesses of the French democracy and the reactionary spirit that resulted from the Napoleonic wars checked this tendency and made the conservative doctrines of Burke the dominant theory in England for over a quarter of a century.

REFERENCES

Boorstin, D. J., *The Mysterious Science of Law; an Essay on Blackstone's Commentaries* (Cambridge, Harvard Univ. Press, 1941).

Gignoux, C. J., *Turgot* (Paris, Fayard, 1945).

Hubert, René, *D'Holbach et ses amis* (Paris, Delpeuch, 1928).

Laski, H. J., *Political Thought in England from Locke to Bentham* (New York, Holt, 1920), Chap. 5.

Maestro, M. T., *Voltaire and Beccaria as Reformers of Criminal Law* (New York, Columbia Univ. Press, 1942).

Sabine, G. H., *A History of Political Theory*, rev. ed. (New York, Holt, 1950), pp. 563-567, 568-570.

Stephen, Leslie, *History of English Thought in the Eighteenth Century*, 2 vols. (New York, Putnam, 1927), Vol. II.

Wickwar, W. H., *Baron d'Holbach* (London, G. Allen, 1935).

——, "Helvétius and Holbach," in F. J. C. Hearnshaw, ed., *The Social and Political Ideas of Some Great French Thinkers of the Age of Reason* (New York, Barnes & Noble, 1950), Chap. 8.

[19] In his *Treatise on Civil Government* (1781).

CHAPTER XIX

Political Theories of the American and French Revolutions

Nature of the American and French Revolutions

For fifty years before the American Revolution there was constant political controversy between the American colonists and the representatives of the British government in the colonies. These disputes were, however, local and personal, dealing with such questions as the extension of the franchise, the importation of convicts, the issue of paper money, and the taxation of proprietaries' lands. No serious hostility had arisen, because the colonists trusted the justice of the British government and because Walpole and his successors had carefully avoided issues that would arouse opposition at home or in the colonies.

The ambition of George III to reëstablish the power of the monarch led to the fall of the old governing aristocracy in England and to the adoption of a vigorous colonial policy. The opposition to the king in England championed the cause of the colonists, hence the reëstablishment of royal power became closely bound up with the maintenance of authority over the colonies. The conflict began with an attempt to enforce the Navigation Acts, which had been largely ignored, especially by the New England merchants, who had built up a profitable trade with Africa and the West Indies. The issuing of writs of assistance, or search warrants, for the seizure of suspected goods was viewed in the colonies as an unwarranted extension of the powers of the British parliament.

The real conflict arose over the efforts of England to assess upon the colonists a portion of the expenditure required for the maintenance of troops in Canada. The passing of the Stamp Act in 1765 marked the beginning of this policy, and led to the claim in the colonies that taxation without representation was tyranny. The colonists held that their assemblies alone could levy internal taxes; and bitter differences of opinion over the nature of the British Empire and the powers of parliament began to appear. While the Stamp Act was replaced by taxes on colonial imports, these also were opposed, and were met by colonial agreements to boycott English goods. The sending of troops to America to enforce British policy led to violence, to more repressive legislation, and to war. State governments were set up and a Continental Congress was assembled. Beginning with a demand for the redress of grievances, the war led to the independence and unification of the colonies.

The American Revolution attracted much attention in Europe, especially in France. The French king and his advisers, smarting over the humiliation of the Seven Years' War, rejoiced in England's difficulties, took up the cause of the Americans, and gave substantial aid in winning their independence. French political philosophers saw in the American Revolution a practical application of current doctrines. A people, close to nature, had deliberately, on the grounds of natural rights, overthrown one government and, by voluntary agreement, had set up another. The doctrines put forward by Americans to justify their actions were thoroughly familiar in French thought; and a powerful stimulus was thus given to French revolutionary ideas.

French intervention in the American Revolution hastened the course of events in France itself, where the government was rapidly becoming bankrupt. The financial reforms of Turgot and Necker failed because of the opposition of the nobility and clergy, who were unwilling to bear their share of taxation. Various plans of reform were proposed; finally in 1789 the ancient Estates-General was called together, proclaimed itself a national assembly representing the general will of the French people, and assumed the power to govern and to reorganize the state. Special privileges were abolished, an elaborate bill of rights was issued, and a new constitution for the kingdom put into effect.

However, the revolution soon got beyond the control of the moderate element that began it. The spread of revolutionary ideas to the masses, especially in Paris, led to anarchy and brought into prominence the more radical leaders. The execution of the king, the establishment of a republic, the experiments of the Directory, and the enlightened despotism of Napoleon followed in rapid succession. During this period a number of written constitutions were prepared and put into effect. This device, drawn from America, and furthered by the general belief of the period in legislative codes and fundamental documents, spread later to all parts of

Europe. The nature of a written constitution and the method of its creation became, therefore, an important issue in political theory.

The National Assembly of France in 1790 solemnly declared that "the
French nation renounces wars of conquest and will never use force
against the liberty of any people." The Abbé Gregoire in 1794 presented
a project for a declaration of the law of nations as an appendix to the
Declaration of the Rights of Man of 1789. It contained advanced ideas
of international justice and represented the idealistic spirit of the early
French Revolution. However, the effort of neighboring rulers to restore
the French monarchy, and fear of the French efforts to spread their revolutionary doctrines led to a general European war. In this the revolution
proved false to its principles, and France entered upon a career of aggression and conquest which culminated in the Napoleonic empire. Great
Britain, at first inclined to a policy of neutrality, became the leader of a
series of coalitions that finally reduced France to her former boundaries.
During these struggles the fundamental principles of international law,
especially of maritime law, were ignored by both France and England,
and the rights of neutral commerce were outrageously violated. This
called forth the opposition of the United States, the leading maritime
neutral, and led to the War of 1812. The Congress of Vienna, at the close
of the Napoleonic wars, based its work upon the principle of legitimacy,
ignored the powerful forces of democracy and nationality, and was animated by a reactionary spirit that lasted until well into the nineteenth
century.

Political Theory of the American Revolution

The political theory of the American Revolution was not put forward
in any systematic treatise. It appeared in the form of pamphlets, ad-
dresses from platform and pulpit, newspaper discussions, resolutions, and
constitutions. Its upholders were not disinterested political philosophers,
but promoters of a revolutionary program. In the early part of the struggle the argument of the colonists was mainly constitutional, dealing with
the legal relation of the colonies to the home government. Against the
claim of parliament to tax the colonists, they appealed to the king, to
their charters, to the long recognition of their autonomy in taxation, and
to the traditional rights of Englishmen. In the later period, arguments
based upon the more general theory of natural rights and social contract
were prominent; and the inalienable rights of the colonists as men rather
than their legal rights as Englishmen were stressed. Some claimed that
the king had broken his contract with the people and that they were

accordingly justified in resistance. Others claimed that the social contract itself had been broken and the state of nature restored. The American people were therefore justified in establishing a new body politic.

The political ideas of the colonists were drawn mainly from the historical precedents of the seventeenth century in England, and from the theory developed by the revolutionary party at that time. The doctrines of natural rights, social contract, popular sovereignty, and the right of revolution, as worked out by Milton, Sydney, Harrington, and Locke, were frequently quoted. Grotius, Pufendorf, and Vattel were also popular because of their emphasis on natural law. A few radical thinkers put forward communistic ideas similar to those of the English Levellers, but in general the colonial doctrines were those that had long been familiar in England. In the practical application of these doctrines in their constructive program after independence, however, the colonists worked out a more democratic system of government than had been possible in England.

In their constitutional arguments, the colonists claimed that the British parliament had no right to tax the colonies. They held that they owed allegiance to the king, from whom they had received their charters, not to parliament; and that their own assemblies held the same position in the colonies that parliament did in Great Britain. Some made a distinction between internal and external taxation, holding that parliament might regulate colonial trade but could not levy taxes within the colonies. It was also argued that the colonists, as Englishmen, could not be taxed by parliament unless they were represented in parliament; and that, since no colonial representatives sat in the British parliament, colonial taxes could be levied only by the colonial assemblies.

The constitutional arguments of the colonists were weak [1] in that they held an antiquated idea of the relative position of king and parliament in the British system, not realizing the enormous growth of parliamentary power. They also held a premature theory of parliamentary representation, which in England was based upon the class system, not upon population as in the colonies, and which left a large part of the British population unrepresented as much as were the colonies. Examples of the early legal arguments [2] used by the colonists may be found in the speeches of James Otis and Patrick Henry; in the writings of John Adams,[3] James

---

[1] In his book, *The American Revolution* (1923), Professor C. H. McIlwain makes a strong case for the constitutional arguments of the colonists.

[2] Similar constitutional principles, denying the right of the British parliament to legislate for Ireland, were put forward as early as 1644 in an anonymous pamphlet entitled *A Declaration setting forth How, and by what Means, the Laws and Statutes of England, from Time to Time, came to be of Force in Ireland.*

[3] See his *Works*, Vol. IV, pp. 1-177.

Wilson,[4] Stephen Hopkins,[5] and Richard Bland;[6] and in the resolutions adopted by the Virginia Assembly (1765).

Concurrently with the constitutional arguments appeared others based upon the abstract doctrine of natural rights.[7] These were elaborated as the constitutional arguments were shown to be vulnerable. They included the usual belief in an original state of nature in which men were free and equal, the establishment of political society by voluntary agreement for the purpose of promoting general welfare, the possession of rights with which the government must not interfere, the ultimate sovereignty of the people, and the right of revolution in case of misgovernment. The natural and inalienable rights of men were usually defined as those of life, liberty, property, and the pursuit of happiness. To these were usually added freedom of worship and freedom of expression, and a guarantee of fair and speedy trial by jury for those accused of crime. It was generally held that those who showed "sufficient evidence of permanent common interest with, and attachment to, the community"[8] had a natural right to vote and hold office. Since the security of individual liberty and of property was the great end of government, more attention was given to what the government should not do than to what it should do. Governmental interference was generally disliked, and it was held that a large measure of civil liberty and freedom of action should be left to the individual.

Since men were born free and equal, no authority could claim their allegiance except by voluntary agreement. Hence government rested upon the consent of the governed. All legislation, especially the levying of taxes, must rest upon the consent of those who obeyed the laws. Hence "taxation without representation was tyranny." Sovereignty resided in the people, though no clear statement was made as to just whom the "people" included. American theory, like that of Althusius in the seventeenth century, was inclined to view a sovereign people over a large area as a collection of groups rather than a collection of individuals. This idea was closely associated with the states' rights doctrine of the period and with the later federal principle. Those who exercised governmental powers were the agents of the people and were accountable to them for their conduct. If they abused their power or infringed upon the natural rights

---

[4] *Considerations on the Nature and Extent of the Legislative Authority of the British Parliament* (1774).

[5] See the *Rights of the Colonies Examined* (1764).

[6] See *An Inquiry into the Rights of the British Colonies* (1766).

[7] An impetus to these ideas was given by the popularity of the *Vindication of the Government of New England Churches* by John Wise, a new edition of which appeared in 1772.

[8] *Virginia Declaration of Rights.*

of the people, they should be removed. Revolution was a duty as well as a right for those who loved freedom.

The best statement of the natural rights theory of the colonists was made in the Declaration of Independence. Similar statements appeared in the resolutions of the colonial assemblies and in the bills of rights of the early state constitutions. As early as 1761, James Otis had suggested revolutionary doctrines.[9] John Dickinson,[10] Samuel Adams,[11] John Adams,[12] James Wilson,[13] and Thomas Jefferson[14] also made clear presentations of the philosophy of the times.

In the early period of the controversy there was little opposition in America to the monarchical principle in government, and little desire for independence. Writers in America as in England were inclined to view the British system of government as the best in the world. The influence of Blackstone was strong in the colonies, and both James Otis and John Adams warmly praised the excellent features of the British constitution. The growth of republican sentiment was stimulated by the war, and especially by the writings of Thomas Paine (1737-1809).[15] Paine bitterly attacked the institutions of monarchy and of hereditary nobility. He viewed kings as expensive and useless figureheads. He ridiculed the idea of the divine right of monarchs, and said that one honest man was worth more than all the crowned ruffians that ever lived. The principle of hereditary succession seemed to him an absurd method of choosing governing officials. Paine urged the colonists to declare their independence, arguing that foreign nations would not intervene on the side of the colonists so long as they acknowledged allegiance to the British crown. The later American attitude toward monarchy and the system of nobility, the emphasis on popular elections, and the idea of independence owed much to the influence of Paine.

Paine also attacked the nature of the British government, and criticized the check and balance system that Montesquieu had praised. He held that there are but two functions of government, the creation of law and

[9] In his speech in opposition to the Writs of Assistance. See also his *Rights of the Colonies Asserted and Proved* (1764), and his *Vindication of the British Colonies* (1765).

[10] *Letters of a Pennsylvania Farmer* (1768).

[11] *Rights of the Colonists as Men and as British Subjects; Natural Rights of the Colonists.*

[12] *Thoughts on Government* (1776).

[13] *Considerations on the Nature and Extent of the Legislative Authority of the British Parliament* (1774).

[14] *Summary View of the Rights of British America* (1774); *Virginia Declaration of Independence* (1776).

[15] *Common Sense* (1776); *The Foresters' Letters* (1776); *The American Crisis* (1776-1783). For Paine's ideas concerning the French Revolution, see below.

the execution of law; and that the judiciary exercises merely one phase of executive power. On this point he differed from the leaders of American thought. He believed that the absence of a written constitution was a serious defect in the British system, arguing that the traditions and practices upon which its government was based could not properly be called a constitution. The American idea of a definite written document, created by a process distinct from the usual method of legislation, he considered an epoch-making advance in political method. To Paine, government at its best was a necessary evil. Its functions therefore should be narrowly limited. The rights of man were more important than any positive benefit that government could confer.[16]

Opinion in America was by no means unanimous in favor of resistance. Many Loyalists opposed the Revolution, on grounds of expediency, for personal reasons, and on political principle. The Tory point of view was represented in the writings of the Virginia clergyman, Jonathan Boucher (1738-1804).[17] Boucher followed, in general, the doctrines of Filmer's *Patriarcha*. He held that government was from God and that kings ruled by divine right. He denied that government was an evil, viewing it rather as the source of great blessings. Ideas of natural equality and popular sovereignty he held in abhorrence. He believed that democracy was equivalent to anarchy, and that the established authority should receive respectful obedience. The right of revolution seemed to him a "damnable doctrine, derived from Lucifer, the father of rebellion."

American Documents and Constitutions

The period of the revolution in America and in France gave rise to numerous important governmental documents in which the current political philosophy was crystallized. In America, the Declaration of Independence, the resolutions of the colonial assemblies and the continental congresses, the state constitutions, the Articles of Confederation, and the Federal Constitution were most important. In so far as these contained a statement of individual liberties, they followed the English tradition that came down through Magna Carta, the Petition of Right, the Bill of Rights, the Habeas Corpus Act, and the like, with added emphasis derived from the theory of Locke concerning inalienable natural rights. The Declaration of Independence was accepted as the classic statement of civil liberty and the right of revolution.

In so far as they were frameworks of government, they suggested the

---

[16] He later qualified this idea. See the second part of the *Rights of Man* (1792), published while Paine was in England.
[17] In his *View of the Causes and Consequences of the American Revolution* (1797).

Instrument of Government of Cromwell. The colonial charters had also been made to serve as written constitutions; and the theory of social contract gave a philosophical basis for the establishment of a body politic by popular covenant, which had already been applied in the Mayflower Compact and in the Fundamental Orders of Connecticut. The American constitutions represented the first successful attempt of a people to create, consciously and deliberately, a system of government, and to enact the principles of a political philosophy into law. The idea of a fundamental document, created by a special representative body created for the purpose, and formally approved by the people, was one of the most important contributions of the period. The fear of governmental oppression led the American democracy to place upon their governments the additional check of a fundamental law which the ordinary government could not change, and to make a Bill of Rights guaranteeing their liberty a part of this law.

The written constitutions of the Americans represented not only the political ideas derived from English and French sources, but also certain principles resulting from peculiarly American institutions. The general equality of social and economic conditions, the absence of feudal customs, and the congregational system of church organization were important factors in determining the nature of American governmental ideas. Accordingly, monarchy and privileged aristocracy were prohibited, as was the hereditary principle in office holding. The system of checks and balances was adopted with elaborate devices to prevent any organ of government from exercising undue power. Government was viewed as an untrustworthy servant, constantly under suspicion, and needing limitation at every point. Executive authority was especially feared, and chief confidence was placed in the representative assemblies. Popular election and short terms were provided as additional safeguards against tyranny. Large standing armies were considered dangerous, and provision was made for the subordination of the military to the civil authority. Centralized authority was opposed, and chief emphasis was laid on local self-government. The difficulty of union was greatly intensified by this attitude.

While the destructive theory of the revolution was extremely democratic, certain limitations were placed upon the practical application of its principles. Property qualifications, preferably in real estate, were generally required for voting and for officeholding, thus limiting the political "people" to a decided minority. Religious qualifications, such as the exclusion of Catholics or atheists from the higher offices, were found in most of the states. In order to prevent too close a union between church and state, the clergy were generally forbidden to hold office. The existence of a large slave population was not considered incompatible with the theory of natural equality, and woman's suffrage was practically unheard of.[18]

The American documents were closely studied by political philosophers in Europe. In England, Richard Price [19] spoke of the American Revolution as opening a new era in the history of the world. In France, largely through the influence of Benjamin Franklin,[20] American ideas spread rapidly—thinkers such as Turgot, Mably, Condorcet, and Mirabeau giving them careful attention.[21] Many Frenchmen, some from the noblest families, fought along with the Americans during the war and returned to France as ardent advocates of the American views on liberty and equality. Lafayette framed the American Declaration of Independence with a vacant space left for a similar declaration of the rights of the French people. Numerous books of the period show the interest in France in American affairs.[22]

The American Revolution seemed to Europeans to signify the dawn of liberty. Even in Germany, the sympathies of the government and of the educated classes, partly because of the dislike of England and of the traffic in Hessian soldiers, was with the colonies. American speeches and documents were given wide publicity in the German press, and returning Hessians were often enthusiastic over conditions in America. The American idea of a Declaration of Rights met with especial favor in Europe. The attempt to apply a republican form of government over so large a population and so wide an area, in contradiction to the political axiom that democracy was possible only in small states, led to much discussion. American ideas were largely responsible for the rapid spread of revolutionary doctrines in France, and for the general demand for written constitutions and representative assemblies that appeared in Europe in the early nineteenth century. The meeting of the Philadelphia convention in 1787 for the purpose of creating a new American union, the document they drew up, and the able exposition of its principles in *The Federalist*, were directly influential in the assembling of the Estates-General in 1789.

[18] In England, Mary Wollstonecraft, the wife of Godwin, argued for woman's rights in her *Vindication of the Rights of Women* (1792).

[19] In his *Observations on the Importance of the American Revolution* (1777).

[20] Franklin had the Declaration of Independence, the constitutions of the states, and other papers relating to American affairs translated and spread throughout France.

[21] The criticisms of the American system put forward by these writers led John Adams to reply in his *Defense of the Constitution of the United States* (1787-8), and his *Discourses on Davila* (1790).

[22] For example, Clavière and Brissot, *De la France et des États-Unis* (1787); Abbé Raynal, *Observations on the Government and Laws of the United States* (1785); Mirabeau, *Considerations on the Order of Cincinnatus* (1785); and the volumes of travels by the Marquis de Chastellux.

Political Theory of the French Revolution

In France, as in America, the philosophy of the revolution, after the work of Rousseau, appeared mainly in the form of political pamphlets. Radical ideas were published anonymously, and old institutions were defended by the nobility, the clergy, and the magistrates. Numerous writers believed that they could solve the problems of social and political life by the application of pure reason, if only other men would abandon their prejudices. The calling of the Estates-General and the reform of feudal abuses and of legal procedure were chiefly discussed. Book-sellers' shops were crowded, reading rooms were opened, and political clubs, after the English fashion, were set up. The deluge of pamphlets in Paris was so great that the price of printing was doubled, several thousand appearing in the last months of 1788 alone.[23]

Somewhat more moderate than the pamphlets were the *cahiers* of the spring of 1789. These were statements of grievances and suggestions of reform prepared in the local election districts, and intended to serve as instructions for the Estates-General. While they showed wide variations and often dealt chiefly with local abuses, certain features frequently appeared. General complaint was made of inequality and over-taxation; and the natural-law philosophy, with its belief in the social contract, the rights of men, and the sovereignty of the people was usually stated. While the *cahiers* of the peasants were mainly concerned with demands for social and economic reform, and those of the clergy dealt with their own affairs, those of the nobles gave chief attention to a political program. All classes were agreed that a new political system must be set up; in some cases deputies were instructed not to consider details of reform until a constitution had been adopted.

The main features of the system of government which they desired to establish were generally agreed upon. The king should remain, but his legislative powers should be shared by the nation as represented in a general assembly. Whether the representatives of the three estates should vote separately or in a single body was a much disputed point. The executive power of the king was to be exercised through ministers who could be held responsible by the civil tribunals or by the Estates-General. The Estates-General should meet at frequent intervals and vote taxes for limited periods. Local assemblies were to be established in the provinces, with large administrative powers. Court procedure was to be simplified

[23] Characteristic titles were *Plan for a Matrimonial Alliance between Monsieur Third Estate and Madam Nobility; Te Deum of the Third Estate as it will be sung at the First Mass of the Estates General, with the Confession of the Nobility.*

and accused persons given better treatment. A codification of the laws was frequently demanded.

The political thought of the reformers was well represented by the famous essay of the Abbé Siéyès (1748-1836).[24] He attacked the special privileges of the nobility and the clergy and held that the third estate, which composed the greater part of the population and did all the useful work of the nation, should be given its fair share of political power. Following the political philosophy of Rousseau, Siéyès believed that the state was composed of individuals who voluntarily combined their separate wills to form a general will. He differed from Rousseau in holding that in a large state the general will might be expressed by representatives acting for the people as a whole.

The proper procedure in the organization of a state was to call a national convention to draw up a written constitution. This fundamental law could not bind the sovereign people, who might change it through the action of a later convention; it would, however, bind the government which was established according to its provisions. Writing his pamphlet at the time of the controversy over the proper organization of the Estates-General, Siéyès urged the representatives of the third estate to meet separately and form a national constitution-making assembly. While the Americans had already put into practice the idea of a national constitutional convention, the clarity with which Siéyès worked out the doctrine of the expression of popular sovereignty through a special constitution-making assembly was a valuable contribution to political thought. The actual process by which the French Estates-General was transformed into the Constituent Assembly followed closely the procedure which he laid down.

The theory of a written constitution was worked out in more detail by the Marquis de Condorcet (1743-1794).[25] He was familiar with American practice and believed thoroughly in the expression of national will, through a constitutional convention, in the form of a written document. He held that through the application of rational philosophy a perfect system of government and a perfect guarantee of natural liberty could be achieved. He believed that a declaration of rights should be included in the constitution, and that an amending clause, providing for an automatic assembling of the national convention, should also be included. He held that no generation could bind its successor; each should determine for itself the nature of its institutions. The American system of checks and

[24] *Qu'-est-ce que le Tiers-État?* (1788). See also his *Essai sur les Privilèges* (1788).
[25] In his *Plan de Constitution* (1788). See also his *Esquisse d'un tableau des progrès de l'esprit humain* (1795).

balances he criticized as interfering too much with a free and direct expression of the general will.

In contrast to Rousseau's idea that the golden age was in the past and that civilization brought vice and the corruption of rational institutions, Condorcet held an optimistic view of history, believing that change was beneficent and that the course of human development made for progress. The American and French revolutions seemed to him marked examples of advance resulting from the application of human reason. He made a remarkable forecast of the course of events in Europe, predicting the spread of liberal ideas, the growing importance of the American nation, the abolition of commercial restrictions, and the extension of European influence in Asia and Africa.

French Documents and Constitutions

The French Revolution also produced a remarkable series of documents and constitutions. Before the meetings of the Estates-General, Lafayette, Siéyès, Condorcet, and Mirabeau had published model Declarations of Rights. Like the Americans, many French leaders believed that a statement of their political philosophy should form a part of their fundamental law. Many of the *cahiers* contained an injunction to the Estates-General to draw up a guarantee of civil rights after the American fashion; and Lafayette strongly urged the French assembly to imitate the Americans in preparing a statement of their natural rights. The clergy, led by Malouet and the Abbé Gregoire, opposed the idea, arguing that conditions in France were different from those in America, that a reform of institutions and of laws was more important than metaphysical theories of equality impossible of realization, and that a statement of duties was as important as a statement of rights.

However, a *Declaration of the Rights of Man and of Citizen* was drawn up (1789) and made a part of the constitutions that appeared in the following years. The French declaration followed closely the American bills of rights, being, however, somewhat more elaborate and precise, and more logically arranged. It also tended to emphasize equality more than liberty, and to confuse liberty with democracy. As a result, the absolute power vested in the sovereign people resulted, in practice, in a considerable interference with liberty. The French felt that the eyes of the world were upon them and that their "principles of 1789" would survive the vicissitudes of the ages. The influence of this document on the political thought of Europe was enormous.

The first written constitution for France was issued in 1791. It followed Rousseau in locating sovereignty in the people, Montesquieu in setting up a system of checks and balances, and Siéyès in delegating the exercise of sovereign power to representatives and in providing for a complex method of constitutional amendment. The king was retained, but an assembly of a single chamber became the real governing body. The historic provinces were wiped out, and France was divided into artificial local subdivisions, each with large powers of self-government. The franchise was limited by property qualifications and by a system of indirect elections.

The growth of factional parties in the legislature, the outbreak of war, the attempt of German princes to interfere in the internal affairs of the French people, and the growing influence of the masses in Paris destroyed the control of the moderates and strengthened the leaders that demanded a republic. In 1792 the first constitution was set aside, with scant regard for the legal method of amendment, by a decree of the legislative organ; and a new Girondist document was framed in which the influence of Condorcet and Paine was prominent. This draft was soon set aside by the success of the Jacobins, the king was put to death, and a republic established. In the Constitution of the Year I (1793) suffrage was extended to all adult males, and an annual parliament of a single chamber was given practical control of the government, its acts being subject to popular veto. The principle of separation of powers was abandoned for the theory of direct popular control. Administration was vested in a council responsible to the legislative body. This constitution was ratified by popular vote but never put into effect, the Convention suspending it unconstitutionally by a decree that, as France was in danger, the government must be revolutionary until the war was over.

In 1795, after remarkable military victories, the Convention turned again to constitution-making, issuing a much more conservative document. Numerous provisions were omitted from the bill of rights, the property qualification for voting was restored, the separation of powers again appeared, a bicameral legislature was set up, and an independent executive with more centralized power was provided for in the Directory. During the period of the Consulate and Empire of Napoleon, which soon followed, the enactment of constitutions based upon political theory ceased. The documents put forward during this period were based upon the doctrine that the emperor ruled as the representative of the French people; and the constitution of 1800, devised in the main by Siéyès, but revised to suit the ideas of Napoleon, was a cleverly planned scheme to secure an efficient system of centralized administration. With the establishment of a hereditary empire and a new system of nobility, the revolutionary philosophy seemed completely obscured and the principles of reaction gained the upper hand.

English Response to the American and French Revolutions

Political opinion concerning the American Revolution was much divided in England. There were many Whigs who felt that the colonists, in resisting George III, were fighting the same battle for the rights of Englishmen that was being waged in England. With the arguments of natural rights and the right of revolution they were in hearty sympathy. On the other hand, the Tory supporters of the king saw in the revolutionists only rebels against the crown.[26] In general, the constitutional arguments of the colonists concerning the nature of the British Empire, the system of representation, and the right of taxation received little support in England. There were, however, many who felt that the English colonial policy was tyrannous even though it might claim legality, and who opposed the use of force to coerce the Americans. This point of view was best represented by Chatham and by the writings and speeches of Edmund Burke (1729-1797).[27]

Like Montesquieu, Burke approached the study of the state through history, not through philosophy. He appealed to experience against dogmatism. He had no sympathy with the theory of social contract, which made the state an artificial structure. He saw it as an organic growth whose roots stretched deep into the past; as a partnership between the living, the dead, and the yet unborn. Neither could he endure the idea of natural rights, which seemed to him to split the community into individual fragments and to lead to anarchy. Burke began his career as a publicist with a satirical attack,[28] after the style of Bolingbroke, on the natural-law philosophy and on the belief that society could be reformed by abstract human reason. Burke believed in facts rather than theories and held that ideals must be applied to practical conditions and made applicable in practical politics in order to be effective. He realized that politics must rest upon expediency; at the same time he tried to make what was expedient correspond to what was just and right. Behind his practical political ideals was a mystic belief in a Divine Providence that shaped human affairs.

While essentially conservative in his political ideas, Burke showed a decided strain of liberalism. He was the ablest spokesman of the Whigs in their contest with George III; and his views on Ireland, India, and America showed political sagacity. He protested against the confusion of legality with convenience, and argued that no matter what the legal

[26] See Samuel Johnson, *Taxation no Tyranny* (1775).

[27] See his *Speech on Conciliation with America* (1775), and his *Speech on American Taxation* (1774).

[28] In his *Vindication of Natural Society* (1756). This was taken seriously and led to Godwin's *Political Justice*.

rights of parliament might be, its colonial policy could not be justified. He believed that the success of the American colonists was essential to the maintenance of British liberties. His theories of colonial administration and of the treatment of subject races were a half-century in advance of his time. Nevertheless, his chief interest was in order and stability. He believed that reform must come slowly, by legislating in accordance with the natural trend of events. He had no confidence in the masses; his ideal was a state governed by a landed aristocracy, in which property was safe and an established church was respected. He saw in the British constitution a slow and natural evolution and believed it far better than any document that men could devise. Its system of checks and balances, its adjustment of liberty to authority, and its representation of various classes and interests seemed especially valuable.[29]

Accordingly, Burke was a bitter opponent [30] of the French Revolution, with its disorder, its fondness for abstract theory, its attack on the religious system, and its attempt to wipe out the past in France and begin anew. He upheld the cause of the French aristocracy and invoked British hatred of French radical ideas. The writings of Rousseau he stigmatized as "blurred shreds of paper about the rights of man"; the French Declaration of Rights was a "digest of anarchy." Burke criticized keenly the doctrines of equality, of popular sovereignty, and of the right of revolution. He held that men were naturally unequal and that those who are best fitted for public functions should naturally rule. Duties were as important as rights, and duties rested upon men whether or not they gave their consent. Men were born into the state and were under obligation to respect its institutions and its authority. The state existed to provide for men's wants, rather than to safeguard their rights, and whatever methods were best adapted to this purpose were justifiable. The state must be viewed as a practical concern, making necessary adjustments and compromises, rather than as an abstract concept of pure reason. Burke insisted that each state had its peculiar national genius, based upon its own history and traditions, and that any attempt to imitate other peoples or to adopt novel devices based upon theoretic dogmas was doomed to failure. He prophesied that the French democracy would result in a dictatorship.

Burke's contribution to political thought was his insistence on the value of studying actual institutions and on the evolutionary nature of successful reform. No other writer of the time possessed so full an understanding of the complexities of political life. His limitation was his

[29] See his *Causes of our Present Discontents* (1770).

[30] See his *Reflections on the Revolution in France* (1790); *Appeal from the New to the Old Whigs* (1791); *Thoughts on French Affairs* (1791).

tendency to worship the system that existed and to underrate the value of ideas as a stimulant to progress. He did not realize that many of the institutions he praised were already outworn. His attitude was expressed in his assertion, "We fear God—we look with awe to the king, with affection to parliament, with duty to magistrates, with reverence to priests, and with respect to nobility." He represented in England the reactionary philosophy which set in all over Europe after the Reign of Terror and the Napoleonic wars. In his exaltation of passion and imagination over the logical reason of man, he was in line with the school of Hegel and Savigny in Germany, and De Maistre and Bonald in France.[31]

In the early period of the French Revolution, the leaders of the Whig party, the non-conformist ministers, and the English poets justified the movement and believed that an era of enlightenment and freedom was appearing on the continent. A revolutionary society was formed in England, and men like Fox approved the acts of the revolutionary leaders. The radical doctrines of the French Revolution were supported in England by Thomas Paine, who returned from America in 1787, by William Godwin, and by James Mackintosh.[32]

Paine wrote his defense of the French Revolution [33] in reply to Burke. Burke insisted upon the maintenance of tradition and the continuous growth of the state, whose unity he considered more important than the interests of its individual members. Paine declared that each generation must be free to act for itself. It was under no obligation to respect old institutions and laws when they became burdensome or unjust. He distinguished carefully between state and government, which Burke had confused. The state he viewed as the necessary result of man's nature and needs, but government was an artificial creation, necessary to restrain man's vices. It might easily fall into wrong hands or usurp power. There was, therefore, nothing sacred about the existing form of political institutions.

Paine held that the contract upon which the state was based was one among equal individuals, not between ruler and people as Burke had said. A republican form of government and a written constitution were necessary for the proper organization of popular consent. Kings, priests, and diplomatic war-mongers were artificial and dangerous creations. Paine strongly upheld the natural-law philosophy of the *Declaration of the Rights of Man*. He believed that men are free and equal, that they possess the natural rights of security, liberty, and property, and that all

[31] See below, Part VI. Burke could have been considered equally well with the reactionary groups which aided the growth of fascism. But his close connection with the American and French revolutions suggested his inclusion here.

[32] See his *Vindiciae Gallicae* (1791).

[33] *The Rights of Man* (1791). Second part in 1792.

authority is derived from the people. He insisted that the state was made for man and that government should be his servant. If it were properly organized, it might do considerable good in the way of reform. In the second volume of the *Rights of Man,* he put forward a practical and constructive program, including compulsory education, the reform of the Poor Law, and a plan for a league of nations.

William Godwin (1756-1836) [34] was a philosophical anarchist, and was unwilling to make any compromise with the state. He held that all government, even if free from superstition and tyranny, was undesirable. He had a passion for justice, defined in terms of public utility, and believed in the perfectability of man under proper education and institutions. The source of all vices he found in social institutions that kept men ignorant and servile. If men were intelligent, the need for coercion of all kinds would disappear. Accordingly, Godwin had little interest in the controversy over the social contract and the natural rights of man. Under existing conditions of ignorance, he held that some authority was necessary, but that it should be local in nature and should limit its activities strictly to the preservation of peace and order. Godwin disliked especially the ambitious schemes of national wealth and glory that enabled governments to exercise large powers.

Godwin also attacked the system of private property, holding that inequality of wealth was contrary to the principle of natural equality among men. The growth of intelligence would, he believed, lead to a voluntary removal of the evils of wealth and poverty, as well as those that resulted from the injustice of law and government. Godwin's work was an interesting combination of the utopias of Plato and More, the natural-law philosophy of the eighteenth century, and the utilitarian and individualistic ideas accompanying the Industrial Revolution. His doctrines, though adopted by continental thinkers,[35] were never popular in England. His influence there was exerted mainly through the writings of his son-in-law, the poet Shelley, whose passion for humanity and hatred of oppression he inspired.

As the Napoleonic wars changed the spirit of the French Revolution from a revolutionary idealism to an aggressive imperialism, English sympathy with natural law and the rights of man disappeared. The radical and utopian ideas of Paine and Godwin were unsuited to the mood of a country engaged in a desperate war; the conservatism of Burke more nearly represented the general temper of the nation. The decree of the National Convention (1792), which attacked the institutions of all monarchical countries and threatened war for the overthrow of kingdoms

[34] In his *Enquiry Concerning Political Justice* (1793).
[35] Especially Saint-Simon and Proudhon.

and the establishment of republics, caused great excitement in England. The execution of Louis XVI sent a thrill of horror through England and silenced the Whigs, even Fox considering it an act of cruelty and injustice. As a result all attempts at reform in England were silenced. The aristocratic leaders, fearing that republican ideas would take root, repressed every proposal to extend the franchise or otherwise to reform parliament. Fearing a revolution, parliament passed laws against foreigners, checked freedom of discussion, and severely punished those who protested against the laws.

At the same time, the economic changes which were creating industrial cities and a new manufacturing class were in the long run opposed to the conservative attitude and to the dominance of the landed nobility. While the manufacturers were not philosophic doctrinaires and had no use for the anarchism of Godwin and Shelley, they were intolerant of the old régime and the clumsy legal system that Blackstone had praised. They desired freedom of trade and the removal of legal interference. Their desire for political liberty was the result of their commercial doctrine of *laissez faire*. This point of view was represented in the doctrines of English Utilitarianism and found its full development in the creed of the Manchester School and in the reform movements of the middle nineteenth century.

REFERENCES

BARKER, Ernest, *Essays on Government* (Oxford, Clarendon Press, 1945), Chap. 7.

BECKER, C. L., *The Declaration of Independence* (New York, Knopf, 1942).

BEST, M. A., *Thomas Paine, Prophet and Martyr of Democracy* (New York, Harcourt, 1927).

BRAILSFORD, H. N., *Shelley, Godwin, and Their Circle* (New York, Holt, n. d.).

BURNS, C. D., *Political Ideals* (London, Oxford Univ. Press, 1936), Chap. 7.

COBBAN, Alfred, *Edmund Burke and the Revolt against the Eighteenth Century* (London, G. Allen, 1929), Chaps. 1-4.

HEARNSHAW, F. J. C., ed., *The Social and Political Ideas of Some Representative Thinkers of the Revolutionary Age* (New York, Barnes & Noble, 1950).

JELLINEK, Georg, *The Declaration of the Rights of Man and Citizens,* trans. by Max Farrand (New York, Holt, 1901).

LASKI, H. J., *Political Thought in England from Locke to Bentham* (New York, Holt, 1920), Chap. 6.

McILWAIN, C. H., *The American Revolution* (New York, Macmillan, 1923).

MERRIAM, C. E., "Thomas Paine's Political Theories," *Political Science Quarterly,* Vol. 14 (1899).

OSBORN, A. M., *Rousseau and Burke* (London, Oxford Univ. Press, 1940).

SABINE, G. H., *A History of Political Theory,* rev. ed. (New York, Holt, 1950), pp. 607-619.

WOODWARD, W. E., *Tom Paine: America's Godfather* (New York, Dutton, 1945).

CHAPTER XX

The English Utilitarians

Utilitarian political philosophy was based upon the English tradition in psychology as worked out by Locke and Hume. Its beginnings appeared in the seventeenth century in the writings of Richard Cumberland (1632-1719),[1] who denied the rationalist doctrine of innate moral ideas and who regarded general welfare as the highest good. The formula of "the greatest happiness of the greatest number" was first used by Francis Hutcheson (1694-1747).[2]

The Basic Doctrine

The first proposition of Utilitarianism, to present the doctrine in outline form, is that "there is a science of the mind." [3] The mind is at first composed of scattered sensations drawn from the environment in which it finds itself. The sensations are soon grouped, however, by a simple law —the law of attraction. Two similar sensations, having previously appeared together, will tend to reappear associated. A baby, to illustrate, will associate its mother with a sense of security. In its mind the two go together, and the presence of one will recall the other. Commonly, to go on, these grouped sensations can be characterized as agreeable or painful. Those that are agreeable become the objects of our desires; those that are painful, the objects of our aversions. All men consequently seek pleasure and avoid pain, and from this results the whole mechanism of our moral life. Truth and morality in fact have no other meaning. A thing is "true" or good if it promotes happiness.

Turning to the legal aspects of Utilitarianism, all men want to be

---

[1] In his *De Legibus Naturae* (1672).

[2] See his *System of Moral Philosophy* (1755).

[3] The following analysis of Utilitarian philosophy follows closely the outstanding work in this field of Elie Halévy. See *The Growth of Philosophic Radicalism* (1928), pp. 486 ff.

happy, but the means various individuals employ to promote happiness are often contradictory. "Two individuals who both wish to live from the product of their labor may dispute the ownership of the same piece of land." [4] One, the lawful owner, wishes to enjoy his land in peace. The other wishes to find happiness through usurping another's property. In this case the greatest happiness (and consequently the greatest good) results from upholding the established property holder [5] by threatening the usurper with the infliction of a pain which will equal the intensity of the pleasure for which he hoped. This can best be done by the government through its legislators. They determine that certain actions are harmful to public happiness and constitute these actions as crimes, providing appropriate punishments. Legislation is thus a science of intimidation and the general utility (happiness) is its justification.[6] Granted that human nature is about the same in all men, classes of crimes can be established and these can be codified into written laws by the legislator. Through these codes of law the legislator creates in effect a moral order based on a balance of pleasures and pains. Society thus becomes the work of his artifices.

It should be observed that in the legal part of this philosophy the Utilitarians adopted the principle of artificial identification of interests. This means that the legislator (or government) must interfere in the lives of the people to artificially reconcile their interests. The government must take positive actions to promote happiness as it has done in the United States during recent years. In its economic aspects, however, Utilitarianism adopted a contradictory principle—the principle of natural harmony of interests. It occurred to these social philosophers when they considered economic phenomena that happiness might be better promoted by allowing nature to take its course. If the legislator refrained from interfering in economic matters, a natural order would arise spontaneously based on two fundamental laws—division of labor and the automatic mechanism of exchange. These would promote a natural harmony of interests which would excel anything artificially created by

---

[4] *Ibid.,* p. 487.

[5] The reason that this course of action promotes the general happiness, rather than the opposite course, is built around what Bentham called "the feeling of expectation." The established owner would expect to enjoy his property and would be extremely disappointed and unhappy were he not allowed to do so. The usurper would have no such feelings involved. To avoid this disappointment and unhappiness on the part of the owner, the general utility requires, therefore, that property be upheld. It can be observed that in this part of their philosophy the Utilitarians were not as scientific as they pretended to be. By giving such importance to the feeling of expectation in regard to property, they weighted their system in favor of the propertied classes. They might with equal science have given the property to the most hungry of the two men.

[6] Halévy, *op. cit.,* p. 487.

government. From this beginning, David Ricardo and others worked out the theories of English classical economics.

Politically, this doctrine proved an invaluable aid to democracy. On the basis of its suppositions, democracy was undeniable. Its first supposition was that all individuals are perfectly egoistical. Its second was that the greatest happiness of the greatest number ought to be the goal of any government. Granting this, it followed that "an absolute ruler is the least safe of all masters: for being, on this hypothesis, absolutely free to do what he wishes, he will follow his own interest and not the interest of the greatest number." [7] A democratic majority, on the contrary, is the best of all masters: "for since each individual is the best judge of his interests, it is the majority of individuals which will be able to estimate the interests of the greatest number." [8]

Some Further Comments

Utilitarianism was thus closely associated with psychology, with law, with economics, and with politics. It taught, to highlight significant points, that each individual is largely determined by the social environment within which he lives. It held that men are moved chiefly by the desire to obtain happiness and to avoid pain, that the happiness of each individual involves relations with other persons; hence that it is necessary for limitations to be set upon the freedom of all by legislation. In the field of economics, however, it held that such legislation is not necessary because of the operation of a providential order. And in politics it taught that only through democracy can the greatest happiness of the greatest number be realized.

Utilitarianism, more practical than competing philosophies, taught also, as the term itself implies, that actions must be judged by their results or by their usefulness. In this sense Utilitarianism was revolutionary. It had no more respect for the old and traditional, worshipped by Burke, than it had for the theory of natural rights and social contract. It viewed the state neither as a mystical social organism nor as an association created to guard the natural rights of its citizens.

The state existed because it was necessary. Its duty was to promote general welfare. If its laws failed to accomplish this end, they should be changed. Utilitarianism had no use for vague phrases or abstract principles. It was concerned with the actual experiences and difficulties of living human beings.[9]

[7] *Ibid.*, p. 491.
[8] *Ibid.*
[9] See Graham Wallas, *The Life of Francis Place*, 3rd ed. (1919).

The Utilitarian point of view in political theory represented a rational and practical interest in the welfare of mankind, combined with the belief that it was possible to improve the conditions of human life through state legislation. The Utilitarians were not abstract philosophers standing aloof from the world; they kept in close touch with concrete problems. The leaders of the movement were active in public life. The reform of the legal and penal systems, the improvement of conditions in factories and mines, and the reform of parliamentary suffrage and representation were largely due to their efforts. The reform of the Poor Law, the repeal of the Corn Laws, the gradual adoption of universal suffrage were based on the principles of the Utilitarian philosophy. The Utilitarians opposed tyranny and injustice, and championed individual freedom, believing in the possibility of human progress. They were concerned primarily with the problem of the activities of the state in its relation to its individual members, only secondarily with the question of the proper organization of the state and the location of sovereignty within it.

The political theory of Utilitarianism was developed in the writings of Jeremy Bentham and James Mill. In the work of John Stuart Mill it went through a decided transformation. The historian, Grote, and the psychologist, Alexander Bain, adopted its fundamental arguments. On the side of jurisprudence, John Austin developed the Utilitarian principles; Ricardo upheld them in political economy. The doctrines were applied in practical politics through the work of such men as Romilly, Brougham, Hobhouse, and Cobbett, and in the demand for free trade, by Cobden and Bright.

Bentham

The intellectual leader of English Utilitarianism was Jeremy Bentham (1748-1832), whose active interest in public affairs covered the period from the American Revolution to the Reform Bill of 1832. The young Bentham scorned the education he received at unreformed Oxford, but had an instinctive interest in science and a marked talent for introspective psychology. From his youth he showed a passionate devotion to social welfare, identifying himself, in imagination, with the hero in Fénelon's *Télémaque*, and determining to apply to the social sciences the methods that were being worked out in the natural sciences. At the age of twenty-three he read Priestley's *Essay on Government*, and was impressed by the statement that the happiness of the majority of its members is the standard by which a state should be judged. Following Helvetius and Beccaria, Bentham believed that happiness consisted in the presence of pleasure and the absence of pain. Institutions, therefore, should be so contrived that social conduct was conducive to the greatest happiness.

In his most comprehensive political work,[10] Bentham worked out this psychology in its application to morals and law, holding that mankind's "two sovereign masters, pain and pleasure" pointed out what ought to be done and determined what actually was done. He held that all human instincts are equally natural, and that they are good or bad depending upon their results. The "principle of utility" approved or disapproved of actions in accordance with their tendency to promote or to oppose happiness. Bentham believed that men have no duties to abstractions, such as states, churches, or parties, but only to other human beings who are capable of feeling pleasure and pain.

Trained in the law, Bentham was much interested in the theory of jurisprudence and in the problem of the ends aimed at by legislation. As a student he had rebelled against the lectures of Blackstone; and when Blackstone's lectures were published, he replied in a scathing criticism.[11] He bitterly attacked Blackstone's pompous generalizations concerning the glories of the English constitution and the English law and his sentimental optimism concerning conditions in England, and he completely demolished Blackstone's theory that the original source of law was found in a social contract. The Tories praised the English law as a natural growth in accordance with divine providence; Bentham attacked it as a tyrannical and elaborate mechanism by which the powerful kept down the ignorant and oppressed. Bentham denied every form of the contract theory, arguing that the state was based, not upon consent, but upon the habit of obedience. It existed because of its obvious utility. This doctrine left no room for the mystical theory of the state as a super-person, held by the idealists and the reactionaries.

Bentham denied the existence of natural law, holding that law is the expression of the sovereign will of a political society in the form of a command. Against this authority individuals possessed no natural rights; nor had they any legal right to resist it. A right, he taught, implied a correlative duty and the existence of an authority that was able to enforce rights by imposing penalties in case of violation. The extent to which the sovereign saw fit to exercise its unlimited legal authority would be determined by expediency and utility. The right to resist the supreme power could be only a moral right, but might become a moral duty in case the benefit to be secured was greater than the evil of revolution. The development of this phase of the Utilitarian philosophy, in separating jurisprudence from the historical and ethical foundations of political society, was carried on by John Austin.

[10] The *Introduction to Morals and Legislation* (1789).
[11] The *Fragment on Government* (1776), published anonymously. This short work contains the clearest and simplest expression of Bentham's ideas.

The English constitution Bentham considered far from perfect; he urged especially the need for universal manhood suffrage, annual parliaments, and vote by ballot. Bentham came gradually to realize that the implications of his doctrine of the greatest good of the greatest number led in the direction of democracy and radical reform. He opposed the House of Lords and the king, and believed that the best form of government was a republic with a single legislative chamber. He was in thorough sympathy with the democratic spirit of the American and French revolutions, but not with the natural-law philosophy upon which it was based.[12] He strenuously opposed the doctrine of natural and inalienable rights, which he called "rhetorical nonsense upon stilts." He held that men possess such rights as are given them or allowed them by law, and that the test of proper law is the degree in which it conduces to the greatest happiness of the greatest number. The practical legislative reforms urged by Bentham were numerous, and aimed, among other things, at public education, public health, reform of the Poor Laws, and reform of the civil service.

In his economic theory, Bentham was an ardent follower of Adam Smith, dissenting however at several points. He agreed that the government should interfere as little as possible with the law of supply and demand,[13] and was a staunch supporter of free trade. He praised the value of unrestricted competition and contended against monopolies and bounties. He had no sympathy with the imperial ideal, believing that the possession of colonies was not essential to carrying on trade with them, and that capital invested in such trade might be applied equally well elsewhere.[14] He agreed that British control in some cases was for the best interests of mankind, but denied that colonies could be a source of wealth to the home country. In 1828 Bentham drafted a petition for the Canadians, asking for complete separation. In general, the Utilitarians would have seen the colonies go without compunction. Nevertheless, in his later years, Bentham turned rather to the idea of colonial self-government within the empire. Through the Mills he became interested in India, and contributed to the working out of a system of legal and judicial institutions for that empire. He also prepared a draft for the scientific settlement and self-government of the Australian colonies.

Bentham's interest in practical social reform as a means of increasing human happiness led him to devote the major part of his attention to

---

[12] Bentham opposed natural-law theories in his political and legal philosophy, but accepted these theories in his economic philosophy. See immediately below.

[13] In opposition to Adam Smith, Bentham held that the government should not even legislate against usury. See his *Defense of Usury* (1787).

[14] See *Emancipate your Colonies* (1793).

the problems of legislation and punishment.[15] He criticized existing laws and the machinery and methods of executing them and proposed detailed schemes of his own. Most of the law reforms since Bentham's day can be traced to his influence. He also laid down principles of value regarding international law. He attacked the chaotic system of the English law of his day and placed great emphasis on the need of simplification in phraseology and procedure, and on the value of codification. The English system of allowing country gentlemen to be administrators of justice he especially condemned.

The injustice and severity of punishment provided in the criminal law, and the system of prison administration, Bentham considered intolerable. He held that the end of punishment was the prevention of crime, that it should be proportioned to the offense, and that the reform of the criminal should also be aimed at. Certainty and impartiality in enforcement he considered essential. He attacked conditions in the English prisons and was in thorough sympathy with Howard's efforts at prison reform. He urged a system of education and of useful labor for criminals and gave years of effort to induce parliament to adopt his scheme of housing criminals in a wheel-shaped building, or *Panopticon*, in which the governor, from his lodge in the center, could keep the lives and actions of all the inhabitants under his observation. Partial efforts to apply Bentham's plans were made outside Great Britain, and the reform of prisons and the institution of reformatories and industrial schools derived its impulse largely from his principles.

Bentham's influence early spread abroad. He was actively interested in the French Revolution, and his writings on legislation were translated into French in 1802 by Étienne Dumont, secretary to Mirabeau. The procedure of the French Assembly was based largely on a sketch by Bentham; many of his political and legal proposals were put forward in the speeches of Mirabeau; and in 1792 Bentham, with Paine, was made a "citizen of France." Bentham's doctrines were widespread in Russia, Portugal, Spain, and parts of South America, and his ideas were used by the leaders of the national movements that defeated the Holy Alliance and created new nations on the ruins of the Spanish and Turkish empires.

Bentham contributed, sometimes on request, sometimes as a volunteer, to the revision of the legal codes of many countries. In 1811 he made a formal proposal to President Madison to draw up a scientific code of law for the United States. Later he made a similar offer to the czar of Russia

---

[15] See his *Discourse on Civil and Penal Legislation* (1802); *Theory of Punishments and Rewards* (1811); *Treatise on Judicial Evidence* (1813); and his *Constitutional Code* (part published, 1830; finally published, 1841).

and to the governor of Pennsylvania; and in 1822 he appealed to "all nations professing liberal opinions." His confidence in his ability to create a system of laws guaranteed to promote the greatest good of the greatest number was unbounded.

Bentham's early writings were clear and terse; his later works were over-elaborated and were loaded with clumsy, technical terms largely of his own coining.[16] Some of these terms, however, such as "international," "utilitarian," "codification," and "minimize," have permanently enriched the English language.

James Mill

The most vigorous disciple of Bentham was James Mill (1773-1836),[17] who applied to the Utilitarian principles the strong support of the associationist psychology.[18] Mill agreed with Bentham that the distinction between moral and immoral acts lies in their utility, and that it is the function of law to bring the pressure of the community to bear in order to secure the performance of acts conducive to general happiness and to prevent those that destroy happiness. He also shared Bentham's belief in the fundamental importance of education, practically adopting the principle of Helvetius that men are born with an equal capacity for improvement and that inequalities result from differences in environment and education.

Mill was tireless in urging representative government and freedom of discussion as essential to proper political life. Believing that every man, in seeking his own happiness, tended to encroach upon others, he held that government was necessary to prevent such encroachment. At the same time, it was desirable to prevent the government itself from unduly expanding its power. This could be best accomplished by placing chief authority in the body that best represented the community as a whole. Mill had great confidence in the middle class and disagreed with those who valued the British system because of its balance of power among monarchic, aristocratic, and democratic elements. He argued that mutual interest led king and Lords to combine against the Commons. He held that the Commons must be powerful enough to counterbalance both Lords and king, and proposed an arrangement almost identical with the

---

[16] The tendency to coin words, usually from Greek roots, was characteristic of the period. Compare the course of study prepared by Jefferson for the University of Virginia.

[17] James Mill's political ideas appeared in numerous essays, especially those on *Government, Jurisprudence,* and *Laws of Nations* in the supplement to the fifth edition of the *Encyclopedia Britannica.*

[18] In his *Analysis of the Phenomena of the Human Mind* (1829), and his *Fragment on Mackintosh* (1835).

Lords' Veto Bill of 1911. In order to keep the representatives in touch with their constituents, short terms were considered desirable; and manhood suffrage for those above the age of forty was urged. Mill's writings were widely read and exerted a considerable influence on the events leading to the Reform Bill of 1832.

Mill shared Bentham's enthusiasm for law and legal reform, but made little advance beyond him. He discussed jurisprudence under the heads of definition of rights, punishment for wrongs, constitution of tribunals, and mode of procedure in tribunals. In his discussion of international law, he pointed out the lack of any authority with power of final decision in controversies among nations. He held that the sanction of international law was public sentiment, and that not even the most powerful nation could afford to ignore its pressure, especially if the nation were democratic. Mill urged, however, the creation of a code of international law and the establishment of an international judicial tribunal. He believed that if such a body, properly representing the nations, gave an impartial decision, the pressure of public opinion would compel obedience. To strengthen public sentiment, he urged that the study of international questions should be made a part of every man's education.

Austin

The combination of general Utilitarian principles with positivism in jurisprudence was the work of John Austin (1790-1859).[19] Austin wished to give clearness and precision to the confused mass of English law that Bentham had criticized. For this purpose a definite theory of legislation and of sovereignty was necessary. Utilitarianism furnished the ethical basis for legislation. Conditions in England were favorable to a legal theory of sovereignty, since the supremacy of parliament, unrestrained by royal veto or by constitutional limitations, was unquestioned. Moreover, sovereignty could be discussed in nineteenth century England apart from the controversy between king and people that had led Bodin to place absolute power in royal hands and Rousseau to vest in it the community as a whole.

Austin studied in Germany, but disliked the metaphysical political theory of the German idealists. He was, however, influenced by the German jurists, especially Gustav von Hugo,[20] from whom he drew his term "philosophy of positive law." Austin's method, like that of Hobbes, was logical and formal, placing much emphasis on clear definition, fine

[19] In *Lectures on Jurisprudence* (1832); *A Plea for the Constitution* (1859); *On the Study of Jurisprudence* (1863).
[20] *Lehrbuch des Naturrechts als einer Philosophie des positiven Rechts* (1798).

distinctions in the use of terms, and close deductive reasoning. He separated the theory of sovereignty from its ethical and historical background, and by a process of abstraction built up the science of positive law. He assumed the sovereign authority of the state as the source of law, which he analyzed and classified, regardless of the influences which led the sovereign to create or approve it.

Austin rejected the social contract, holding that the state was the result of a slow process of growth in which men came to a realization of the utility of government and preferred obedience to anarchy. Men are bound together in political society, not by formal consent, but by the habit of obedience. The person or persons who habitually receive obedience from the bulk of the people in any society, but who render no obedience to any superior, is the sovereign. The sovereign and the state Austin considered identical. Sovereignty was thus vested, not in the king, nor in the whole people, but in a determinate part of the people who actually exercised supreme governing power. The authority of the sovereign was legally absolute, since supreme lawmaking power could not be limited by any higher law. The sovereign was the source of all legal rights, and the creator and guarantor of all civil liberty.

For the doctrine of natural rights Austin had great contempt. He insisted that all rights are created by law and that political restraint is as important as civil liberty. While a radical in law reform, Austin was essentially conservative. He disliked extreme democracy and opposed parliamentary reform in 1859. He denied that government rests upon the consent of the governed, arguing that only a small proportion of highly enlightened men give conscious attention to such questions, the majority of persons supporting authority and obeying law through habit and sentiment.

Austin defined law as a command given by a superior to an inferior, binding by reason of the power of the superior to enforce penalties. Commands issued by a political superior, that is, by the sovereign in a state, are *positive* law, or law proper; all other human commands, set by indeterminate or non-sovereign superiors, are positive morality. Within this latter class would fall custom, laws of fashion and of honor, the mass of understandings and conventions that form international law, and the principles and precedents of constitutional law. International law is not positive law, since there is no sovereign power to enforce it; constitutional law is not positive law, since no legal authority can establish the rules by which the sovereign itself was created. For reasons of convenience, Austin admitted that a large part of constitutional law must be treated as if it were a part of the *corpus juris*. The sovereign cannot possess legal rights or be bound by legal obligations, since there is no higher authority to enforce them.

The legal rules to which habitual obedience is given might be statutes created by the sovereign will, court decisions created by the sovereign's agents, or customs permitted by the sovereign, but which it might at any time supersede. To these the principle that "what the sovereign permits, it commands" was applied. Austin drew a sharp line between law and custom; custom was not law until the sovereign formally or tacitly assented. Jurisprudence and ethics were carefully separated. Jurisprudence was limited to the field of positive law. Austin realized that many forces were actually operative in social life, determining the actions of men; and that only in the abstract field of positive law was his theory of sovereignty tenable.

Austin insisted that sovereignty must be unlimited and indivisible, in contrast to Bentham, who held that sovereignty in federal states and in confederations is limited by expressed agreements. Austin said that political associations held together in governmental union are either confederations, in which each member is sovereign, or composite states, in which a determinate body in the union possesses sovereignty. Austin disagreed with the prevalent American theory of divided sovereignty and considered the United States a composite state with sovereignty residing in the voters that chose the state legislatures.

Austin's ideas did not receive approval from the jurists of his day. Not until later was the value of his contribution to political theory realized. On the continent he exerted practically no immediate influence.[21] His relegation of the principles of constitutional and international law to the field of political morality was bitterly opposed, and his theory of sovereignty was criticized, especially by the historical school of jurisprudence, as being too rigid and formal and as not applicable to all political societies.

John Stuart Mill

By the middle of the nineteenth century Utilitarian liberalism was generally accepted in England. The democratic efforts of the earlier Utilitarians had been largely successful, and political power had been extended to a considerable proportion of the population. Many of the old evils and inequalities had been removed. In this process some of the

[21] In the United States Calhoun followed the analytical-legal method, and a modified form of analytical political theory appeared in W. W. Willoughby's *The Nature of the State* (1896).

dangers of democracy became apparent, and the tendency toward state centralization led political theory to give attention to the scope of state activities and to the liberty of the individual. The leader in the intellectual life of the period was John Stuart Mill (1806-1873).[22]

In his youth Mill was an energetic supporter of Bentham's doctrines and of radical politics. In his later years he took a wider and more sympathetic attitude, realized the importance of the emotions as well as that of the intellect, and modified the somewhat narrow and rigid principles of Utilitarianism and its confidence in democratic reform. To Bentham and James Mill, one form of happiness was as good as another. Pleasures differed in quantity only. John Stuart Mill drew a distinction between different kinds of pleasure, considering some as higher, others as lower. He said that "it is better to be Socrates dissatisfied than a fool satisfied." Mill rebelled against the selfish idea of each individual devoting himself to a deliberate attempt to secure his own happiness, and pointed out that directly aiming at pleasure may fail to secure it. He realized more clearly than his predecessors the essentially social nature of morality and the fact that justice and altruism were its chief supports. Mill, therefore, laid stress upon the idea that every individual should aim to promote the general happiness. Social well-being was the end of government; the fostering of virtue and intelligence was the test of its success.

In his general attitude toward the nature and method of the social sciences, Mill was much influenced by the French positivists, especially by August Comte's philosophy of history and interest in creating a science of society. Mill, however, was more interested in the individual, and less in society in general, than Comte. He realized the complexity of social phenomena and pointed out the errors of reasoning into which politicians were most likely to fall. The first was the tendency to argue that a policy which worked successfully in one country should be adopted by another, without considering differences in conditions which would prevent similar results. The other was the failure to take into consideration the fact that conditions are constantly changing. While Mill admitted the impossibility of scientific prediction in the field of politics, he believed that the study of history, combined with a knowledge of human nature and a careful analysis of political phenomena, would result in a gauging of tendencies of great value to legislators and statesmen. Mill was an ardent believer in the possibility of hastening progress through intelligent human effort. Influenced no doubt by the speculations of

[22] Especially his *On Liberty* (1859); *Considerations on Representative Government* (1860). See also *Thoughts on Parliamentary Reform* (1859); *Utilitarianism* (1863); and *The Subjection of Women* (1869).

H. T. Buckle,[23] which had just appeared, he recommended especially the use of statistics. Buckle hoped to make the science of human society as certain as the physical sciences, and urged the collection and interpretation of data in accordance with the methods of natural science. His belief that government was a blundering enemy of progress also strengthened Mill's individualistic point of view.

Mill's attitude toward political questions was distinctly practical. He was interested as much in social reform as in political speculation. His sense of justice was early stirred by the social and legal disabilities of women. In the mid-Victorian period women were excluded from higher education, from most occupations that offered any opportunity for a career, and from public life. In their legal status, moreover, they were decidedly inferior. Mill argued that woman's nature was the result of centuries of "subjection" and lack of opportunity. He was eager to "emancipate" women, and was the first to plead their cause in parliament. He believed that if women were given equal opportunities with men the result would be beneficial to women, since freedom alone gives happiness, and valuable to the community in general, since society would benefit from the contributions made by the mental capacities characteristic of women. The higher education of women, the increased opportunities open to their talents, and the extension to them of the franchise and of eligibility to public office were largely aided by his arguments and his efforts.

In his attitude toward the laboring classes, Mill at first urged education and a greater degree of independence. Later he approved of trade unions and of voluntary coöperation between capital and labor. He believed in private property, but urged the mitigation of inequalities, especially those resulting from the ownership of land. At the same time, Mill was fearful of governmental interference in economic questions. He believed that state control should be restricted to the narrowest limit, and that the government should intervene only when the interests of the community as a whole made it necessary. In his later years, however, his confidence in ultimate improvement led him to look forward to the socialistic ideal when there might be "a common ownership in the raw material of the globe, and an equal participation of all in the benefits of combined labor." [24] Mill showed a strong adherence to the *laissez-faire* principles of the past. At the same time he recognized the evils that had developed under them and the insufficiency of individual effort to effect a cure. Adam Smith's belief in natural law made his application of *laissez faire* absolute; Mill's principle of utility justified him in making important exceptions when demanded by social welfare.

[23] In his *History of Civilization in England* (1857-1861).
[24] See his *Autobiography* (1873), pp. 230-234.

Mill supported democracy as the best form of government, on the grounds that any work is done best by those whose interests are immediately involved, and that active political life develops the moral and intellectual faculties of those taking part. He agreed with Austin that there must be a single, supreme depository of political power, and that such power in England was vested in the British parliament. The proper function of such a body, however, was not active legislation or interference in administration, but a general policy of control and criticism.

At the same time, Mill feared that the growth of democracy and the expanding legislative powers of the state tended to reduce individuals to a common type and to swamp them in the tyranny of collectivism. He believed that social progress depended upon giving to each individual the fullest opportunity for free development. Accordingly, Mill favored freedom of thought, speech, and action. He believed in toleration of opinions and unhampered freedom of discussion. He had confidence that truth would survive in the struggle of ideas. Arguments put forward by Milton, Sydney, and Humboldt were restated from the Utilitarian point of view. Mill argued that individuals and associations should be left unmolested unless their actions seriously interfered with the interests and rights of others. He laid stress upon the value of originality and the social benefits resulting from a variety of ideas and actions. He even opposed state education on the ground that it was a "contrivance for molding people to be exactly like one another."

Mill was especially disturbed by the danger in a democracy that the majority will tyrannize over the minority. He believed that minorities were insufficiently represented in the British parliament. He therefore supported the system of proportional representation, first proposed in England by Thomas Hare,[25] in order that the distribution of parliamentary seats might correspond more closely to the votes cast by the party groups. Mill also emphasized the importance of trained leaders in politics, and feared that the extension of the franchise would lead to a deterioration in the quality of public officials. Hence, while favoring universal suffrage for all taxpayers, he advocated plurality of votes for those citizens that were distinguished by superior intellect and high character. Besides drawing up a classification of citizens, he proposed that voluntary examination should be open to any citizen in order that he might prove his intelligence. Mill opposed payment to members of parliament, in the interest of purity of government, and opposed the secret ballot, on the grounds that it tended to selfish and irresponsible voting. He believed that final legislative authority should rest with the

---

[25] In his *On the Election of Representatives* (1859).

House of Commons, but suggested that the House of Lords, containing men of legal ability, should be entrusted with the power to draft the bills that came before parliament.

In spite of the narrowness and materialism of its ethics, and the formalism and abstractness of its theory of sovereignty and law, that led later writers to seek for a political sovereign behind the legal sovereign of Austin, the Utilitarian theory was valuable, both in the field of practical politics and in political philosophy. Many of the most needed reforms of the nineteenth century are traceable directly to its influence. The simplicity and definiteness of its political terms and its interest in the concrete realities of political life were a refreshing contrast to the vague generalities of the natural-rights philosophy, and to the metaphysical concepts of the idealists. And its emphasis on the individual and on liberty served as a counterbalance to the growth of communism and to the glorification of the state as the highest form of person, beyond all restraints of morality and law.

REFERENCES

ADAMS, K. M., "How the Benthamites Became Democrats," *Journal of Social Philosophy and Jurisprudence,* Vol. 7 (January, 1942).

ASHTON, T. S., *The Industrial Revolution, 1760-1830* (London, Oxford Univ. Press, 1948).

DEWEY, John, "Austin's Theory of Sovereignty," *Political Science Quarterly,* Vol. 9 (1894).

HALÉVY, Elie, *The Growth of Philosophic Radicalism,* trans. by Mary Morris (New York, Macmillan, 1928).

HOLLOND, H. H., "Jeremy Bentham," *Cambridge Law Journal,* Vol. 10 (1948).

KEETON, G. W. and SCHWARZENBERGER, Georg, eds., *Jeremy Bentham and the Law* (London, Stevens, 1948).

LEVI, A. W., *A Study in the Social Philosophy of John Stuart Mill* (Chicago, Univ. of Chicago Press, 1940).

PLAMENATZ, John, *Mill's Utilitarianism* (Oxford, Blackwell, 1949).

SABINE, G. H., *A History of Political Theory,* rev. ed. (New York, Holt, 1950), Chaps. 31-32.

VINER, Jacob, "Bentham and J. S. Mill: The Utilitarian Background," *American Economic Review,* Vol. 39 (March, 1949).

WALLAS, Graham, *The Life of Francis Place,* 3rd ed. (New York, Knopf, 1919).

———, *Men and Ideas* (London, G. Allen, 1940), pp. 19-48.

CHAPTER XXI ⚓

Political Theory of Constitutional Democracy

Democracy and the Demand for Written Constitutions

In spite of the efforts of the reactionaries at the Congress of Vienna to restore Europe to its former condition, most of the ideas of the French Revolution survived. Chief among these was the confidence in written constitutions and in representative institutions. Besides, the Napoleonic wars had given a stimulus to national unity and autonomy. The overthrow of Napoleon had been accomplished partly as a result of popular uprisings, and rulers had made repeated appeals to national patriotism and had promised constitutional liberties. The attitude of the Congress of Vienna was a bitter disappointment to European liberals, and the failure of the monarchs to keep their promises soon led to popular demonstrations and to the formation of secret revolutionary societies. As a result, the greater part of the nineteenth century in Europe was occupied with revolutions and with wars which had for their general purpose the creation of national states, in accordance with the ethnic and geographic divisions of Europe, and the establishment of constitutional governments within these states.

In the twenties, popular uprisings secured the beginnings of constitutional government in Italy, Spain, and Portugal; and the Greeks won national independence from Turkey. In 1830 the Bourbon king was again driven from the French throne, the Poles attempted unsuccessfully to break away from Russia, and the unnatural union of Belgium and Holland was destroyed. In 1848 all central Europe was in turmoil. France changed rapidly from a limited monarchy to a republic, then to an empire. The German people tried hard but in vain to secure union and

322

liberal government. In the third quarter of the century, international wars hastened the unification of Germany and Italy and the independence of the Balkan peoples. Nationality and constitutional democracy were the disturbing factors in nineteenth century European politics.

A liberal party in each state desired a written document in which there should be some guarantee of individual rights and some provision for a deliberative assembly that represented the mass of the population. Belief in the value of a separation of the powers of executive, legislative, and judicial organs was also widespread. The anarchy of the French Republic served as a warning against too radical change, and there was little demand for republican government. What was desired was an adjustment of powers between the monarch and the peoples' representatives that would prevent tyranny. The demand for a definite statement of constitutional principles was given an impetus by the general confusion following the overthrow of Napoleon's empire, and by the necessity of reorganizing the system of government under the restored monarchs. In many cases constitutions were issued by the rulers in response to popular demand or through fear of revolution. In some instances constitutions resulted from a formal agreement between the monarchs and the estates-general. Occasionally revolutionary bodies took the creation of constitutions into their own hands. Austria, Prussia, and Russia offered the strongest resistance to the movement; but by 1880 practically every state in Europe except Russia and Turkey had made some provision for a definite constitutional system and for the extension of a share in government to a considerable part of its population.

These constitutions showed wide variations, but the political theory upon which they were based centered in the controversy over the position of the monarch in the new system, especially over his power to change the constitution, and his share in legislation. The monarchs and the conservative lawyers that supported them maintained that the king could modify or set aside constitutional provisions which he had created. Revolution was frequently invoked before the theory was accepted that the consent of the legislature as well as of the crown was necessary for constitutional revision.

The monarchs also claimed the residuary power of lawmaking, holding that the peoples' assemblies merely deliberated over the content of a law, but that the sovereign act of the state by which the new rule became law was performed when the rule was promulgated by the king. The royal power to issue ordinances in connection with the exercise of administrative functions was also liberally interpreted and sometimes abused. Later constitutions contained the provision that the ordinance power of the king must not interfere with the execution of laws passed by the legislative assembly. Continental theory, however, was not willing to reduce the king to the position of a figurehead in the state. The monarch remained during the nineteenth century a real directing power in most of the states of Europe. In the German states especially, the doctrine was held that the kingship developed naturally with the nation and that king and people formed the state.

The supporters of liberal constitutionalism and of popular sovereignty upheld the theory of separation of powers in an attempt to check the efforts of determined monarchs to maintain their royal prerogatives. The conservatives attacked the principle of separation of powers as historically inaccurate and as unsound in its analysis of the functions of government. In the United States and in Germany the constitutional theory of the period dealt mainly with the nature of a federal state, the location of sovereignty within it, and the distribution of powers between the union and its component members. The controversy between kings and parliaments and, in federal states, between the union and its parts both tended to oppose the Austinian theory of absolute sovereignty located in a definite organ. As a result, it was generally held that sovereignty resided in a somewhat abstract and impersonal way in the nation or in the people.

Theories of Constitutional Government in Europe

The political philosophy of the effort to reconcile monarchy with constitutional institutions in Europe was best expressed in the compromise theory of sovereignty worked out by the *Doctrinaires* in France. French thinkers, since Bodin, had been accustomed to a definite location of sovereignty within the state. The supporters of the Bourbons found it in the will of a divine-right king. The revolutionists located it in the general will of the whole people. Since neither king nor people were supreme under the Charter of 1814, final authority was held to be found in reason or abstract justice. Sovereignty was placed above all human aspirants, and was derived from intelligent thought rather than from will. The conception of absolute sovereignty was thus avoided. The sovereignty of reason admitted the rights of both king and people, but denied the exclusive authority of either.

The ablest defender of the sovereignty of reason was Victor Cousin (1792-1867).[1] He held that sovereignty was the same as absolute right, and that right could not be based upon force or upon general will, but must rest upon absolute reason. Since men were liable to error, absolute

---

[1] *Cours d'histoire de la philosophie morale au dix-huitième siècle* (1839-40).

reason was unattainable; hence neither king nor people could claim absolute sovereignty. Certain principles of reason might be attained, and these were best represented in constitutional government.

Similar views were held by François P. Guizot (1787-1874).[2] He opposed both the sovereignty of divine right and that of general will and declared his belief that reason and justice alone could furnish the basis for absolute power. Like Cousin, he attacked the doctrine of supreme will in either a single individual or in a number of individuals. He believed that the conception of sovereignty as worked out by Hobbes, Rousseau, and Austin led to tyranny, and that political authority was derived from abstract truth rather than from human volition. He believed that all governments that attributed absolute sovereignty to human beings were despotic; only those that placed extensive checks and balances upon the authority of every organ could approach justice. Representative government, in which those who represented the best reason of the community were chosen to govern, was best adapted to maintain true liberty. Power possessed by king or people alone was dangerous; a balance between them must be justly maintained. Guizot wished to secure for the constitutional system set up in France after 1814 something of the reverence felt by Englishmen for their unwritten constitution. He realized, however, that the English system, a result of slow and evolutionary growth, had a decided advantage over the artificially created French charter.

The *Doctrinaires* hoped that the constitutional compromise between king and people would be permanent; the Liberals looked upon it as a transitional stage between monarchy and republicanism. The leader of the latter group was Benjamin Constant (1767-1830).[3] He believed in the sovereignty of the people, in the sense that the general will was superior to the individual will of the monarch, but denied that the authority of the people was unlimited. The only true sovereignty was justice; the jurisdiction of the government ended where the liberty of the individual commenced. In practice, the absolute exercise of sovereign power should be prevented by public opinion and by checks and balances among the organs of government. Constant made a new classification of the departments of government. He found an executive power in the ministers, a judicial power in the courts, a power representing permanence in a hereditary assembly, and a power representing opinion in an elective assembly. The king he considered a neutral organ holding the balance of power in government. The distinction between king and ministry was

[2] *Du Gouvernement répresentatif* (1816); *Du Gouvernement de France depuis la Réstoration et le Ministère actuel* (1821).

[3] *Principes Politiques* (1815); *Réflexions sur les Constitutions et les Garanties* (1814-18).

an important feature in Constant's theory, although he clung to the earlier view of a ministry responsible to the king rather than to the later system of parliamentary responsibility.

The Revolution of 1830 in France broke down the compromise arrangements of 1814, and the Chamber of Deputies declared that the people of France called Louis Philippe to the throne. The newly manifested power of the nation led to a modification of the earlier theory of the sovereignty of reason in which reason was viewed not as an abstraction but as the calm and deliberate opinion of the French nation. The organized people were sovereign, but their authority was not unlimited. They must act within the bounds of the constitution. The reason of the nation rather than the will of the people was supreme.

An impetus was given to democratic ideas in Europe by the work of Alexis de Tocqueville (1805-1859).[4] Basing his political philosophy on a close observation of conditions in America, Tocqueville helped to correct the belief in Europe that popular government necessarily resulted in anarchy or in a military despotism. The federal system of the United States, in which authority was divided between the states and the union, and an additional set of checks and balances thus created, was especially praised. Likewise, the decentralized administration, in which towns and counties exercised a considerable degree of local self-government, and the important political function performed by the judiciary in passing upon the constitutionality of legislative enactments were given careful consideration. Like Montesquieu, Tocqueville taught that the environment and the social conditions of a people determine their institutions. He believed that democracy would ultimately prevail throughout the civilized world as a result of natural development. Although Tocqueville feared the tyranny of the majority in a democracy, he showed Europe that it was possible to work popular government over a large area, and he gave to Americans the benefit of a critical estimate of their government from the outside. Many of the traditional conceptions in American politics can be traced to his work.

After the Revolution of 1848, the doctrine of popular sovereignty was more definitely restored in France. The new constitution declared that sovereignty rested in the general body of the citizens; and the rise of socialistic doctrines strengthened the idea of authority exercised by the community as a whole. French political theory of the nineteenth century was eager to check absolute power. The doctrines of the sovereignty of reason, of the individual rights which sovereignty cannot destroy, and of the limited sovereignty of the organized nation all aimed to prevent a

---

[4] *Democracy in America* (1835), trans. by H. Reeve.

recurrence, on the one hand, of absolute monarchy, and, on the other, of uncontrolled popular will.

The best statement of this point of view appeared in the writings of J. P. Esmein (1848-1913).[5] He defined the state as the juridical personality of the nation, and laid emphasis upon its internal and external sovereignty. At the same time he insisted upon the rights of the individual, which the state was bound to respect. The individual has, however, no right of resistance. Sovereignty is the will of the nation politically organized. It is legally supreme, but morally bound to protect the liberty of the individual.

Growth of Democratic Ideas in America

The early part of the nineteenth century was marked by a decided expansion of democratic ideas in America. Republics were established in Latin America with constitutions modeled on that of the United States. In the United States liberal ideas of government made rapid progress. During its first twelve years, the government of the United States was controlled by the Federalists,[6] the group of conservative leaders who had secured the adoption of the constitution. They were determined to keep the common people in a subordinate place and to assure political power to men of quality and substance. They aimed to invest the president with the trappings of monarchy and to give a decidedly aristocratic cast to the government. They had no sympathy with the doctrines of the French Revolution, and passed the Alien and Sedition Acts, giving the president power to punish those who criticized the government and to deport summarily troublesome foreigners. They favored a strong national government and, through their control of the Supreme Court, determined the main lines of constitutional development for a generation after they lost control of the executive and legislative branches. Under the able leadership of John Marshall,[7] the doctrine of implied powers was developed and the right of the court to declare unconstitutional both federal and state statutes was assured.

In 1800 a new period opened with the election of Jefferson to the presidency. This event was hailed by his followers as a return to the principles for which the war for independence had been fought. By the

---

[5] *Éléments de droit constitutionnel français et comparés* (1896).

[6] In the early period of the constitutional convention, the term "federal" had been applied to the plan of the small states, which desired a weak union, in contrast to the "national" plan of the large states. Later, all supporters of the constitution called themselves "Federalists," in opposition to the "Antifederalists" who opposed ratification.

[7] See C. G. Haines, *The American Doctrine of Judicial Supremacy* (1914).

Federalists it was viewed as ushering in a period of anarchy and of rule by the rabble. Numerous causes contributed to the fall of the Federalist group. After the violent agitation for a strong government that secured the adoption of the constitution, a natural reaction set in in favor of individual and state rights. The early years of the French Revolution also gave a stimulus to democratic spirit in America, and the Federalist administration was unpopular because it refused to aid republican France against monarchic England. The quarrel between the military faction, led by Hamilton, and the congressional faction, led by Adams, split the Federalist party. The invention of the cotton gin and the growing importance of the planters and the upland cotton growers shifted economic control from the merchants and bankers of New England to the landed aristocracy of the South. The westward movement of population increased the number of those who sympathized with the individualistic views of Jefferson and who felt that the New England leaders had no sympathy with their interests. Political power was shifted from a mercantile aristocracy, following English models, to a landed aristocracy, more purely American in spirit. For six administrations, the "Virginia dynasty" remained in control.

The political philosophy of the new aristocracy differed from that of the old. It discarded the ostentation of the Federalist régime and its cynical contempt for the masses. It regarded itself as the protector of the people, governing in their interests, although unwilling to entrust to them actual control. Its theory of democracy was in advance of its practice, but it looked forward to a continuous process of democratic development. It feared a strongly centralized government, and opposed a large standing army, the assumption of state debts, and the establishment of a national bank. Its theory was represented in the writings of H. St. George Tucker,[8] John Taylor,[9] Joel Barlow,[10] and, especially, Thomas Jefferson.[11]

Jefferson made little original contribution to political theory. His ideas were drawn largely from Sydney and Locke, liberalized somewhat by the influence of Paine. His chief work was to give the ideas of these men a form suitable to American conditions. Jefferson believed in human equality, natural rights, the establishment of government by social contract to protect individual liberty, and the right of revolution in case of misgovernment. He disliked energetic government, fearing that it tended to oppression. He believed that the consent of the people should be made

[8] *Commentaries on Blackstone* (1803).

[9] *Inquiry into the Principles and Policy of the Government of the United States* (1814).

[10] *Joel Barlow to his Fellow Citizens in the United States of America* (1801).

[11] See *The Papers of Thomas Jefferson* (1950-   ), now being edited by Julian P. Boyd.

the constant basis of government and argued that an occasional revolution was a medicine necessary to the health of the state. He suggested as a regular procedure the periodic revision of fundamental law at nineteen-year intervals.

Jefferson opposed monarchy, but was inclined to believe in a natural aristocracy of ability and intelligence. He advocated education and local self-government as the "two hooks" upon which republican institutions depend; and he believed that the masses, if intelligent, would select those best fitted to rule. He realized that democracy was not for peoples unqualified to exercise it, but he had confidence in the future of democratic development. He opposed a large standing army, associating it with oppressive government; and he argued for the subordination of the military to the civil power. He favored argiculture as against industry and commerce, believing that the growth of cities led to corruption and made successful democracy difficult.

The practical application of radical democratic principles came a generation later in the form of Jacksonian democracy. The growth of population and the admission of new states on the western frontier, together with the increase of the industrial population of the eastern cities, were largely responsible for this movement. Frontier conditions promoted independence, individuality, and a strong sense of equality. Urban conditions created a set of interests hostile to the landed aristocracy. Special privilege became unpopular and the idea of natural aristocracy was ridiculed. The extension of suffrage, by the removal of property qualifications, and the direct control of the people, in the national government as well as in local affairs, was demanded. The protective tariff, which favored the northern manufacturing interests, and the national bank, which was accused of maintaining the power of a financial oligarchy, were bitterly opposed by the new party. The removal of surviving religious qualifications and the complete separation of church and state were desired.

The election of Jackson in 1828 marked the success of this movement. Power was transferred from the landholding class to the mass of the population, and the older leaders again believed that "King Mob" had triumphed and that republican institutions were threatened with anarchy. The development of party organization and of the national nominating convention focused attention upon the president as the outstanding figure in national politics. Considering himself the direct representative of the people, Jackson took a vigorous attitude toward the rights of the executive department of government. The Whig doctrine that the legislature represents the people most closely and should be given chief power, while the executive should be distrusted and checked, was ably upheld by congressional leaders, such as Clay, Webster, and Calhoun; but the president, supported by the people, was able to increase the power of the executive in opposition to the entrenched aristocracy of Congress. A similar expansion of executive power was noticeable in the states, where the governor was made popularly elective, with a longer term and with larger powers of appointment and of veto.

The democratic movement also laid emphasis upon popular election of officials formerly appointed, especially judges; upon short terms and rotation in office; and upon the idea that special training and experience were not essential to public leadership. It taught that any man of average intelligence was competent to hold high office, and that long service led to bureaucracy and to loss of sympathy with the people. The institution of slavery, however, survived the democratic tendencies of the period.

The Jacksonian democracy added little to political theory. It was mainly devoted to the carrying out of ideas formerly stated. At the same time, the doctrines of natural law and social contract, upon which American theory had been based, began to lose ground. John C. Calhoun (1782-1850) [12] repudiated the theory of natural rights and of human equality, holding that government was a natural outgrowth of human instincts and of necessity, and that inequality was essential to human progress. He taught that government arose naturally because of the necessity of restraining the selfish interests of individuals. The written constitution, in turn, was a device for checking the selfish tendencies of government. Calhoun believed that ultimate sovereignty in the United States resided in the separate states, as organized in their constitutional conventions. The states were originally sovereign and had formed the union by ceding to the national government certain powers which they could at any time withdraw. They might at any time assert their sovereign prerogative and secede from the union. Calhoun feared the tyranny of the majority which might result from unlimited popular sovereignty and desired to place checks upon the unrestrained exercise of governing power. He argued for a "concurrent" rather than a "numerical" majority. On the basis of this principle he argued the right of any state to nullify an action of the federal government. If, however, three-fourths of the states upheld the federal government, the nullifying state must yield or withdraw from the union.

The doctrines of natural rights and social contract were also opposed, though on different grounds, by the German refugee, Francis Lieber (1800-1872),[13] who wrote the first systematic treatises on political science that appeared in the United States. His work introduced a more scientific

[12] See his *Disquisition on Government* (1851).
[13] *Manual of Political Ethics* (1838-9); *Legal and Political Hermeneutics* (1839); *On Civil Liberty and Self-Government* (1853).

method and represented a decided reaction against the individualistic philosophy of the earlier period. Lieber boldly asserted that the state should take whatever measures were necessary to social welfare that could not or would not be taken by individual initiative. While Lieber held to a modified doctrine of natural law, as a body of rights deduced from the essential nature of man, and believed that under this law men possess certain natural rights, he did not interpret these rights after the fashion of the eighteenth century revolutionists. He condemned the theory of a state of nature and a social contract, holding that it was artificial and inadequate. Men were essentially social and no artificial process to create political society was needed. The state was an organic unit, created by an evolutionary process. Lieber pointed out the difference between English and French ideas of liberty, holding that the English emphasized civil liberty, or a sphere of immunity against governmental interference; the French emphasized political liberty, or the right of all persons to share in political authority. Lieber also influenced American ideas on international law, preparing, at President Lincoln's request, a code of land warfare for the guidance of the Union armies. Lieber's influence on American thought was reinforced by a line of thinkers, many of whom were trained in Germany and were deeply affected by the historical and comparative method of studying political institutions.[14] They were also somewhat impressed by the German theory of the importance of the national state and of the political mission of the Teutonic peoples.

The analytical jurisprudence of the Austinian school was represented in the work of W. W. Willoughby.[15] He criticized the theory of social contract, argued that rights cannot exist except under the law in the state, and viewed the state as a legal personality, with rights and duies of its own. He upheld the idea of absolute and indivisible sovereignty, and located it in all the organs through which the state expresses its will.

Nineteenth Century Anti-Democratic Theories

In the early part of the nineteenth century democracy was associated with Rousseau's theory of general will. It assumed the direct exercise of sovereign power by the people. It was viewed in the light of the experience of ancient Greece, and was supposed to be best suited to small states. Critics, such as Burke, Hamilton, and John Adams, believed that

---

[14] Especially O. A. Brownson, *Constitutional Government* (1842); E. Mulford, *The Nation* (1870); T. D. Woolsey, *Political Science* (1877); J. W. Burgess, *Political Science and Comparative Constitutional Law* (1890).

[15] *The Nature of the State* (1896).

democracy was essentially violent, excessive in its use of physical force, anarchic, and short-lived. The disorder of the French Revolution and of the American Confederation was associated with popular control. The founders of the American Constitution distinguished between a democracy and a republic. In the former, the people exercised government in person; in the latter, they administered it through representatives and agents. The extensive use of representation and of various devices of indirect popular government in the American system, and the widespread interest in De Tocqueville's description of American government, led to the acceptance of the United States as the typical democracy. Direct popular government came to be considered exceptional; the normal democracy was a representative republic.

The general tendency of nineteenth century development was toward the extension of democracy.[16] This was manifest in the abolition of slavery and serfdom, the removal of religious and property qualifications for voting, the adoption of written constitutions and of representative institutions, the abolition of hereditary monarchy, the extension of suffrage to women, and the revival of direct popular legislation by means of initiative and referendum. At the same time, critics of democracy were not lacking.[17] After the middle of the century, their arguments were no longer based on the divine right of hereditary monarchy or on the necessary degeneration of popular government into mob rule, revolution, and anarchy. They were rather inclined to emphasize the inefficiency, extravagance, and inconsistency of democratic governments, and their tendency to crush out excellence and to use a resistless public opinion to reduce individuals to a uniform level of mediocrity. They feared the rise of the demagogue and the corruption in government that resulted from the influence brought to bear by business interests. The weakness of popular government in large cities was especially noted by numerous observers. Many argued that democracy did not necessarily safeguard liberty, that it excluded its ablest leaders from public office, and that it was hostile to progress in science and art. The tendency of democracy to overlegisla-

[16] On modern democracy see: J. Bryce, *Modern Democracies* (1921); C. F. Dole, *The Spirit of Democracy* (1906); A. L. Lowell, *Public Opinion and Popular Government* (1913); L. T. Hobhouse, *Democracy and Reaction* (1904); H. Adams, *The Degradation of Democratic Dogma* (1919); W. Weyl, *The New Democracy* (1912); F. Cleveland, *Organized Democracy* (1913); J. H. Hyslop, *Democracy* (1899).

[17] Among the leading critics of modern democracy were H. Maine, *Popular Government* (1886); W. E. H. Lecky, *Democracy and Liberty* (1896); J. Stephen, *Liberty, Equality, Fraternity* (1873); E. L. Godkin, *Problems of Modern Democracy* (1896); *Unforeseen Tendencies of Democracy* (1898); E. Faguet, *The Cult of Incompetence* (1911); E. Lavéleye, *Le Gouvernement dans la Démocratie* (1891); A. M. Ludovici, *Defence of Aristocracy* (1915); W. S. Lilly, *First Principles in Politics* (1899); W. H. Mallock, *The Limits of Pure Democracy* (1918).

tion, the organization and methods of political parties that arose behind the ordinary machinery of government, and the methods used to influence public opinion also came under attack. During the first part of this century the basis upon which representation rested came under criticism, and a demand arose for proportional representation or for the political recognition of the functional groups that compose the state.

As a result, in those countries longest familiar with popular government, efforts have recently been made to prevent corruption in elections and in legislation and to secure greater efficiency, especially in administration. Appointment and permanence of tenure were found to have certain advantages over short elective terms, and civil service examinations were introduced to remedy the evils of the spoils system. With the expansion of governmental functions, the ability of the average man was found incompetent to deal intelligently with the complicated problems of modern life, and special commissions of experts were created and given large powers formerly exercised by popularly chosen representative assemblies. A concentration of responsibility was found necessary in order to secure real popular control; and the result was to increase further the power of the executive. The theory of separation of powers, especially in its extreme application in the United States, also came under severe criticism.[18] The value of the expert in government was given more consideration; modern reform is as likely to aim at efficient and business-like government as at further popular control.

The political theory of democracy was chiefly influenced during the second half of the nineteenth century by the economic development of the period. It was a time of rapid accumulation of capital and enormous development of manufactures, transportation, and trade. This development took place under a *laissez-faire* policy in which the state made little effort to control competition or combination. In this process the gap between capital and labor was widened, the former combining into powerful corporations, the latter into organized unions. Both brought their influence to bear upon government, especially upon the party system which had come to be the chief factor in modern democracies. Conservatism and liberalism came to be expressed in terms of attitude toward the relation of the government to the contest between capital and labor. Conservatives, while favoring government aid in business, opposed the effort to bring business under government regulation. Liberal and radical thought urged strict public control and in some cases public ownership and operation of services that affected public welfare.

The successful establishment of democracy reversed the attitude of a

[18] F. J. Goodnow, *Politics and Administration* (1900); T. R. Powell, "The Separation of Powers," *Political Science Quarterly*, Vols. 27-28 (June, 1912; March, 1913).

century earlier. At that time, liberal thought favored individualism as a means of limiting the authority of an undemocratic government. At present, conservative thought favors individualism in economic matters, as a means of preventing a government controlled by the masses from interfering with private interests.

REFERENCES

BELOFF, Max, *Thomas Jefferson and American Democracy* (New York, Macmillan, 1949).

BOORSTIN, D. J., *The Lost World of Thomas Jefferson* (New York, Holt, 1948).

BOWERS, C. G., *Jefferson und Hamilton* (Berlin, Henssel, 1948).

BURGESS, J. W., *Recent Changes in American Constitutional Theory* (New York, Columbia Univ. Press, 1923).

COIT, M. L., *John C. Calhoun, American Portrait* (Boston, Houghton, 1950).

COKER, F. W., *Recent Political Thought* (New York, Appleton-Century, 1934), Chap. 11.

HAINES, C. G., *The American Doctrine of Judicial Supremacy* (New York, Macmillan, 1914).

HOFSTADTER, Richard, *The American Political Tradition and the Men Who Made It* (New York, Knopf, 1948).

LASKI, H. F., *Authority in the Modern State* (New Haven, Yale Univ. Press, 1919), Chap. 4.

LEROY, Maxime, "Alexis de Tocqueville," *Politica*, Vol. 1 (August, 1935).

NICOLSON, H. G., *Benjamin Constant* (New York, Doubleday, 1949).

NYS, E., "Francis Lieber, His Life and Work," *American Journal of International Law*, Vol. 5 (April, 1911).

SPAIN, A. O., *The Political Theory of John C. Calhoun* (New York, Bookman, 1951).

SOLTAU, Roger, *French Political Thought in the Nineteenth Century* (New Haven, Yale Univ. Press, 1931).

WATKINS, Frederick, *The Political Tradition of the West* (Cambridge, Harvard Univ. Press, 1948), Chap. 6.

WEYL, W. E., *The New Democracy* (New York, Macmillan, 1912).

CHAPTER XXII ⟶

Rise of Democratic Socialism

Before turning to the development of democratic socialism, perhaps a word should be said about the term itself. This form of socialism is to be distinguished from the type now practiced in the Soviet Union on two major counts. Western socialism is evolutionary and democratic. Socialism as practiced by the followers of Marx, Lenin, and Stalin is revolutionary and authoritarian. The first, with which we are here concerned, has resulted in democratically organized welfare states in Britain and the Scandinavian countries. The second, which will be considered in later chapters, has resulted in dictatorship in Russia and those countries dominated by her.

Causes of Democratic Socialism

Democratic socialism owes its beginnings to the Industrial Revolution and to the conditions created by it.[1] This period was dominated by the view that the best state is the one that governs least. Freedom *from* government rather than freedom *through* government was the prevailing belief. Government had merely to mind its own business, which was to maintain order, and this negative concept of freedom would result in general happiness. If people pursued their own advantage free from restraints they would secure not only their individual happiness, but the well-being of the community as well. Alexander Pope expressed this view in the following couplet:

> Thus God or nature formed the general frame
> And bade self-love and social be the same.

[1] As does Marxian socialism or communism as it is more commonly called. See below, Part VII.

335

This was individualism in its most extreme form. It made the economic man an important and respectable member of society. It worked hand in hand with the new biology to teach evolution toward a better world through the struggle for existence and through the survival of the fittest. And it, of course, aided and abetted the fight for political freedoms. During the first half of the nineteenth century, then, powerful forces in society were moving in the direction of undiluted individualism.

The result of this movement was twofold. The production of material goods increased tremendously. Individual resourcefulness, goaded on by the promise of great wealth, transformed the economy of Europe and America. But at the same time, misery and poverty assumed unequaled proportions. The Industrial Revolution was followed by the factory system and the era of *Oliver Twist*, which has been so well dramatized by Charles Dickens.[2] Workers, huddled into urban slums, lived on that same level of starvation predicted for them by Malthus.[3] Children, often only eight or nine years old, worked much longer than men work today.[4] Workers were considered to be commodities to be hired at the lowest possible rate and to be laid off as soon as their use was no longer profitable. In keeping with classical economic theory, the worker was to be paid the rate acceptable to those workers who needed employment most. And as there was always a large reservoir of unemployed, this rate was never high. Beyond this, the worker, being essentially a commodity, had no right to further value which his labors might create. This was the return due to the enterpriser, the person who had taken the risks. Under these conditions it was possible to talk about freedom for all, but in reality freedom existed for just the few. The great majority of people were free only in the sense of being "free to sleep under a bridge," as noted by Carlyle.

In reaction to this situation, a new group of writers arose who urged greater concern for the social welfare of the people. They argued that public well-being depended not on the economic laws of Smith and Ricardo, but on a positive program aimed at greater economic equality, better working conditions, and other social improvements.

The Utopian Socialists

Early in this period a number of these writers proposed such sweeping changes that they have since become known as the utopian socialists.

[2] See also Benjamin Disraeli, *Sybil* (1895).
[3] See above, Chapter XVII.
[4] They were told, incidentally, that this was good for them because it kept them off the streets.

They were influenced by the prevalent optimistic ideas of human perfect-ability, and they expected to regenerate mankind by educational experi-mentation. They reasoned from ideal speculations and hoped to establish an ideal social order. They opposed revolution and class conflict, were broadly humanitarian in their outlook, and appealed to the dominant classes to aid the poor from above.

One of the first of these was Jean de Sismondi (1773-1842).[5] He opposed the prevailing belief in *laissez faire* by urging government intervention to redistribute wealth and to regulate the use of labor. He suggested that economics was too concerned with the means of increasing wealth, rather than increasing human happiness. He foreshadowed the humanitarian point of view of the Christian Socialists by suggesting that human compassion replace the cold calculation of economic gain. He also opposed the growing use of machinery in place of hand labor.

A more famous figure was Robert Owen (1771-1858).[6] As early as 1800 Owen, a shrewd man of business as well as an idealist, attempted to base the relations of employer and employed upon coöperation rather than competition and suggested a reform of society in order to remedy the poverty and misery of the wage earners. He believed that men are naturally good, but that evils resulted from the capitalist system; private property, religion, and the institution of marriage were considered bar-riers to the natural order. Owen proposed a communal system in which man's natural goodness could find free expression. He organized utopian communities, especially at New Lanark in Scotland and at New Harmony in Indiana, in which industrial and educational experiments were tried. General councils were to direct the internal affairs of the community and other councils were to carry on relations with similar communities. Unions of communities into larger areas, also under councils, were urged. The influence of Owen and his followers in England was an important element in creating coöperative societies, in bringing about legislation in the interest of the working classes, and in removing the restrictions upon labor unions.

The most important follower of Owen was William Thompson,[7] an Irish socialist. In his writings he argued that the laborer produced all value in exchange, and that he was entitled to the full product of his labor. He suggested a reconstruction of social institutions along the lines laid down by Owen, being unwilling to push his ideas to the logical con-clusion in abolishing property rights and in taking away the unearned

[5] *Nouveaux Principes d'Économie Politique* (1819).
[6] *A New View of Society* (1812); *The Book of the New Moral World* (1820).
[7] *Inquiry into the Principles of the Distribution of Wealth most Conducive to Human Happiness* (1824).

surplus from capitalists and land owners. Coöperation was expected to solve the difficulties of employer and laborer.

Turning to France, economic conditions there, being even worse in some ways than those in Britain, gave rise to a distinctly French school of utopian socialists. This group approached social reform by way of philosophic speculation, not from the practical point of view of Owenism. Count Henri de Saint-Simon (1760-1825) [8] taught that the goal of social activity is "the exploitation of the globe by association." He viewed the French Revolution as a class war and was chiefly interested in the welfare of the workers. He believed that politics was primarily the science of production, and that it would ultimately be absorbed in the field of economics. He proposed a new social order resting upon the leadership of the producing class and aiming at progress in industry. Authority should be vested in a parliament of three houses: a house of invention, composed of engineers, poets, and artists; a house of examination, made up of mathematicians and physicists; and a house of execution, comprised of captains of industry. The first house should suggest laws; the second, pass upon them; the third, carry them into effect. His ideal was a society modeled on a factory, a nation transformed into a productive association.

Saint-Simon believed that successful social and political reform must rest upon a spiritual basis. He suggested the abolishment of existing forms of religion and the establishment of a new ethical order, based upon the teachings of Jesus, and having for its object the amelioration of the conditions of the poor. He made his appeal especially to the cultured classes. His ideas represented the generous aspirations of the new *bourgeoisie*. They represented industrialism mixed with socialism, and served later as a foundation for the positivism of Comte.

After his death, Saint-Simon's teachings were taken up by a band of devoted disciples,[9] who pushed his doctrines further in the direction of collectivism. They formed a society to promote his religious ideas, and were a conspicuous center of radical agitation. They worked out a philosophy of history, believing that careful observation of the past would furnish a clue to the future. They believed that history taught the gradual progress of human association in a peaceful exploitation of the material world; and that religion, science, and industry, properly harmonized in a régime of coöperation, would solve the problems of the times. Religion, based on love and sympathy, was the highest coördinating force. Religious rulers, suggestive of Plato's guardian philosophers, should possess supreme governing power. Fanatical leadership demoralized the movement and the Saint Simonian society was abolished by the police.

[8] *L'Industrie* (1817); *Le Nouveau Christianisme* (1825).
[9] Especially B. P. Enfantin and St. A. Bazard.

While Saint-Simon suggested a socialization of the entire nation, which would lead logically to state socialism, other utopian socialists sought reform in voluntary, local communities. Charles Fourier (1772-1837),[10] in spite of his eccentric ideas, possessed a wide intellectual outlook, and combined a keen criticism of the existing social order with an uncanny ability to foretell the future. He condemned the wastefulness of production and appealed to the material interests of men, urging order and harmony. He regarded the universe as God's harmonious creation and urged men to create a social organization equally well ordered and harmonious. Association was the principle of attraction among men, as gravitation was in the physical world. Like Saint-Simon, his social theories were closely related to his religious conceptions.

His project for the establishment of harmony in the economic and political world was the creation of a number of "phalanges" or groups of 500 families, united into communities. Each should include capitalists, laborers, and persons of creative imagination. Labor should be made attractive, monotonous employment and overwork should be prevented, and unpleasant tasks should be most highly rewarded. A minimum income was guaranteed to all, with the surplus divided according to a fixed ratio. Each phalanx should dwell in a communal palace and control a square league of land. The various phalanges should be united in a great federation with a capital at Constantinople. Under this system, Fourier believed that poverty would be abolished and the natural liberty of every man assured. With the establishment of natural harmony, the need for coercive authority would disappear. Fourier's ideas thus led logically to philosophical anarchy.

The leader of the last great utopian movement was Étienne Cabet (1788-1856). Influenced by Owen, he published his famous romance,[11] in which he outlined a plan of agricultural colonies and national workshops. He advocated progressive income taxes, the abolition of inheritance, and free education. His work created great enthusiasm in France and resulted in the setting up of a communistic colony, under his personal direction. Like Fourier, Cabet appealed to the altruistic feelings of men and held an optimistic view of the possibility of reforming human nature through education.

The utopian literature of socialism was thrown into the background by the rise of the Marxian movement. A number of recent writers have, however, put forth interesting ideas, showing imaginative power of a high order and expressed in excellent literary form. Some of these works

[10] L'Association domestique agricole ou attraction industrielle (1822); Nouveau Monde Industriel et Societaire (1829).
[11] Voyage en Icarie (1839).

have exerted an important influence on the development of the practical socialist movements. Among the most important of this group are Edward Bellamy,[12] William Morris,[13] William Dean Howells,[14] Samuel Butler,[15] H. G. Wells,[16] and Graham Wallas.[17]

Nineteenth Century Social Movements

Between 1830 and 1848 the working class throughout Europe was becoming politically active. The factory system had created a large laboring, non-propertied class and, in bringing the workers together, had made possible mass thought and mass action. The widening of commercial relations had extended the area of those having common interests. The workers increasingly demanded a share in the benefits of the great economic improvements. They agreed on the general policy that society should control land and capital, should regulate industry, and should provide opportunity for education. The accession of the "citizen king" in France in 1830 and the passage of the Reform Bill in England in 1832 marked the declining importance of the old governing class. The contest between the landed aristocracy and the manufacturers was replaced by a contest between capitalists and laborers.

In England the workers demanded political democracy. They formed the Working Men's Association, and, with the aid of radical members in the House of Commons, drew up the People's Charter, demanding an extension of the franchise and better distribution of parliamentary representation. Whereas the coöperative socialism of Owen drew its inspiration from experience and from the Utilitarian ideal, the Chartist movement broke with Benthamism and reverted to the natural-law ideals of Rousseau and the French Revolution. In its spirit it suggested the peasant revolts of the Middle Ages and the Levellers of the seventeenth century. The Benthamite creed had become associated with the wealthy Whigs who formed the right wing of the Liberals. The Chartists represented the radical labor wing who believed that men had been robbed of their natural heritage. While the mass of the English people remained impervious both to the utopian propaganda of Owen and to the Chartist revival of natural rights, the Chartist movement prepared the way for the Reform Acts of 1867 and 1884 and was later merged in the general Liberal movement.

[12] *Looking Backward* (1887).
[13] *News from Nowhere* (1892).
[14] *A Traveller from Altruria* (1894).
[15] *Erewhon* (1872); *Erewhon Revisited* (1901).
[16] *New Worlds for Old* (1908); *A Modern Utopia* (1905).
[17] *The Great Society* (1914).

In France the workers supported Louis Blanc (1813-1882) [18] in his agitation for social workshops to be set up by the state and managed by the workers under state supervision. He taught that all men had the right to subsistence and the right to work, and that each should produce according to his ability and receive according to his need. Unlike earlier socialists who depended upon voluntary association and who believed that education would lead to the adoption of their doctrines, Blanc appealed to the state to carry out his system. He looked to a democracy that should replace the capitalistic monarchy of Louis Philippe. The unsuccessful reform wave of 1848 followed his teachings. The Young Italy movement and the Young Europe Association, growing out of Mazzini's work for Italian freedom, and the Young Germany Society, founded by German refugees in Paris, were additional manifestations of such socialistic ideas.

Another important movement of the middle of the nineteenth century was an attempt to apply the precepts of Christianity to the solution of social problems. This tendency was especially pronounced in Catholic Europe where Catholic political parties were formed. The teachings of the Bible concerning the duties of the rich to the poor seemed particularly applicable to the conditions of the period. The Christian Socialists, as these parties were called, believed in coöperation, not competition. They attacked the individualistic doctrine that the natural man, acting from selfish motives, should be given freedom of action. At the same time, they opposed the doctrines of scientific socialism, which tended to become materialistic and anti-Christian. They attacked the existing organization of society, but believed that the chief remedy lay in the moral reform of the individual. They aspired to a society in which all men were brothers.

Present-day Social Catholics desire to bring about an understanding between the church and democracy. They urge the necessity of social reform, but believe that thoroughgoing socialism is destructive of religion, morality, and social progress. They favor the formation of unions, permeated by the Christian spirit, among Catholic workingmen, sometimes with the coöperation of employers. They attack with special bitterness the communist doctrines of Russia and her satellites, having learned from experience that Soviet control ends the freedom of unions as well as freedom of religion.

German Revisionism

During the formative years of the Christian Socialist movement, another type of party was springing up in Europe. This was the Social Democratic party. In its beginnings this group was controlled by the strong influence

[18] *Organization du Travail* (1841).

of Karl Marx.[19] It became in the long run, however, a bulwark of liberalism through the work of three German socialists—J. K. Rodbertus (1805-1875), Ferdinand Lassalle (1825-1864), and Edward Bernstein (1850-1932). These men were instrumental in revising Marxian philosophy to conform with a milder pattern of social, but democratic, reform.

Rodbertus [20] was one of the liberal figures caught up in the revolution of 1848 in Prussia. As a member of the Prussian National Assembly of that year he urged social and constitutional reform. He felt that while the eighteenth century had given workers legal freedom, the accompanying economic system had stripped this freedom of any meaning. It was necessary, if social justice were to be achieved, for the state to bring about a better distribution of production. In contrast to Marx, however, he felt that this could be accomplished without the violence of class warfare. Rodbertus' socialism was drawn from both French and German sources. His ideas represent a mixture of the ideas of the French utopian socialists with those of the German idealists, with their emphasis on the value of the state.

He viewed society as an organism created by division of labor, but did not believe that the free play of natural laws would be beneficial. He held that the state was an historical creation, with its organization determined, not spontaneously, but by the efforts of its own individuals. Each state must pass its own laws and develop its own system. Hence, Rodbertus favored state direction rather than natural liberty. His ideal was a socialist party confining its attention wholly to social questions. In German affairs he favored national unity under a constitutional monarchy. Much of his later life was spent in an effort to reconcile monarchical policy with a practical socialistic program.

Lassalle [21] was a brilliant spokesman for German labor. Through his eloquence and through his activities as an agitator and propagandist, the first worker's association was formed in Germany in 1863. This organization, which was a precursor of the Social Democratic party, was called the Universal German Workingmen's Association. Lassalle believed that the workers should control the state, and that governmental intervention rather than private initiative should direct economic life. He taught that the state was the outcome of an historical process in which helpless individuals were forced to combine in order to overcome nature and to put down oppression. Through the state alone could mankind realize its destiny and attain a high degree of culture. The state therefore must actively further the welfare of humanity. Again in contrast to Marx, how-

[19] See Part VII.
[20] *Forderungen* (1837); *Sociale Briefe* (1850-51).
[21] *Das System der Erworbenen Rechte* (1861).

ever, he fought for these changes through democratic channels. His chief political demand was for universal suffrage.

While Rodbertus and Lassalle did much to pave the way for a democratic form of socialism in Europe, the most important work was done by Edward Bernstein.[22] It is to him that the term "revisionist" is best applied, and it was he who worked within the ranks of the Social Democratic party after its formation in 1869 to keep it from following the leadership of its more extreme wing.

To Marxian philosophy Bernstein raised the following objections: [23]

(1) There is no evidence to support Marx' belief that the collapse of capitalism is imminent.
(2) The opposition of class to class is not so acute as that depicted by Marx because social conditions have not eliminated the middle class.
(3) A social reaction has set in against the exploiting tendencies of capital which has ameliorated the condition of the working class without the need of violence.
(4) There is greater chance of lasting success in a steady advance toward social reform rather than in the possibilities offered by a head-long rush on an all or nothing basis.

With these views in mind, Bernstein led the socialist movement toward immediate and obtainable goals. His aim was to secure political rights for workingmen, to guarantee the right of workers to unionize, and to promote safety devices to reduce occupational hazards. "Unable to believe in finalities," he concluded, "I cannot believe in a final aim of socialism [as envisaged by Marx]. But I strongly believe in the socialist movement, in the march forward of the working classes, who step by step must work out their emancipation by changing society from the domain of a commercial landholding oligarchy to a real democracy which in all its departments is guided by the interests of those who work and create." [24]

REFERENCES

BRANDES, George, *Ferdinand Lassalle* (New York, Richards, 1925).

BUBER, Martin, *Paths in Utopia,* trans. by R. F. C. Hull (London, Routledge and Paul, 1949).

COKER, F. W., *Recent Political Thought* (New York, Appleton-Century, 1934), Chaps. 1, 3.

COLE, G. D. H., *The Life of Robert Owen* (New York, Macmillan, 1930).

[22] See his *Evolutionary Socialism* (1909).

[23] These objections were contained in a letter which Bernstein sent to a meeting of the German Social Democratic party at Stuttgart in 1898. Marxism itself is discussed below, Part VII.

[24] *Evolutionary Socialism,* pp. xxii-xxiii. For a detailed discussion of Bernstein and revisionism, see H. W. Laidler, *Social-Economic Movements* (1948), Chap. 20.

DURBIN, E. F. M., *The Politics of Democratic Socialism* (London, Labour Book Service, 1946).

HALÉVY, Elie, *Histoire du socialisme européen* (Paris, Gaillimard, 1948).

HEBERLE, Rudolf, *Social Movements* (New York, Appleton-Century-Crofts, 1951), Chap. 4.

HERTZLER, O. J., *History of Utopian Thought* (New York, Macmillan, 1923).

KAUTSKY, Karl, *Social Democracy versus Communism* (New York, Rand School Press, 1946).

LAIDLER, H. W., *Social-Economic Movements* (New York, Crowell, 1948), Chaps. 8-10, 19-20.

LOCKWOOD, G. B., *The New Harmony Movement* (New York, Appleton, 1905).

MARKHAM, S. F., *A History of Socialism* (New York, Macmillan, 1930).

RUSSELL, Bertrand, *Freedom versus Organization* (New York, Norton, 1934), pp. 146-175.

WAGNER, D. O., *Social Reformers* (New York, Macmillan, 1934).

CHAPTER XXIII ⟿

British Socialism

In today's world, the most important experiments in democratic socialism are taking place in Great Britain.

British socialism, like most things British, has never taken an extreme form. Karl Marx wrote several of his manuscripts while living in London, but his ideas were never very successful there. Socialism in Britain owes more, rather, to a mild-mannered Oxford don, Thomas Hill Green. Through his lectures and through contact with students who were later to become leaders in public life, Green contributed immeasurably to the growth of Fabianism, guild socialism, and the British Labor party.

Green

The singular contribution of T. H. Green (1836-1882) [1] to political philosophy and to the development of liberalism is to be found in his doctrine of positive freedom. What he conceived was a means of combining social responsibility with democratic freedom. And this in essence has become the present meaning of liberalism.

The old liberalism of *laissez-faire* economics and negative notions of political freedom was becoming bankrupt during Green's day. The chief spokesman for complete individualism, Herbert Spencer (1820-1903), had carried the doctrine to the absurdities of its logical limits. In one of his works, *Social Statics*, he even went so far as to suggest that public education, poor relief, factory legislation, and state-controlled monetary and postal systems were wrong.

Green's answer to this sort of negativism was to reassert the integral relationship of the individual to the community. Following the leader-

[1] See especially his lectures published as the *Principles of Political Obligation* (1879-1880).

345

ship of Rousseau and Kant,[2] he undertook to demonstrate that individual personality or what he called the "moral self" could only be realized through the state, not apart from it. Green felt strongly the injustice of a state which condemned so many of its members to abject poverty. These members had a rightful share in the well-being created by the society of which they were a part. Yet they were being refused not only the material goods of society, but the spiritual goods as well. Material poverty carried moral degradation with it, leaving the underprivileged citizen unqualified "to fulfil any social function, [or] to contribute anything to the common good." [3]

Green proposed, consequently, that the negative freedom of Spencer be replaced by a more meaningful positive freedom. This he defined as "a positive power or capacity of doing or enjoying something worth doing or enjoying." It was thus not enough, argued Green, to grant people legal equality and freedom. Freedom had to imply the "actual possibility, in view of existing circumstances, of developing human capacities, a genuinely increased power on the part of an individual to share in the goods which society has produced and enlarged ability to contribute to the common good." [4]

Because these views corresponded in part to the idealism of Kant, Green and his followers were often referred to as English idealists or as the Oxford idealists. It should be noted, however, that Green never accepted the authoritarian elements of German idealism. He stressed instead the social nature of man and the value of collective responsibility and well-being through democratically controlled agents of government. He viewed political theory as moral theory, writ large, and upheld the state as the indispensable champion of individual rights rather than as their enemy. The assimilation of the individual and the state, and the insistence upon the unity of ethics and politics were the basic doctrines of the school.

Green started with the principle that the state is a natural growth and that its purpose is essentially ethical. Individual rights thus were not the result of contractual bargaining; they were the necessary conditions of free moral will and were represented by the crystallization of the general moral will into law. The conscious realization of a common end among men creates sovereignty, the power that uses force to guarantee rights and to safeguard freedom. Consequently, unless the state plainly acts in

---

[2] Green was also much influenced by the later views of John Stuart Mill. Mill had rejected in later life many of the economic aspects of Utilitarianism, suggesting the need for less egoism and more social concern.

[3] *Principles of Political Obligation,* section 155.

[4] G. H. Sabine, *A History of Political Theory,* rev. ed. (1950), p. 729.

contravention to generally accepted moral ideas, individuals should render it obedience because it is promoting their interests. Green did not push this theory to an extreme idealization of state sovereignty, however. He distinguished between legal rights and moral rights, and realized that the law always expressed moral ideals imperfectly. He preferred to limit state action to a policy of removing obstacles to freedom; he was willing to recognize the rights of associations within the state; and he welcomed the ideal of a world federation within which the rights of the separate states would be distinctly limited. War he considered an undesirable attribute of an imperfect state system.

Fabian Socialism

The Fabian Society, which was formed in England in 1884, represented a further extension of socialized liberalism. Like Green, the Fabians were appalled by the inhumanity of man to man that accompanied an industrial society. They proposed through state legislation to improve the conditions of the working class, but to do it in the manner of General Fabius [5]—through slow, but certain stages.

The Fabian Society was comprised during its early years of a small, vigorous band of intellectuals. Included were George Bernard Shaw, H. G. Wells, Sidney Webb, Graham Wallas, and Ramsay MacDonald. They were influenced by the collectivist revision which John Stuart Mill had made in his earlier Utilitarian philosophy, by certain aspects of Marxism, and by the American author of *Progress and Poverty*, Henry George. Their objective was to spread the doctrine of evolutionary socialism through pamphlets,[6] plays, novels, or any other effective medium.[7]

They agreed that "the Competitive system assures the happiness and comfort of the few at the expense of the suffering of the many and that Society must be reconstituted in such a manner as to secure the general welfare and happiness." [8] To this end they proposed the following principles which were issued in 1887 as "The Basis for the Fabian Society": [9]

[5] General Fabius was the Roman general who defeated Hannibal through his delaying tactics.

[6] See the *Fabian Tracts* (Nos. 1-174), published by the Fabian Society from 1884 to 1914.

[7] They were especially interested in reaching the governing classes. Mass propaganda they left to others.

[8] E. R. Pease, *The History of the Fabian Society* (1916), p. 32. Pease was the secretary of the Fabian Society for twenty-five years.

[9] *Ibid.*, p. 269. This statement can also be found in many of the Fabian Society tracts.

The Fabian Society consists of Socialists.

It therefore aims at the reorganization of Society by the emancipation of Land and Industrial Capital from individual and class ownership, and the vesting of them in the community for the general benefit. In this way only can the natural and acquired advantages of the country be equitably shared by the whole people.

The Society accordingly works for the extinction of private property in Land and of the consequent individual appropriation, in the form of Rent, of the price paid for permission to use the earth, as well as for the advantages of superior soils and sites.

The Society, further, works for the transfer to the community of the administration of such industrial Capital as can conveniently be managed socially. For, owing to the monopoly of the means of production in the past, industrial inventions and the transformation of surplus income into Capital have mainly enriched the proprietary class, the worker being now dependent on that class for leave to earn a living.

If these measures be carried out, without compensation (though not without such relief to expropriated individuals as may seem fit to the community), Rent and Interest will be added to the reward of labour, the idle class now living on the labour of others will necessarily disappear, and practical equality of opportunity will be maintained by the spontaneous action of economic forces with much less interference with personal liberty than the present system entails.

For the attainment of these ends the Fabian Society looks to the spread of Socialist opinions, and the social and political changes consequent thereon. It seeks to achieve these ends by the general dissemination of knowledge as to the relation between the individual and Society in its economic, ethical, and political aspects.

These principles were augmented from time to time by analyses of legislation pending before parliament and by broader studies of socialism. Of the latter, perhaps the most interesting was George Bernard Shaw's *The Fabian Society: Its Early History.*[10] In 1893 the Society joined with elements of the trade union movement to form the Independent Labor party. They have been active in the Labor movement since that date and continue today to promote through study and research the belief that socialism is but the "economic side of the democratic ideal."

The Guild Socialists

Guild socialism arose in England during the early years of the twentieth century as an offshoot of the Fabian movement. Its members were dissatisfied with the stand of the Fabians on the question of centralization of power. They shared many of the fears which motivated the

---

[10] Fabian Society Tract, No. 41 (1909). See also the *Fabian Essays* (1899), which Shaw edited.

French syndicalists, believing that too much government was bad whether it be socialist or not. They proposed a form of socialism keyed to the idea of decentralization and divided responsibility.

Concretely, they proposed and continue to propose that the state, representing consumers, own the means of production, but that guilds, representing the workers, control the means of production. In addition they suggest that each church, industry, educational organization, or other functional group have direct control of its own affairs; and that the state should interfere only as a last resort, or should stand on a par with other natural groups, with final authority to adjust disputes resting in a body that represents all essential interests.

Guild socialists believe that state control of industry results in a bureaucratic and undemocratic system because it creates a self-interested electorate partly controlled by and partly controlling a governing bureaucracy. Hence they prefer to set up a federal system in which the state looks after only such matters as public conduct, international relations, and the promotion of art and higher education—other matters being left to autonomous, coöperating occupational groups. These organizations will determine wages and prices; they will control all industrial matters; and they will have charge of the national income, paying to the state a certain sum to enable it to perform its duties. There will thus be established two democracies—one economic, one political.

From another point of view, guild socialism represents a reaction against the large-scale machine industry of the present day, as well as against the state. It looks back to the medieval period, with its small, decentralized, handicraft industry, which developed the personality of the workers and made possible pride in workmanship.

Perhaps for this reason, guild socialism has made little progress in Britain and is considered somewhat academic by its critics. In a world striving for mass production, its approach to Britain's problems has seemed less realistic than that of the Fabian Society. In any case the policies followed by the Labor party have been Fabian policies in the main, rather than those of the guild socialists.

The British Labor Party

The Labor party was officially formed in 1906. It grew out of a welter of allied social movements of which the chief were the British Trade Union Congress, the Independent Labor party, the Fabian Society, and the Social Democratic Federation. During the following half-century it grew from a party with a handful of members into one of Britain's two largest political organizations.

It has from its inception been a party devoted to democratic socialism, rather than to class warfare and proletarian dictatorship. The Labor party has always had a high respect for the quality of rank-and-file workingmen. It has never shared Lenin's belief that this vast group of people could be led to salvation only by a small, tightly knit band of professional revolutionaries.

Another distinguishing quality of the Labor party is its religious humanitarianism. Clement Attlee, the present leader of the party, was converted to socialism through contact with the poverty he encountered in London's slums from 1905 to 1922. He stated later that conditions were so bad in the Limehouse district where he served as a social worker that they aroused his Christian beliefs in the dignity of the individual, leading him to enlist in the socialist cause.

In the field of economics, the Labor party prides itself on following a middle course between capitalism and communism. They have nationalized industries considered vital to the national welfare, but have not eliminated free enterprise in other fields. Taxes have been high and have fallen heavily on the well-to-do, but compensation, they point out, has been provided for nationalized property and there have been no purges or extra-legal actions taken against large property owners.

The Labor party thinks of its program as revolution by consent, and suggests it is the democratic answer to today's problems. In this program,[11] three major features stand out. They are nationalization of basic industries, redistribution of income, and social and economic planning. The object of nationalization is twofold. It is considered essential that basic industries be owned by the state in order that they can be made socially responsible.[12] It is also felt that nationalization removes, "step by step, the source from which major unearned incomes are derived." [13] Redistribution of income is justified as leading to greater social equality. This means a heavily graduated income tax on the one hand and higher wages and social benefits for the working classes on the other. As for social and economic planning, this is the Labor party's answer to depressions and ineffective utilization of the nation's resources. They pride themselves especially on taking the "boom and bust" out of their economy.

Members of the British Labor party thus believe with Keir Hardie [14] that capitalist liberalism must now give way to a social form of liberalism wherein the labourer shall be rewarded in proportion to his work.[15] And

[11] For a recent statement of official policy, see *Labour and the New Society* (1950).
[12] John Strachey, *The Just Society* (1951), p. 6.
[13] *Ibid.*
[14] Hardie was the first socialist elected to parliament.
[15] Strachey, *op. cit.*, p. 4.

they suggest that against capitalism in decline, "against communism which has no appreciation of human values," the wise choice is Labor's "creed of free social democracy." [16]

The Future of Liberalism

Nearly two hundred years after Rousseau, liberalism is still searching for its full meaning. It has, however, taken some remarkable strides toward the goal of translating men's desires, ambitions, and fears into social and political realities.

The most notable advance of recent years has taken place in the economic and social fields. The political liberty of the nineteenth century has been augmented by the economic and social equality of the twentieth century. Great inequalities of wealth no longer deprive political equality of meaning.

In simplest terms, the steps leading to this, our present form of liberalism, can be summarized as follows: During the latter part of the eighteenth century, the hereditary, landowning nobility found itself losing ground to a rising class of enterprisers who convinced the masses of people that they had no common interests with the ruling few. They promised a community of interest which would improve conditions for all. The ensuing revolutions, both political and industrial, were followed, however, by a new form of control in which the interests of the commercial classes proved antithetical to rather than identical with those of the working classes. Following a period of unparalleled economic growth, accompanied by a corresponding increase in conscious poverty, a new movement arose seeking the social justice which had not been previously achieved. This centered in the condition of the workers, or the proletariat as Marx called them. Practically it took the form of trade unionism; its ideas were supplied by an intellectual leadership. In those countries not possessing established channels of constitutional government and democracy, this movement resulted in communism (or fascism as a reaction to communism) and a continuation of control by an elite. In Britain and the United States, the forces seeking social and economic change succeeded in replacing the former ruling classes through democratic means. The result has been the New Deal and Fair Deal in the United States and a mild form of socialism in Britain.

Seemingly, the control of the government has at last passed in these latter countries to the great majority of the people, who have come of age politically and economically for the first time. Doubts remain, however,

[16] From a speech by Clement Attlee, quoted in the *New York Times Magazine*, October 19, 1952.

whether this new form of liberalism will not lead ultimately to another type of controlling elite, which will be more powerful than ever because it will have all economic as well as political controls in its hands. The danger lies in centralizing power so much that those in control will be able to create an automatic majority for their decisions or that they will come to identify their own (bureaucratic) interests with the public interest, dispensing with really effective popular controls.

Whether these doubts are well founded is a question which deserves much thought and discussion. A return to the principles of the last century is not now possible. We live in an age which will continue to emphasize social responsibility. The problem for us is how to live with the machinery social responsibility makes necessary without losing control of the machinery we create.

REFERENCES

ATTLEE, Clement R., *The Labour Party in Perspective—and Twelve Years Later* (London, Gollancz, 1949).

BRADY, R. A., *Crisis in Britain: Plans and Achievements of the Labour Government* (Berkeley, Univ. of California Press, 1950).

CHIN, Y. L., *The Political Theory of Thomas Hill Green* (New York, Gray, 1920).

COKER, F. W., *Recent Political Thought* (New York, Appleton-Century, 1934), Chaps. 4, 9, 15.

COLE, G. D. H., *A History of the Labour Party from 1914* (London, Routledge and Paul, 1948).

CRIPPS, Stafford, *Towards Christian Democracy* (New York, G. Allen, 1946).

HALLOWELL, J. H., *Main Currents in Modern Political Thought* (New York, Holt, 1950), pp. 463-476.

HUTCHISON, Keith, *The Decline and Fall of British Capitalism* (New York, Scribner, 1950).

LAIDLER, H. W., *Social-Economic Movements* (New York, Crowell, 1948), Chaps. 17-18, 23, 31.

LEWIS, W. A., *The Principles of Economic Planning: A Study for the Fabian Society* (London, Dobson, 1949).

PEASE, E. R., *A History of the Fabian Society* (New York, Dutton, 1916).

SABINE, G. H., *A History of Political Theory*, rev. ed. (New York, Holt, 1950), pp. 725-749.

STRACHEY, John, *The Just Society* (London, The Labour Party, 1951).

TAWNEY, R. H., *The British Labor Movement* (New Haven, Yale Univ. Press, 1925).

WATKINS, Frederick, *The Political Tradition of the West* (Cambridge, Harvard Univ. Press, 1948), Chaps. 9, 12.

PART VI

The Growth of Fascism

CHAPTER XXIV ~

German Idealism

Nature of Idealist Thought

The beginnings of fascism are to be found in the conservative reaction which followed the French Revolution. German idealism,[1] as one aspect of this reaction came to be known, culminated in the doctrines of Georg Wilhelm Hegel, sometimes called the father of fascism.[2]

Idealism was an outgrowth of Greek philosophy and of the confused but fertile ideas of Rousseau. It was also a reaction to Hume's theory of knowledge. From Greek philosophy, the idealists adopted the view that political philosophy was essentially an ethical study, which considered the state as a natural society and which inquired into the methods by which it sought to attain its moral aims. They taught, as did Plato and Aristotle, that man, by his very nature, is a member of the political community, that law is the expression of pure reason, and that the good life consists in each man performing his proper duties in the life of the community.

From Rousseau, the idealists adopted the concept of the general will. They also learned to distrust any brand of "reason" but their own.[3] The

---

[1] While important relationships between German idealism and fascism are emphasized in the following pages, it should be noted that the two are by no means identical. German idealism, for example, contained a moral element which never found its way into fascist doctrine.

[2] Ernst Cassirer observes on this score that Hegel in spite of intentions to the contrary "unchained the most irrational powers that have ever appeared in man's social and political life. No other philosophical system," he declares, "has done so much for the preparation of fascism and imperialism." *The Myth of the State* (1946), p. 273.

[3] The idealists were critical of reason in the then accepted scientific sense. This did not lead them to profess irrationalism, however, as was the case with later fascists. Hegel considered his philosophy as the epitome of reasonableness in the sense that it depended on a dialectical argument that was considered strictly logical.

general will, for its part, became in Kant's philosophy a moral imperative to will a self-imposed duty, leading to a philosophy not incompatible with liberalism. But in Hegel this will became the will of the state which absorbed the will of the individual, leaving the state as the new Leviathan. In regard to reason, Rousseau had characterized the arts and sciences as a source of moral decay and demanded a return to the simplicity of nature. He had based man's worth, not on his intelligence, but upon his moral nature, and placed dependence upon emotion rather than on reason. Building on these views, the idealists sought a higher kind of truth than that offered by scientific intelligence. A clear distinction was drawn between truth discovered by observation of phenomena and truth arrived at by abstract thought. In this process political theory became part of a transcendental metaphysics.

The importance of Hume rests in this struggle to reassert the existence of *a priori* truths. His destructive theory of knowledge served as a goad to the idealists. Hume had asserted in his *Treatise of Human Nature* that the absolute truths of philosophy were not truths at all but only opinions. About such matters no certain knowledge existed. Man could be led only by his experience and by utilitarian self-interest. The detailed answer of Kant and other idealists to this proposition is beyond our scope, but essentially they argued a higher form of truth resting on such fundamental moral obligations as good will, which were prior to experience and therefore not dependent on it. These elemental obligations served as the core of a healthy personality and bound men together in a community of well-being.

The Political Thought of the Idealists: Kant and Fichte

These ideas were represented in the writings of Kant, Fichte, and Hegel. Immanuel Kant (1724-1804) [4] did not take an active part in politics,[5] nor did he make an original contribution to political thought,

---

[4] Kant's political ideas are found chiefly in his *Metaphysical First Principles of the Theory of Law* (1796), trans. by W. Hastie; and his *Perpetual Peace* (1795), trans. by M. C. Smith. See also his essays on *The Principles of Political Right* and *The Natural Principle of the Political Order*.

[5] Heinrich Heine has drawn a famous picture of Kant which indicates that he took little part in anything. "The history of Immanuel Kant's life is difficult to portray, for he had neither life nor history. He led a mechanical, regular, almost abstract bachelor existence in a little retired street of Königsberg, an old town on the northeastern frontier of Germany. I do not believe that the great clock of the cathedral performed in a more passionless and methodical manner its daily routine than did its townsman, Immanuel Kant. Rising in the morning, coffee-drinking, writing, reading lectures, dining, walking, everything had its appointed time, and the neighbours knew that it was exactly half-past three o'clock when Immanuel Kant stepped forth from his

though his innovations in philosophy are well known. His political principles were derived mainly from Rousseau and Montesquieu, and his work consisted in fitting their ideas into the categories of his critical philosophy. He was more interested in the analysis of fundamental concepts than in practical questions of politics and administration.

Kant held that men are by nature free and equal, and that the state represents in principle a contract by which the natural rights of each individual are placed under the guarantee of the whole people. The social contract as an historical fact he rejected. Sovereignty resides in the people, whose general will is the source of law, a just law being one to which the whole people can reasonably give assent. The adoption of a constitution represents the process by which the state is established and the general will expressed. The functions of the state are legislative, executive, and judicial; and the separation of legislative and executive power is essential to liberty. The authority of the people may be represented by elected deputies, or may be represented by a king and a nobility. Conditions in Prussia led Kant to attempt to reconcile the doctrine that the general will of the people is sovereign with the belief that this sovereignty could be exercised through a monarchic form of government. His philosophical distinction between the ideal and the actual led him into some confusion. His ideal state was formed by voluntary agreement, and its sovereignty, manifest in abstract law, was derived from the will of all. His practical state, resulting from historical conditions, was based on force and reason, its sovereignty resting with those who had the actual power. Disliking violence and disorder, and alarmed by the excesses in France, Kant denied the right of revolution, holding that changes in the constitution must be made in a legal way by the sovereign itself.

Kant had little idea of the corporate life of a national state, as did later fascists. The free will of the individual was uppermost in his thought. He tried to discover the abstract principles that underlie morals, law, and politics. These he found in the right of each individual to will and to impose limitations upon himself. Mutual limitations upon the life of men in association were imposed by law, which represented the general will. In this way Kant tried to reconcile authority with perfect freedom. Freedom was essentially subjective, and the individual was an end in

---

house in his grey, tight-fitting coat, with his Spanish cane in his hand, and betook himself to the little linden avenue called after him to this day the 'Philosopher's Walk.' Summer and winter he walked up and down it eight times, and when the weather was dull or heavy clouds prognosticated rain, the townspeople beheld his servant, the old Lampe, trudging anxiously behind him with a big umbrella under his arm, like an image of Providence." *Religion and Philosophy in Germany* (1891), p 108.

himself. The supreme value of the rational man was the dominant idea in his philosophy. Accordingly, his attitude toward the state was individualistic; it must not attempt to determine the whole life of its citizens.

The same ideas were applied to the relations among states. Kant held that the European system of a balance of power could never be the basis of a lasting peace, and that states could never be entirely independent in their external dealings. He advocated the subordination of the state to a federal league of nations, in which each state should be subject to the adjudication of a general European will. He held that it was the divine intention that mankind should ultimately be united in a world-state. The remedy for European anarchy was a "system of international right, founded upon public laws conjoined with power, to which every state must submit." Kant believed that economic conditions would compel reasonable men to eliminate war. The period through which he lived, covering the Seven Years' War and the Napoleonic wars, in both of which Germany suffered severely, no doubt influenced his attitude toward international relations.

Johann Fichte (1762-1814) agreed with Kant in his idealistic philosophy. He was, however, more actively interested than Kant in problems of practical politics, and was much influenced by the disasters of Prussia under the Napoleonic conquest, and by the strong revival of national feeling that followed. In his earlier writings [6] he followed the liberal and individualistic doctrines of Rousseau, emphasizing the law of nature, the rights of the individual, and the sovereignty of the people. In his later writings [7] he emphasized the importance of the national state and justified the extension of its activities into a system of state socialism, leading to future fascist doctrines.

In his earlier writings, Fichte developed the Kantian concept of free, rational beings, realizing that their freedom is limited by the freedom of others, uniting their wills into a general will by means of a social contract, in order that the restrictions placed by law upon their free activities might be self-imposed. Fichte rejected, however, the idea of a prepolitical state of nature, holding that the state is itself the natural condition of mankind. The social contract he subdivided into three processes: the property contract, by which men mutually agreed to limit their rights of free action in the external world of sense; the protection contract, by which each agreed to contribute his share of the force necessary to maintain the former agreement; the union contract, by which all united to form a sovereign state, whose duty it was to enforce the

[6] *Beiträge zur Berichtigung der Urteile des Publikums über die Französische Revolution* (1793); *Grundlage des Naturrechts* (1796), trans. by A. E. Kroeger.
[7] *Der Geschlossene Handelsstaat* (1800); *Die Staatslehre* (1813).

previous agreements. Beyond the protection of individual rights, the state should not interfere with the free actions of its citizens.

In his later writings, Fichte permitted a much wider sphere of authority to the state, holding that individual property had no existence except through the state, and that it was the duty of the state to give each individual what properly belonged to him and to protect him in its possession. Influenced by political and economic conditions in Germany, he believed that each state should be economically self-supporting. The state should distribute its population among the several classes of producers, farmers, artisans, and merchants, should fix prices, and should insure to each individual his proportionate share of the national wealth. As far as possible, foreign trade should be avoided; when necessary, it should be carried on through the government itself. Economic independence he held to be a natural corollary of the existence of separate national states. The English idea of free trade, ruinous to the undeveloped economic system in Germany, he bitterly opposed. The rational state was an economic unit, enclosed within natural geographical boundaries, having only such relations with neighboring states as could not be avoided. The ambitions and rivalries of world commerce he considered the chief cause of war.

Just as each individual should have his proper place and employment in the state, so, Fichte believed, each nation has its peculiar contribution to make to the progress of civilization. The cause of Prussia's weakness in the contest with Napoleon, Fichte found in the lack of political consciousness among the people. Accordingly, he appealed [8] to the patriotism of his countrymen and held up the ideal of German unity, teaching that it was Germany's mission to regain her national existence and to assume a place of leadership in the world. To this end he urged the state to undertake an elaborate system of moral and intellectual training.

For the problem that had led Kant into difficulties—the reconciliation of the theory of popular sovereignty with the existence of a powerful and irresponsible monarch—Fichte offered an unusual solution. Realizing that there was danger that the sovereign will of the people, as represented in the fundamental law, or constitution, might be ignored by some organ of the government, he suggested the creation of a board of Ephors,[9] whose sole duty it should be to determine whether the constitution was

[8] In his *Reden an die deutsche Nation* (1807-8).

[9] Note the Spartan system of Ephors, the Ephors of Althusius, and the Council of Censors provided for in the first constitutions of Pennsylvania (1776) and Vermont (1777). These latter were charged with the duty of inquiring whether the constitution had been preserved inviolate. The Censors were abolished in Pennsylvania in 1790; in Vermont they existed until 1870; having met thirteen times and having ten times proposed constitutional changes.

being observed and to provide means when necessary by which the sovereign will of the people might find expression. If this check on governmental usurpation failed, the people as a whole had the right to revolt, since they were the source of all power, responsible to God alone.

Hegel

The climax of German idealistic political thought was reached in the writings of Georg Wilhelm Hegel (1770-1831).[10] Kant's theory of freedom and his ideal of perpetual peace were inspired by the French revolutionary ideas of 1789. Hegel wrote when the reaction had set in against Napoleon and when allegiance to the national state and to monarchy was restored. International morality, therefore, received little consideration, and the personality of the national state, superior in importance to its individual members, was exalted to a mystical height.

In contrast to the revolutionary doctrine of the artificial origin of the state by contract, Hegel held that the state was a natural organism, representing a phase of the historical "world process." [11] In contrast to the collection of separate individuals each with his natural rights and his share of the general will or sovereignty, Hegel viewed the state as the real person, its will as the manifestation of perfect rationality—the synthesis of universal and individual freedom. Only as a member of the state had the individual reality; a perfect life consisted in living in accordance with the universal will. He endeavored to reconcile the inwardness of morality with the externality of law, and to show that true freedom involved the outward realization of what was subjectively demanded by reason. He believed that this could be accomplished only through law, through the rules of morality, and through the system of institutions that made for righteousness. In this category the state, as the harmonizer of all social functions, occupied the highest place.

Sovereignty resided in the state as a legal person, not in the people of the state as collective individuals contrasted with their ruler. However, Hegel held that personality must find expression in an individual; the monarch thus became the bearer of the state's personality. By emphasizing the monarch as the personification of the state, the immediate effect of his teaching was to divert attention from his theory of state sovereignty to its apparent identification of sovereignty with the monarch. Hegel idealized the state and considered constitutional monarchy decidedly superior to democracy.

[10] In his *Grundlinien der Philosophie des Rechts* (1821), trans. by S. W. Dyde.
[11] This idea was first stated by Friedrich Schelling in his *System of Transcendental Idealism* (1800).

Hegel asserted that the constitution of each state should be the result of its historical evolution, and that to debate over the best form of constitution or to attempt to create a constitution was futile. In his analysis of government, he discovered three powers: the legislative; the administrative, which included the judicial; and the monarchic. The differentiation of legislative and administrative powers represented the valuable principle of diversity; the monarchic power represented the equally valuable principle of unity. The legislature represented the many; the administration the few; the king, the one. Thus monarchic, aristocratic, and democratic elements were happily combined. Hegel opposed the principle of separation of powers, holding that king and administration should share in lawmaking in order to preserve the organic unity of the state's will.

In its external relations, Hegel taught that each state was independent and subject to no law but its own will. He emphasized the complete individuality of each member of the family of nations and asserted that the ordinary rules of morality that obtained among individuals could not be applied in the relations among states. Agreements made among states were only provisional. The object of a treaty was to secure the particular interests of the state; in consequence of changing circumstances, treaties might be ignored. War was an inevitable, and not wholly undesirable, activity of the state in creating and maintaining its national existence. War, in fact, was the crucible out of which a state's "true personality" developed. Perpetual peace led to internal corruption; successful war prevented internal unrest and strengthened the power of the state. A special class of citizens, distinguished by courage, devoted to war, and ready to sacrifice itself in the service of the state, was highly desirable.

Hegel followed Fichte in believing that each nation has its peculiar spirit and culture and makes its peculiar contribution to world civilization. The progress of history thus portrayed the gradual unfolding of the universal spirit; [12] in each age some people represented the world spirit as thus far revealed. Viewing ideal freedom as the goal toward which state life moved, Hegel found four stages in political evolution: the Oriental, in which the despot alone was free; the Greek and the Roman, in which some were free; and the German, in which all were free. The institutions of his own land and of his own time were idealized as the highest achievements of human progress.

The German idealists based their political principles upon concepts of pure thought rather than on observation and experience. They developed

[12] See his *Philosophie der Geschichte* (published in 1832 after his death), trans. by J. Sibree.

the idea of will as the ultimate element in politics. Starting with the liberal and cosmopolitan doctrines of the French Revolution, they developed in the opposite direction toward a glorification of the national state and a mystic belief in the divine mission of the German people. Authority rather than freedom came into the foreground. Their ideas gave a marked stimulus to the demand for German unification, to the growth of fascism, and to the aggressive ideas of German dominance put forward by later political writers.

REFERENCES

Bosanquet, Bernard, *The Philosophical Theory of the State,* 3rd ed. (London, Macmillan, 1920).

Cairns, Huntington, *Legal Philosophy from Plato to Hegel* (Baltimore, Johns Hopkins Press, 1949), Chaps. 12-14.

Cassirer, Ernst, *The Myth of the State* (New Haven, Yale Univ. Press, 1946), Chap. 17.

Dewey, John, *German Philosophy and Politics* (New York, Holt, 1915).

Engelbrecht, H. C., *Johann Gottlieb Fichte* (New York, Columbia Univ. Press, 1933).

Foster, M. B., *The Political Philosophies of Plato and Hegel* (Oxford, Oxford Univ. Press, 1935).

Heine, Heinrich, *Religion and Philosophy in Germany,* trans. by John Snodgrass (London, Kegan Paul, 1891), Part III.

Hobhouse, L. T., *The Metaphysical Theory of the State* (London, G. Allen, 1918).

Lindsay, A. D., *Kant* (London, Oxford Univ. Press, 1934).

Lukacs, György, *Der junge Hegel* (Zurich, Europa Verlag, 1948).

Marcuse, Herbert, *Reason and Revolution: Hegel and the Rise of Social Theory* (New York, Oxford Univ. Press, 1941).

McGovern, W. M., *From Luther to Hitler* (Boston, Houghton, 1941), Part II.

Rosenzweig, F., *Hegel und der Staat* (Munich, Oldenbourg, 1920).

CHAPTER XXV ✒︎

From Wagner to Chamberlain

Continuation of the Reaction

The philosophical reaction to the French Revolution was accompanied by reaction in other forms.

In the arts, romanticism became the order of the day. The exploits of characters of fiction like the Count of Monte Cristo, the works of Carlyle, and the operas of Wagner helped prepare the way for fascism by sowing the seeds of hero worship and by creating a belief in the destiny of the *Volk*.

As a reaction to the breakdown of the community inherent in liberal notions of individualism, a new interest in nationalism was created. People turned with greater pride to their common national origins and to the spirit or genius of their particular nation. There was also, as a consequence, a revival of interest in history and the historical approach to political problems. The historical school attacked the idea that the state was a deliberate, artificial creation, and that political institutions might be made at will. They emphasized the element of unconscious growth and viewed the state as the product of historical development, rather than of contract among individuals. Burke in England, and Treitschke and Savigny in Germany supported this view.

As a reaction to rationalism and the atheistic tendencies of the revolution, a strong revival of religious theory appeared. This declared that human power was insufficient to serve as a sanction for authority and that the sovereignty of the state came from God. It held that the state was the result of a divine command, not of a human contract. De Maistre, the Marquis de Bonald, and Lamennais—all French Catholics—upheld this position.

This distrust of human reason was also evident in the development of a school of irrationalism in philosophy. Led by Nietzsche and Pareto, this school taught the inadequacy of reason as a solution to the world's problems. The irrationalists believed that most men possessed little reason, were essentially irrational, and were in any case up against a mystery that "reasonable" methods could not conquer. In politics they scoffed at parliamentary institutions and at the assumptions of democracy, promoting the fascist belief that "We think with our blood."

Finally, there was a reaction to the liberal idea of equality in the doctrine of racial superiority put forward by Gobineau and Chamberlain.

Wagner and Carlyle

Richard Wagner (1813-1883) represents perhaps more closely than any other figure the climax of romanticism in Germany. Through his music he helped to combine the cult of the *Volk* with a belief in the great leader or hero.

Building on the work of Herder, he romanticized the importance of the *Volk* by returning to the greatness of medieval Germany. He recreated through his operas the music, poetry, and folk myths of Germany's past, leaving his audiences welded together in a common feeling of pride. The hero he pictured as the rare leader who caught the spirit of the *Volk*. He was in a sense the soul of the people, leading them on to greater glories. Through him the true meaning of life was to be found. Never mundane, Wagner's heroes despised the masses individually though the masses might reach great heights collectively. Utilitarian morality and the pettiness of the *bourgeoisie* were also to be despised as was anything commonplace. A restless surge of basic emotions, a primitive strength, were the real ingredients of greatness.[1]

In England, similar ideas were advanced by Thomas Carlyle (1795-1881)[2] who preached against the averageness of democracy and the uninspiring creed of Utilitarianism. Carlyle early developed a profound respect for German literature and philosophy which colored his thinking. He was impressed by the gospel of a hero with a special mission to perform. Democracy needed to be taken out of itself by something bigger than it could ever become alone. In his essay on *Chartism*, Carlyle called for a leader who would intuitively know the right path. People left to their own devices were little better than madmen. They needed to be laid hold of and pushed if necessary toward their destiny.[3] "Carlyle

---

[1] For an interesting and more complete discussion of these views, see Peter Viereck, *Metapolitics* (1941), Chaps. 5-6.

[2] *Chartism* (1839); *Past and Present* (1843); *Shooting Niagara* (1867).

[3] *Past and Present*, p. 212.

thought that good government meant wise government and wisdom was not to be found in the ignorant mob. To find out truth and wisdom by counting noses was ridiculous. To him the twenty-seven millions who then inhabited England were 'mostly fools.' To seek from them or their elected representatives the answers to the complicated problems of government was senseless. As for women, 'the Lord made them fools to match the men.'" [4]

The Prussian Historians

The emphasis on nationalism which played so large a part in the development of fascism is best represented in the writings of the Prussian historians, Heinrich von Treitschke (1834-1896) and Friedrich Karl von Savigny (1779-1861). [5]

Treitschke, [6] more than any other figure, was responsible for the patriotism surrounding Bismarck's successes in Prussia and for the aggressive form of nationalism identified with Germany during this century. He taught that Germany should fill out her natural boundaries, assimilate her various elements, and extend her culture over inferior peoples by war if necessary. [7] The constant theme of Treitschke's works was that state building justified all necessary measures, whether they be at the expense of individuals or other nations. Only a strong state could successfully conserve Germany's culture and bring stability and unity to her people.

Treitschke was a professor of history for many years at the University of Berlin, where his lectures attracted large and distinguished audiences. To all who would listen he preached the historic greatness of Germany and the exalted destiny that lay before her. [8] As an historian he was not concerned with such a pale thing as searching out the truth. Everything he said or wrote was aimed at the goal of German unification under an aggressive military leadership. Like Hegel, he often spoke of this as the true aim of liberalism and freedom. But liberty for him was always the liberty of the state, never of the individual.

In domestic affairs, Treitschke supported the Hohenzollern monarchy and an aristocratic Prussian leadership. He also advocated measures curtailing the freedom of Jews, doing much to advance anti-Semitism.

[4] W. M. McGovern, *From Luther to Hitler* (1941), p. 198. By permission of the Houghton Mifflin Company.

[5] Edmund Burke, who represented this approach in England, is discussed above, Chapter XIX.

[6] *Die Politik* (1899-1900). An English translation appeared in 1916.

[7] War, stated Treitschke, knitted a nation more closely together than anything else. "It makes it worthy of the name of nation as nothing else can, and the extension of existent states is generally achieved by conquest." *Politics* (1916), Vol. I, p. 108.

[8] F. W. Coker, *Recent Political Thought* (1934), p. 441.

The way for Treitschke had been made easier by the work of Savigny.[9] He was the leading influence in the formation of the German historical school.

As early as 1814 [10] he laid down the principles which were accepted by the historical school as to the nature and origin of law. He viewed law as a creation of the collective national mind, closely interwoven with national life and character. It was the work of many generations, not the product of an arbitrary will. It evolved out of the changing social, economic, and moral conditions of the people. In contrast to the philosophical school, which desired reform in accordance with its ideals, Savigny urged the force of tradition, the danger of change, and the necessity of a careful study and understanding of historical conditions. He believed that reform should wait until science and theory had created trustworthy legal principles for the legislator. He denied that law could be made at the behest of men and aimed to overthrow the rationalism by which the eighteenth century had been distinguished. His theory of legislation was the antithesis of that of the Utilitarians. Savigny insisted upon the superiority of the life of the state to that of its individual members, and he strengthened the tendency in Germany toward a thoroughgoing absolutism. He held that the people could possess no political power unless they were organized into the state, through which they obtained personality and sovereignty. Even then, sovereignty resided in no single generation. The state included many generations in the past and others yet unborn. It sprang organically from the life and history of a nation; it resulted from a creative power working from within.

Savigny's historical conception of law became a part of the intellectual background of the nineteenth century. It met the natural-rights philosophy on its own terms. It admitted that rights were founded in nature, but it identified nature with history and held that the institutions of a nation were the crystallization of its tradition and experience. It opened the door to gradual progress in terms of nationality, but refused admission to revolutionary methods. Writers ceased to search for natural rights common to all men, or to construct ideal institutions suitable for all peoples. They sought for what was distinctive in each nation, and believed that the political organization and legal system of each state were the necessary products of the social process through which the national genius had developed.

[9] *Geschichte des römischen Rechts in Mittelalter* (1815-1831); *System des heutigen romischen Rechts* (1840-1849).

[10] *Von Beruf unserer Zeit für Gesetzgebung und Rechtswissenschaft,* written in answer to a pamphlet by Thibaut urging a new civil code for Germany.

Religion and Politics

The political philosophy that opposed the principles of the French Revolution mainly because of their anti-religious tendencies was best represented in the writings of the French Catholics, Joseph de Maistre (1753-1821),[11] the Marquis de Bonald (1754-1840)[12] and Robert de Lamennais (1782-1854).[13] Not in direct line with fascist tradition, these writers are nonetheless of interest as leading figures in the conservative reaction of the nineteenth century. Their doctrines represented the point of view of the exiled nobles and of persons who resented the hostility of the revolution to the church and the effort of Napoleon to subordinate the church to his political ambitions. They saw in the revolution only the enthronement of anarchy; in the Rights of Man, the execution of the king and the exile of the nobility; in the sovereignty of reason, the persecution of the church. They aimed to restore monarchy, to free the church from state control, and to establish the ultimate sovereignty of the papacy. They returned to the doctrines of Bossuet and held that all power is derived from God. Terrified by the anarchy of individualism in politics and in religion, they revived the doctrine of authority and of divine right. They emphasized tradition and dogma, rather than reason, believing that the will of the state should reflect the mind of God rather than the theories of men. They viewed the restoration of the Bourbon monarchy as a return to God's plan, and the French Revolution as an episode during which the nation had turned away from God.

De Maistre believed that the application of human reason to the framing of laws and constitutions was futile. Institutions should develop gradually in accordance with natural conditions; law should represent accumulated customs and traditions. Artificial schemes will never work as expected. A democratic constitution cannot make a free nation, nor a declaration of rights give a people liberty. The documents of the American and the French revolutions and the written constitutions of the period excited his scorn, as did the prevalent belief in fundamental and universal principles of governmental organization. De Maistre believed, with Montesquieu, that the laws of a people should grow out of their peculiar circumstances; and he drew upon his wide knowledge of history to find instances to support his views.

[11] In his *Essays on the Natural Laws of the Social Order; Primitive Legislation; Theory of Political and Religious Power.*
[12] In his *Considérations sur la France* (1797); *Essai sur le principe générateur des constitutions politiques* (1814); *Du Pape* (1817).
[13] In his *Essay on Indifference in Matters of Religion* (1817-1821).

At the same time, De Maistre's political philosophy was essentially medieval and theological. He believed that monarchy was essential in church and state and upheld the infallibility of the pope and the absolute sovereignty of the king as representing two phases of the divine plan for ruling the earth. Authority came from God; the state could not owe its existence to the deliberate choice of human wills. Men were not free. Only in so far as they acted in harmony with the divine will was achievement possible. Authority based upon religion was the remedy for the evils of the time; the Roman Catholic religion alone possessed the unity, the permanence, and the authority upon which order could be safely based; the pope must possess ultimate sovereignty. The ultramontanism by which the papacy sought to restore its prestige in the nineteenth century was based upon the work of De Maistre.

De Bonald discussed the state in accordance with his trinity of categories: cause, means, and effect. Family, church, and state each illustrated the three-fold principle of sovereign power, of a ministry to carry out its will, and of subjects to obey. In the state, sovereignty came from God and was represented in the monarch. The agent of the sovereign power was the nobility, whose function it was to serve the state. Passive obedience was the duty of subjects. Natural rights were little better than deceitful dreams; inequality was the law of nature. The deliberate efforts of men to create new institutions and to devise new constitutions were futile. The Bible and the established traditions should be followed. Change was viewed as an evil; religious and political uniformity was considered necessary. The doctrines of the seventeenth century and the authoritative methods of scholastic logic found their last great representative in De Bonald.

Lamennais, drawing largely upon the doctrines of Bonald, also opposed the individualism of the period and insisted upon authority based upon religion. He disliked especially the efforts of Napoleon to use the church for political ends; and after the restoration of the monarchy, he attacked the Gallican doctrine of federalism between church and state, because he believed it would result in the subordination of the church. His ideal was an ecclesiastical imperialism centering at Rome, in which the church would be independent of the state. In contrast to De Bonald and De Maistre, who were concerned chiefly with the state and who adopted the theocratic point of view to support the monarch, Lamennais had little interest in secular politics. Religion alone held his allegiance; he aimed to free the church from state control. Knowing that he could expect no support from the French monarchy or clergy, to whom the Gallican arrangement was mutually advantageous, and finally realizing that the papacy, because of complicated political considerations, was unwilling to adopt his policy, Lamennais turned to more liberal views,[14] appealing to the people and to the collective priesthood, and urging freedom of conscience and of education. Condemned by the church, his ideas grew more radical [15] until they approached the communistic doctrines of his contemporary, Louis Blanc.

Nietzsche and Pareto

Closer to fascist doctrine were the writings of Friedrich Nietzsche (1844-1900) [16] and Vilfredo Pareto (1843-1923).[17] Nietzsche is best known for his concept of the superman which led to the idea of the super state and to such elitist organizations in Hitler Germany as the S. S. Elite Guard. He believed that a Darwinian process of evolution would ultimately divide the human race into two classes—supermen and those who were physically, morally, and mentally inferior. The domination of the first class was as inevitable as it was natural and Nietzsche's "millennium" waited only for this change to take place.

Following ideas suggested in Schopenhauer's The World as Will and Idea, Nietzsche [18] also placed great emphasis on the irrational element in men's lives. The world was controlled by something far more basic than reason—by the will to power. All things, he stated, were constantly struggling to overcome their natural enemies. In this struggle those with the greatest will to power succeeded in subduing their opponents who were rightfully removed from the path of social progress. Progress was in fact nothing more than this struggle for power in which only the most daring [19] and able survived.

Nietzsche had little respect for conventional ideas or morality. Through a desperate sort of genius he attacked both Christianity and democracy as servile doctrines created by servile men. Christianity thwarted the process of evolution by opposing the triumph of the strong over the weak. Democracy taught a false belief in reason and equality.

Pareto belonged to a group of Italian and Swiss university professors [20] who advanced the thesis that all organizations were in reality ruled by an inner group or elite, whether they pretended to be democratic or not. Pareto's particular contribution to this school was to demonstrate that all groups were not only organized in this fashion, but that most

[14] In his Progrès de la Révolution (1829).
[15] In his Paroles d'un Croyant (1834); La Question du Travail (1848).
[16] Also sprach Zarathustra (1883-1885).
[17] Trattato di sociologia generale (1916), trans. by A. Bongiorno and A. Livingston as The Mind and Society (1935). See especially secs. 2239 ff.
[18] Nietzsche was also influenced by a personal friendship with Richard Wagner.
[19] Nietzsche often advised his readers "to live dangerously."
[20] Others in this group were Gaetano Mosca and Robert Michels.

of their activities were controlled by irrational factors. In his major work, *The Mind and Society*, Pareto argued that the most constant factors influencing conduct were those resting on a subconscious or instinctive level. These factors included the "instinct of combinations" or desire to be a part of a larger whole, the tendency of people to protect their "status," the need of self expression, and the desire to conform to accepted sex patterns.[21]

In view of these facts, Pareto concluded that talk of democracy or constitutional government was wasted. "We need not linger," he stated, "on the fiction of popular representation—poppy cock grinds no flour."[22]

Racism

Of all the aspects of fascism thus far mentioned, none had more revolting consequences than the doctrine of racial superiority taught by Arthur de Gobineau (1816-1882)[23] and Houston Stewart Chamberlain (1855-1926).[24] Because of this doctrine untold thousands of Jews were put to death in Germany or were driven from their homes.

Gobineau, the founder of this school, was more poet than scientist, but he was not deterred by this from proclaiming a new "science" based on the inequalities of human races.

Mankind, he said, could be divided into three distinct races—Negro, Chinese, and European. Each race was marked by qualities peculiar to it and was superior or inferior to the other races in accordance with the quality compared. In regard to intellect, the Negro ranked lowest, the European highest. In artistic and musical capacity, however, Gobineau found the Negro to excel. The Chinese he believed to be practical and law abiding but incapable of producing great leaders or great geniuses.[25] The white peoples were, according to him, rich in reason, energy, resourcefulness, and creativeness,[26] but were not uniformly excellent. The Semites, for example, were "somewhat inferior to the other white groups," as they were really a combination of white and black races.[27] The purest and best of the white groups was the Aryan race which was to be found in Germany and England, and among the aristocrats of France.[28]

[21] *The Mind and Society*, secs. 888-889.
[22] *Ibid.*, sec. 2244.
[23] *Essai sur l'inégalité des races humaines* (1853-1855), trans. by Adrian Collins as *The Inequality of Human Races* (1915).
[24] *Die Grundlagen des neunzehnten Jarhunderts* (1899), trans. by John Lees as *The Foundations of the Nineteenth Century* (1911).
[25] McGovern, *op. cit.*, p. 501.
[26] *Ibid.*
[27] *Ibid.*
[28] Among whom Gobineau numbered himself.

Gobineau felt that while complete purity of race was not desirable [29] the Aryan race was being ruined by being polluted with the blood of inferior races.[30] If this process were allowed to continue, the future of civilization would be jeopardized.

Chamberlain, who was an Englishman by birth but a German by adoption,[31] popularized these views in Germany. His most famous work, *The Foundations of the Nineteenth Century*, was so widely read that it is difficult to overestimate its influence. Kaiser Wilhelm II read the book aloud to his children and was instrumental in putting copies of it into every library in Germany.

Chamberlain argued in the fashion of Gobineau that races vary as much in their characteristics as do animals. "The human races are in reality," he said, "as different from one another in character ... as a grey-hound, bulldog, poodle, and Newfoundland dog." [32] The Aryan race, and more particularly the Teutonic division of the Aryan race, has proved so superior to other races in essential qualities that all modern advances in art, science, philosophy, religion, and politics can be traced to it. The Teuton, he stated, "is the soul of our culture. ... If we look around we see that the importance of each nation ... is dependent upon the proportion of genuinely Teutonic blood in its population." [33] The nation having the most Teutonic blood was of course Germany. The Germanic peoples were so superior in this regard that they constituted a master race which was predestined to be the cultural and political leader of the world for centuries to come.[34]

REFERENCES

BARKER, Ernest, *Nietzsche and Treitschke, the Worship of Power in Modern Germany* (London, Oxford Univ. Press, 1914).

BORKENAU, Franz, *Pareto* (New York, Wiley, 1936).

BUTLER, Rohan, *The Roots of National Socialism* (New York, Dutton, 1942).

COKER, F. W., *Recent Political Thought* (New York, Appleton-Century, 1934), Chaps. 11-12.

HANKINS, F. H., *The Racial Basis of Civilization*, rev. ed. (New York, Knopf, 1931).

HOMANS, G. C. and CURTIS, C. P., *An Introduction to Pareto* (New York, Knopf, 1934).

JACKSON, Holbrook, *Dreamers of Dreams: the Rise and Fall of 19th Century Idealism* (London, Faber, 1948).

[29] He believed that slight mixtures of other bloods with those of the Aryan race had resulted in some of the great periods of history.

[30] McGovern, *op. cit.*, p. 502.

[31] He married the daughter of Richard Wagner.

[32] *The Foundations of the Nineteenth Century*, Vol. I, p. 261.

[33] *Ibid.*, Vol. I, p. 257.

[34] McGovern, *op. cit.*, p. 505.

LEHMAN, B. H., *Carlyle's Theory of the Hero* (Durham, Duke Univ. Press, 1928).

McGOVERN, W. M., *From Luther to Hitler* (Boston, Houghton, 1941), Part III.

MORGAN, G. A., *What Nietzsche Means* (Cambridge, Harvard Univ. Press, 1941).

SNYDER, L. L., *Race, a History of Modern Ethnic Theories* (New York, Longmans, 1939).

SYMONS, Julian, *Thomas Carlyle* (New York, Oxford Univ. Press, 1952).

VIERECK, Peter, *Metapolitics* (New York, Knopf, 1941).

CHAPTER XXVI ✐

Fascism

Nature of Fascism

Fascism, like communism, is essentially a reaction to Western individualism [1]—to what is considered "corrupt, hypocritical, and decadent *bourgeois* democracy." It was spawned in the economic and military strife which grew out of the apparent peace of the nineteenth century, culminating in World War I. Most Europeans had never really welcomed the disorganization of *laissez fairism*. They had never really accepted the principles of parliamentary democracy. Both seemed to work for weakness rather than strength. Strength lay in organization and organization depended on a doctrine to which everyone could adhere. It depended on a creed which could be a new "religion." The two primary tenets of fascism thus became totality and authority—the whole against the parts and "truth" against opinion.

To bring fascism to fruition, however, something more than this longing for organization and strength was needed. The forces of liberalism succumbed only to the added pressures of communism and depression.

Communism, having gained a foothold in Russia in 1917, menaced the propertied classes of both Italy and Germany and instilled fear into the hearts of thousands of white-collared, middle class people who later supported fascism. These people were afraid that democracy could not stop this new tide. First in Italy and then in Germany they became disgusted with the halfhearted measures taken by the Italian Chamber of Deputies and the Reichstag. New leadership and a different approach were needed to save Europe from the "Red Terror."

As a child of depression, fascism also developed out of squalor and

[1] This is well illustrated in an official nazi publication entitled *A Revolution in Thought* (1939), written by Otto Dietrich.

want. Men driven to hunger have little time for parliamentary procedures and talk about liberty. Consequently, when Italy faced the bleak prospect of coming out of World War I on the winning side with nothing to show for it but disastrous economic consequences, and Germany faced the burden of inflation followed by depression, conditions were at last ripe for a new political God to take the stage.

Idealism and Fascism

In one sense fascism developed a political philosophy as an after-thought. This was particularly true in Italy where Mussolini drew up the tenets of his movements as an aftermath to his political success. But in a larger sense fascism, like other political phenomena, has grown out of an ideological past to which it ultimately owes its life. The scribblings of Rousseau, interpreted by the idealists and augmented by writers like Nietzsche and Chamberlain, thus made possible the posturing of Mussolini and prepared the way for the nazi chant of "One People, One Reich, and One *Führer*."

The ideological traditions of fascism, discussed in previous chapters, need only be summarized here: Foremost among them was the Hegelian belief in the state as the highest form of association and as the agency of fulfillment for all members of the *Volk*. Of nearly equal weight was the belief in leadership, the rare mind, and the heroic figure, come to lead the children out of the wilderness. A third factor was the growth of irrationalism, the acceptance of authoritarianism, and the rejection of democracy. The popular will expressed in free elections became the "real will" of the people caught in the spirit of the state and of the leader. Nationalism and greed for world power were also present, as was the cohesive factor of common racial hatreds.

Mussolini

The political beginnings of fascism date from 1922. In that year Benito Mussolini (1883-1945) [2] led his followers in a march on Rome, bent on seizing control of the government. He could easily have been turned back by the army or even the police, but forces previously mentioned conspired to assure his success. On his arrival he was asked by the king to form a government. During the ensuing years he consolidated his position by brutally eliminating all opposition. The trade unions came under his control as did the parliament. By 1932 he felt secure

[2] *The Doctrine of Fascism* (1932). This early statement of fascist theory was written by Mussolini for the *Enciclopedia Italiana*.

enough to turn his attentions to other things, bringing forth *The Doctrine of Fascism* as the official apology for the actions he had taken.

In general form this doctrine was a reaction to the two competing doctrines which the fascists faced. Since their "chief opponents, the Marxists, were self-proclaimed materialists, fascism must stand for an exalted form of political idealism. Since the Marxists held all forms of politics to be a reflection of economic relations, fascism must regard the state as the leader and director of the industrial system." [3] And since Marx had taught progress through class warfare, fascism must teach progress through being a cog in the all-inclusive state.[4] Against their other opponents, the democrats, prating about freedom must be met by a higher form of freedom. And old-fashioned and inefficient theories of parliamentarism must be replaced by a new form of society based on corporate organization.

These views were set down by Mussolini in the first section of *The Doctrine of Fascism:*

The world seen through Fascism is not this material world which appears on the surface, in which man is an individual separated from all others and standing by himself, and in which he is governed by a natural law that makes him instinctively live a life of selfish and momentary pleasure. The man of Fascism is an individual who is nation and fatherland, which is a moral law, binding together individuals and the generations into a tradition and a mission, suppressing the instinct for a life enclosed within the brief round of pleasure in order to restore within duty a higher life free from the limits of time and space: a life in which the individual, through the denial of himself, through the sacrifice of his own private interests, through death itself, realizes that completely spiritual existence in which his value as a man lies.[5]

Fascism, he continued, is a reaction against the flabby doctrines of the nineteenth century. It "desires an active man, one engaged in activity with all his energies: it desires a man virilely conscious of all difficulties" that face him.[6] "Life, therefore, is serious, austere, religious.... The Fascist disdains the comfortable life." [7]

More than this, fascism is a "Will that transcends the particular individual and raises him to conscious membership of a spiritual society." [8] It is also an historic conception. "Outside history man is nothing." [9] The

[3] G. H. Sabine, *A History of Political Theory* (1937), p. 748.
[4] *Ibid.*
[5] Translated by Michael Oakeshott, *The Social and Political Doctrines of Contemporary Europe* (1949), p. 164. By permission of the Cambridge University Press.
[6] *Ibid.*, p. 165.
[7] *Ibid.*
[8] *Ibid.*
[9] *Ibid.*

individual is important only as he plays his part in the state which is the

conscience and universal will of man in his historical existence. . . . Liberalism denied the State in the interests of the particular individual; Fascism reaffirms the State as the true reality of the individual. . . . Therefore, for the Fascist, everything is in the State, and nothing human or spiritual exists, much less has value, outside the State. In this sense, Fascism is totalitarian, and the Fascist State, the synthesis and unity of all values, interprets, develops and gives strength to the whole life of the people.[10]

Fascism is also opposed to socialism which teaches class conflict, ignoring the unity of classes under one leader.[11] It likewise opposes democracy. Democracy makes the mistake of equating the nation with the numerical majority. The nation must be conceived of qualitatively, not quantitatively. It must be conceived of as the "most powerful idea which acts within the nation as the conscience and the will of a few, even of One." [12]

Fascism is finally a will to power which recognizes that the state dies if its expansion is arrested.

Therefore the State is not only the authority which governs and gives the form of laws and the value of spiritual life to the wills of individuals, but it is also a power that makes its will felt abroad, making it known and respected, in other words, demonstrating the fact of its universality in all the necessary directions of its development. It is consequently organization and expansion, at least virtually. Thus it can be likened to the human will which knows no limits to its development and realizes itself in testing its own limitlessness.[13]

German Fascism: National Socialism

These ideas, which sound so strange and even frightening to us, did not seem so discordant to millions of Germans. They had been prepared by a hundred years of philosophy, by war, by depression, by communism in Russia, and by weak government to accept a similar ideology, known in Germany as national socialism.

The *Nationalsozialistische Deutsche Arbeiterpartei*, as Adolf Hitler's (1889-1945) [14] party was officially called, was founded in 1919. In the beginning it was only one of many dissident factions competing for the loyalties of the disillusioned. Under Hitler's leadership, however, and because of his genius for organization and a frenzied form of oratory, the party soon outstripped its competitors. It established branches through-

[10] *Ibid.*, p. 166.
[11] *Ibid.*
[12] *Ibid.*, p. 167.
[13] *Ibid.*, pp. 167-168.
[14] *Mein Kampf* (1925-1927), especially Vol. I, Chap. 11; Vol. II, Chaps. 1, 2, 4. English translations appeared in 1939.

out Germany, founded a newspaper, and formed a quasi-military organization known as the Storm Troopers.[15]

Led on by initial success Hitler undertook his ill-fated Munich *Putsch* in 1923. For his trouble he was sentenced to a term in the prison fortress of Landsberg-am-Lech where most of *Mein Kampf* was written. On being pardoned in December, 1924, Hitler found his movement in pieces and Germany enjoying a period of prosperity not conducive to change. Until 1930 his party made little progress, but the depression of that year quickened interest in national socialism. The nazis elected 107 deputies to the Reichstag in the September, 1930, election, and in the presidential election of March, 1932, Hitler received over 13,000,000 votes. In January, 1933, Hitler was named chancellor by Hindenburg, who had been convinced that Hitler alone could remove the spectre of communism.

Once in power Hitler lost no time solidifying his position. He blamed the communists for the burning of the Reichstag, and on a wave of reaction he defeated the democratic parties in the election of March, 1933. With Hindenburg's death, the way was clear for his unquestioned ascendance to power. In 1934 the Third Reich was proclaimed, parliamentary institutions were dissolved, and Hitler named himself *Reichsführer*.

The Master Race

The two most authoritative statements of nazi ideology appear in Hitler's *Mein Kampf* and in Alfred Rosenberg's *Der Mythus des 20. Jahrhunderts*. Of the two, the latter is infinitely more clear and to the point. Of *Mein Kampf*, one observer remarks that no autobiography in history can match its fantastic qualities. "Reading it we are in a universe of grotesque proportions—a nightmare Wonderland in which we are all Alices watching the distorted perspectives. World movements like Christianity, socialism, democracy, are reduced to items in the ego-displacement of a little Austrian water-color dauber. Whole nations and continents become the stamping-ground for his restless personality. His tastes and traumata are expanded into universals to decide the destiny of millions." [16] Hitler in truth gives little reasoned thought to the basic principles of national socialism in *Mein Kampf*. His primary interest is to trace the growth of national socialism from its inception and to describe the role he personally played in its development. In a chapter entitled "People and Race" [17] Hitler does, however, discuss one subject at length

[15] W. M. McGovern, *From Luther to Hitler* (1941), pp. 603-604.
[16] Max Lerner, *Ideas Are Weapons* (1939), p. 356. By permission of The Viking Press.
[17] Vol. I, Chap. 11.

—his concept of the master race—and this becomes the key to much else contained in his writings.

Building on the principles of social Darwinism and on the racial theories of Gobineau and Chamberlain, Hitler reordered the foundations of political philosophy. History was not a struggle of emancipation for the individual. It was not a struggle of class against class. It was the unfolding of the genius of a superior race—the Aryan race. Out of the chaos of races which were struggling for survival, the races which were most pure [18] were certain to be the strongest. And by far the purest was the Aryan race or more particularly the Aryan race as it existed in Germany.[19] This race was so in advance of other races in this respect that it constituted civilization's only hope of survival. Every time this race mixed with inferior races, alarming results followed.

Historical experience offers countless proofs of this. It shows with terrifying clarity that in every mingling of Aryan blood with that of lower peoples the result was the end of the cultured people. North America, whose population consists in by far the largest part of Germanic elements who mixed but little with the lower colored peoples, shows a different humanity and culture from Central and South America, where the predominantly Latin immigrants often mixed with the aborigines on a large scale. By this one example, we can clearly and distinctly recognize the effect of racial mixture. The Germanic inhabitant of the American continent, who has remained racially pure and unmixed, rose to be master of the continent; he will remain the master as long as he does not fall a victim to defilement of the blood.[20]

It is the will of nature, concluded Hitler, that distinctions in races be kept, because transgressions are always punished with inferiority.

Races are not only to be kept distinct, but some are manifestly superior to others apart from the question of purity. Of these the Aryan race is again outstanding. "All the human culture, all the results of art, science, and technology that we see before us today, are almost exclusively the creative product of the Aryan." [21] Examination of other races shows the fact that none are creators: they are only sustainers. Something like the following picture of their development always results:

[18] *Mein Kampf*, pp. 284 ff. References are to the 1943 English translation by Ralph Manheim, published by the Houghton Mifflin Company. By permission.

[19] Hitler was willing to concede a certain superiority to all branches of the Aryan race, but he felt that the purest Aryan stock existed in Germany. The Germans were consequently the ultimate racial group.

[20] *Mein Kampf*, p. 6.

[21] *Ibid.*, p. 290. Rosenberg stated in *Der Mythus des 20. Jahrhunderts* that "the meaning of world history has radiated out from the North over the whole world, borne by a blue-eyed blond race which in several great waves determined the spiritual face of the world." p. 114.

Aryan races—often absurdly small numerically—subject foreign peoples, and then, stimulated by the special living conditions of the new territory (fertility, climatic conditions, etc.) and assisted by the multitude of lower-type beings standing at their disposal as helpers, develop the intellectual and organizational capacities dormant within them. Often in a few millenniums or even centuries they create cultures which originally bear all the inner characteristics of their nature, adapted to the above-indicated special qualities of the soil and subjected beings.[22]

But eventually, Hitler warned, the conquerors violate the fundamental rule of racial purity. They intermingle with inferior races, even as they are today intermingling in Germany with the Jews. This must be stopped.

To Hitler, as to Rosenberg, the Jew was the incarnation of all that was wrong with Germany. The Jews were defiling the race. They were conspiring in international intrigues against Germany. They were greedily lapping up all profits and property. For true nazis, the Jew was the common enemy. He welded their movement together by giving it a common hatred which knew no bounds.[23] In one of history's most inhuman demonstrations the nazis undertook to drive all Jews from Germany or literally to exterminate them. And when cries arose in England and the United States against such action, the nazis replied that objections to their policy of anti-Semitism were too stupid to demand refutation. The Jews were little better than parasitic animals which must be wiped out. As long as one Jew remained in Germany, the world's greatest culture was in danger because "History demonstrates that all nations receiving the Jews among themselves and giving them the same rights sooner or later perish from the Jewish poison." [24]

[22] *Mein Kampf,* pp. 291-292.

[23] Frederick Watkins comments that this attack was especially effective in welding the lower middle class together as a bulwark of fascism. "For desperate members of the lower middle classes, eager to bolster up their threatened sense of social superiority, the idea of belonging to the master race, and the possibility of joining a permanent party elite, were definitely beguiling. By destroying the Jews, whose competition was most keenly felt by small shopkeepers, professional men, and other middle-class elements, and by reducing the Marxist-indoctrinated proletariat to impotence, fascist movements promised an immediate improvement in the social and economic position of the middle classes, while the prospect of future imperial expansion, with its vista of innumerable administrative and other white-collar jobs for members of the master race, gave room for even brighter long-range ambitions." *The Political Tradition of the West* (1948), pp. 337-338. By permission of the Harvard University Press.

[24] Rolf Tell, ed., *Nazi Guide to Nazism* (1942), pp. 114 ff. Later, during World War II, the racial doctrines of the nazis were made to appear as ridiculous as they actually were when the Italian and Japanese peoples were suddenly raised to a new status as "superior" races.

Der Führer and the Totalitarian State

A second aspect of national socialism which deserves mention is the principle of personal leadership. In the person of the *Führer*, Adolf Hitler, all elements in German society were expected to find a common bond. He was to be the infallible leader who would catch the spirit of the people.

An excellent exposition of this principle is contained in a work by Ernst Huber entitled *Verfassungsrecht des grossdeutschen Reiches*,[25] published in 1939. Huber makes it clear that a leader is necessary because "the true will of the people cannot be disclosed through parliamentary votes." [26] In its pure and uncorrupted form, the will of the people or *Volk* can only be expressed through the *Führer*.[27] The will of the people in democracies represents in reality only a clash of selfish interests. In the Third Reich the collective will, expressed through the leader, represents the objective, historical greatness of the German people. Selfish interests are lost in the common interest.

> The Führer is no 'representative' of a particular group whose wishes he must carry out. He is no 'organ' of the state in the sense of a mere executive agent. He is rather himself the bearer of the collective will of the people. In his will the will of the people is realized. He transforms the mere feelings of the people into a conscious will. . . . Thus it is possible for him, in the name of the true will of the people which he serves, to go against the subjective opinions and convictions of single individuals within the people if these are not in accord with the objective destiny of the people. . . . He shapes the collective will of the people himself and he embodies the political unity and entirety of the people in opposition to individual interests.[28]

In the *Führer* all authority was to be centered. It was he who was to make all laws and set up the "great ends which were to be attained." It was he who was to make all plans for the utilization of the powers of the nation. In this great work the *Führer* rightfully expected and must receive the total coöperation of the German people. Nothing was to be beyond the power of the state because everything must be bent to the single purpose of German greatness. Education, industry, culture were all a part of the nation's strength and so must come under the control of the

[25] *Constitutional Law of the Greater German Reich*. References to this work are to excerpts contained in a State Department publication entitled *National Socialism* (1943).

[26] *Ibid.*, p. 34.

[27] *Ibid.*

[28] *Ibid.*, p. 35. Compare Rousseau's discussion of the general will in the *Social Contract*.

government. No form of organization, be it religious or political, had any right of existence except as a part of the total scheme. Regimentation was complete.

From a period of democratic government under the Weimar constitution the German government became in less than ten years one of the most authoritarian, total governments in human history. And in spite of all our wishes to the contrary, the people of Germany seemed to have had few regrets.

Anti-Intellectualism and the Artist in Politics

If the nazis had little regard for constitutional government, they had even less regard for Western "intellectualism." "One energetic man," stated Hitler, "is worth more than a thousand intellectual babblers who are useless waste products of the nation." [29] The nazis rightly suspected the intellectuals. The doctrines of national socialism could stand little scrutiny even from "babblers." Nazism depended instead on mass emotions which could be controlled by Hitler and Goebbels. What better then, than a philosophy based on action rather than thought, on emotion rather than reason!

Philosophic support for these views was not difficult to find. Rousseau's distrust of reason and the revolt against reason of the nineteenth century [30] were only a step removed from the familiar nazi cry, "We think with our blood." Against Western intellectualism, national socialism turned therefore with relative ease to another set of principles. These were the genius of the great leader, the strength of primitive emotions, and the creativeness and "assertiveness of will and action." [31]

The nazis contrasted their philosophy with "barren intellectualism" as being "creative rather than critical, profound rather than superficial, natural rather than conventional, uncontrollable and demonic rather than methodical." [32] Discussion and examination of evidence were "bourgeois virtues beneath the dignity" of the New Order.[33] It is a principle of national socialism, stated Hitler, that some things are beyond discussion. "Who dares with his small average brain" to discuss eternal values. These things are to be judged by the centuries, not by the "intellect of small ordinary beings." [34] It is better, Hitler argued, to give yourself in loyalty

[29] Speech before Reichstag, January 30, 1939. Quoted by Tell, *op. cit.*, p. 48.
[30] See above, Chapter XXV.
[31] G. H. Sabine, *A History of Political Theory*, rev. ed. (1950), p. 865.
[32] *Ibid.*
[33] *Ibid.*
[34] From a speech made by Hitler at the opening of the Architecture Exposition, Munich, January 22, 1938. Quoted by Tell, *op. cit.*, p. 49.

to the common cause and to be led beyond your own small reason by the genius and artistry of the leader.

The nazi leaders were convinced that they had captured something beyond reason—the "art of politics," which they alone understood. Hitler believed that he was the greatest of all artists, creating by his mastery a great nation out of the masses which he despised. He believed that politics without art lacked inspiration and inspiration was everything. Leaders without a feeling for art were always second-rate. Hitler once stated, thinking largely of himself, that "He who is called by Providence to reveal the soul of a people to the world around ... suffers beneath the power of the almighty driving force which is his master, he will speak, even if the world does not understand, or has no wish to do so, he will suffer all things, rather than even once prove unfaithful to the star which burns within his breast and leads him on." [35]

Practical men have long been wary of the theorist in politics. Today, with the advent of fascism, they are faced with a new and much more frightening spectre—the artist in politics.

Lebensraum

From theories of the blood, from the leader in a totalitarian state, and from the artist in politics, the nazis turned finally to a theory of the soil. This was best expressed by the term *Lebensraum*. It was based on the goal of a Germanic state situated in the "heartland" of Europe and surrounded by a ring of conquered non-Germanic states.[36]

For decades this notion had been festering in the German mind. The geopolitics of Ratzel, Kjellen, and Haushofer had given currency to the belief that a nation is a living organism which must expand or die. To realize its historical destiny it needed living space or *Lebensraum* in which to grow. Friedrich Ratzel (1844-1904) [37] stated in his now famous *Political Geography* that a nation's growth was conditioned more by geography than by political organization. The dynamics of history were to be explained by the struggle for living space among the world's cultural areas. Rudolf Kjellen (1864-1922),[38] a Swedish political scientist, popularized these views in Germany by outlining a plan of German conquest—as the nation best suited to win in this struggle for space. While

[35] Speech before National-Socialist Party Congress, 1933. Quoted in Richard Monnig, ed., *Adolf Hitler from his Speeches* (1938).

[36] Sabine, *op. cit.*, p. 891.

[37] *Anthropogeographie* (1882-1891); *Politische Geographie* (1897).

[38] *Stormakterna* (1905); *Staten som lifsform* (1916); *Grundriss zu einem System der Politik* (1920).

Karl Haushofer (1869-1946) [39] became the official nazi apologist for geopolitics by developing the "heartland" idea of the British geographer, H. J. Mackinder. Mackinder had warned Britain that the *maritime* powers, would lose to the *land* powers in any struggle for domination if Germany or Russia were allowed to control Europe's heartland, an area including Eastern Europe and Western Asia. "Who rules this area," cautioned Mackinder, "commands the Heartland. Who rules the Heartland commands the World-Island [Europe, Asia, and Africa]. Who rules the World-Island commands the World." [40] To Haushofer, the moral was clear. Germany's future lay toward the east. If she were successful there, her horizon would be limitless.

Under Haushofer's prompting, the nazis accepted this as the official party line. Hitler wrote in *Mein Kampf* that the duty of the foreign policy of a racial state was to safeguard the existence of that race. This could best be done in Germany's case by enlarging the state's territory [41] at the expense of nations toward the east. Germany previously had made the mistake of expanding south and west. Germans, Hitler said, must direct their eyes toward Europe's heartland. "We can...have in mind only Russia and her vassal border states." [42]

The nazis accepted other aspects of these doctrines with equal relish. They not only provided the answer to the problems of over-population,[43] but they complemented their racial theories. Believers in the superiority of the German race were by implication committed to two further policies. One was that all Germans must be liberated from foreign domination and incorporated into a greater Germany.[44] The second was that inferior races must be brought under the control of the Germanic race and made to do its bidding. Germany's world mission thus became that of the greatest of imperial powers, carrying culture and organization to inferior peoples. Through war, conquest, and "space politics" Germany was destined to rule the world.

The Future of Fascism

There is great comfort in the fact that war prevented these aims from being realized. But it would be a mistake to think that fascism is now dead. Fascism represents an aspect of a fundamental problem we have not

[39] See the *Zeitschrift für Geopolitik*, a publication which Haushofer controlled.
[40] *Democratic Ideals and Realities* (1919), p. 150.
[41] *Mein Kampf*, pp. 642-643.
[42] *Ibid.*, p. 654.
[43] See Rudolf Frercks, *German Population Policy* (1938).
[44] Franz Neumann, *Behemoth* (1944), p. 130.

yet solved. Western liberalism has created a form of individualism which has in large measure replaced community, authority, and purpose. It has given men their freedom, but it has left them alone without the comforts of belonging, without the guidance which makes individual decisions unnecessary, and without gleaming goals to call men on. Liberalism has also suffered from the apparent weaknesses of interminable discussion, constitutional procedures, and corruption and inefficiency. Italians used to boast that at least the trains ran on time under Mussolini.

To countless millions liberalism seems so expensive that few people are willing or able to pay the price. We are willing, but are the Germans and Italians even yet? Ideas existing in the minds of men are never defeated by war. And at this writing there is little reason to believe that Germany or Italy [45] has developed a genuine desire to renounce dictatorship. Fascism, in truth, awaits only a greater swing to the right in opposition to communism to re-emerge as a formidable force.

REFERENCES

BAYLES, W. D., *Caesars in Goose Step* (New York, Harper, 1940).

CHANDLER, A. R., *Rosenberg's Nazi Myth* (Ithaca, Cornell Univ. Press, 1945).

COBBAN, Alfred, *Dictatorship* (New York, Scribner, 1939).

DIETRICH, Otto, *A Revolution in Thought* (Berlin, Terramare, 1939).

EBENSTEIN, William, *Fascist Italy* (New York, American Book, 1939).

——, *The Nazi State* (New York, Farrar and Rinehart, 1943).

FRERCKS, Rudolf, *German Population Policy* (Berlin, Terramare, 1938).

KNELLER, G. F., *The Educational Policy of National Socialism* (New Haven, Yale Univ. Press, 1941).

LERNER, Max, *Ideas Are Weapons* (New York, Viking, 1939), Part III, Chap. 9.

LICHTENBERGER, Henri, *The Third Reich* (New York, Greystone, 1937).

MATTHEWS, H. L., *The Fruits of Fascism* (New York, Harcourt, 1943).

McGOVERN, W. M., *From Luther to Hitler* (Boston, Houghton, 1941), Part IV.

MONNIG, Richard, ed., *Adolf Hitler from His Speeches* (Berlin, Terramare, 1938).

MONTAGUE, M. F. A., *Man's Most Dangerous Myth: The Fallacy of Race* (New York, Columbia Univ. Press, 1942).

NEUMANN, Franz, *Behemoth* (New York, Oxford Univ. Press, 1944).

NEUMANN, Sigmund, *Permanent Revolution* (New York, Harper, 1942).

PITIGLIANI, F., *The Italian Corporative State* (New York, Macmillan, 1935).

SABINE, G. H., *A History of Political Theory*, rev. ed. (New York, Holt, 1950), Chap. 35.

SCHINNERER, Erich, *German Law and Legislation* (Berlin, Terramare, 1938).

SCHMIDT, C. T., *The Corporate State in Action: Italy under Fascism* (New York, Oxford Univ. Press, 1939).

---

[45] Fascism continues in Spain as well. And in South America it is gaining new adherents almost hourly.

SCHUMAN, F. L., *Hitler and the Nazi Dictatorship*, 3rd ed. (London, Hale, 1936).

————, "The Political Theory of German Fascism," *American Political Science Review*, Vol. 28 (April, 1934).

TELL, Rolf, ed., *Nazi Guide to Nazism* (Washington, American Council on Public Affairs, 1942).

U. S. State Department, *National Socialism* (Washington, Government Printing Office, 1943).

WATKINS, Frederick, *The Political Traditions of the West* (Cambridge, Harvard Univ. Press, 1948), Chap. 11.

PART VII

The Legacy of Marx

PART VII

The Legacy of Marx

CHAPTER XXVII ⟞⟞⟞

Communism

The Life and Works of Marx and Engels

Communism, which we may define as a philosophy of history based on a materialistic conception of human development, owes its beginnings to Karl Marx and Friedrich Engels. They are now revered, together with Lenin and Stalin, as the prophets of a new gospel based not on brotherly love, but on the dogmas of class conflict and revolt.

Marx (1818-1883) was born in Treves, Germany, the son of a Jewish lawyer who became converted to Christianity. As a university student he gave early evidence of the brilliant mind and dogged perseverance for which he is now famous. He immersed himself in the philosophy of Hegel and in the history of Savigny. He wrote volumes of poetry to "his Jenny," a beautiful girl with an aristocratic background whom he later married. And he completed a doctoral dissertation on the materialistic philosophy of Epicurus.

From his study of Hegel he had already perceived what he considered a basic fallacy in idealistic thinking. For Hegel the mainspring of history was the unfolding of the "world idea" or "absolute spirit." For Marx the meaning of history lay in the material world about him. In a letter to his father he wrote that "A curtain had fallen, my holy of holies [Hegel] had been shattered, and new gods had to be found for the vacant shrine. Setting out from idealism . . . I proceeded to seek for the idea in the real itself. If in earlier days gods had dwelt above the world, they now became its centre." [1] Hegel's "grotesque craggy melody" was unpleasing. "I wished," he stated, "to dive into the ocean again . . . to bring pure pearls into the sunlight." [2]

- Quoted by Otto Rühle, *Karl Marx: His Life and Work* (1929), pp. 20-21. This is the standard biography of Marx. By permission of The Viking Press.

[2] *Ibid.*

389

Marx would have liked to follow an academic career, but his views proved too radical for university authorities, leading him instead into the field of journalism. In 1842 he became the editor of a newspaper in Cologne, but his radical views, this time on the subject of religion, again hastened his departure for Paris. Marx chose Paris because he wished to know more about French socialism. He had heard a great deal about men like Proudhon and Blanc, but on his arrival in Paris he became quickly disillusioned. The French socialists had created a dissatisfaction with capitalism, but they had not been able to give socialism a philosophy or a program. Laski states that the vital fact about Marx was that he found socialism "a chaos and left it a movement. . . . Through him . . . it became an international organization laying continuous emphasis upon the unified interest of the working classes of all countries." [3] Marx, unlike most French socialists, believed that theory and practice had to meet in political action if the conditions of the working class were ever to be improved. The proletariat was lost without theory, but theory was as surely lost without the proletariat. To socialists who disdained politics, Marx replied that it was not enough to announce a new theory and expect everyone to bow down. The real struggle was down in the street where victory alone could be won.

While still in Paris, Marx renewed an acquaintance with Friedrich Engels (1820-1895), beginning one of history's most famous partnerships. Engels at twenty-four was only two years younger than Marx and came from a similar background. He was employed as a manager in one of his family's cotton mills, but for him this merely provided an income necessary to sustain his intellectual and political interests. Factory and slum conditions in England, where most of his later life was spent, so troubled him that he had already accepted the tenets of revolutionary socialism before he met Marx. His quick mind and ready understanding led Marx to write to him "you know that I am slow to grasp things, and that I will always follow in your footprints." [4] Engels for his part discounted his own importance to this partnership, writing that he was glad to do what he "was meant for, to play second fiddle" to Marx's exceptional genius. [5] Which of them played the greater part, it is difficult to say. The books they wrote together were a joint product in every sense. And Engels would probably have become famous had Marx never lived. But history has chosen to give Marx the greater credit, ascribing to Engels the role of junior partner.

In 1845 Marx was banished from Paris at the insistence of the Prussian

[3] H. J. Laski, *Communism* (1927), p. 22.
[4] Gustav Mayer, *Friedrich Engels* (1936), p. 57.
[5] *Ibid.*

government. He went first to Brussels, where the *Communist Manifesto* was written; then to Cologne, where he edited a revolutionary newspaper; and finally to England, where the remainder of his life was spent.

England has often been called the Mother of Exiles, but she was never very good to Marx. During his years there he experienced first hand the poverty and distress about which he wrote. He lived with his large family in a two-room flat. His wife was often ill and in later life he was himself unwell. Food was scarce and Marx was able to continue only because of the generosity of his friend Engels. Rühle recounts that his life was a succession of unpaid bills, illness, and worse misfortune. In a letter to a friend Marx's wife wrote:

Let me describe only one day of this life, as it actually was, and you will see that perhaps few other refugees have had to suffer as much. Since wet-nurses are exceedingly expensive here, I made up my mind, despite terrible pains in the breasts and the back, to nurse the baby myself. But the poor little angel drank in so much sorrow with the milk that he was continually fretting, in violent pain day and night. Since he has been in the world, he has not slept a single night through, at most two or three hours. Of late, there have been violent spasms, so that the child is continually betwixt life and death. . . . One day I was sitting [nursing the poor dear] when our landlady suddenly appeared. In the course of the winter we had paid her more than two hundred and fifty thalers, and then it had been agreed that in future we were not to pay her but her landlord, who had put in an execution. Now she repudiated this agreement, and demanded the five pounds which we still owed her. Since we could not pay this sum instantly, two brokers came into the house, and took possession of all my belongings—bedding, clothes, everything, even the baby's cradle and the little girls' toys, so that the children wept bitterly. They threatened to take everything away in two hours. If this had happened, I should have had to lie on the floor, with my freezing children beside me, and with my aching breast. Our friend Schramm hastened forthwith to seek help. He took a cab, the horses fell down, he jumped out, and was brought back into the house bleeding, the house where I was lamenting and my poor children were trembling.[6]

But even in the face of such hardships Marx continued his unrelenting efforts to "free the working classes from the bondage of capitalism." He worked long hours in the British Museum developing the economic theories of *Capital*. Through voluminous correspondence he maintained a position of leadership in the socialist movement. He wrote numerous pamphlets defending himself and criticizing his opponents. He sold a series of articles to the *New York Tribune*, then edited by Horace Greeley. And with Engels he founded the first International Working Men's Association in 1864. Poverty and struggle perhaps became him because in the end he achieved his ambition to "unleash the forces of history."

[6] Rühle, *op. cit.*, pp. 202-203.

The two most important works published by Marx were the *Communist Manifesto* and *Capital*. The *Communist Manifesto*, written with the aid of Engels, has been called the best thing Marx ever did.[7] For force and clarity it has few competitors. As an instrument of propaganda it has none. It concludes with the words "Communists scorn to hide their views and aims. They openly declare that their purpose can only be achieved by a forcible overthrow of the whole extant social order. Let the ruling classes tremble at the prospects of a communist revolution. Proletarians have nothing to lose but their chains. They have a world to win. Proletarians of all lands, unite!"

Capital was planned by Marx as his life's work. He wrote to a friend that he had sacrificed comfort, happiness, and even his family to this *magnum opus*. To all but the most intent reader, the work will seem ponderous; yet for the true Marxist, *Capital* remains the "gospel" of communism. It is filled with a unique combination of theory, description, and analysis. A most abstract analysis of surplus value is followed by a detailed description of the operations of a Manchester carding machine operator. *Capital* consists of three volumes, the first published in 1867. The other volumes were edited and published by Engels after Marx's death.

Other works deserving mention include the *Poverty of Philosophy*, *Contribution to the Critique of Political Economy*, and *Eleven Theses on Feuerbach*. The *Poverty of Philosophy* was published in 1847 as an answer to Proudhon's *Philosophy of Poverty* and is a thorough-going indictment of utopian socialism. Marx accuses Proudhon of thinking like a peasant with no understanding of history or economics. The *Critique of Political Economy*, published in 1859, is noteworthy as the only work containing an explicit statement of Marx's doctrine of historical materialism. We will have cause to turn to this statement shortly. The *Eleven Theses on Feuerbach* (1845) sets forth Marx's philosophical materialism. He concludes that philosophers have only interpreted the world in various ways, but the real task is to alter it.

From Hegel to Marx

The theory of communism was derived by Marx and Engels from a curious mixture of German idealism, English economics, and French revolutionary and social thought. Marxism rests first on the doctrines of historical materialism and class warfare, which are closely related to

[7] Bertrand Russell, *Freedom versus Organization* (1934), p. 181.

Hegelian philosophy. It depends secondly on Marx's theory of surplus value, which is based on English classical economics. And it contains lastly elements of the French Revolution and of French socialism in its theory of progress through revolt and its assumptions concerning the withering away of the state.

To understand what Marx meant by the first of these terms, historical materialism, it is necessary to know something about Hegel and his use of the dialectical method. Marx, though he rejected the substance of Hegel's philosophy, adopted the dialectical method as the context for his historical materialism. For Hegel [8] history gained its meaning from the interaction of ideas which alone were real. History depended upon the gradual unfolding of the "world spirit" or "absolute idea" according to a divine plan which was imminent in the universe. Ideas struggled with other ideas for dominance, and out of the dynamics of struggle arose new ideas corresponding more closely to the ultimate perfection of God himself.

No idea, in consequence, could be considered static or complete. All things were in a state of flux (or what Hegel called a state of becoming). Every idea (thesis) because of its incompleteness or inherent contradictions led naturally to its opposite (antithesis). And from the two there emerged the truth embraced by both (synthesis).[9] The resulting synthesis then became a new thesis, and the process repeated itself in an unending chain.[10]

Marx agreed that history unfolded according to a dialectical plan, but he did not believe the controlling factors to be ideas. Hegel, he declared, had turned history on its head. *Ideas* did not control reality. They were rather the result of *material* conditions. In a famous passage in *Capital* he stated, "To Hegel ... the process of thinking, which, under the name of 'the Idea,' he even transforms into an independent subject, is the demiurgos [creator] of the real world, and the real world is only the external, phenomenal form of 'the Idea.' With me, on the contrary, the ideal is nothing else than the material world reflected by the human mind, and translated into forms of thought." [11] Marx believed that all things depend upon material conditions and that this provides the real clue to the working of the dialectic. In the interaction of thesis, antithesis, syn-

[8] See above, Chapter XXIV.

[9] Hegel thus denied formal logic which is based on the law of contradictions. (A thing is proved untrue by demonstrating its opposite.) Hegel asserted that reality is not static. All things are in a state of becoming. So that which is, is becoming.

[10] Hegel believed the process would be completed only when the "absolute idea" itself was reached.

[11] *Capital,* Vol. I, p. 25. References are to the Kerr edition (1926). By permission.

thesis, and thesis, the dominant factors are material in nature and arise out of the relation of man to the means of production.

Historical Materialism

Marx argued that two basic factors are to to found in every society. They are the material forces of production and the knowledge necessary to their use. These form the "conditions of production." To utilize effectively these conditions of production, society becomes organized into what Marx calls the "relations of production." These are always dependent on the conditions of production and are to be found in the property relationships of any society. In a capitalist society, to illustrate, the effective use of the conditions of production implies the protection of private property and the existence of a large class of wage laborers. It also implies certain legal, political, religious, and philosophical forms reflecting basic economic relations.[12] But to continue in Marx's own words:

In the social production which men carry on they enter into definite relations that are indispensable and independent of their will; these relations of production correspond to a definite stage of development of their material powers of production. The sum total of these relations of production constitutes the economic structure of society—the real foundation, on which rise legal and political superstructures and to which correspond definite forms of social consciousness. The mode of production in material life determines the general character of the social, political and spiritual processes of life. It is not the consciousness of men that determines their existence, but on the contrary, their social existence determines their consciousness. At a certain stage of their development, the material forces of production in society come in conflict with the existing relations of production, or—what is but a legal expression for the same thing—with the property relations within which they had been at work before. From forms of development of the forces of production these relations turn into their fetters. Then comes the period of social revolution. With the change of the economic foundation the entire immense superstructure is more or less rapidly transformed.

It should be observed, however, that

no social order ever disappears before all the productive forces, for which there is room in it, have been developed; and new higher relations of production

[12] "In acquiring new productive forces," Marx stated, "men change their mode of production, and in changing their mode of production, their manner of gaining a living, they change all their social relations. The windmill gives you society with a feudal lord; the steam mill, society with the industrial capitalist." *The Poverty of Philosophy* (1847), p. 119. References to this work are to the Quelch translation published by the Twentieth Century Press (1900).

never appear before the material conditions of their existence have matured in the womb of the old society. Therefore, mankind always takes up only such problems as it can solve; since, looking at the matter more closely, we will always find that the problem itself arises only when the material conditions necessary for its solution already exist or are at least in the process of formation.[13]

The four broad stages through which society had evolved were designated by Marx as Asiatic, ancient, feudal, and *bourgeois*. Each had been characterized by antagonisms resulting from the forces of production outrunning the relations of production. But in each case this disharmony was overcome by a solution which was engendered through conflict.

The Class Struggle

Although this conflict took many forms, it was in essence an unrelenting struggle between opposing classes—between those who had benefited from the old relations of production and those who were to benefit from the new and expanding forces of production. Marx believed that every society is divided into oppressors and oppressed and that "The history of all hitherto existing societies is the history of class struggle." [14] This is particularly true of the *bourgeois* epoch. Modern capitalism develops its full powers only through creating a large proletarian class which depends wholly on wages for its livelihood. The capitalist needs a reservoir of manpower which he can hire at the going price in the same sense as a miller purchases wheat. Modern capitalism also depends on a lust for profits which heightens the class problem. Capitalist lust is insatiable and the accumulation of profit is only a spur to gain greater profits. Consequently history must record the few getting richer and the proletariat becoming poorer and more numerous as weaker members of the owning class are broken by their stronger brothers and forced into the proletariat.

As this happens, however, the exploited class begins to solidify and to become conscious of its own size and importance. It becomes acutely aware of its poverty compared to the increasing riches of the owning class. And with the aid of the social philosopher (Marx) it is led to the realization that it is producing all of society's material goods, but receiving in return only a meager share of the goods produced. Marx discusses this latter problem at great length in *Capital*.

[13] *Critique of Political Economy* (1859), pp. 11-13. International Library edition (1904). As this is the only statement of this doctrine which Marx ever committed to print, it is quoted at length.

[14] *Communist Manifesto* (1848), p. 8. References are to the Regenery edition (1949).

The Theory of Surplus Value

The economic aspects of Marxism hinge on the doctrine of surplus value, and this in turn depends on the labor theory of value of English classical economics.

Ricardo had maintained,[15] as did Locke earlier,[16] that the value of any commodity is determined by the labor expended in its production. A pair of shoes which takes fifteen hours to produce has the same exchange value as a bushel of wheat representing an equal expenditure of labor. To this Marx gave his wholehearted assent. "A useful article," Marx asserted, has value only because human labor . . . has been embodied or materialized in it. How, then, is the magnitude of this value to be measured? Plainly by the quantity of the value-creating substance, the labor contained in the article." [17] Those who expend labor in the production of any commodity therefore create its value and have a right to the full value of their production. The capitalists, however, are unwilling to allow laborers the full return for their industry. Through rents, interest, and profits they extort from the worker a part of his production.

They take this unearned share from what Marx calls surplus value. A labourer is able to produce in a day more than is necessary to his own survival, but he is paid by the employer a wage commensurate with a subsistence level of existence.[18] The difference, called surplus value, is appropriated by the employer.

The owner of money buys labour power at its value, which is determined, like the value of every other commodity, by the socially necessary labour time requisite for its production (that is to say, the cost of maintaining the worker and his family). Having bought labour power, the owner of money is entitled to use it, that is to set it to work for the whole day—twelve hours, let us suppose. Meanwhile, in the course of six hours ("necessary" labour time), he produces a "surplus" product for which the capitalist does not pay him.[19]

Marx allows that the capitalist may be usefully employed and should receive a commensurate share of the value produced. But he has no right to this surplus value which he actually steals from the mouths of the worker's family.

To rectify this injustice the capitalist must be eliminated from society and private property must give way to a collectivist economy in which each will produce according to his ability and receive according to his need. Only a socialist regime can return to the worker what is rightfully

[15] *Principles of Political Economy* (1817).
[16] See above, Chapter XIV.
[17] *Capital*, Vol. I, p. 45.
[18] Compare the position of Malthus. See above, Chapter XVII.
[19] V. I. Lenin, *The Teachings of Karl Marx* (1930), p. 21. International Publishers edition.

his by abolishing interest, profits, and rents. But although socialism is clearly the answer to the problem of economic exploitation, its achievement is made difficult by the type of state erected by capitalist societies.

Theory of the State

As we have previously observed, Marx regarded the state as a reflection of prevailing economic forces. It is part of the class struggle. Engels observed that the state comes into being when the governing class finds it needs the protection of an organized coercive power to maintain existing property relationships.[20] The state is nothing more than organized oppression.[21] The ruling economic class "by force of its economic supremacy becomes also the ruling political class, and thus acquires new means of subduing and exploiting the oppressed masses. The ancient state was therefore the state of the slave-owners for the purpose of holding the slaves in check. The feudal state was the organ of the nobility for the oppression of the serfs and dependent farmers. The modern representative state is the tool of the capitalist exploiters of wage labour." [22]

As the executive committee of the *bourgeoisie,* the state's primary task is to provide law, order, and stabilized economic relationships. This is made increasingly difficult, however, by the previously mentioned self-consciousness of the working classes and by their growing militancy. The state, through its police power and through hired armies, will seek to continue oppression because no ruling class will voluntarily relinquish such an advantage; but it must ultimately fail in the face of the unrelenting dialectical forces of history. At a point when proletarian pressures equal the forces of the *bourgeoisie* a revolution will follow.

Revolution

Marx believed revolution to be inevitable,[23] but he did not for this reason wish merely to await its coming. He argued that it was not enough

[20] Friedrich Engels, *Origin of the Family, Private Property, and the State* (1884), p. 211. Untermann translation (1902).

[21] Lenin, *op. cit.,* p. 31.

[22] *Ibid.*

[23] It is a much discussed question whether Marx did not foresee in later life the possibility of overturning capitalism without resort to revolution and violence. "Engels tells us that Marx reached the conclusion that in England at any rate 'the inevitable revolution might be effected entirely by peaceful means'; and in a letter of 1880 to Hyndman he [Marx] stated that his party did not hold such a revolution to be 'necessary', but only, on historic precedents, 'possible'." (R. N. Carew Hunt, *The Theory and Practice of Communism* (1951), pp. 69-70). It is clear, however, that the great weight of Marx's writings is in line with the call to arms of the *Communist Manifesto,* and that even in his later writings Marx continued to believe that revolt would prove necessary in all but the most democratic countries.

for philosophy to understand the world. It must change it. He was especially critical of Hegel on this score. Hegel had written that the role of philosophy was only to understand what had happened, not to interfere with the Divine plan. "Philosophy," Hegel stated, "comes too late to teach the world what it should be. . . . The owl of Minerva begins its flight when the shades of twilight have fallen." With this Marx wholly disagreed.[24] He considered the philosopher to be a midwife to history. He could not alter the basic design, but he could ease the pain and hasten the process of dialectical materialism. Marx hoped that he might personally lead a revolution. His theoretical works were always geared to "the coming revolt." And his correspondence with Engels is filled with speculation about when the hour would be at hand.

Marx wrote with confidence about the coming revolt because he believed its success was assured. He shared the belief of the French Revolution in the certainty of progress and he viewed the working of the dialectic as a science beyond challenge. The laws of history, which he had discovered, were as inexorable as the law of gravity. Once *bourgeois* society reached the point of maturation its doom was inevitable.[25]

Marx defined revolution as the class struggle carried to its ultimate conclusion.[26] Combination among the workers first occurs to maintain wages and resist exploitation.[27] But the workers soon discover that of all the "instruments of production the greatest productive power is the revolutionary class itself." [28] In combination they are able to alter the forces of production and overthrow their old masters. With a change in the forces of production a corresponding dialectical change takes place in the political order, and the working class comes finally into its birthright.

After Capitalism

Marx has little to say about the form of society which will replace capitalism. But he does conclude that between the defeat of capitalism

[24] Hunt, *op. cit.*, pp. 15-16.

[25] This feeling that communism is riding the new wave of history has had a profound effect. The success of communism first in Russia and then in Eastern Europe and China has been due in no small measure to an almost religious conviction that communism has success on its side. It has been customary for us to wish for God's support in our major undertakings. The communists think they have no need for God or any formal religion; they have Marx and history on their side. They also draw tremendous strength from the conviction that if they do not have a refrigerator or an electric stove today, tomorrow they will have two of each.

[26] *The Poverty of Philosophy*, p. 159.

[27] *Ibid.*, p. 157.

[28] *Ibid.*

and the realization of true communism [29] a transitional stage will be necessary. He refers to this phase as the "dictatorship of the proletariat." This stage is necessary in order to secure the victory, to destroy the last vestiges of the old order, and to eliminate any remaining traces of class distinction.

During the dictatorship of the proletariat it will be necessary to retain the state and to be satisfied with a diluted form of communism. But when the work of the dictatorship has been done the state will have no further purpose. It will "wither away." There will be no class conflicts and no exploitation. All classes will have been merged into one. And the age of true communism will be at hand. Marx was very critical of the utopian socialists, but he never outlived his years in France. The ultimate goal of society is a voluntary association where economic cares are unknown. "Freed from capitalist slavery, from the innumerable horrors, savagery, absurdities and infamies of capitalist exploitation, people will gradually become accustomed to the observation of the elementary rules of social life, known for centuries, repeated for thousands of years in all sermons. They will become accustomed to their observance without force, without constraint, without subjection, without the special apparatus for compulsion which is called the State." [30]

In the highest phase of Communist society, after the enslaving subordination of the individual under the division of labor has disappeared, and therewith also the opposition between manual and intellectual labor; after labor has become not only a means of life, but also the highest want in life; when, with the development of all the faculties of the individual, the productive forces have correspondingly increased, and all the springs of social wealth flow more abundantly—only then may the limited horizon of capitalist right be left behind entirely, and society inscribe on its banners: "From everyone according to his faculties, to everyone according to his needs." [31]

Lenin

After the death of Marx and Engels, leadership in the communist movement fell to Nikolai Lenin (1870-1924).[32] Lenin had in no sense been designated as the heir-apparent, nor was he the most faithful of

[29] In strict Marxian terms, the communist stage is reached only when class conflict ceases and a golden, stateless society is achieved. Prior stages, such as that in which Russia now finds herself, are described as socialist in character.

[30] V. I. Lenin, *The State and Revolution* (1917), p. 94. Marxian Educational Society edition (1924).

[31] Karl Marx, *Critique of the Gotha Programme* (1891), p. 31. International Publishers edition (1933).

[32] *State and Revolution* (1917); *Imperialism: The Highest Stage of Capitalism* (1916).

Marx's interpreters. His succession was due rather to the fact that communists first came to power in Russia rather than in Germany or England as predicted by Marx, and to an extraordinary talent for revolutionary manipulation which Lenin possessed. Prior to the Bolshevik coup of October, 1917, there was more reason to believe that Kerensky's Constitutional Democrats, the Mensheviks,[33] or even the Social Revolutionaries [34] would benefit from the revolutionary situation brought on in Russia by war and mismanagement. But the only group to fully exploit the situation was the Bolshevik party led by Lenin.

Lenin, whose real name was Vladimir Ilyich Ulyanov, had gained his revolutionary insight from long and bitter experience. He was expelled from the University of Kazan and placed under police surveillance when he was not yet twenty. A year prior to this his brother had been executed for plotting against the life of Alexander III. While studying for the bar at the University of St. Petersburg, Lenin worked in the trade union movement, often defying the police. He later edited *Labor's Work* and *Iskra* (the *Spark*), both underground journals aimed at fomenting revolution among the urban working classes. From 1903 onward he led with zeal the fight against what he termed half-way measures being advocated by more moderate socialist elements. He missed the revolution of 1905, arriving from Switzerland where he had been in exile too late to do more than observe the mistakes that had been made. But the October Revolution of 1917 found him ready.

His first action when he again returned to Russia in April, 1917,[35] was to issue his *April Theses,* calling on Bolsheviks not to support the floundering provisional government which had taken over after the February Revolt. Instead he called for "peace, liberty, bread, and land" for the workers and peasants. He anticipated that people would follow the

[33] The Mensheviks ("minority") were originally a part of the Social Democratic party, as were the Bolsheviks ("majority"). The two groups split, however, in 1903 over questions of procedure, the Mensheviks disavowing the revolutionary temperament of the Bolsheviks.

[34] The Social Revolutionaries drew their support chiefly from the peasant classes.

[35] Lenin succeeded in reaching Petrograd only because Germany allowed him to cross her borders. Bertrand Russell, in discussing the limitations of Marx's philosophy of history, comments in this regard: "Admitting that the great forces are generated by economic causes, it often depends upon quite trivial and fortuitous events which of the great forces gets the victory. In reading Trotsky's account of the Russian Revolution, it is difficult to believe that Lenin made no difference, but it was touch and go whether the German Government allowed him to get to Russia. If the Minister concerned had happened to be suffering from dyspepsia on a certain morning, he might have said 'No' when in fact he said 'Yes,' and I do not think it can be rationally maintained that without Lenin the Russian Revolution would have achieved what it did." *Freedom versus Organization* (1934), p. 198. By permission of W. W. Norton & Co.

leader who promised them the most and he succeeded in convincing both workers and peasants that the provisional government was incapable of reform or of keeping the promises it had made. Sensing late in October that conditions were ripe for a second revolt, he proclaimed that it was now or never! In a matter of hours the Bolsheviks consummated carefully laid plans. During the night of October 24, the Bolsheviks surrounded the Winter Palace and other government buildings; and on the morning of October 25, members of the provisional government were placed under arrest as they came to work—Kerensky alone escaping.

Lenin's remarkable faculty for revolutionary intrigue was nearly equaled by an ability in theoretical analysis. One of Lenin's admirers has remarked that "there is probably nothing in the history of political thought that equals in dramatic power Lenin's achievement in linking in his own life the analysis and enactment of revolution. He was one of those rare persons in whom life drives no paralyzing wedges and in whom therefore there is no gap between the idea and the act." [36] As a theorist, Lenin is best known for his analysis of revolutionary tactics and for his study of imperialism. [37]

In discussing revolution Lenin stressed the inadvisability of compromise with the *bourgeois* liberals and the necessity of violent change. For many years he carried on a pamphlet war with Marxists whom he accused of turning Marx into a "hackneyed liberal." According to Lenin, success for the toilers could only be achieved by action and action meant revolt. Any other course was illusory. To wait for evolutionary change or to talk about democratic procedures and freedoms reduced Marxism to an armchair philosophy. No ruling class would give up more than the appearance of freedom for the working classes without resort to the "arbitrament of forces." The exploited must take what they want if they are ever to have it. And if in the process liberal-democratic ideas are trampled on, what does it really matter? The state is only a temporary institution at best. Its use by the revolutionists in confiscating the property of the former ruling classes is only to be expected. " 'So long as the proletariat still needs the state, it needs it, not in the interest of freedom, but in order to suppress its opponents, and when it becomes possible to speak of freedom, the state as such ceases to exist.' " [38]

To suppose, Lenin continued, that revolutionists have time or interest

[36] Max Lerner, *Ideas Are Weapons* (1939), p. 326.

[37] Stalin said of his predecessor that Leninism is Marxism in the era of revolt and of imperialism. *Foundations of Leninism* (1924), p. 10. International Publishers edition (1939).

[38] V. I. Lenin, *The Proletarian Revolution and the Renegade Kautsky* (1918), p. 24. Foreign Languages Publishing House edition (1947). Lenin is quoting from a letter written by Engels to Bebel, March 28, 1875.

in such democratic notions as majorities and minorities is the acme of stupidity. Revolution has little to do with large popular followings or with party membership.[39] Lenin split with the Mensheviks over the question of admitting casually interested members into the communist movement. He proposed to admit only such members as were prepared to work actively for party goals. He wanted the party to be a tightly knit band of professional revolutionaries who could move with a unity of will, incompatible with the existence of factions.[40] The Party was the advanced guard of the working classes, and on it rested the responsibility for the transitional period envisaged by Marx when the last vestiges of the old society would be liquidated by a dictatorship of the proletariat.

Through the Party, the proletariat takes power, becomes the ruling class, smashes *bourgeois* parliamentarism and democracy, suppresses all the attempts of other classes to return to capitalism, gives real liberty and equality to the toilers (which is made possible only by the abolition of private ownership of the means of production), and gives them not only the right to but the real use of that which has been taken away from the *bourgeoisie*. Only in this way can the exploitation of man by man be stopped and the way prepared for the classless, stateless society of pure communism.

Lenin's views on imperialism are contained in his *Imperialism: The Highest Stage of Capitalism*, written in 1916. In this work Lenin expanded on the economic aspects of Marxism. Marx, he believed, had accurately described the nationalist phase of capitalism, but he had not accounted for capitalism's imperialist or final stage. The growth of capitalism in any country continues, he stated, until all of the best markets have been utilized and all of the most lucrative investments made. Capitalism then enters a monopoly stage in which competition at home ceases and combinations become the dominant form of industrial organization. These national monopolies exploit the home market to the fullest extent, but they become increasingly aware that greater profits are to be made by turning their attentions to the world's underdeveloped areas. Trade consequently becomes global in scale and competition between national combines takes the form of a struggle for raw materials and world markets. In this scramble economic commitments involve political commitments because a nation's strength rests ultimately on its economy, and international politics turns more and more on the control of exploitable areas of the world. International fencing is inevitably followed by armed contests of strength, and capitalism enters the stage of the imperialist war.

[39] *Ibid.*, pp. 22 ff.
[40] Hunt, *op. cit.*, p. 147.

Lenin believed that he was witnessing such a war as he wrote in 1916. Germany, England, and France, he stated, were locked in a struggle of imperialist robber-barons to see which would control the world's economic resources. It was a struggle between one young robber and two old ones,[41] and as such it was of no concern to the working classes. What interest had they in serving the cause of their capitalist masters? *Bourgeois* patriotism was an empty form used to deceive the toiling masses. The purpose of the workers should be to use imperialist wars to their own advantage. If such a conflict could be turned into a proletarian revolution, then communism would be at hand. It was the hope of Lenin's life [42] that proletarian revolt would follow from imperialist war.

Stalin

History is more likely to record Joseph Stalin (1879-1953) [43] as a master politician than as a political philosopher. But he has made one contribution to communist theory for which he will be remembered. This is his doctrine of "socialism in one country," which he announced rather abruptly in 1924 during his struggle for power with Leon Trotsky.

Trotsky in his speeches and writings had urged Russia to carry immediately the torch of revolution to other nations on the peril of seeing her own beginnings snuffed out by the capitalist enemy. His approach was radical and internationalist. Stalin on the other hand, sensing the strength of Russian nationalism, successfully advised a cautious and nationalist approach. It is possible, he argued, for socialism to succeed in a single country in spite of capitalist encirclement.[44] All that is needed is the sympathy and indirect support of Europe's workers. This, combined with the might of the Red Army and the readiness of the workers and peasants to defend their socialist fatherland, will assure Russia the time she needs to face any enemy.[45]

By this Stalin did not imply that world revolution was to be given up. It was merely to be postponed. The final stage of communism would not be reached, he stated, until the encircling enemy was defeated by proletarian revolt. But the success of these revolutions depended on welding Russia into a bastion from which communism could then be spread to the rest of the world.

[41] G. H. Sabine, *A History of Political Theory*, rev. ed. (1950), p. 819.

[42] *Ibid.*

[43] *Foundations of Leninism* (1924); *Problems of Leninism* (1926); *Economic Problems of Socialism in the U.S.S.R.* (1952).

[44] Joseph Stalin, *Leninism* (1942), p. 17. References are to the International Publishers edition. This work is an abridged edition of *Problems of Leninism*.

[45] *Ibid.*, p. 20.

The Future of Communism

The importance of this doctrine does not lie in a change of objective. Russia's leaders still purport to be headed towards world-wide communism in its utopian, stateless form. But the change in approach is significant. The internationalism of Marx and the *Communist Manifesto* has now given way to the nationalism of a Russianized brand of communism, leading to a two-fold effect.

In international politics, the Russians are now carrying out their delayed program of aiding the working classes of other nations to revolt. But as they move from Rumania, to Bulgaria, to Poland, to Czechoslovakia, freeing the toiling masses, it is difficult to distinguish the type of freedom they bring from the freedom Western nations have long brought to under-developed peoples under the guise of assuming the "white man's burden." The Russianization of communism has meant in fact that a new form of imperialism has been created. It sends few armies across state lines, and it turns governments into "people's democracies," but the control from Russia is no less real nor is the exploitation less apparent.[46]

In the national sphere, nationalized communism has meant greater regimentation and an indefinite postponement of communism in its pure form, even though the socialist phase of communism was proclaimed complete as early as 1936. Stalin and his successors have insisted on un-limited power at home to drive back the encircling capitalist enemy. And with this as their excuse, they have used such well known dictatorial devices as the big lie and the purge. Their constitution can talk about democracy and civil rights and communist propaganda can condemn fascist dictatorship, but there is truth in the observation that communism has proved to be the Red bed-fellow of fascism. Both rest ultimately on the twin concepts of authority and totality and both are profoundly reactionary in character, though we continue through default to allow communists to call themselves "truly progressive."

As to what lies ahead, only speculation is possible. It seems improbable, however, that communism will be crushed in the near future, as some of its critics suppose, by its own dead weight or by internal rebellion. Communism is too deep-rooted to disappear overnight; its philosophical traditions go back too far; it breeds on unsolved problems. Nor is there reason to suppose a dark future in which communist tentacles will slowly encircle the earth, strangling democratic government and liberal traditions. This places too little value on the vitality of liberalism. A more likely prognosis is that, short of total war, the world will continue to be

[46] In 1952, to illustrate, Rumania turned 95 per cent of her oil production over to Russia. *Washington Post*, February 12, 1953.

divided for the foreseeable future into two armed camps which are ideologically incompatible and which await in consequence the other's failures and shortcomings.

REFERENCES

BERLIN, Isaiah, *Karl Marx* (London, T. Butterworth, 1939).

CARR, E. H., *Karl Marx* (London, Dent, 1934).

CHANG, Sherman H. M., *The Marxian Theory of the State* (Philadelphia, 1931).

COKER, F. W., *Recent Political Thought* (New York, Appleton-Century, 1934), pp. 35-65 ff.

COLE, G. D. H., *What Marx Really Meant* (New York, Knopf, 1937).

HOOK, Sidney, *Towards the Understanding of Karl Marx* (New York, Day, 1933).

HUNT, R. N. Carew, *The Theory and Practice of Communism* (New York, Macmillan, 1951).

KELSEN, Hans, *The Political Theory of Bolshevism* (Berkeley, Univ. of California Press, 1948).

KOESTLER, Arthur, *The Yogi and the Commissar* (New York, Macmillan, 1945).

LASKI, H. J., *Communism* (New York, Holt, 1927).

——, *Karl Marx* (London, G. Allen, n.d.).

LERNER, Max, *Ideas Are Weapons* (New York, Viking, 1939), pp. 319-337.

LEROSSIGNOL, J. E., *From Marx to Stalin* (New York, Crowell, 1940).

MAYER, Gustav, *Friedrich Engels* (London, Chapman, 1936).

ROBINSON, Joan, *An Essay on Marxian Economics* (London, Macmillan, 1942).

RÜHLE, Otto, *Karl Marx* (New York, Viking, 1929).

RUSSELL, Bertrand, *Freedom versus Organization* (New York, Norton, 1934), Chaps. 17-20.

——, *The Practice and Theory of Bolshevism* (London, G. Allen, 1920).

SABINE, G. H., *A History of Political Theory,* rev. ed. (New York, Holt, 1950), Chaps. 33-34.

WINSLOW, E. M., *The Pattern of Imperialism* (New York, Columbia Univ. Press, 1948), Chaps. 6-9.

INDEX

Academy of Plato, 49n, 61
Accursius, Irnerius, 116
Achaean League, 71
Adams, John, 209, 238, 285, 292, 294, 328, 331
Adams, Samuel, 238, 294
Aeschylus, 72
Aetolian League, 71
Agobard, 113
Agreement of the People, 205
Ahab, 29
D'Alembert, Jean, 248
Alexander the Great, 48n, 61
Alien and Sedition Acts, 327
Althusius, Johannes, political theory of, 174, 199, 215, 253, 293
American Revolution, nature of, 289-290; political theory of, 291-295; documents and constitutions, 295; English response to, 302-306
Amyntas II, 60
Anabaptists, 163-164, 212
Anarchism, Godwin, 305; Fourier, 339
Anarchy, 201, 367
Anti-democratic theories, nineteenth century, 331-334
Anti-intellectualism, Hitler, 381-382
Anti-Semitism, Hegel, 365; Gobineau, 370; Hitler, 379
Apostolicans, 163
Aquinas, St. Thomas, 16, 60, 101, 113; political theory of, 120-123; definition of law, 121; forms of law, 121; precedence of Church, 122; 126, 160, 167, 179, 181, 188
d'Argenson, Marquis, 223, 247, 281
Aristides, 72
Aristocracy, Montesquieu, 250
Aristophanes, 44, 46
Aristotle, 8, 16, 34; life of, 60-61; political theory of, 60-68; method compared to Plato, 62; character and method of writings, 62; respect for tradition, 62-63; economic basis of political institutions, 64; criticism of Plato's ideas, 65; definition of state and citizens, 65; distinction between state and government, 65; classifica-

tion of governments, 66; revolution, 67; value of moderation and stability in the state, 67; contribution to political thought, 68; 84, 85, 121, 124, 126, 155, 181, 182, 184, 207, 215, 249, 252, 263, 355
Armada, 166, 200
Articles of Confederation, 295
Artist in politics, Hitler, 382
Aryan race, Chamberlain, 371; Gobineau, 371; 378
Associationist psychology, James Mill, 314
Athens, social classes, 36; government of, 37-38
Attlee, Clement, 350
Aubrey, John, quoted, 217n
Augustine, St., political theory of, 100-102; 112, 116, 121, 181, 188
Austin, John, 286, 310, 311; political theory of, 315-317; 321, 325
Authoritarianism, and German idealism, 257; 374
Authority, obligation to, 7; location of within the state, 9; in primitive society, 22; in Hindu thought, 26-27; Aristotle's discussion of basis of, 66-68; St. Thomas Aquinas, 121-122; Dante, 126; Hegel, 362
Avignon, 110, 123, 125, 135
Ayala, Balthazar, 190

Bacon, Francis, 199, 240, 247
Bain, Alexander, 310
Baldus, 116
Ball, John, 137
Barclay, William, 170, 178, 182, 200
Barker, Ernest, quoted, 61
Barlow, Joel, 328
Bartolus, 116
Bazard, St. A., 338n
Beard, C. A., quoted, 16
Beccaria, Cesare, 278; political theory of, 282-283; 310
Bechers, J. J., 267
Bellamy, Edward, 4, 340
Bellarmine, Robert, 177-178, 179

(¹)

WITHDRAWN